t4

THE
NEW FEMALE
INSTRUCTOR

or

YOUNG WOMAN'S

GUIDE TO DOMESTIC

HAPPINESS

First published 1834 by Thomas Kelly, London.
This edition 1988 by Rosters Ltd. 60, Welbeck Street, London W1

Published by Rosters Ltd., 60, Welbeck Street, London W1.

ISBN 0–948032–13–8

Reproduced from the original with additional typesetting by
Lovell Baines Print Ltd., Newbury, Berkshire.

Printed and bound in Great Britain by
William Clowes Limited, Beccles and London

PREFACE

"It has been often remarked, that the rank which the female sex holds in any country, is a just criterion of its advance in knowledge and civilization. If we assume this as a test, it will assign to Great Britain no ordinary elevation in the scale of nations. There is, perhaps, hardly a spot in the world in which a more just estimate is formed of the female character, than in our own happy country. Exempted in great measure from the fulsome and frivolous attentions which characterise the manners of a neighbouring country, or the despotic tyranny to which they are exposed in the East; it is highly desirable that the moral and mental culture of the women of Great Britain should keep pace with the rank they are destined to hold in society."

These are the opening sentences of the original preface the The New Female Instructor when it was published over one hundred and fifty years ago. They put into perspective the book you are about to read. The original edition ran to some 670 pages containing the following:

- General rules for the regulation of female conduct and formation of moral habits
- The elements of science
- Geography, astronomy, natural history and botany
- Important hints in regard to domestic economy
- Advice to servants
- Complete art of cookery
- A great variety of medicinal and other useful recipes
- An epitome of all the acquirements necessary to form the female character in every class of life

In this edition we have concentrated on the chapters which discuss the appropriate conduct for a young lady of good standing as well as the practical hints on how she should run her household. Inside you will discover that women are particular prone to the "vice of detraction" and that "great intimacies are both foolish and imprudent". That "reading novels is liable to produce mischievous effects".

On courtship we learn that "love should proceed from the attachment of the man" plus dire warnings of the adverse effect on women if they become "attached" to men who are indifferent to their suit. There are also warnings about men who may pretend to be in love, with the practical advice that women can distinguish the "real thing" as true love makes a man "extremely timid". Even when women agree to marry the man they love they must make sure their feelings are suitably restrained. The instructor advises: "never to let him know how much you love him, even though you may marry him".

Unlike modern manuals of the twentieth century we pass quickly from courtship to duties of the married state, which include – as if by immaculate conception – how to behave during pregnancy. Mixed in with good sound practical advice about fresh air is much nonsensical talk of "longings" and the fact that "cards, or any kind of gaming, should be particularly avoided during pregnancy".

To the modern reader the book provides a smile on one page, provokes a scowl of reproach on the next and produces a practical idea on another. It takes us back to a bygone era when men were men and women were "objects of love and desire".

Rosemary Burr, London 1988.

CONTENTS

THE NEW

FEMALE INSTRUCTOR;

OR,

YOUNG WOMAN'S

GUIDE TO DOMESTIC HAPPINESS.

"GIVE ear, fair daughter of LOVE, to the instruction of PRUDENCE, and let the precepts of TRUTH sink deep into thine heart; so shall the *charms of thy mind* add lustre to the elegance of thy *form;* and thy beauty, like the rose it resembleth, shall retain its sweetness when its bloom is withered."

INTRODUCTION.

BY the arts of *pleasing* only it is, that WOMEN can attain to any degree of consequence or of power: and it is by pleasing only that they can hope to become objects of *love* and *affection*. These are attainments, which, as they are of all others the most dear to them, prompt them to cultivate, most assiduously, the arts of pleasing; arts for which they are well qualified by nature. In their forms lovely, in their manners soft and engaging, they can infuse, by their smiles, air and address, a thousand nameless sweets into society, which, without them, would be insipid, and barren of sentiment and feeling.

When we consider the two sexes into which the human species are divided, it appears in the most conspicuous manner, that the Author of Nature has placed the balance of power on the side of the male, by giving him not only a body more large and robust, but also a mind endowed with greater resolution, and more extensive powers. But are these qualities without their counterpoise in the other sex? Have women nothing left to balance this superiority of our nature? Have they no powers to exert, whereby they can reduce this seeming superiority to a more equal footing? If they have not, they may justly complain of the partiality of nature, and the severity of their lot But let us attentively conside: the matter, and we shall find, that the Author of our being is no such partial parent · To each sex he has given its different qualifications; and these, when properly cultivated and exerted, put both nearly on an equal footing, and the advantages and disadvantages of life are impartially shared between them. To bend the haughty stubbornness of man, is given to woman BEAUTY; and to BEAUTY is added that *inexpressible softness and persuasion*, of which but few know the extent, and still fewer have the power of resisting. Thus an insinuating word, a kind look, or even a smile, conquered Alexander, subdued Cæsar, and decided the fate of empires and of kingdoms. The intercession of the mother or Coriolanus saved Rome from impending destruction, and in one hour brought about a happy event, which the senate and people despaired of ever seeing accomplished.—Thus it is evident, that though the power of women, in bending the stronger sex to their will, is no doubt greatly augmented, when they have youth and beauty on their side ; even with the loss of these, it is not altogether extinguished; of which this last circumstance is an indubitable proof.

It were easy to multiply instances of the ascendency which WOMEN OF SENSE have always gained over men of feeling;—but I shall now proceed, to enumerate all those qualities which will enable you to attain the much desired art of pleasing, which will entitle you to the character of WOMEN OF SENSE, and which will bestow on you all that power of which I have just spoken. The charms of person, without the charms of mind will hold but a short and fleeting dominion—UNITED, their reign will be permanent. Those on whom nature has *not* lavished her choicest gifts, if they cultivate their minds, and improve their understandings, will often supplant BEAUTY ITSELF; and they will ALWAYS BE PREFERRED by men of sense, to those who boast the utmost regularity or harmony of features, and the highest peach-bloom of complexion, when unaccompanied by solid and lasting accomplishments.

A young girl, vain of her beauty, and whose chief study and employment is the decoration of her person, is a most contemptible character; and the more a woman is distinguished for the charms of her face, and the graces of her form, the more she is exposed to censure and to danger. The rose is torn from its parent stem in all its pride of beauty ; the jessamine is scarcely permitted to blossom before it is plucked; and no sooner are their beauties faded, than the merciless hand which was eager to obtain them throws them away with contempt; whilst the primrose, the humble violet, the lily of the valley, and the snow-drop, less exposed to observation, escape unhurt, and uninjured by the spoiler's hand.

Neglect not, my fair readers, in the halcyon days of youth to *make your mind a fit companion for the most lovely form.* Personal charms may please for a moment; but the more lasting beauties of an improved understanding, and intelligent mind, can never tire. We are soon weary of looking at a picture, though executed in the most masterly style: and the woman who has only beauty to recommend her, has but little chance of meeting a lover who will not grow indifferent to a mere portrait, particularly when its colours are faded by the subduing hand of time. Then it is that *modesty and sweetness of temper* are to be particularly observed; and the loss of beauty will not be regretted even by the man it first made your captive.

> See, lovely fair, yon blushing rose :
> All hail the beauty as it blows.
> Vain of her charms, she courts the sun,
> And soon her gaudy race is run.
> Observe in yonder pensive dale,
> The white-rob'd lily of the vale :
> Pure emblem of this spotless maid,
> Adorn'd with flow'rs that cannot fade.
> Virtue, bright ornament of youth,
> Sincerity, unblushing truth :
> Through all life's seasons these will please,
> In all life's storms secure heart's ease.

CHAPTER I.

DRESS AND FASHION

In things which in themselves, and in their attendant circumstances, are indifferent, *custom* is generally the proper guide;
and obstinately to resist its authority, with respect to objects
in reality of that description, is commonly the mark either of
weakness or of arrogance. The *variations of dress*, as in
countries highly polished frequent variations will exist, fall
within its jurisdiction. And as long as the prevailing modes
remain actually indifferent; that is to say, as long as in their
form they are not tinctured with indelicacy, nor in their costliness are inconsistent with the station or the fortune of the
wearer; such a degree of conformity to them, as is sufficient
to preclude the appearance of particularity, is reasonable and
becoming. It is modesty to acquiesce in the decision of
others, on a subject upon which they have at least as good a
title as ourselves to decide, and upon which they have not
decided amiss. When other unobjectionable modes are generally established, the same reasoning indicates the propriety
of acceding to them. But it neither suggests nor justifies the
practice of adopting fashions, which intrench either on the
principles of decency, or on the rules of reasonable frugality.
Fashions of the former kind are not unfrequently introduced
by the shameless, of the latter by the profuse; and both are
copied by the vain and the inconsiderate. But deliberately to
copy either, is to shew that delicacy, the chief grace of the
female character; or that economy, the support not merely
of honesty alone but of generosity, is deemed an object only
of secondary importance. To copy either inadvertently,
denotes a want of habitual liveliness of attention to the native
dictates of sensibility, or to the suggestions of equity and
kindness.

Beauty, it is true, may remain attractive in the midst of
absurd and uncouth decorations. It is attractive, however,
not in consequence of them, but in spite of them; and it attracts with force singularly diminished by the medium
through which it has chosen to operate. And those men,
who expect in women qualities more estimable than personal
charms, feel themselves impelled to draw conclusions not
very favourable to the understanding or to the dispositions
of one, who proves herself so little attached to the proprie-

ties natural to her sex; and if they are betrayed by inadvertence into the language of compliment, can scarcely restrain
emotions of disgust from rising in their hearts.

Fashions in dress, which in the two particulars already
specified are irreprehensible, are yet sometimes of such a
nature as to be *extremely inconvenient* to the wearer. Modes
of this description may seldom be likely to be very long prevalent. But, while they continue, every practicable discou-
ragement should be pointed against them; and similar care
should be employed to discountenance all such methods of de-
corating the person as involve in their operation the surrender
of any considerable portion of time.

In the next place, it is to be observed, that the principles,
which recommend such a degree of compliance with established
fashion of an unobjectionable nature as is sufficient to prevent
the appearance of particularity, cannot be alleged in defence
of those persons, who are solicitous to pursue existing modes
through their minute ramifications, or who seek to distinguish
themselves as the introducers or early followers of new
modes. Fickleness, or vanity, or ambition, is the motive
which encourages such desires : desires which afford pre-
sumptive evidence of feebleness of intellect ; though found
occasionally to actuate and degrade superior minds. It happens,
in the embellishment of the person, as in most other instances,
that wayward caprice, and a passion for admiration, deviate
into those paths of folly which lead from the objects of
pursuit. So preposterous and fantastic are the disguises of the
human form which modern fashion has exhibited, that her
votaries, when brought together in her public haunts, have
sometimes been found scarcely able to refrain from gazing
with an eye of ridicule and contempt on each other. And
while individually priding themselves on their elegance and
taste, they have very commonly appeared in the eyes of an
indifferent spectator to be running a race for the acquisition
of deformity.

It is a frequent and a just remark, that objects in their own
nature innocent and entitled to notice may become the
sources of disadvantage and of guilt, when, by being raised
from the rank of trifles to ideal importance, they occupy a
share of attention which they do not deserve ; and when
they are pursued with an immoderate ardour, which at once
indisposes the mind for occupations of higher concern, and
clouds it with malignant emotions. There are few subjects,
by a reference to which it is more easy to illustrate the observation; there are none to which it is more evidently necessary to apply it, than fashions in attire in equipage, in

furniture, in the embellishments of the table, and in other
similar circumstances. Thus, to speak of the topic immediately under consideration, if, in addition to that reasonable
degree of regard to propriety of attire which ensures the
strictest neatness, and a modest conformity in unobjectionable points to the authority of custom, a young woman per-
mits her thoughts to be frequently engaged by the subject
of exterior ornaments ; occupations of moment will be pro
portionably neglected. From the complacency natural to
all human beings, when employed in contemplating objects
by means of which the flattering hope of shining is presented to them ; she will be in the most imminent danger
of contracting a distaste to serious reflection, and of being
at length absorbed in the delusions of vanity and self-love.
It is undoubtedly a matter of indifference, whether a lady's
ribands be green or blue ; whether her head be decorated
with flowers or with feathers ; whether her gown be composed of muslin or of silk. But it is no matter of indifference, whether the time which she devotes to the determination of one of these points, is to be reckoned by hours or by
minutes ; nor whether, on discovering the elevation of her
bonnet to be an inch higher or lower, and its tint a shade
lighter or darker, than the model which prevails among her
acquaintance, she is overwhelmed with consternation and
disappointment, or bears the calamity with the apathy of a
stoic.

I have not scrupled in the preceding pages explicitly to
inculcate the duty of refraining from compliance with
fashions in dress, which would be accompanied with a degree of *expense inconsistent with the present circumstances of
the individual.* Let not the admonition be conceived as intended to countenance a niggardly disposition. To prevent
the danger of contracting such a disposition, has been one
of the principal reasons for offering the advice. Young
women who accustom themselves to be lavish in matters of
personal decoration, easily proceed to think, that so long
as they restrain their expensiveness within the limits of the
resources supplied by their parents and friends, they are not
chargeable with blame on the subject. If they pay their
bills punctually, who is entitled to find fault ? Those persons will discern just cause of reprehension, who do not
consider the honest payment of bills at the customary times,
as comprising the whole of human duty with regard to the
expenditure of money. The demands of justice may be si-
lenced : but has benevolence no claims to be satisfied ? The
fact is, that an unguarded fondness for ornament has been

known, in a multitude of examples, to overpower the native
tenderness of the female mind; and to prevent the growth
and establishment of dispositions pronounced in the Gospel
to be indispensably requisite to the Christian character. If
the purse be generally kept low by the demands of milliners,
of mantua-makers, of jewellers, and dealers in trinkets, and
of others who bear their part in adorning the person; little
can be allotted to the applications of charity. But charity
requires, in common with other virtues, the fostering influence of habit. If the custom of devoting an adequate portion of the income to the relief of distress be long inter-
mitted, the desire of giving relief will gradually be impaired. The heart forgets, by disuse, the emotions in which it
once delighted. The ear turns from solicitations now become unwelcome. In proportion as the wants and the griefs
of others are disregarded, the spirit of selfishness strikes
deeper and stronger roots in the breast. Let the generous
exertions of kindness be tempered with discretion; but let a
disposition to those exertions be encouraged on principles of
duty; and confirmed, in proportion to the ability of the
individual, by frequency of practice. Before the world
has repressed, by its interested lessons, the warmth of youthful
benevolence; let experience establish a conviction, that the
greatest of all pleasures is to do good. She who has accustomed herself to this delight, will not easily be induced to forego
it. She will feel, that whatever she is able, without penu-
riousness or improper singularity, to withdraw from the
expense of personal ornament, is not only reserved for much
higher purposes, but for purposes productive of exquisite and
permanent gratification.

Another, and a very important benefit which results from
fixed habits of moderation as to dress, and all points of a
similar nature, will be clearly discerned by adverting to the
irreparable evils into which young women are sometimes
plunged by the contrary practice. The lavish indulgence
in which they have learned to seek for happiness, becoming,
in their estimation, essential to their comfort, is able to bias
their conduct in every important step. Hence, in forming
matrimonial connexions, it exercises perhaps a secret but
a very powerful influence. The prospect of wealth and
magnificence, of the continuance and of the increase ot
pleasures supposed to flow from the pomp of dress and equipage, from sumptuous mansions, shewy furniture, and numerous attendants, dazzles the judgment; imposes on the
affections; conceals many defects in moral character, and
compensates for others. It frequently proves the decisive

circumstance which leads the deluded victim to the altar, there to consign herself to splendid misery for life.

There are yet other consequences which attend an immoderate passion for the embellishments of dress. When the mind is fixed upon objects which derive their chief value from the food which they administer to vanity and the love of admiration; the aversion, which almost every individual of either sex is prone to feel towards a rival, is particularly called forth. And when objects, attainable so easily as exterior ornaments, occupy the heart, there will be rivals without number. Hence it is not very unusual to see neighbouring young women engaged in a constant state of petty warfare with each other To vie in ostentatiousness, in costliness, or in elegance of apparel; to be distinguished by novel inventions in the science of decoration; to gain the earliest intelligence respecting the changes of fashion in the metropolis; to detect, in the attire of a luckless competitor, traces of a mode which for six weeks has been obsolete in high life; these frequently are the points of excellence to which the force of female genius is directed. In the mean time, while the mask of friendship is worn on the countenance, and the language of regard dwells on the tongue, indifference, disgust, and envy, are gradually taking possession of the breast; until, at length, the unworthy contest, prolonged for years under confirmed habits of dissimulation, by which none of the parties are deceived, terminates in the violence of an open rupture.

There is no set of people, however envied, more to be pitied than the fluttering votaries of that capricious dame, called FASHION; whose vagaries are endless, and whose taste and humour is so uncertain, it is scarcely to be relied upon for an hour: ever fertile at invention, her mazy and tempting wiles are dangerously alluring to the young, the artless, and beautiful: many a spotless character has been sacrificed at her gaudy decorated shrine; many a fair reputation lost, to obtain the feathers and the flowers of Fashion; so difficult is it to set proper bounds to vanity, or to say to pride, so far you shall lead me, and no farther.

However trifling or unpleasant this subject may appear to the lovers of dress, who study more to adorn their persons than improve their minds, it is, in my opinion, become, at this period, a matter that deserves their most serious consideration: it is an epidemical disease that appears to have affected all ranks of people. Numerous are the evils it has occasioned, from the peer to the humble mechanic, from the *duchess* to the *chambermaid*. Many unhappy young women has the love of dress brought upon the town, more the victims to their own vain pride, than to the artifices and designs of mankind.

Ever, therefore, cautiously avoid the extravagance and extremes of fashion, and let your appearance be directed by your circumstances and situation. Can any thing be more absurd and out of character, than to see a young girl at an assembly, or any other public place, drest in a style as if entitled to expect *ten thousand pounds* to her marriage portion, when perhaps, if inquiries are made, a *few hundreds* are all that her friends will have it in their power to give her? Such an improper appearance, instead of being any recommendation, is almost the certain method of preventing her making a decent and comfortable establishment in life. What prudent man would think seriously of uniting himself with a young woman sò likely to spend his fortune, or the produce of his industry, upon the decoration of her person? which, if pretty, requires not the borrowed aid of ornament, and, if plain, would be less exposed to observation, by being simply and plainly drest.

Consider, how trifling is the value of that respect which dress extorts! Look at the vain peacock; you may admire his plumage for a moment, but you are soon weary of doing so. Observe the gaudy butterfly; but recollect how short its stay, how trifling and useless its life, how unlamented and unmarked its departure! Learn industry of the humble ant; contemplate the bee, and be taught wisdom.

There is a MODESTY in dress that should also be attended to. Dress is an important article in female life. And here I wish you to aim at propriety, neatness, and elegance, rather than affectation or extravagance : the one is always commendable, while the other is the object of contempt. Virtue itself is disagreeable in a sloven ; and that woman who takes no care of herself, will find nobody will care for her. The chief fault in dress is excess ; mind your persons, but mind your understandings too, and do not be *fools* in order to be *belles.* Above all things consult decency and ease ; never expose nor torture nature. That dress is most elegant, which is apparently the most easy, and seems to be the least studied. As extravagant and ridiculous as fashions are in general, there is no dressing elegantly without some attention to them : but be always within the fashion, rather than exceed it ; you will be admired for the one, but laughed at for the other. Have a better opinion of yourself than to suppose you can receive any additional merit from the adventitious ornaments of dress. Leave the study of the toilet to those who are adapted to it : I mean that insignificant set of females, whose whole life, from the cradle to the coffin is only a varied scene of trifling, and whose understandings fit them not for any thing beyond it.   Remember that it is not dress, however sumptuous, which reflects dignity and honour on the person; but the rank and merit of the person, that gives consequence to dress.

Men are apt to judge of your characters from your dress Indeed, vanity, levity, filthiness, and folly, shew themselves in nothing more.   An elegant neatness is the strongest proof of taste and delicacy.

If you wish to please, your attention to dress should not be confined to your appearing abroad.   Study to be neat at all times; accustom yourselves to it, so that in your most unguarded hours, in your most careless undress, you will never be afraid of being seen.   Study,

> Still to be neat, still to be drest,
> As tho' you were going to a feast.

In regard to your appearance, my fair readers, a nice medium should be observed, and all extremes carefully avoided: the fewer whimsical caprices or ornaments, amongst the middling class of people, in the article of dress, the better   Neatness, simplicity, and frugality, should be the only counsellors consulted by those, whose situations are such as demand a proper attention to economy.   Even the sons and daughters of rank and affluence, would be less exposed to, and often escape ridicule, did they confine their appearance to the rules laid down by reason and common sense.   The example of the great will ever be followed by the little.   An expensive fashion, has often proved a heavy tax upon the industrious father of a numerous family.

Nor are the lordly sex exempt from this epidemical vanity; the effeminately ornamented figures we often see amongst our young men, contrasted with the more masculine appearance of many of our young women, makes it a matter of some difficulty to distinguish (since this strange innovation of dress took place) one sex from the other.   So various and unaccountable are the deceptions lately practised, that nature seems to be entirely out of fashion, and *her* lilies and roses thought of but little value.

I much admire to see a fine exhibition of pictures; but never wish to see any painting on the human face; it is the destroyer of beauty, the enemy of health, and a kind of pantomimical trick; which, whilst it destroys the most brilliant eyes, renders those of others very clear-sighted in discovering the cause of their defect.

This subject reminds me of Hamlet's speech to Ophelia. " I have heard of your painting, too ; well enough:—God has

" given you one face, and you make yourselves another:—
" You jig, you amble, and you lisp, and nick-name God's
" creatures, and make your wantonness your ignorance—Go to,
" I'll no more on't; it doth make me mad."

Artifice is not likely to please. A false face may be supposed the covering to a false heart. It would be infinitely less
trouble to make yourselves by nature, what you vainly attempt
by art. Were any one of these self-destroying beauties to lose
by necessity what they do by choice, they would think themselves the most wretched beings on earth.

What renders an improper and extravagant fondness for dress
more absurd is, that it does not go off with youth, but appears to
increase and gather strength with our years. To attempt appearing young when we are no longer so, only serves to expose
old age to ridicule, and deprive it of that respectful attention to
which it has a just claim.

Before I take leave of my readers on this subject, I must entreat they will endeavour to appear like what they really are,
and forsake the mean practice of deception, not only in their
dress, but in their actions. It would soon produce an amazing
but pleasing and useful alteration in the world. Do not mistake me, my young friends; for I do not mean, by what I have
said on this subject, that young women should neglect, or become totally indifferent to the decoration of their persons: by
no means; but they should carefully avoid all extremes, particularly when inimical to neatness. Pyramids of frippery and
false taste, paints, powders, wool, and a number of *et-ceteras*,
should be left to the Hottentots: they only serve to disguise and
disfigure beauty, and may be justly called a provoking innovation on nature. One of our poets says, and I cordially join
him in the sentiment,

Give me a look, give me a face,
Which makes simplicity a grace;
This, this, more taketh me
Than all th' adult'ries of art,
Which charms the eye, but not the heart.

Let therefore a too great love of vanity and dress be banished from every mind—a desire of useful knowledge, good
humour, humility, and cautious prudence—fill up the vacancy.
Marriage will then regain its former honours, consequence, and
respect—modesty re-assume its original fascinating power, and
virtue again be reckoned the brightest and most becoming ornament of woman : whilst inconstancy, seduction, pride, repentance, and shame, shall be sentenced to hide their baleful heads
in the *cave* of *oblivion*.

CHAPTER II.

BEHAVIOUR AND MANNERS.

AFTER *modesty,* dignity of manner is the highest ornament of the female character.   It gives a distinguishing lustre to every look, every motion, every sentence you utter; in short, it gives that charm to beauty, without which it generally fails to please. By dignity of manner I would not be understood to mean *pride,* nor the least tincture of haughtiness; but a care not to let yourself down in the opinion of the rational part of your acquaintance.   You certainly may possess dignity without pride, affability without meanness, and elegance without affectation.

As mariners steer clear of the shoals and quicksands laid down in their charts, I shall now draw a picture of a character to be especially avoided by young females—that of *a vain woman.*

When a woman once becomes vain, her thoughts are so much employed on her own dear person, that, when with others, she neither sees nor hears any thing that passes.   She takes such pains in her conversation to bring in herself upon all occasions, that the artifice is readily seen through, and sneered at. It is highly laughable to see her angling for praise, and rise so dissatisfied with the *ill-bred* company, if they will not bite; to observe her throwing her eyes about to catch admirers.   She cruises like a privateer, and is greatly out of countenance if she returns without a prize.   She is so eager to draw respect, that she always misses it: yet thinks it so much her due, that when she fails she grows waspish ; not considering that the opinions of others cannot be taken by storm.

If the world, instead of admiring her imaginary excellencies takes the liberty to ridicule them, she appeals to herself, gives sentence in her own favour, and proclaims it wherever she goes.   On the contrary, if encouraged by a single word, she is so very obliging and grateful, that she will thank you again and again, though in fact you are only laughing at her.   She construes a compliment into a demonstration; thinks herself *divine,* because she is told so in gallantry ; and believes it sooner than she would her looking-glass.   But the good lady forgets all this while, that the men, against whom she directs her artillery, would not submit to her impertinence, but with views she little thinks of.   Every civil thing they say to any other lady in company, is a dagger to her.   It makes her so uneasy, that she cannot keep her seat, but up she rises, and goes home, half burst with anger. She looks on rules, as things made for common people, and not for persons of her rank. If, by great fortune, she happens, in spite of her vanity, to be honest, she is quite troublesome with it. Her bragging of her virtue looks as if it cost her so much pains to get the better of her inclination, that the inferences are very ridiculous. Her good humoui is chiefly employed in laughing at good sense; and it is pleasant to see how heartily she despises any thing that is fit for hei to do. Her fancy is chiefly taken up in the choice of a gown, or some such thing; and so faithful and obsequious is she to the fashion, that she would be reconciled even to virtue, with all its faults, if she thought it was practised at court.

To a woman so composed, when *affectation* comes in to heighten the character, she is the very summit of absurdity. She first sets up for something extrao linary, and on this account will distinguish herself, right or wrong, and is particular in every thing she does. She would have it thought, that she is formed of finer clay than other people, and that she has no common earth about her. Hence, she neither moves nor speaks like other women, because it is *vulgar*; and as ordinary *Englisł* is too coarse for her, she must have a language of her own, and the words of that she minces.

Her looking-glass, in the morning, directs all her motions for the day. She comes into a room as if her limbs were set on with ill-made screws, which puts the company in a panic, lest the pretty thing should drop some of its artificial person as she moves. She does not like herself as God Almighty made her; of course colours her face, and pencils her eyebrows. She falls out with nature, against which she is ever at war, except in those moments when her gallant is with her When she wishes to be soft and languishing, there is something in her affected easiness, so unnatural, that her frowns are fai more engaging. When she would appear humble, it is carried to an uncommon length, and, at the same time, she is so exceedingly proud, that there is no enduring it.

There is such an impertinent *smile*, such a satisfied *simper* when she faintly disowns some fulsome compliment, made her perhaps at the sacrifice of truth, that her thanks for it are more visible under this disguise, than they could be, were she to declare them openly. If a handsome woman takes the liberty of dressing herself out of the fashion, *she* immediately does the same, and makes herself uglier than ever. Her discourse is a senseless chime of empty words; a heap of compliments, so equally applied to very different persons, that they are neither valued nor believed. Her eyes keep pace with her tongue, and are therefore always in motion. She thinks that paint and sin are concealed by railing at them. In short, divided between her beauty and her virtue, she is often tempted to give broad hints, that somebody is dying for her ; and of the two, she is less unwilling to let the world think she may be sometimes profaned, than that she is never worshipped.

This picture, strange as it is, is a striking likeness of some of our modern ladies. Their deformity, well considered, is instruction enough ; for the same reason, that the sight of a drunkard is a better sermon against that vice, than the best that ever was preached upon it.

The men are too apt to indulge themselves in a species of refined luxury to which the ladies are yet strangers, and I hope will continue so. I mean that of eating. It is despicable enough in men, but it would be beyond expression indelicate and disgusting in women. However valuable may be the blessings of health, it is indelicate in a lady to boast of it ; to talk of her great appetite or her strength ; to say she eats heartily, can walk several miles, or can bear a good deal of fatigue. Softness is a charm of *your* sex, to which we annex a delicacy of constitution ; and any expression which reverses that idea, is disgusting to *ours*. It is also indelicate and exceedingly illiberal for a young lady to talk of being hot, or to say she sweats, &c.; such things will lessen her in the opinion of gentlemen, who wish the female sex to be all attraction.

Never *receive a present* of any considerable value from a gentleman who is indifferent to you; for we are apt to put unfavourable constructions on the acceptance of such presents ; few men give them but with particular views, and the giver generally concludes, that the girl who accepts his presents, would, if offered, as readily receive his hand.

If invited by a gentleman, at any shop, to accept a present, and you cannot, without affronting him, refuse it ; be sure to fix on something of little value ; and let no persuasions tempt you to alter your choice : not only for the reasons assigned above, but that you may not be thought ill-bred, covetous, or mercenary.

Should a gentleman, on proper occasions, politely approach to salute you, modestly receive his salute ; as drawing back, or a refusal would be the highest affront you could shew him but never *return it*, except it be to a very near relation, lest improper constructions be put upon it.

Be careful of being too familiar, especially with the men, who are apt to take advantages of it. Be as affable as you please, but do not be familiar : nay, it is safer for a woman to be thought too proud than too familiar. The advantages of being reserved are too many to be here enumerated: I shall only say, that it is a guard to a *good woman*, and a disguise to an *ill one*. It is of so much use to both, that such as refuse to practise it as a *virtue*, would do well to use it as an *artifice*.

A lady's *civility*, which is always to be preserved, must not be carried to a *compliance*, which may betray her into irrecoverable difficulties. The word *complaisance* has led your sex into greater errors, than all other things put together. It carries them by degrees, into a certain thing called a *good kind of woman*, which is an easy, idle creature, that does neither good nor harm but by chance, and has no choice but that of the company she keeps. She thinks it a rudeness to refuse, when civilly requested, either her service, in person, or her friendly assistance to those who wish for a party, or want a confidant. There is nothing very criminal indeed in this character; but it is far from being a respectable one.

There is another not less ridiculous, which is that of the *good-humoured woman*, who, as good-humour is an obliging quality, thinks she must always be laughing; hence she wears upon her face an insipid, unmeaning simper, smiling upon all alike. Rather than be silent in company, which she considers as dulness, she will chatter without end; and if applauded for any thing she says, she is so encouraged, that like a ballad-singer, when commended, she will strain her voice, talk louder and faster, till no one is heard but herself. She idly conceives that mirth should have no intermission, and therefore she carries it about with her, though it be to a funeral. Nay, let her hear what she will, or see what she will, she is never offended, that being inconsistent with her character. Thus does she expose herself to the derision of her acquaintance, who would not fail to shew it openly, but out of charity to her. It is highly absurd in a lady to suppose that she cannot be good company unless she shews herself at all times infinitely pleased. In a handsome woman, this kind of attraction is unnecessary, and in one who is not so, ridiculous. Not that I want to throw every spark of nature out of your composition and make you entirely artificial; no, I would have you cheerful and pleasing, but, at the same time, easy and unaffected. Fools *are always painted* LAUGHING, sufficient, I should imagine, to deter a wise person from it; much more from laughing loud, which is disgustful in men, but abominable in women. This boisterous kind of mirth is as contrary to good humour and good-manners, as it is to modesty and virtue.

If at any time an improper conversation should be started in your presence, seem not to hear it; or withdraw. I

you keep good company you will not often find yourself in such a disagreeable situation; but it may sometimes happen, as fools will occasionally intrude themselves where their company is despised.

Industriously avoid every thing that is masculine, either in your dress or your behaviour. Many things unnoticed in the men are disgustful in women; such as sitting cross-legged, spitting, blowing their noses, which last *may* be avoided in company by habit and attention; but if necessity obliges you, where you can, retire. The power of a fine woman over the hearts of men, if she is perfectly delicate, is beyond conception; but still it is in her power to dispel the charm; and if she is not careful, she may soon reduce the angel to a very ordinary girl.

The female sex are accused of being particularly addicted to the vice of *detraction;* why they are so, I cannot take upon me to say; in my opinion, the men are equally guilty, where their interests interfere. However let me advise you to guard against it at all times, but especially where your own sex are concerned; and where you may chance to have a rival, and to be speaking of her, be nicely tender of her reputation : it will dignify you in our minds more than you are aware of. Were you to speak degradingly of her, it would be attributed to meanness and jealousy; but if you mention her with respect, it would give a high opinion of your greatness of mind.

Sympathize in the distress of unfortunate women, particularly those who fall by the artful villany of men. Sink them not lower by any severity of censure, or ungenerous upbraidings; but pride yourself in being the friend of the unhappy, and pity where you can.

Great intimacies are both foolish and imprudent; for when once broken, of which they scarce ever fail, the bag of secrets is untied; they fly about like birds let loose from a cage, and become the entertainment of the town. Besides, they are not only imprudent, but lead to ill manners; for when an intimate friend comes into company where you are, there is such a distinction shewn her, that is offensive and affronting to all the rest.

Never suffer any one, under the pretence of friendship, *to take unbecoming liberties* with you. Never submit to be teazed by them, where it is disagreeable to you; but exert a proper spirit, and support that dignity that will always entitle you to respect. No friendship whatever will authorize unbecoming freedoms, and I should doubt the affection of any one, who would take pleasure in making me unhappy.

But yet, I would not have you formal. There is a medium

to be preserved. Be reserved, but do not seem so. If formality is allowable in any instance, it is in resisting the intrusion of such forward women, as shall attempt to force them selves into your friendship; for, if admitted, they will either be a snare or an incumbrance.

I must further caution you against forming any friendship with men. Many a valuable young woman has been ruined by men, who approached them under the sanction of friendship. Even admitting a man to have the strictest honour, yet is his friendship to women so near akin to love, that often, where they looked for a friend only, they have found a lover

MODESTY

The principal beauty and basis of the female character is modesty : I mean that modest reserve, that delicacy, that retires from the public eye, and is disconcerted even at being admired. It is of itself so beautiful, as to be a charm to hearts insensible of every other charm ; and has conquered, when a fair face has been overlooked. Though art and nature shall conspire to render a woman lovely, still if she wear the appearance of boldness, it blots out every trace of beauty, and, like a cloud that shades the sun, intercepts the view of all that is amiable. Blushing in man may be a weakness, but in woman it is peculiarly engaging.

There cannot be a more captivating or interesting object than a young girl, who, with *timid modesty,* enters a room filled with a mixed company. The blush, which diffuses its crimson on her cheek, is not only the most powerful charm of beauty, but does honour to the innocence of her heart, and has a peculiar claim on the tender and generous feelings of every susceptible mind. Her artless confusion and retiring delicacy merit indulgence, and demand universal respect. To insult or distress modesty, is too commonly the degrading humour of unblushing vice.

Modesty, however, is not confined to the face ; there it is merely the shadow ; would we look for the substance, it is in actions and in words : in amusements and in dress. I will not suppose a young lady, who has had a liberal education, can be bold in her actions ; but so nice is the distinction with respect to her conversation, her amusements, and her dress, that there are few, on their first outset in life, but need advice in this particular.

Modesty not only refines the language, but often modulates the voice and accent. A woman by no means should talk loud ; her tongue should be, like the music of the spheres, sweet and charming, but not heard at a distance. A loud talker

conveys the idea of a scold, and scolding is the strongest mark
of low breeding.

It has of late years been thought necessary to introduce
young people early into what is called LIFE, in order that this
rustic and beautiful diffidence might not expose them to the
observation and ridicule of the fashionable world.   Mistaken
notion ! cruel innovation on the sweet simplicity of youth and
innocence ! What an opinion does it give a rational and thinking mind of modern refinements, which have so dangerous a
tendency !

In former ages, a modest and diffident woman was sure to
meet with general respect, and appeared to have a just demand on every one for protection.   Vice then fled, to conceal
its ugliness and deformity from the penetrating eyes of the
world ; and the wily libertine, the unprincipled gambler, or
the known votary of Bacchus, were shunned, as monsters
formed to destroy ; whilst the poor victims of their baseness,
unable to support the humiliating distresses which their own
weakness and the frailties of others had brought upon them,
atoned, by years of penitence and voluntary obscurity, for a
few hours of guilt, folly, and believing tenderness.

But the countenance and indulgence which has for so long a
period been extended to fashionable seduction, has rendered too
many regardless of censure and fearless of consequences.   The
unhappy daughters of frailty, by being often seen, seldom rob
us of tears ; and at the same time their miseries are beheld with
contempt or indifference by their own sex, and are either encouraged or insulted by the other ; they are deprived of hope
by cruelty, or bribed into a continuance in guilt, till they become
too hardened for repentance ; and often, after a life of misery,
end their wretched existence--the victims of folly, persecution,
despair, and want.

Hapless children of indiscretion ! Whilst the good, humane,
and benevolent behold your sufferings with an eye of tender
compassion, and pray for your reformation, your own hearts
will not be so indulgent to your failings; you will ever, at times,
in the bitterness of anguish, lament your first deviation from the
safe, serene, and pleasant paths of modest innocence; and in the
serious moments of reflection (for such moments there will be
found to steal upon you, could you even secure yourselves a
constant residence in the house of joy,) regret the heart-rending
pangs of imprudence brought on your unfortunate parents :
and till the cold hand of death has closed those eyes which
once sparkled with the soft emanation of unsullied purity, lament
your disregard of the divine precepts of religion, the basis of
every virtue.

May this true, though painful description, of those unhappy females, who have fallen into the snares of guilt, check too eager a desire after pleasure in the youthful mind unspotted with a crime! May it suppress all impatient desires of being early introduced into a world from which they have so much to fear, and so little to hope!

Look into yourselves, learn wisdom, and acquire experience, before you venture into the dangerous vortex of beguiling pleasure. *If you cannot find contentment in the sweet security of domestic enjoyments, be assured you will never find happiness abroad.*

Many women have lost their characters through indiscretion only. With respect to the world, it is as bad to appear wicked, as to be really so. She who throws off her modesty either in her words or her dress, will not be thought to set much value upon it in her actions.

Some women unfortunately know themselves to be handsome, and rather than not make the most of their beauty, learn the art of *languishing;* and flatter themselves that the tenderness they affect, may pass for innocence, and their languishing for modesty. There is an impudence in the very bashful part of such women's behaviour; the *flutter of the fan, the awkwardness of the look, the disorder of the gesture,* at hearing what they should know nothing of, warm the imagination of those men that see them, and lay them open to their attacks.

Fear not the being reproached with *prudery.* Prudery is the affectation only of delicacy. I do not mean that you should *affect* it, but *possess* it in reality. At any rate, it is better to be thought ridiculous than loose.

Possibly you may be called *reserved,* and may be told by the men, that a more open behaviour would render you more amiable. Believe me, they are false who tell you so. As companions, indeed, it may make you more agreeable, but as women, less amiable. However, I mean not to forbid your being easy and frank in conversation; but to guard you against too great freedom, or the least tincture of indelicacy.

There is an innate dignity in ingenuous modesty peculiar to *your* sex, which naturally protects you from the freedom of *ours.* This sense of virtue should be felt by every woman, prior to the reflection that it is her interest to keep herself sacred from familiarities with the men. That a woman may admit of innocent freedoms, provided she keeps her virtue sacred, is a notion, not only indelicate in the highest degree, but dreadfully dangerous and has proved so to many of your sex.

I shall close my advice to my fair readers, on this important subject, with the following beautiful description of that *inestimable jewel*,—a MODEST WOMAN.

" Lo ! yonder she walketh in maiden sweetness, with innocence in her mind, and modesty on her cheek.

" Her hand seeketh employment, her foot delighteth not in gadding abroad.

" She is clothed with neatness, she is fed with temperance; humility and meekness are as a crown of glory circling her head.

" On her tongue dwelleth music, the sweetness of honey floweth from her lips.

" Decency is in all her words, in her answers are mildness and truth.

" Submission and obedience are the lessons of her life, peace and happiness are her reward.

" Before her steps walketh Prudence, and Virtue attendeth at her right hand.

" Her breast is the mansion of goodness, and therefore she suspecteth no evil in others.

" Happy were the man that should make her his wife, happy the child that shall call her mother."

CHAPTER III.

INTRODUCTION INTO COMPANY.

EMANCIPATED from the shackles of instruction, the young woman is now to be brought forward to act her part on the public stage of life. And as though liberty were a gift unattended with temptations to inexperienced youth ; as though vivacity, openness of heart, the consciousness of personal accomplishments and of personal beauty, would serve rather to counteract than to aggravate these temptations ; the change of situation is not unfrequently heightened by every possible aid of contrast. Pains are taken, as it were, to contrive, that the dazzled stranger shall step from the nursery at once into a flood of vanity and dissipation ; stimulated with desire to outshine her equals in age and rank, she burns with impatience for the hour of displaying her perfections : till, at length intoxicated beforehand with anticipated flatteries, she is launched, in the pride of ornament, on some occasion of festivity; and from that time forward thinks by day, and dreams by night, of amusements and of dress, and of compliments and of admirers.

I believe this picture to convey no exaggerated representation of the state of things, which is often witnessed in the higher ranks of society. I fear too, that it is a picture to which the practice of the middle ranks, thought at present not fully corresponding, bears a continually increasing resemblance. The extreme, however, which has been described, has, like every other extreme, its opposite. There are mothers who profess to initiate their daughters, almost from the cradle, into the knowledge, as they are wont to express themselves, of life; and pollute the years of childhood with an instilled attachment to the card-table; with habits of flippancy and pertness, denominated wit; with an " easiness" of manners, which ought to be named effrontery; and with a knowledge of tales of scandal, unfit to be mentioned by any one but in a court of justice. Both these extremes are most dangerous to every thing that is valuable in the female character; to every thing on which happiness in the present world and in a future world depends. But of the two the latter is the most pernicious. In that system war is carried on almost from infancy, and carried on in the most detestable manner, against female delicacy and innocence. In the former, that delicacy and that innocence are exposed under the greatest disadvantages to the sudden influence of highly-fascinating allurements. It may be hoped, however, that, coming to the encounter as yet little impaired, they may have some chances of escaping without severe injury. At any rate, be this chance ever so small, it is greater than the probability, that when assailed from their earliest dawn by slow poison incessantly administered, they should ultimately survive.

To accustom the mind by degrees to the trials which it must learn to withstand, yet to shelter it from insidious temptations, while it is unable to discern and to shun the snare, is the first rule which wisdom suggests with regard to all trials and temptations whatever. To this rule too much attention cannot be paid in the mode of introducing a young woman into the common habits of social intercourse. Let her not be distracted in the years by nature particularly designed for the cultivation of the understanding and the acquisition of knowledge, by the turbulence and glare of polite amusements.

Let her not be suffered to taste the draught which the world offers to her, until she has learned that, if there be sweetness on the surface, there is venom deeper in the cup; until she has acquired a right judgment and a well-directed taste as to the pursuits and pleasures of life, or, according to the language of the apostle, has become disposed " to approve the things which are excellent;" and is fortified with those principles of Christian temperance and rectitude, which may guard her against unsafe indulgence. Let vanity, and other unwarrantable springs of action, prompt at all times to exert their influence on the female character, and at no time likely to exert an influence more dangerous than when a young woman first steps into public life, be curtailed, as far as may be safely practicable, of the powerful assistance of novelty. Altogether to preclude that assistance is impossible.

But it may be disarmed of much of its force by gradual familiarity. Let that gradual familiarity take place under the superintendence of parents and near relations, and of friends of approved sobriety and discretion. Let not the young woman be consigned to some fashionable instructress, who, professing at once to add the last polish to education, and to introduce the pupil into the best company, will probably dismiss her thirsting for admiration; inflamed with ambition; devoted to dress and amusements; initiated in the science, and the habits of gaming; and prepared to deem every thing right and indispensable, which is or shall be recommended by modish example.

Let her not be abandoned in her outset in life to the giddiness and mistaken kindness of fashionable acquaintance in the metropolis; nor forwarded under their convoy to public places, there to be whirled, far from maternal care and admonition, in the circles of levity and folly, into which even had maternal care and admonition been at hand to protect her, she ought not to have been permitted to step. At this very important season, while the mother selects with cautious discrimination, and limits within narrow bounds, both as to time and expense, the scenes of public resort and entertainment, to which her youthful charge is now to be suffered to have access; let her cultivate in the mind of the latter with augmented solicitude, those principles, dispositions, and habits, which may lead her not only cheerfully to acquiesce in the course adopted, but even spontaneously and decidedly to prefer it to a system of less guarded indulgence.

Let a double share of attention be exerted to preserve and strengthen in her breast a sense of the sinfulness of human nature; of the necessity of constantly looking up for divine support; of the transitory and inconsiderable worth of temporal things compared with eternity; of the superiority of the peaceful and heartfelt joys, which flow from the discharge of duty and the animating hopes of the favour of God through Christ, over every other gratification. All these principles are menaced, when fresh inlets of insnaring pleasures are opened.

Let parental vigilance and love gently point out to the daughter, on every convenient occasion, what is proper or improper in the conduct of the persons of her own age, with whom she is in any degree conversant, and also the grounds of the approbation or disapprobation expressed. Let parental counsel and authority be prudently exercised in regulating the choice of her associates. And at the same time that she is habituated to regard distinctions of wealth and rank, as circumstances wholly unconnected with personal worth; let her companions be in general neither much above her own level, nor much below it: lest she should be led to ape the opinions, the expensiveness, and the fashionable follies of persons in a station higher than her own; or in her intercourse with those of humble condition, to assume airs of contemptuous and domineering superiority. Solicitude on the part of parents, to consult the welfare of their child in these points, will probably be attended with a farther consequence of no small benefit to themselves; when it persuades them to an increased degree of circumspection as to the visitors whom they encourage at home, and the society which they frequent abroad.

CHAPTER IV.

CONVERSATION AND LETTER-WRITING.

Canst thou be silent?   No ; for wit is thine ;
And wit talks most, when least she has to say,
And reason interrupts not her career.   YOUNG.

CONVERSATION is one of our most rational and highest enjoyments ; it is very necessary, therefore, that our readers should acquire an easy and pleasing manner of conversing on every subject proper for their sex and age ; but never to attempt those in which their want of knowledge would expose them to ridicule.

A *good memory* is a very necessary requisite to make an agreeable and intelligent companion. Diffidence is sometimes an impediment to young people's shewing their abilities in conversation ; but that will wear off, after associating a little time with the polite world. Yet, however brilliant your powers of conversing, they must be kept under the nicest restrictions. If so fortunate as to have a good understanding, united with the happy art of shewing it to advantage, you must never attempt to monopolize too much of the conversation to yourselves : but be content very often to wait till called upon to give your sentiments on the subject discussed : and then, be sure to give it with modest diffidence, which will not appear to enforce upon your hearers a certainty of being right in your opinions If you find you have been wrong in your sentiments or that you have mistaken the subject, be not captious, or displeased with those who endeavour to set you right; but le your mind be open to conviction, and be ever ready to acknowledge any error you have committed. Such an ingenuous proceeding, so far from being considered as a proof of your wanting judgment, will assuredly prove the contrary, and you will find every one ready to find excuses for you, and to prevent your making any future mistakes.

The *babbler* is a perpetual nuisance to society. It commonly happens that shallow streams make the loudest noise; so those who talk the most, very often talk the greatest nonsense. People who are fond of hearing themselves, have but few opportunities of improving from the conversation of others; and though they weary their hearers, they will not be prevailed upon to believe it possible. To talk much and well, requires a sound judgment, retentive memory, and good understanding, with a vast command of temper : for be assured, if you talk much, you will meet with many severe attacks for the innovation you are making on the time, patience, and pleasure of others.

Another ridiculous folly which the love of talking makes many people fall into, is *telling marvellous and improbable stories;* which, by being often repeated, grows tiresome, and frequently brings a reproach on the person's veracity. Some, indeed, have the happy art of telling a story well, and by the introduction of a good anecdote, or witty bon-mot, will set the table in a roar. But where one succeeds in this way many will fail, and find their endeavours to amuse, repaid, with a yawn or a dead silence. This is often owing to a slowness and formality in their manner, or by the improper introduction of a number of useless and unnecessary words: never attempt being witty by design, lest you meet with as severe a retort, as that given by Dean Swift to a young gentleman ; who, on hearing that bright genius, by his wit and pleasantry, enliven and produce the most violent bursts of laughter from his companions, started up on a sudden, and addressing the Dean—' You must know, Sir,' said he, ' I have a great mind to set up for a wit myself.'—' Have you so, young man?' replied Swift; ' then let me advise you to set down again.'

Let me caution you against *laughing too much* in company. Nothing serves to render any one more disagreeable, than a perpetual giggling, without any visible or ludicrous cause. It often excites the fears and apprehensions of those that are present, that they are the objects of your ill-timed mirth—a suspicion, to which perhaps some defect of person or appearance may have given rise. I have seen many worthy and sensible people hurt in this way, by the unthinking levity of youth, who came out for amusement, and were sent home by folly, with the thorn of discontent rankling in their bosoms.

A young gentleman, much addicted to laughing, happened to get into Swift's company; and, having heard much of the Dean's pleasantries, was upon the titter at every thing he said. ' Where is the jest?' said one that was present.—' There!' said Swift, pointing at the laughing gentleman.

Mankind being in general less solicitous to gain instruction than applause, we are certain of displeasing in conversation, when we appear more attentive to ourselves than to the company around us.

There is one offence committed in conversation, of much too serious a nature to be overlooked, or to be animadverted on without sorrow and indignation; I mean the habitual and thoughtless profaneness of those who are repeatedly invoking their Maker's name on occasions the most trivial. It is offensive in all its variety of aspects; it is pernicious in its effects; it is a *growing* evil; those who are most guilty of it, are, from habit, hardly conscious when they do it; are not aware of the sin; and for both these reasons, without the admonitions of faithful friendship, are little likely to discontinue it. It is utterly INEXCUSABLE; it has none of the palliatives of temptation which other vices plead, and in that respect stands distinguished from all others, both in its nature and degree of guilt. Like many other sins, however, it is at once cause and effect; it *proceeds* from want of love and reverence to the best of Beings, and *causes* the want of that love both in themselves and others Yet with all these aggravations, there is, perhaps, hardly any sin so frequently committed, so slightly censured, so seldom repented of, and so little guarded against. On the score of *impropriety* too, it is additionally offensive, as being utterly repugnant to female delicacy, which often does not see the turpitude of this sin, while it affects to be shocked at swearing in a man. Now this species of profaneness is not only swearing, but perhaps in some respects swearing of the worst sort; as it is a *direct* breach of an express command, and offends against the *very letter* of that law which says in so many words, THOU SHALT NOT TAKE THE NAME OF THE LORD THY GOD IN VAIN. It offends against politeness and *good-breeding*; for those who commit it, little think of the pain they are inflicting on the sober mind, which is deeply wounded when it hears the holy name it loves dishonoured; and it is as contrary to good breeding to give pain, as it is to true piety to be profane. It is astonishing that the refined and elegant should not reprobate this practice for its coarseness and vulgarity, as much as the pious abhor it for its sinfulness.

I would endeavour to give some faint idea of the grossness of this offence, by an analogy (oh! how inadequate!) with which the feeling heart, even though not seasoned with religion, may yet be touched. To such I would say: Suppose you had some beloved friend—to put the case still more strongly, a departed friend—a revered parent, perhaps, whose image never occurs without awaking in your bosom sentiments of tender love, and lively gratitude; how would you feel if you heard this honoured name *bandied about* with unfeeling familiarity, and indecent levity; or, at best, thrust into every pause of speech as a vulgar expletive? Does not your affectionate heart recoil at the thought? And yet the hallowed name of your truest Benefactor, your heavenly Father, your best Friend, to whom you are indebted for all that you enjoy; who gives you those very friends in whom you so much delight, those very talents with which you dishonour him, those very organs of speech with which you blaspheme him; is treated with an irreverence, a contempt, a wantonness, with which you cannot bear the very thought or mention of treating a human friend. His name is impiously, is unfeelingly, is ungratefully, singled out as the object of decided irreverence, of systematic contempt, of thoughtless levity. His sacred name is used indiscriminately to express anger, joy, grief, surprise, impatience, and, what is still more unpardonable than all, it is wantonly used as a mere unmeaning expletive, which, being excited by no temptation, can have nothing to extenuate it; which causing no emotion, can have nothing to recommend it, unless it be the pleasure of sin.

Among the deep, but less obvious mischiefs of conversation, *misrepresentation* must not be overlooked. Self-love is continually at work to give to all we say a bias in our own favour. The counteraction of this fault should be set about in the earliest stages of education. If young persons have not been discouraged in the natural but evil propensity, to relate every dispute they have had with others to their own advantage; if they have not been trained up to the bounden duty of doing justice even to those with whom they are at variance; if they have not been led to aim at a complete impartiality in their little narratives, and instructed never to take advantage of the absence of the other party, in order to make the story lean to their own side more than the truth will admit; how shall we in advanced life look for correct habits, for unprejudiced representations, for fidelity, accuracy, and unbiassed justice?

Yet how often in society, otherwise respectable, we are pained with narrations, in which prejudice warps and self-love blinds! How often do we see, that withholding a part of the truth answers the worst ends of a falsehood! How often regret the unfair turn given to a cause, by placing a sentiment in one point of view, which the speaker had used in another! the letter of truth preserved, where its spirit is violated! a superstitious exactness, scrupulously maintained in the under parts of a detail, in order to impress such an idea of integrity as shall gain credit for the *misrepresenter*, while he is designedly mistaking the leading principle! How often may we observe a new character given to a fact, by a different look, tone, or emphasis, which alters it as much as words could have done! the false impression of a sermon conveyed, when we do not like the preacher; or when, through him, we wish to make religion itself ridiculous! the care to avoid literal untruths, while the mischief is better effected by the unfair quotation of a passage divested of its context; the bringing together detached portions of a subject, and making those parts ludicrous, when connected, which were serious in their distinct position! the insidious use made of a sentiment by representing it as the *opinion* of him who had only brought it forward in order to expose it! that subtle falsehood which is so made to incorporate with a certain quantity of truth, that the most skilful moral chemist cannot analyze or separate them! for a good *misinterpreter* knows that a successful lie must have a certain infusion of truth, or it will not go down. And this amalgamation is the test of his skill; as too *much* truth would defeat the end of his mischief; and too *little* would destroy the belief of the hearer. All that undefinable ambiguity and equivocation; all that prudent deceit, which is rather implied than expressed; those more delicate artifices of the school of Loyola and of Chesterfield, which allow us, when we dare not deny a truth, yet so to disguise and discolour it, that the truth we relate shall not resemble the truth we heard! These, and all the thousand shades of simulation and dissimulation, will be carefully guarded against in the conversation of vigilant Christians.

Again, it is surprising to mark the common deviations from strict veracity, which spring not from enmity to truth, not from intentional deceit, not from malevolence or envy, not from the least design to injure; but from mere levity, habitual inattention, and a current notion that it is not worth while to be correct in little things. But here the doctrine of habit

comes in with great force, and in that view no error is small
The cure of this disease in its more inveterate stages being next
to impossible, its prevention ought to be one of the earliest objects of education.

Some women indulge themselves in sharp raillery, unfeeling
wit, and cutting sarcasms, from the consciousness, it is to be
feared, that they are secured from the danger of being called to
account; this licence of speech being encouraged by the very
circumstance which ought to suppress it. To be severe, because they can be so with impunity, is a most ungenerous reason.
It is taking a base and dishonourable advantage of their sex;
the weakness of which, instead of tempting them to commit
offences because they can commit them with safety, ought
rather to make them more scrupulously careful to avoid indis-
cretions, for which no reparation can be demanded. What
can be said for those who carelessly involve the injured party
in consequences from which they know themselves are exempted, and whose very sense of their own security leads them to
be indifferent to the security of others.

The grievous fault of gross and obvious calumny or detraction which infests conversation, has been so heavily and justly
condemned by divines and moralists, that the subject, copious
as it is, is nearly exhausted. But there is an error of an opposite complexion, which we have noticed, and against which the
peculiar temper of the times requires young women should be
guarded. There is an affectation of candour, which is almost
as mischievous as calumny itself; nay, if it be less injurious in
its individual application, it is, perhaps, more alarming in its
general principle, as it lays waste the strong fences which separate good from evil. They know, as a general principle,
(though they sometimes calumniate) that calumny is wrong;
but they have not been told that *flattery* is wrong also; and
youth, being apt to fancy that the direct contrary to wrong
must necessarily be right, are apt to be driven into violent extremes. The dread of being only suspected of one fault,
makes them actually guilty of the opposite, and to avoid the
charge of harshness, or of envy, they plunge into insincerity
and falsehood. In this they are actuated either by an unsound
judgment, which does not see what is right, or an unsound
principle, which prefers what is wrong. Some also com-
mend, to conceal envy; and others compassionate, to indulge
superiority.

In fine, to recapitulate what has been said, with some additional hints:—Study to promote both intellectual and moral
improvement in conversation; labour to bring into it a disposition to bear with others, and to be watchful over yourself;

keep out of sight any prominent talent of your own, which, if indulged, might discourage or oppress the feeble-minded ; and try to bring their modest virtues into notice.   If you know any one present to possess any particular weakness or infirmity, never exercise your wit by maliciously inventing occasions which may lead her to expose or betray it; but give as favourable a turn as you can to the follies which appear, and kindly help her to keep the rest out of sight.   Never gratify your own humour by hazarding what you suspect may wound any present, in their persons, connexions, professions in life, or religious opinions ; and do not forget to examine whether the laugh your wit has raised be never bought at this expense Cultivate true politeness, for it grows out of true principle and is consistent with the gospel of Christ; but avoid those feigned attentions which are not stimulated by good-will, and those stated professions of fondness which are not dictated by esteem.   Remember, that the pleasure of being thought *amiable* by strangers may be too dearly purchased, if it be purchased at the expense of truth and simplicity: remember, that simplicity is the first charm in manners, as truth is in mind ; and could truth make herself visible, she would appear vested in simplicity.

Remember also, that *true Christian goodness* is the soul, of which politeness is only the garb.   It is not that artificial quality which is taken up by many when they go into society, in order to charm those whom it is not their particular business to please ; and is laid down when they return home to those, to whom to appear amiable is a real duty.   It is not that fascinating, but deceitful softness, which, after having acted over a hundred scenes of the most lively sympathy, and tender interest, with every slight acquaintance—after having exhausted every phrase of feeling, for the trivial sicknesses or petty sorrows of multitudes who are scarcely known—leaves it doubtful whether a grain of real feeling or genuine sympathy be reserved for the dearest connexions ; and which dismisses a woman to her immediate friends with little affection, and to her own family with little attachment.

In concluding these remarks upon conversation we shall add a few words on a kindred subject—

LETTER WRITING.

Letters which pass between men commonly relate, in a greater or less degree, to actual business.   Even young men, on whom the cares of life are not yet devolved in their full weight, will frequently be led to enlarge to their absent friends on topics not only of an interesting nature, but also of a serious cast: on the studies which they are respectively pursuing; of the advantages and disadvantages of the profession to which the one or the other is destined; on the circumstances which appear likely to forward or to impede the success of each in the world. The seriousness of the subject, therefore, has a tendency, though a tendency which, I admit, is not always successful, to guard the writer from an affected and artificial style.

Young women, whose minds are comparatively unoccupied by such concerns, are sometimes found to want in their correspondence a counterpoise, if not to the desire of shining, yet to the quickness of imagination, and, occasionally, to the quickness of feeling, natural to their sex. Hence they are exposed to peculiar danger, a danger aggravated sometimes by familiarity with *novels* and *theatrical productions;* sometimes by the nature of the fashionable topics, which will proceed, from engrossing conversation, to employ the pen; of learning to clothe their thoughts in studied phrases; and even of losing simplicity both of thought and expression in florid, refined, and sentimental parade. Frequently, too, the desire of shining intermingles itself, and involves them in additional temptations They are ambitious to be distinguished for writing, as the phrase is, *good* letters.

Those letters only are good, which contain the natural effusions of the heart, expressed in unaffected language. Tinsel and glitter, and laboured phrases, dismiss the friend and introduce the authoress. From the use of strained and hyperbolical language, it is but a step to advance to that which is insincere. But though that step be not taken, all that is pleasing in letter-writing is already lost. And a far heavier loss is to be dreaded, the loss of *simplicity of manners and character* in other points. For when a woman is habitually betrayed into an artificial mode of proceeding by vanity, by the desire of pleasing, by erroneous judgment, or by any other cause; can it be improbable that the same cause should extend its influence to other parts of her conduct, and be productive of similar effects? In justice to the female sex, however, it ought to be added, that when amiable women, and especially amiable women of improved understandings, write with simplicity, and employ their pens in a more rational way than retailing the shapes of head-dresses and gowns, and thus, however without intention, encouraging each other in vanity, their letters are in many respects particularly pleasing. A few specimens of letters on common subjects are here added for the use of those who have been prevented from practising epistolary correspondence, and we shall conclude with some hints for avoiding vulgarisms and improprieties.

A Daughter to her Mother.

My dear mamma will, I hope, forgive this complaint, when I secretly inform her of the cause—though I confess myself frequently negligent, yet my governess's severity discomposes me in such a manner, that I am really incapable of attending to my work. I am frequently deprived of my breakfast—sometimes of my dinner—and have often supperless gone to bed, because I have not drunk large basons of camomile tea, which is so exceedingly obnoxious to me. If my dear mamma would remove me to another school, or prevail upon my governess to moderate her cruelty, my future conduct, I hope, will prove me—A dutiful daughter

The Mother's Answer.

Dear Mary,—The cause of complaint is ample excuse for your writing. I wish my dear girl had been earlier in her communication, for I should deem myself more cruel than your governess, did I connive at such unwarrantable usages. You shall leave the school immediately. I am, your affectionate mother.

A young Lady to her Mamma.

Dear Mamma,—The great pleasure I see other young ladies take in the study of arithmetic, and the advantage it seems to give them in conversation, render me desirous to be similarly accomplished. I throw myself with confidence on the kindness of my dear and ever-indulgent mamma, to favour me in this particular, and flatter myself that her approbation of my proficiency in this branch of education will be equal to that she was pleased to bestow on me in the last holidays, and which contributed so much to the felicity of—My dear mamma's most dutiful and affectionate daughter.

Dr. Johnson to Miss Thrale.

Dearest Miss Sophy,—By an absence from home, and from one reason or another, I owe a great number of letters, and I assure you, that I sit down to write your's first. Why you should think yourself not a favourite, I cannot guess; my favour will, I am afraid never be worth much; but, be its value more or less, you are never likely to lose it, and less likely if you continue your studies with the same diligence as you have begun them.

Your proficiency in arithmetic is not only to be commended, but admired. Your master does not, I suppose, come very often nor stay very long: yet your advance in the science of

numbers is greater than is commonly made by those who, for as
many weeks as you have been learning, spend six hours a day
in the writing-school.

Never think, my sweet, that you have arithmetic enough;
when you have exhausted your master, buy books. Nothing
amuses more harmlessly than computation, and nothing is
oftener applicable to real business or speculative inquiries. A
thousand stories, which the ignorant tell and believe, die away
at once, when the computest takes them in his gripe. I hope
you will cultivate in yourself a disposition to numerical inquiries: they will give you entertainment in solitude, by the practice; and reputation in public, by the effect. Let me hear
from you soon again. I am your's, &c.

Dr. Johnson to Miss Susannah Thrale.

Dearest Miss Susy,—When you favoured me with your letter, you seemed to be in want of materials to fill it, having met
with no great adventures, either of peril or delight, nor done or
suffered any thing out of the common course of life.

When you have lived longer, and considered more, you will
find the common course of life very fertile of observation and
reflection. Upon the common course of life must our thoughts
and our conversation be generally employed. Our general
course of life must denounce us wise or foolish, happy or miserable; if it is well regulated, we pass on prosperously and
smoothly; as it is neglect' we 'ive in embarrassment, perplex-
ity, and uneasiness.

Your time, my love, passes I suppose in devotion, reading,
work, and company. Of your devotions, in which I earnestly
advise you to be very punctual, you may not, perhaps, think it
proper to give me an account; and of work, unless I understood
it better, it will be of no great use to say much; but books and
company will always supply you with materials for your letters
to me, as I shall always be pleased to know what you are reading, and with what you are pleased, and shall take great delight
in knowing what impression new modes or new characters make
upon you, and to observe with what attention you distinguish
the tempers, dispositions, and abilities, of your companions.

A letter may be always made out of the books of the morning, or talk of the evening; and any letters from you, my dearest,
will be welcome to your, &c.

Dr. Johnson to Miss Jane Langton.

My dearest Miss Jenny,—I am sorry that your pretty letter
has been so long without being answered; but when I am not-

well, I do not always write plain enough for young ladies. I am glad, my dear, to see you write so well, and hope that you mind your pen, your book, and your needle, for they are all necessary: your books will give you knowledge, and make you respected; and your needle will find you useful employment when you do not care to read. When you are a little older, I hope you will be very diligent in learning arithmetic; and, above all, that through your whole life you will carefully say your prayers, and read your Bible. I am, my dear, your most humble servant.

Hints for avoiding Vulgarisms and Improprieties.

1. *Spelling.*—It is now usual to dismiss the *u* from the final syllable of words ending in *our*, as *honour, labour,* &c., and the concluding *k* from words ending *ck*, as *almanack, tragick, comick; compleat,* is now more properly written *complete,* &c

2. *Vulgarisms.*—*I comes, I goes,* &c., for *I come, I go. Learn* is frequently used for *teach, set* for *sit, laid* for *lay, mistaken* for *mistaking,* &c. *Was* is used for *were,* and the power of conjunctions is little attended to, viz., if *he was,* instead of if *he were* Adjectives are commonly used for adverbs; *he wrote agreeable to your order,* should be *he wrote agreeably*
Proverbial expressions and trite sayings are the flowers of the rhetoric of a low-bred person; instead of saying, *My friend was compelled by necessity,* he would say, *Necessity has no law,* &c.; such vulgar aphorisms ought to be rejected which are common and in familiar use. An attentive writer would not say, *It was all through you it happened,* but *It happened through your inattention.*

3. *Punctuation,* inasmuch as it is necessary to the proper division of sentences, is of very great importance. It may easily be acquired by looking at the position of points in books, and by consulting good treatises, as *Stackhouse on Punctuation,* &c. In general, points are the pauses which a correct orator would use in speaking, and as a knowledge of their powers is to be acquired with very *little care,* the neglect of them is unpardonable.

4. *Miscellaneous.*—The art of *writing well* is an indispensable requisite to complete epistolary communications. Various opinions prevail respecting the use of *capital letters;* but all writers agree that every sentence should begin with one, and that proper names, and the emphatical words in a sentence, should only be distinguished by them.
There should be a margin on the left hand of your paper, some distance from the top of the sheet where you begin, and

a place for the date; but these being regulated entirely by fashion, written rules would only puzzle the reader. Regard to the straightness of your lines ought to be strictly attended to, and if you rule lines with a lead pencil, take care to efface them before your letter is sent away. In making up a letter, fold it so as to leave room to conceal the wafer, or display the seal intended for it: the folds ought to be strongly pressed with an ivory folder, or with the hand.

CHAPTER V.

ON VISITING AND AMUSEMENTS.

I love my house, and seldom roam;
Few visits please me more than home.
I pity that unhappy elf
Who loves all company but self.

There is nothing more irksome, and unprofitable, both to health, spirits, and a proper use of that short portion of time which is allotted us, than for young people to be constantly engaged in a *round of visiting*, in which too often neither the heart nor any of its tender affections are interested : it is, at best, to sacrifice a real good, to a frivolous and unsatisfying use of those precious moments which might be better and more serviceably employed. In early youth, the more limited your acquaintance the better, and the less danger you will be in of finding yourselves deceived. You will, in the progress of life, meet with many you will feel a propensity and generous inclination to love, and a number with whom you cannot bring yourselves to associate with pleasure, or to make yourselves acquainted. If therefore you are blessed with two or three real friends, consider yourselves as being particularly fortunate, and rest satisfied with having drawn such invaluable prizes in the lottery of life.

It is not necessary that we should be secluded from the world; but to be always engaged would be a still greater misfortune. The mind by that means would be rendered so dissipated, and the taste so vitiated as to lose all relish for the retired hour of sober reflection, which ought to be frequently set apart to enable you to look into yourselves, to read your own hearts, to inspect your affairs, and to correct whatever has been thought-less or faulty in your conduct.

To people in the middle rank of life, keeping too much company has often been attended with consequences fatal to

then affairs; and the ridiculous ambition of little folks associating with the great, has, no doubt, added many a name to
the list of bankrupts.

Many a fond couple are happy and contented, till this *unfortunate ambition* takes possession of their minds : from that
ill-fated period every thing goes wrong, and their affairs, like
their ideas, are equally unfortunate. Their house must be
altered, their room enlarged : plain furniture gives place to a
profusion of ornament, glass and silver glitter on the sideboard,
the smell of tallow candles becomes offensive, and therefore *wax lights* must be introduced. In the article of *dress*, the
whole family must be improved: the young ladies and gentlemen
are never seen but in the most extravagant and costly
dresses.

Their house becomes burthened with servants to attend the
crowds of company which constantly fill their rooms, and who
secretly despise their imprudence, and publicly laugh at their
vanity. A carriage too is kept, for the convenience of returning their numerous visits; and what is, if possible, still more
ridiculous, while the real good of a competent fortune is wasting,
and happiness sacrificed to the unmeaning and unsatisfactory
folly of parade and show, this unhappy and foolish couple feel
themselves awkward and uncomfortable from having stept out
of their place, and from acting out of their real character. A few
fleeting years terminate their career of folly and extravagance—
an execution is entered on their goods—and a commission of
bankruptcy settles the whole account.

Being reduced to the necessity of beginning the world anew,
they are taught by dear-bought experience, to set a proper
value upon the necessaries of life; they therefore carefully
avoid venturing again to taste any of its luxuries. Industry and
care take place of idleness and dissipation; show is banished
for substance; perseverance and success once more bless
them with ease and plenty ; solid sense keeps pride from making
any innovations in their way of living ; and they are content to
pay a proper respect to their smiling superiors, without wish-
ing to be enrolled amongst the lists of their acquaintance : the
young masters and misses thrive as well, and feel as much at
their ease, in plain dresses, as they had ever done in the most
expensive ones, while their mother finds herself very comfortable,
and is now content to visit her neighbours in a white dimity
gown.

To mix with our superiors is undoubtedly very desirable on
many accounts, if we have a sufficient command over ourselves to keep our wishes and desires within the proper bounds
of prudence and discretion ; but never let a vain ambition of

being noticed by the great, render you meanly servile to their humours, or subservient to their vices. The character of a toad-eater, flatterer, or sycophant is truly detestable; it is a degradation of human nature, and those who can meanly stoop to sacrifice their principles to their ambition, could as easily, and with less trouble, sacrifice their best friend to any one who could pay a higher price for their adulation and hypocrisy.

To associate with those of an equal station with yourselves, or even those of a rank immediately above you, is undoubtedly commendable: but of all absurdities it is the first, to copy the manners of the great, by endeavouring to appear upon an equality with them beyond what your income will afford; it is worse than living in a desert.

We must not let the desire of associating with the higher ranks of life, or of appearing what we are not, mislead us from the safe and peaceful path of unaspiring rectitude. Envy not the splendor of the great, covet not their enjoyments, look not upon their diamonds with a desire to possess them; wish not for their luxuries, which too often are the introduction of various diseases; be not desirous of feeling the weight of their magni-ficent clothes, or lolling in a splendid equipage: a coach is often the gilded vehicle which conveys many a languid body that conceals an aching, discontented, or guilty heart. If you have not so much wealth as many others, be assured you have fewer cares; and though you are obliged to walk many a weary step, remember that exercise is the parent of health, and that health is the first of human blessings, and gives a pleasing relish to every innocent pleasure.

" Home's home, however homely," wisdom says,
And certain is the fact, though coarse the phrase.
To prove it, if it needed proof at all,
Mark what a train attends the Muse's call;
And, as she leads th' ideal group along,
Let your own feelings realize her song.
Clear then the stage; no scen'ry we require,
Save the snug circle round the parlour-fire;
And enter marshall'd in procession fair,
Each happier influence that governs there:

First, love, by friendship mellow'd into bliss,
Lights the warm glow, and sanctifies the kiss,
When, fondly welcom'd to th' accustom'd seat,
In sweet complacence wife and husband meet,
Look mutual pleasure, mutual purpose share,
Repose from labours to unite in care.
Ambition!—does ambition there reside?
Yes, when the boy, in manly mood, astride,
(Of headstrong prowess innocently vain,)
Canters,—the jockey of his father's cane.
While emulation, in the daughter's heart,
Bears a more mild, though not less pow'rful

With zeal to shine her flutt'ring bosom warms,
And in the romp the future housewife forms.
Or both, perchance, to graver sport incline,
And art and genius in their pastime join ;—
This the cramp riddle's puzzling knot invents
That rears aloft the card-built tenements.
Think how joy animates, intense, tho' meek,
The fading roses on their grandam's cheek ;
When proud the frolic progeny to survey,
She feels and owns an int'rest in their play ;
Adopts each wish their wayward whims unfold,
And tells, at every call, the story ten times told.

AMUSEMENTS.

In former ages, when the barbarous combats of gladiators were exhibited in the Roman Circus; and exhibited in so many cities, and with such frequency, as in some instances to cause from twenty to thirty thousand lives to be sacrificed in Europe by this abominable cruelty within the space of a month; the wives and daughters of the citizens of all ranks are represented as having been passionately addicted to these spectacles. To our own countrywomen, whose eyes have not been polluted, nor their hearts hardened by brutish and sanguinary entertainments, this recital may scarcely appear credible. But the fact is confirmed by similar examples.

I mean not to dwell on the concurrent accounts, given by different writers, of the extreme delight which the women among the North American Indians manifest, when vying with each other in embittering the tortures inflicted on the captive enemy: partly because a large share of the pleasure is derived from the triumphant spirit of revenge; and partly because parallels drawn from the untamed ferocity of savage life cannot fairly be applied to illustrate the influence of custom on modern periods of refinement. But a fact, too nearly corresponding to that which has been alleged from the annals of Rome, was very recently to be witnessed, I believe that it is even yet to be witnessed, in one of the cultivated nations of the south of Europe. I allude to the Spanish Bull-feasts. Persons of credit, who have visited Spain, unite in describing the Spanish ladies as beyond measure fond of this barbarous species of entertainment, and as most vehement in their applause when the scene of danger is at the height.

According to Mr. Townsend, the Bull-feasts at Madrid are regularly held one day in every week, and often two days, throughout the summer. On each of these days six bulls are

slaughtered in the morning, and twelve in the evening   Of the
men who engage the ferocious animal, some maintain the com-
bat on foot, some on horseback.   The sanguinary nature and
the danger of the employment may be estimated from two cir
cumstances, mentioned with another view by the author whom
I quote.   First, that *seventeen* horses on an average are killed by
the bulls each day; and that *sixty* horses have been known to
perish in a day.   Secondly, that among the official attendants
on the Bull-feasts, is a priest appointed to administer the sacra-
ment to persons mortally wounded in the conflict.   He concludes his account in the following terms: " The fondness of
the Spaniards for this diversion is scarcely to be conceived.
Men, women, and children, rich and poor, all give the preference to it beyond all other public spectacles."   His testimony
might receive confirmation, were it necessary, from other au-
thorities.

In the former part of the sixteenth century, Bear-baiting is
affirmed to have been a favourite diversion, " exhibited as a
suitable amusement for a Princess."   An amusement thus
countenanced was probably acceptable to English ladies in general.   It appears, at a later period, to have still maintained a
place among the recreations of women of rank.   Among the
spectacles displayed for the diversion of Queen Elizabeth, when
she was entertained at Kenilworth Castle, by the Earl of Lei-
cester, bear-baitings and boxing-matches are enumerated by the
historian of the festivity.

I state these facts as affording an impressive example of the
force of custom; and a warning as to the firmness with which
 he despotism of fashion may in many cases require to be with-
stood, even when it is aspiring to jurisdiction merely over
amusements.   If in the present age, in a Christian country,
among a people which lays claim to considerable refinement,
fashion has power to benumb the sympathetic emotions of humanity which characterize the female heart; to render exhibitions of cruelty and bloodshed, the miseries of tortured animals,
and the dangers of their wretched assailants, not merely tolerable to female eyes, but a spectacle gratifying beyond every
other in the way of amusement: let it not be thought very improbable, that in our own country fashion may, on some occasions, prove herself able to attach women to amusements,
which, though neither stained with blood, nor derived from the
infliction of pain, may be such as for other reasons ought to
be universally reprobated and exploded.   And whenever such
occasions may arise, let every woman remember, that modes
of amusement intrinsically wrong, or in any respect unbecoming the female sex, are not transformed into innocent

recreations by the countenance of numbers, nor by the sanction, if they should obtain the sanction, of nobility, or of a court.

Conscientious vigilance to avoid an improper choice of amusements, and an undue sacrifice of time to them, is a duty of great importance; not only because time spent amiss can never be recalled, but also because, by the nature of the engagements in which the hours of leisure and relaxation are employed, the manners, the dispositions, and the whole character, are materially affected. Let the volume of any judicious traveller through a foreign country be opened in the part where he delineates the pursuits, the general conduct, the prevailing moral or immoral sentiments of the people. He will there be found to bestow attention on their customary diversions, not only because the account of them adds entertainment to his narrative, and is necessary in order to complete the picture of national manners, but also because they form one of the sources to which national opinions, virtues, and vices, may be traced. It is true, that the amusements which prevail in any country will depend, in a considerable degree, on the tone of sentiment and opinion prevailing there; because a conformity to the existing state of general sentiment and opinion is necessary to render public amusements generally acceptable. But it is also true, that the latter exert a reciprocal influence on the former; and are among the most active of the causes by which it may be altered or upheld. If he who affirmed that, were he allowed to compose the ballads of a nation, he would, at pleasure, change its form of government, uttered a boast not altogether unfounded in the principles of human nature; with juster confidence might he have engaged to produce most important effects on the manners, opinions, and moral character of a nation should he be invested with full power over all the public diversions.

The influence of amusements on character is manifest in both sexes. A young woman, however, must be deemed more liable than an individual of the other sex to have the dispositions of the heart essentially affected by favourite modes of entertainment. Her time is not absorbed, nor her turn of mind formed and steadied, by professional habits and occupations: and her superior quickness of feeling renders her the more alive to impressions conveyed through a pleasurable medium. Tacitus, in his description of the manners of the ancient inhabitants of Germany, dwells with merited praise on the *singular modesty* of the women; and assigns as a principal cause of this virtuous excellence their not being corrupted by seducing spectacles and diversion. The remark is made with his usual acuteness of moral reflection. And we cannot doubt, that it was suggested by his experience of the melancholy depravation of conduct in the ladies of Rome, resulting from their attendance on the Amphitheatre and the Circus.

An inordinate love of pleasure often leads us into the most lasting and serious miseries : it involves us in ridiculous distresses, and encompasses us with difficulties from which the toil of years will not set us free. And too often a youth of pleasure and extravagance is followed by an old age of contempt, poverty, and trouble. The most generous minds are sometimes led astray by this unfortunate predilection. To gratify the present moment, they become regardless of the future : virtue, peace, friends, and fortune, are unguardedly sacrificed to the caprices of the hour ; and though warned by the hapless example of thousands, they run heedlessly on in the pursuit of pleasure till they deprive themselves of the power to enjoy .

Unhappy obstinacy !—fatal delusion .—thoughtless propensity !—Pleasure has no charms, when it madly overleaps the bounds of discretion : all her gaudy flowers fade and wither when they approach the baneful presence of that hag called VICE. Even the most innocent pleasures may be pursued till they become a crime in themselves, and a misfortune to our dearest connexions.

To sacrifice too large a portion of our precious time, the interest of ourselves and families, the peace of those who have a just claim upon our most prudent and tender attentions ought to be reprobated and discouraged, and must ever bring a degrading reproach upon the understanding.

Pleasure may likewise be pursued till it becomes a slavery and toil, and the ill effects of an intemperate use of it may be seen in the broken constitutions, the early old age, of many of its unthinking votaries. Late hours and a perpetual round or dissipation, are the well known enemies to youth and beauty, whilst the most brilliant and captivating pleasures are dearly purchased with the loss of health, the first and most invaluable of human blessings, which, like the *sensitive plant*, must be carefully watched to be preserved, and, if once neglected, or too roughly handled, may ever after shrink from the slightest touch.

There cannot be a greater reproach upon our understanding than an immoderate love of *frivolous and idle amusements:* they tend to enervate the soul, and to render it unfit for higher and more rational enjoyments : it gives to the whole behaviour an appearance of levity, makes the mind more easily susceptible of bad impressions, and exposes the young and inexperienced to a multiplicity of dangers; for when the attention is chiefly occupied on the thoughts of pleasure, but little progress can be made in any useful improvement.

But, pleasure is only to be reprobated when it misleads the mind from that steady rectitude which ought to be observed in our conduct; nor is there a single objection to any amusement that does not interfere with our moral and important duties.—We have a just right to fill up our leisure hours with such recreations as are agreeable to our taste, if they are not such as injure our principles, health, or fortune ; but we are highly blameable when we make it our chief business and study, and sacrifice to pleasure not only the social and active duties of this life, but our hopes in that which is to come.

The risk to which a young woman is exposed of contracting a habit of excessive fondness for amusements, depends not only on the particular propensities of her mind, but also on the place and situation in which she principally resides. To the daughter of a country gentleman, though her heart should be fixed on company and diversions, the paternal mansion insulated in its park, or admitting no contiguous habitation, except the neighbouring hamlet, seldom furnishes the opportunity of access to a perpetual circle of amusements. Visitors are not always to be found in the drawing-room; the card-table cannot always be filled up; the county town affords a ball but once in a month; and domestic circumstances perversely arise to obstruct regularity of attendance. Suppose then a young woman, thus situated, to labour under the heavy disadvantage of not having had her mind directed by education to proper objects. Finding herself obliged to procure, by her own efforts, the entertainment which she is frequently without the means of obtaining from others; she is excited to some degree of useful exertion. Family conversation, needle-work, a book, even a book that is not a novel ; in a word, any occupation, is found preferable to the tediousness of a constant want of employment. Thus the foundation of some domestic habits is laid: or, if the habits were previously in existence, they are strengthened, or at least are preserved from being obliterated.

The female who is fixed in a country town, where society is always within reach, and something in the way of petty amusement is ever going forward, or may easily be set on foot, may with greater facility contract a habit of flying from a companion, who, if insipid and unpleasing to her, will be, of all companions, the most insipid and unpleasing,—herself. But it is in the metropolis that amusements, and all the temptations which flow from amusements, are concentred. So various are the scenes of public diversion, so various the parties of private en-

tertainment, which LONDON affords in the EVENING ; so nu
merous are the spectacles and exhibitions of wonders in nature
or in art, and the attractive occupations properly to be classed
under the head of amusement, which obtrude on the leisure of
morning in the capital and its environs ; so magnetic is the
example of wealth, and rank, and fashion ; that she who approaches the stream, with a mind unsteadied by those principles of moderation and sobriety which are essential to the
Christian character, will probably be hurried away far from
her proper course, or even sucked into the vortex, and whirled,
day after day, and year after year, in a never-ending round of
giddiness and dissipation.

If the METROPOLIS be the spot in which the danger of
becoming absorbed in amusements is most formidable ; the
scenes of resort, whether inland or on the SEA-COAST, which
are distinguished by the general denomination of Public
Places, exhibit it in a degree but little inferior.   Of such
places, the predominant spirit is thoughtlessness. And thoughtlessness, ever weary of its own vacuity, flies with restless ardour
from diversion to diversion ; and rouses into action the inhe-
rent love of entertainment, which, in most persons, requires
rather to be moderated than to be inflamed.   The contagion
spreads, in the first place, among those whose presence is
owing to other causes than sickness ; but in a short time, it
extends to many persons who are come in quest of health,
and often affects them so powerfully, that the hurry of the
evening more than counterbalances the salubrious influence
of air and of waters.   Let it be remembered, however, that
there is no place which affords an exemption from the obliga-
tion of rational pursuits and mental improvement ; nor any
place which does not afford opportunities for rational pursuits
and mental improvement to those who are inclined to make use
of them.

I cannot, my readers, dismiss the subject of *amusements*
without a few words on the detestable passion for gaming,
which, I regret to say, but too often pervades the female breast.
The certain miseries of this pursuit are thus ably portrayed
by a lively writer :—

" The most pernicious and scandalous practice which the
female world have fallen into is *gaming*. Notwithstanding
such an ocean of dangerous consequences which attend it, yet
some women particularly distinguish themselves, by following
it with such assiduity, and to such excess, that, could we have
any communication into the minds of those female gamesters,
we should find them full of nothing but *trumps* and *matadores* ;
and were it possible to dive into the secrets of their slumbers,

we should find them haunted by no other order than *kings,
queens,* and *knaves.* The day is irksome to them ; every mi
nute lays a heavy burthen on them, till the season of gaming
returns, which when attained, how wretchedly are their faculties employed ; in how despicable a manner half a dozen
hours, or more, pass away in a continual round of shuffling,
cutting, dealing, and sorting out a pack of cards ; and no
other ideas to be discovered in a soul, which should call itselt
rational, excepting small square figures of painted and spotted
paper ! With submission I would ask those ladies, whether
our understanding (which is the divine part of our composition) was given us for such an infamous use ? Is it thus that
we improve the greatest talent human nature is possessed of ?
What would a superior being think, where he shewn this intellectual faculty in a female gamester, and at the same time
told it was by this she was distinguished from brutes, and allied
to angels ? Who can consider, without a secret indignation,
that all those affections of the mind, which should be conse-
crated to their children, husband, and parents, are thus vilely
prostituted and lavished away, upon a game at loo, while the
husband, and all the family, are neglected and made unhappy.
She takes no manner of delight in the innocent endearments of
a domestic life ; she has a greater regard for pam than her
husband, who is obliged, if he would enjoy her conversation.
to linger out the silent hours, which should be devoted to rest,
in a miserable state of impatience, for her coming home. If
she has been a loser, she is angry with every person about
her; displeased with every thing her husband says or does
and in reality for no other reason but because she has been
squandering his estate. What charming companions for life
are such women ! Have we reason to be surprised, that the
present age is so depraved, and abounds with such multitudes
of worthless and effeminate coxcombs, when they have such
unthinking mothers ? What other race of mortals can be expected from women of such a turn ? There is a kind of apothegm,
that which corrupts the soul, decays the body ;—the beauties
of the face and mind are generally destroyed by the same
means. This consideration should have a particular weight
with the female world, who are designed to please the eye by
nature, not by art. There are no greater enemies to a beautiful face, than the vigils of the card-table, and those cutting
passions which naturally attend them. *Hollow eyes, haggard
looks, and pale complexions,* are the unbecoming indications of
those female worthies. Many a woman of quality have I seen
glide by me, in her chair, at three o'clock in the morning,
half dead, appearing like a spectre, surrounded by a glare of

flambeaux. There is no chance for a thorough-paced gamester to preserve her natural beauty two winters successively.— Notwithstanding the hazardous and dangerous consequences which I have stated, and which undoubtedly prove, that gaming is of a bad tendency, there is still one worse than the rest, in which the body is more endangered than merely by the loss of beauty.—All play debts are falsely styled debts of honour, and must be discharged in specie, or by an equivalent. The man who plays beyond his income, pawns his estate; the woman must find out something to mortgage, when her pin-money is drained; and what resource must she go to? The creditor is importunate; her spirit, softened from its wonted vigour, yields her up to dishonour; she entails an everlasting disgrace upon herself and all her family.—Her future days are miserable.—She is dead to all the sentiments of virtue, from the moment she has given a loose to inclinations which are of the blackest hue, and suffered herself to be entangled in the path of foul dishonour. The succeeding part of her life it is easier to guess than to describe."

CHAPTER VI.

EMPLOYMENT OF TIME.

TO make a proper use of that short and uncertain portion of time allotted us for our mortal pilgrimage, is a proof of wisdom; to use it with economy, and dispose of it with care, the province of prudence and discretion. Consider this address on so important and interesting a subject, with the utmost attention, and let but a very small portion of your time escape without making it subservient to the wise purposes for which it was given you: it is the most inestimable of treasures.

Observe the wary and trembling miser—how carefully he conceals his shining board: with what a brow of anxiety and care, with what guarded caution he secures his beloved gold. Poor, misguided son of error! to lose the substance for the shadow! Whilst watching the riches which his grovelling soul delights to contemplate, but which his niggard spirit will not let him enjoy, time flies unmarked, unnoticed: that far more invaluable treasure is squandered with profuseness and inattention. From the sordid miser, from the unthinking sons and daughters of frolic and dissipation, learn wisdom. Leave the one to lose his precious moments in securing his useless wealth, and the others with pity to their equally pernicious and un-

profitable follies. Be warned by their example, and snatch
the precious minutes as they fly, to improve yourselves in useful knowledge: venture not to waste one hour, lest the next
should not be yours to squander; hazard not a single day in
guilty or improper pursuits, lest the day which follows should
be ordained to bring you an awful summons to the tomb; a
summons which youth and age are equally liable to receive.

You will find a constant employment of your time conducive
to health, happiness, and pleasure: and not only the surest
guard against the dangerous encroachments of vice, but the
best recipe for contentment. SEEK EMPLOYMENT, *languor
and ennui shall be unknown.* AVOID IDLENESS, BANISH
SLOTH; *vigour and cheerfulness will be your enlivening companions;* ADMIT NOT GUILT TO YOUR HEARTS, *and terror
shall not interrupt your slumbers. Follow the footsteps of
virtue; walk steadily in her paths; she will conduct you
through pleasant and flowery scenes to the* TEMPLE OF PEACE;
*she will guard you from the wily snares of vice, and heal the
wounds of sorrow and disappointment which time may inflict.*

VIRTUE has a numerous train of pleasures, a number of
faithful and incorruptible attendants. A mind at peace with
itself, and a stranger to intentional guilt, is not only a never-
failing friend in the hour of trial, but a perpetual source of placid delight, whilst we are rapidly going down the stream of time
Though the world should frown, and the tempest threaten
from afar, all within shall be serenity and harmony: though dis-
cord should walk abroad, though pestilence and famine should
depopulate your native kingdom, the clamours of the one, and
the horrors of the other, however grievous and unpleasant, will
neither impress your souls with fear, nor rob them of conscious
peace.

By being *constantly and usefully employed*, the destroyer of
mortal happiness will have but few opportunities of making his
baneful attacks, and by regularly filling up your precious mo
ments, you will be less exposed to dangers, and in a manner
guarded against the numberless snares and errors in which
idleness would perpetually involve you.

Choose your *companions* with caution, and be not unsteady
in your attachments. Let not rank or situation determine
your choice of them. Let them be such as you can love for
their good qualities, and whose virtues you are desirous to
emulate. If they are humane and benevolent, be assured,
you will not find them envious or prone to what is uncharitable
and mean: if they are good-humoured and unassuming, you
will experience no mortification from their pride; if they will

tell you of your faults with candour and sincerity, cherish them in your bosom as a treasure; they will not basely slander you, or endeavour to lessen your good qualities when you are ab sent If such as I have described like your society, court their friendship, and encourage them to love you by the cheer, fulness and sincerity with which you welcome them to your heart and habitation.

Fly with caution and determined resolution the *slanderer*, the *babbler*, or *malicious railer*, and never venture to repose any confidence in one whom you hear traduce or speak ill of a friend, with whom you have seen them appear on amicable terms: for be assured you will share the same fate, whenever an opportunity offers for the purpose. I remember hearing an anecdote, which is too applicable to my present subject to be omitted:—

A lady, who went to spend an afternoon with a few social friends, was much disappointed, as well as the rest of the party, by the entrance of one remarkable for her talents in the art of detraction. She had not sat long, before she exhibited a spe- cimen of her abilities, by giving the company a ludicrous ac- count of a *friend*, whose house she had just left; and then pro- ceeded to give a similar one of many others, who were so un- fortunate as to be reckoned amongst the number of her *dear friends*.

The lady, whose pleasure had been interrupted by the en- trance of this pest to society, arose, and after taking a polite leave of the mistress of the house, turned to Mrs. Slander, and, with a gentle tone of voice, told her, she would not rob her **of** her time, or longer deprive her of an opportunity of giving a farther proof of her excellent talents, by taking *her off*.—But begged she would speak as *favourable* of her as possible, when she was gone.

The reproof was just:—it was felt for a moment: but minds of that unfortunate turn are not easily cured of a disease which too often proves infectious to the minds of others, and which, in my opinion, chiefly originates from idleness, and the want of knowing how to make a proper use of Time.

To every woman, whether single or married, *the habit of regularly allotting to improving books a portion of each day,* and, as far as may be practicable, at stated hours, cannot be too strongly recommended. I use the term *improving* in a large sense, as comprehending all writings which may contribute to her virtue, her usefulness, her instruction, and her innocent satisfaction; to her happiness in this world and in the next. She who believes that she is to survive in another state of being through eternity, and is duly impressed by the awful conviction, will fix day by day her most serious thoughts on the inheritance to which she aspires. Where her treasure is, there will her heart be also. She will not be seduced from an habitual study of the Holy Scriptures, and of other works calculated to imprint on her bosom the comparatively small importance of the pains and pleasures of this period of her existence, and to fill her with that knowledge, and inspire her with those views and dispositions, which may lead her to delight in the present service of-her Maker, and enable her to rejoice in the contemplation of futurity. With the time allotted to the regular perusal of the word of God, and of performances which inculcate the principles and enforce and illustrate the rules of Christian duty, no other kind of reading ought to be permitted to interfere. At other parts of the day let history, let biography, let poetry, or some of the various branches of elegant and profitable knowledge, pay their tribute of instruction and amusement. But let her studies be confined within the strictest limits of purity. Let whatever she peruses in her most private hours be such as she needs not be ashamed of reading aloud to those whose good opinion she is most anxious to deserve. Let her remember that there is an all-seeing eye, which is ever fixed upon her, even in her closest retirement. Let her not indulge herself in the frequent perusal of writings, however interesting in their nature, however eminent in a literary point of view, which are likely to inflame pride, and to inspire false notions of generosity, of feeling, of spirit, or of any other quality deemed to contribute to excellence of character. Such, unhappily, are the effects to be apprehended from the works even of several of our distinguished writers in prose or in verse. And let her accustom herself regularly to bring the sentiment which she reads, and the conduct which is described in terms, more or less strong, of applause and recommendation, to the test of Christian principles. In proportion as this practice is pursued or neglected, reading will be profitable or pernicious.

There is one species of writings which obtains from a considerable proportion of the female sex a reception much more favourable than is afforded to other kinds of composition more worthy of encouragement. It is scarcely necessary to add the name of novels and romances. Works of this nature not unfrequently deserve the praise of ingenuity of plan and contrivance, of accurate and well supported discrimination of character, and of force and elegance of language. Some of them have professedly been composed with a design to favour the interests of morality. And among those which are deemed to have on the whole a moral tendency, a very few, perhaps, might be selected which are not liable to the disgraceful charge of being occasionally contaminated by incidents and passages unfit to be presented to the reader. This charge, however, may so very generally be alleged with justice, that even of the novels which possess high and established reputation, by far the greater number is totally improper, in consequence of such admixture, to be perused by the eye of delicacy.

To indulge in a practice of reading novels is, in several other particulars, liable to produce mischievous effects. Such compositions are, to most persons, extremely engaging. That story must be singularly barren, or wretchedly told, of which, after having heard the beginning, we desire not to know the end. To the pleasure of learning the ultimate fortune of the heroes and heroines of the tale, the novel commonly adds, in a greater or in a less degree, that which arises from animated description, from lively dialogue, or from interesting sentiment. Hence the perusal of one publication of this class leads, with much more frequency than is the case with respect to works of other kinds, (except perhaps of dramatic writings, to which most of the present remarks may be transferred), to the speedy perusal of another. Thus a habit is formed, at first, of limited indulgence, but that is continually found more formidable and more encroaching. The appetite becomes too keen to be denied ; and in proportion as it is more urgent, grows less nice and select in its fare. What would formerly have given offence, now gives none. The palate is vitiated or made dull. The produce of the book-club, and the contents of the circulating library, are devoured with indiscriminate and insatiable avidity. Hence the mind is secretly corrupted. Let it be observed too, that in exact correspondence with the increase of a passion for reading novels, an aversion to reading of a more improving nature will gather strength. Even in the class of novels least objectionable in point of delicacy, false sentiment unfitting the mind for sober life, applause, and censure distributed amiss, morality estimated by an erroneous standard, and the capricious laws and empty sanctions of honour set up in the place of religion, are the lessons usually presented. There is yet another consequence too important to be overlooked. The catastrophe and the incidents of these fictitious narratives commonly turn on the vicissitudes and effects of a passion the most powerful of all those which agitate the human heart. Hence the study of them frequently creates a susceptibility of impression, and a premature warmth of tender emotions, which, not to speak of other possible effects, have been known to betray young women into a sudden attachment to persons unworthy of their affections, and thus to hurry them into marriages terminating in unhappiness.

In addition to the regular habit of useful reading, the custom of committing to the memory select and ample portions of poetic compositions, · not for the purpose of ostentatiously quoting them in mixed company, but for the sake of private improvement, deserves, in consequence of its beneficial tendency, to be mentioned with a very high degree of praise The mind is thus stored with a lasting treasure of sentiments and ideas, combined by writers of transcendent genius and vigorous imagination; clothed in appropriate, nervous, and glowing language; and impressed by the powers of cadence and harmony. Let the poetry, however, be well chosen. Let it be such as elevates the heart with the ardour of devotion; adds energy and grace to the precepts of morality; kindles benevolence by pathetic narrative and reflection; enters with accurate and lively description into the varieties of character; or presents vivid pictures of the grand and beautiful features which characterize the scenery of nature. Such are, in general, the works of Milton, of Thomson, of Gray, of Mason, of Beattie, and of Cowper. It is thus that the beauty and grandeur of nature will be contemplated with new pleasure. It is thus that taste will be called forth, exercised and corrected. It is thus that judgment will be strengthened, virtuous emotions cherished, piety animated and exalted. At all times, and under every circumstance, the heart, penetrated with religion, will delight itself in the recollection of passages, which display the perfections of that Being on whom it trusts, and the glorious hopes to the accomplishment of which it humbly looks forward. When affliction weighs down the spirits, or sickness the strength; it is then that the cheering influence of that recollection will be doubly felt. When old age, disabling the sufferer from the frequent use of books, obliges the mind to turn inward upon itself; the memory, long retentive, even in its decay, of the acquisitions which it had attained and valued in its early vigour, still suggests the lines which have again and again diffused rapture through the bosom of health, and are yet capable of overspreading the hours of decrepitude and the couch of pain with consolation. If these benefits, these comforts, flow from recollected compositions of man; how much greater may be expected from portions of the word of God deeply imprinted on the mind!

But it is not from books alone that a considerate young woman is to seek her improvement and her gratifications. The discharge of relative duties, and the exercise of benevolence, form additional sources of activity and enjoyment. To give delight in the affectionate intercourse of domestic society; to relieve a parent in the superintendence of family affairs; to smooth the bed of sickness, and cheer the decline of age; to examine into the wants and distresses of the female inhabitants of the neighbourhood; to promote useful institutions for the comfort of mothers, and for the instruction of children; and to give to those institutions that degree of attention, which, without requiring either much time or much personal trouble, will facilitate their establishment and extend their usefulness; these are employments congenial to female sympathy; employments in the precise line of female duty; employments which, so far as the lot of human life allows, confer genuine and lasting kindness on those whom they are designed to benefit, and never fail, when pursued from conscientious motives, to meliorate the heart of her who is engaged in them.

In pointing out that which ought to be done, let justice be rendered to that which has been done. In the discharge of the domestic offices of kindness, and in the exercise of charitable and friendly regard to the neighbouring poor, women in general are exemplary. In this latter branch of Christian virtue, an accession of energy has been witnessed within a few years. Many ladies have shewn, and still continue to shew their earnest solicitude for the welfare of the wretched and the ignorant, by spontaneously establishing schools of industry and of religious instruction; and with a still more beneficial warmth of benevolence, have taken the regular inspection of them upon themselves. May they steadfastly persevere, and be imitated by numbers!

Among the employments of time, which, though regarded with due attention by many young women, are more or less neglected by a considerable portion, *moderate exercise in the open air* claims to be noticed. Sedentary confinement in hot apartments on the one hand, and public diversions frequented on the other, in buildings still more crowded and stifling, are often permitted so to occupy the time, as by degrees even to wear away the relish for the freshness of a pure atmosphere, for the beauties and amusements of the garden, and for those " rural sights and rural sounds," which delight the mind unsubdued by idleness, folly, or vice. Enfeebled health, a capricious temper, low and irritable spirits, and the loss of many pure and continually recurring enjoyments, are among the consequences of such misconduct.

CHAPTER VII.

DOMESTIC ECONOMY

THE best foundation for the health, comfort, and general welfare of a family, will always be found in a well-arranged and long-continued practice of DOMESTIC ECONOMY.

Early rising and a proper disposition of time, are of essentia importance in a family. Besides enabling you to give the necessary orders, and to examine into particular departments or your household affairs, it is productive of health and animation, and it adds many hours to life. They who rise early undoubtedly live much longer than the sluggish mortals who waste their best hours in bed ; and what makes it more wonderful, people take the most effectual means to shorten that existence on which they set so much value.

That early rising is conducive to longevity no one will pretend to deny ; and that morning has abundant sweets to repay those who think it worth their while to observe them, the following lines abundantly evince :

> The dripping rock, the mountain's misty top,
> Swell on the sight, and brighten with the dawn.
> Blue, thro' the dusk, the smoking currents shine,
> And from the bladed field the fearful hare
> Limps awkward ; while, along the forest glade,
> The wild deer trip, and, often turning, gaze
> At early passengers. Music awakes
> The voice of undissembled joy,
> And thick around the woodland hymns arise.
> Rous'd by the cock, the soon-clad shepherd leaves
> His mossy cottage, where with peace he dwells,
> And from the crowded fold in order drives
> His flocks to taste the verdure of the morn.

The following useful hint is well worthy the serious notice of my readers:

" The difference between rising every morning at six and at eight, in the course of forty years, (supposing a person to go to bed at the same time as he otherwise would,) amounts to *twenty-nine thousand two hundred hours,* or THREE YEARS *one hundred and twenty-one days, and sixteen hours,* which will afford eight hours a day, for exactly ten years ; so that it is the same as if ten years of life were added, in which we may command eight hours every day for the cultivation of our minds and the dispatch of business."

Although persons of large fortune may support an expensive establishment without inconvenience, it will be deficient in

every thing that can benefit or grace society, or that is essen
tial to moral order and rational happiness, if it be not conduct
ed on a regular system, embracing all the objects attaching to
such a situation.

What a contrast do two families exhibit, the one living in
the dignified splendour, and with the liberal hospitality that
wealth can command, and ought to maintain ; the other in a
style of tinsel show, without the real appropriate distinctions
belonging to rank and fortune; lavish, not liberal, often sa-
crificing independence to support dissipation, at the cost of
betraying the dearest interests of the community, to support
the follies of domestic mismanagement and personal vices.
The observations here made, are, however, more immediately
addressed to the middle ranks of society, as the most accessi-
ble to such an appeal ; and whose independence and general
discretion are certainly not less important to the welfare of the
state than to that of their own families.

The plan of every family must be adapted to its own peculiar situation, and can only result from the good sense and
early good habits of the parties, acting upon general principles. Thus the practice of one family can never be a safe
precedent for that of another. Each best knows its own resources, and should consult them alone. What may be meanness in one would be extravagance in another, and therefore
there can be no standard of reference but that of individual
prudence. The most fatal of all things to private families, is
to indulge an ambition to make an appearance above their fortunes, professions, or business, whatever these may be. Their
expenses ought to be so restricted within their means, as to
make them easy and independent; for if they are too near
run, the least accident will embarrass the whole system. More
evils may be traced to a thoughtless ambition of appearing
above our situation, than the idle vanity that prompts it ever
pauses to reflect on.

The next point, both for comfort and respectability, is, that
all the household economy should be uniform, not displaying a
parade of show in one thing, and a total want of comfort in
another. Besides the contemptible appearance that this must
have to every person of good sense, it is productive of consequences, not only of present, but of future injury to a family,
that are too often irreparable. How common it is, in great
cities particularly, that for the vanity of having a showy drawing-room for the receiving of company, the family are confined
to a close back room, where they have scarcely either air or
light, the want of which is a very material prejudice to their
health To keep rooms for show belongs to the higher spheres

of life, where the house will accommodate the family property and admit of this also ; but in private families, to shut up, perhaps, the only room in the house which is really wholesome for the family to live in, is to be guilty of a kind of lingering murder; and yet how frequently this consideration escapes persons who mean well by their family, but have a grate, a carpet, and chairs, too fine for every day's use.

Another fruit of this evil, is the seeing more company, and in a more expensive manner than is compatible with the general convenience of the family, introducing with it an expense in dress, and a dissipation of time, for which it suffers in various ways. Not the least of these, is the children being sent to school, where the girls had better never go, and the boys not at the early age they are usually sent; because the mother can spare no time to attend to them at home. Social intercourse is not improved by parade, but quite the contrary; real friends, and the pleasantest kind of acquaintance, those who like to be sociable, are repulsed by it.

A house fitted up with plain good furniture, the kitchen furnished with clean wholesome-looking cooking utensils, good fires in grates, that give no anxiety lest a good fire should spoil them, clean good table-linen, the furniture of the table and sideboard good of the kind, without ostentation, and a well-dressed plain dinner, bespeak a sound judgment and correct taste in a private family, that place it on a footing of respectability with the first characters in the country. It is only the conforming to our sphere, not the vainly attempting to be above it, that can command true respect.

Needle-work is generally considered as a part of good housewifery : many young women make almost every thing they wear, by which they make a respectable appearance at a small expense. The art of properly cutting out female and wearing apparel, is of great importance. There must be a very considerable saving where the mistress of a family cuts out, or at least, superintends the cutting out, those articles which require calculation and exactness.

In purchasing any material, it is cheapest to buy a piece at a wholesale warehouse, provided the proper application is attended to, otherwise, I am sorry to confess, plenty (according to the old adage) makes waste. Who has not heard the following remark continually ?—" Well, we need not grudge making this dress handsome and full, for I am sure there is plenty!" thus, at once, spoiling the shape, instead of adding to its beauty, and wasting that which might be put to other uses.

When whole pieces are bought there is always a certain

quantity over the measure, and the merchant, of course, can afford it cheaper than the retail dealer. It should be observed, in this case, ready money is expected; and I should not do justice if I did not, at the same time, remark, that wher immediate payment can be made, the retail dealer will be glad to lower his price also. Let it be observed, however, I would by no means recommend what are called great bargains, that is, buying things that are not wanted, merely because they may be considered particularly cheap. These bargains generally prove as remarkably extravagant as they have been imagined economical, for the consequence is, they are laid by till the time shall come when they may be wanted, and when that time arrives, the notable purchaser is surprised and mortified to find—they are either quite out of fashion—have entirely lost their colour—or, which often occurs, prove damaged goods ; and frequently those things are put to purposes for which they are but ill adapted, merely because they are at hand.

For a full and complete explanation of this subject, we must refer our readers to an excellent work entitled " *The Lady's Economical Assistant ; or, the Art of cutting out, and making the most useful Articles of wearing Apparel, without waste; explained by the clearest directions and numerous engravings, of appropriate and tasteful Patterns. By a Lady. Designed for domestic use.*" One observation, however, from the introduction to this publication, may prove of such general utility, that we cannot withhold it.

" All persons, I am sure," says this ingenious lady, "have experienced the inconvenience of buttons ill fastened on to shirts and dresses ;—trifling as the observation may appear, it so frequently occurs that I think a hint, to obviate this little difficulty, will be acceptable to the reader. It is not easy to persuade servants to take a little more trouble than they think absolutely necessary, but where they can be prevailed on to observe the following directions, and execute them with care, this little annoyance may be, in a great measure, removed.

" First set the button on, as is usual, by sewing it to the cloth three or four times. Next, when the thread is brought through the cloth, repass the needle, and bring it out under the centre of the button, and then through the button near the edge ; bringing the thread round the outside wire, and return it under the centre through the cloth ; then pass it through again the same on the opposite side, and return it as before ; repeat this twice more, so as to confine the button by the outside ring, in four quarters, after which wind the thread round to enclose these bracing threads, and fasten it off securely."

Regularity in payments and accounts is a very important

branch of female economy:—and, consequently it is highly desirable that every young woman should be thoroughly acquainted with the *four first rules of Arithmetic*. An outline of these will be found in CHAPTER XIII, which treats on the PHYSICAL AND MORAL EDUCATION OF CHILDREN.

FRUGALITY is a virtue that cannot be too often, or too seriously inculcated. Industry, humility, and *frugality*, are riches which neither moth nor rust can corrupt; while those, who make a fortune by their own prudence and activity, generally enjoy it more rationally than those who become possessed of one from the rights of inheritance, or from the care and foresight of others. At a time when we hear so many complaining of hardships and distresses, if we could trace them to their foundation, we should at least find that half of them originated in themselves. The real miseries of life, like its real wants, are but few when compared with those introduced among mankind by luxury, vice, and pleasure. If people will step out of their sphere, and act in a character foreign to that for which they were designed, can it be a matter of surprise that so many are stopped in their career, and become the victims of their own mistaken and heedless conduct?

> *Music* and *French*, when taught in common life,
> Infuse high notions,—spoil the useful wife;
> Miss to *piano* proudly will attend,
> Jabber *bad French*, but stockings blush to mend.
> Ah! that this generation would grow wise,
> Teach girls to make *plain puddings*, and *good pies;*
> Leave to fine ladies the Italian shake,
> And learn—*their husbands' shirts to mend and make!*
> Then men, whose fortunes are confined and small,
> Again would follow nature's sacred call;
> Love, honest love, once more its sweets display,
> Once more to Hymen's temple lead the way.

" Hear the words of prudence; give ear unto her counsels, and store them in thine heart: her maxims are universal, and all the virtues lean upon her: she is the guide and the mistress of human life.

" Furnish thyself with the proper accommodations belonging to thy condition; yet spend not to the utmost of what thou canst afford, that the providence of thy youth may be a comfort to thy old age.

" Let not thy recreations be expensive, lest the pain of purchasing them exceed the pleasure thou hast in their enjoyment.

" From the experience of others, do thou learn wisdom; and from their failings correct thine own faults.

" Yet expect not even from prudence infallible success; for the day knoweth not what the night may bring forth."

Economy such as here recommended, and which every wo-

man, in every station of life, is called to practise, is not merely
the petty detail of small daily expenses, the shabby curtailments
and stinted parsimony of a little mind, operating on little
things; but it is the exercise of a sound judgment exerted in
the comprehensive outline of order, of arrangement, of distri-
bution; of regulations by which alone well-governed families,
great and small, rich and poor, subsist. She who has the best-
regulated mind, will, other things being equal, have the bes·
regulated family.

A woman who is fully sensible of the duties of her situation, will constantly have her eye upon her whole establishment,
and conduct it with uniform prudence. " Her ways are ways
of pleasantness, and all her paths are peace."

CHAPTER VIII.

LOVE AND COURTSHIP.

HARMLESS, unmeaning gallantry, is one of the qualifications
of a well-bred man ; and some accustom themselves to it so
much, that they shew it to every agreeable woman they meet.
Men of this stamp will escort you to public places, and behave to you with the greatest attention. The compliments of
such men, are no other than words of course, which they repeat to every fine woman of their acquaintance. These men,
if they meet with encouragement, will presently become familiar ; and their observances, which before were offered as
marks of politeness, will grow into acts of design. A proper
dignity in your behaviour will presently check their advances;
but if you misconstrue their civilities, and receive them as professions of esteem, you are undone.

These persons will flatter where they may, in order to delude
where they can. And she who lends a patient ear to the
praise of her wit or beauty, may do it at first perhaps to gratify
vanity only ; but the flattery bewitches her in the end, and
she insensibly inclines to a kindness for that person who seems
to value her so much. She will begin with thinking him extremely fond of her, and, as such, will cherish that out of
vanity, which she afterwards will reward out of love. She will
be apt to put the best construction on whatever he says or
does; his rudenesses will be taken for the violence of his passion, and easily obtain pardon. She, by degrees, suffers in
him what she would deem insolence in *another ;* and, idly fan-
cying that one who loves her so much can never have a
thought injurious to her, she forgets that all his compliments
are mercenary, all his passion, desire; that to hear him, is im-

modest; to be pleased with him, wicked; and that, if she does not fly in time, she will catch the flame that is kindled in *him,* and perish in it for ever.

Have a care how you presume on the innocence of your first intentions. You may as well, upon the confidence of a sound constitution, enter a pest-house and converse with the plague, whose contagion does not more subtilely insinuate itself, than this sort of temptation. And as, in that case, a woman would not stay to learn the critical distance at which she might approach with safety, but would run as far from it as she could; so in this, it no less concerns her, to remove from every possibility of danger, and, however unfashionable it be, to put on such a severe modesty, that her very looks may guard her, and discourage the most impudent attack.

This caution, however, should not lead you to be too reserved. I would not have you give up an agreeable acquaintance, under the notion that he may become your lover, nor because idle people may perhaps say he is. It is possible a man may covet your company, without the least design upon your person. All I urge is, that you will be upon your guard, with respect to him, and watch your own heart prudently, lest you unawares become too far engaged to be able to retreat.

Love should by no means begin on your part; it should proceed from the attachment of the man. Some pleasing qualities recommend a man to your notice, and attract your esteem. In time, he becomes attached to you; you perceive it, and it excites your gratitude; thence arises a preference, which perhaps ripens into love. Thus are half the reciprocal attachments first formed; and, when they take place in this manner, there is little to fear: but if a young woman suffers an attachment to steal upon her, till she is sure of a return, or where those qualities are wanting, necessary to make the marriage state happy, her misery is almost sealed.

Although a superior degree of happiness may be attained in marriage, if a young woman gives way to this thought, and thinks matrimony essential to her happiness, she is in a dreadful situation. Besides the indelicacy of the sentiment, the fate of thousands of women has proved it false; but admitting it to be true, an impatience to be married, is the surest method of becoming miserable in that state.

It is difficult to discover the real sentiments of the heart in this particular. The effects of love, in men, are as different as their tempers; and an artful man will sometimes counterfeit them all so well, that he will readily impose on an openhearted generous girl, if she is not exceedingly on her guard.

However we will point out those effects of an honourable passion among the men, which are most difficult to be counterfeited.

True love not only makes a man highly respectful in his behaviour to the woman he loves, but extremely timid. From a fear of not succeeding, he studies to conceal his passion, and yet, from a too great anxiety to conceal it, he often betrays it. Conscious, as of doing wrong, he imagines every eye observes and suspects him; of course, he avoids even those little gallantries that are the polish of his sex, and would be well received; and though to hide the awe in which he stands, he will now and then affect to be cheerful, his cheerfulness looks awkward, and he is presently dull again. His manners, however, improve by his attachment, they become gradually more gentle, and more engaging; but yet, his diffidence and embarrassment before the object of his affection, will make him appear to disadvantage; and if the fascination should hold for any length of time, it will render him inactive, spiritless and unmanly.

When you perceive this in a man, consider seriously how to act. If you approve his attachment, let nature, good sense and delicacy direct you. If his affection for you should have attracted your affection in return, let me advise you, never to let him know how much you love him, even though you marry him. If you give him your hand, that, to a man of delicacy, is a sufficient proof of your affection, and he will want no other. Violent love cannot long subsist; nature, therefore, has laid the reserve on you.

Should his attachment prove disagreeable, and you are determined not to encourage it, tell him so at once, but treat him honourably and humanely. There are various ways, in which you may undeceive him. There is a certain pleasantry, which the ladies can occasionally put on, that will presently tell a man of common discernment, that he has nothing to expect. Unless you wish to preserve his acquaintance, you may in many ways shew a desire to avoid his company; but the best method will be to get some common friend to acquaint him with your sentiments.

If you dislike any of these means, indulge him with an opportunity of explaining himself, and then give him a polite decisive answer. Tell him " you esteem yourself highly honour-
" ed in the opinion he entertains of you, and the preference
" he shews you; but that either your affections are pre-
" engaged, or you are too young, or too unsettled in your
" mind to think of altering your situation or that you shall
" always value him as a friend, but cannot think of him as a

" husband." If he is a man of spirit and delicacy, he will give you no farther trouble; if he continues to tease you after this, any measures you may take to get rid of him will be justifiable.

Coquetry is, of all female conduct, the most infamous ;—I mean that artful coquetry, that strives to fix the hearts of men, in order to wanton in their attachment. It is an act of barbarity and insolence, that deserves the severest punishment. A woman, that would sacrifice a man's happiness to her vanity, would as little scruple to be gratified with the ruin of his reputation or his fortune.

When a man has once made a lady proposals of marriage, and they are rejected, she is too apt to shun his company afterwards, as if he had given her some offence; but in fact, he has paid her the highest compliment in his power, and deserves her future *regard*, if she cannot bestow on him her *love*. A discreet sensible woman, if she cannot give a man her heart, may, if she thinks proper, provided he is a man of sense and candour, make him a steady friend to her for life. If she explains herself to him, with generosity and frankness, he must feel the stroke as a man, but will bear it as a man. His sufferings will be in silence. Though his passion subsides, his esteem will remain. He will view her in the light of a married woman; for he must retain a tenderness for a woman he has once loved, and who treated him well, beyond what he can possibly feel for any other of her sex.

Should this happen to be your case, pray keep it locked within your heart. If he has intrusted no one with it himself, he has a claim to your secrecy. Though you may think proper to communicate to your friends the ill success of your own attachments, in which no one is concerned but yourself; if you have either honour, generosity, or gratitude, you will not betray a secret that is not your own, or that you cannot tell without wounding a person to whom you are under the highest obligations.

Let reason teach what passion fain would hide,
That Hymen's bands by *prudence* should be tied.
Venus in vain the wedded pair would crown,
If *angry fortune* on their union frown.
Soon will the flatt'ring dream of bliss be o'er,
And cloy'd imagination cheat no more :
Then 'waking to the sense of lasting pain,
With mutual tears the nuptial couch they stain,
And that fond love which should afford relief,
Does but increase the anguish of their grief:
For both could easier their own sorrows bear
Than the sad knowledge of each other's care.

Wonderful effects of Love on different Persons.

Eurialus, the young and beautiful count of Augusta, attending the emperor Sigismund at Sienna, fell passionately in love with a beautiful lady in that city, named Lucretia, a virgin, who for her transcendent beauty was generally called the second Venus; she was also no less an admirer and lover of him, and their love grew every day still more vehement, insomuch that when the emperor removed his court to Rome, and Eurialus was obliged to leave his lady behind him, she was so unable to endure his absence, that she died with grief and sorrow. Eurialus having notice of the fatal accident, though, by the advice and consolations of his friends, he was contented to survive her, yet it had such an effect upon him, that from the day he received news of her death to his own, he never was seen to laugh.

Leander was a young man of Abydos, and was deeply in love with Hero, a beautiful virgin of Sestos; these two towns were opposite to each other, and the narrow sea of the Hellespont lay betwixt them. Leander used divers nights to swim over the Hellespont to his love, whilst she held up a torch from a tower, to be his direction in the night; but though this practice continued long, yet at length Leander adventuring to perform the same one night when the sea was rough, and the waves high, was unfortunately drowned. His dead body was cast up at Sestos, where Hero from her tower beheld it; but she, not able to outlive so great a loss, cast herself headlong from the top of it into the sea, and there perished.

Pyramus, a young man of Babylon, was exceedingly in love with Thisbe, the daughter of one that lived next to his father's house; nor was he less beloved by her: their parents had discerned it, and for some reasons kept them both up so strictly, that they were not suffered so much as to speak to each other. At last they found opportunity of discourse through the chink of a wall betwixt them, and appointed to meet together in a certain place without the city. Thisbe came first to the place appointed, but being terrified by a lioness that passed by, she fled into a cave thereabouts, and in her flight had lost her vail, which the lioness tumbled to and fro with her bloody mouth, and so left it. Soon after, Pyramus also came to the same place, and there finding the vail, which she used to wear, all bloody, he over-hastily concluded that she was torn in pieces by some wild beast, and therefore slew himself with his sword under a mulberry-tree, which was to be the place of their meeting. Thisbe, when she thought the lioness was gone, left her cave, with an earnest desire to meet her lover;

but finding him slain, overcome with grief, she fell upon the same sword, and died with him.

Eginardus was secretary of state to Charlemagne, and having placed his affections much higher than his condition admitted, made love to one of his daughters; who, seeing this man of a brave spirit, and a grace suitable, thought him not too low for her whom merit had so eminently raised above his birth: she loved him, and gave him free access to her, so far as to suffer him to laugh and sport in her chamber on evenings, which ought to have been kept as a sanctuary where reliques are preserved. It happened on a winter's night, Eginardus, ever hasty in his approaches, but negligent about returning, had somewhat too long continued his visit: in the mean time a snow had fallen, which troubled them both; he feared to be betrayed by his feet, and the lady was unwilling that such prints should be found at her door. Being much perplexed, love, which taketh the diadem of majesty from queens, made her do an act for a lover, very unusual for the daughter of one of the greatest men upon earth; she took the gentleman upon her shoulders, and carried him all the length of the court to his chamber, he never setting a foot to the ground, that so the next day no impression might be seen of his footing. It fell out that Charlemagne watched at his study this night, and hearing a noise, opened the window, and perceived this pretty prank, at which he could not tell whether he were best to be angry, or to laugh The next day in a great assembly of lords, and in the presence of his daughter and Eginardus, he asked what punishment that servant was worthy of, who made use of a king's daughter as of a mule, and caused himself to be carried on her shoulders in the midst of winter, through night, snow, and all the sharpness of the season? Every one gave his opinion, and not one but condemned that insolent man to death. The princess and secretary changed colour, thinking nothing remained for them but to be flayed alive. But the emperor, looking on his secretary with a smooth brow, said, " Eginardus, hadst thou loved the princess my daughter, thou oughtest to have come to her father, the disposer of her liberty; thou art worthy of death, and I give thee two lives at this present; take thy fair porteress in marriage, fear God, and love one another."

There was among the Grecians a company of soldiers, consisting of three hundred, that was called the Holy Band, erected by Gorgidas, and chosen out of such as heartily loved one another, whereby it came to pass that it could never be broken or overcome; for their love and hearty affection would not suffer them to forsake one another, what danger soever came. But at the battle of Chæronea they were all slain, After the fight, king Philip taking a view of the dead bodies, came to the place where all these three hundred men lay slain, thrust through with pikes on their breasts; and being told that it was the Lover's Band, he could not forbear weeping.

Gobrias, a captain, when he had espied Rodanthe, a fair captive maid, fell upon his knees before Mystilus the general, with tears, vows, and all the rhetoric he could; by the scars he had formerly received, the good services he had done, or whatsoever else was dear unto him, he besought his general, that he might have the fair prisoner to his wife, as a reward of his valour; moreover, he would forgive him all his arrears; " I ask," said he, " no part of the booty, no other thing but Rodanthe to be my wife; and when he could not compass her by fair means, he fell to treachery, force and villany; and, at last, set his life at stake to accomplish his desire.

In the beginning of the thirteenth century, a count of Gleichen was taken in a fight against the Turks, and carried into Turkey, where he suffered a hard and long captivity, being put upon ploughing the ground, &c. But thus happened his deliverance: Upon a certain day, the daughter of the king his master came up to him, and asked him several questions. His good mien, and dexterity, so pleased that princess, that she promised to set him free, and to follow him, provided he would marry her. He answered, " I have a wife and children.' —" That is no argument," replied she, " the custom of the Turks allows one man several wives." The count was not stubborn, but acquiesced to these reasons, and gave his word. The princess employed herself so industriously to get him out of bondage, that they were soon in readiness to go on board a vessel. They arrived happily at Venice. The count found there one of his men, who travelled every where to hear of him; he told him, that his wife and children were in good health: whereupon he presently went to Rome, and, after he had ingenuously related what he had done, the pope granted him a solemn dispensation to keep his two wives. If the court of Rome shewed itself so easy on this occasion, the count's wife was not less so; for she received very kindly the Turkish lady, by whose means she recovered her dear husband, and had for this concubine a particular kindness. The Turkish princess answered very handsomely those civilities, and though she proved barren yet she loved tenderly the children which the other wife bore in abundance. There is still at Erfore, in Thuringia, a monument of this story to be seen in which the count is placed between his two wives. The queen is adorned with a marble-crown : the countess is engraven naked, with children at her feet.

CHAPTER IX.

CONSIDERATIONS BEFORE MARRIAGE.

THE foundation of the greater portion of the unhappiness which clouds matrimonial life, is to be sought in the unconcern so prevalent in the world, as to those radical principles on which character and the permanence of character depend,— the principles of religion. Popular language indicates the state of popular opinion.

If an union about to take place, or recently contracted, between two young persons, be mentioned in conversation ; the first question which we hear asked concerning it is, whether it be *a good match*. The very countenance and voice of the inquirer, and of the answerer, the terms of the answer returned, and the observations, whether expressive of satisfaction or of regret, which fall from the lips of the company present in the circle, all concur to shew what, in common estimation, is meant by being well married. If a young woman be described as thus married, the terms imply, that she is united to a man whose station and fortune are such, when compared with her own or those of her parents, that in point of precedence, in point of command of finery and of money, she is, more or less, a gainer by the bargain. In high life they imply, that she will now possess the enviable advantages of taking place of other ladies in the neighbourhood ; of decking herself out with jewels and lace ; of inhabiting splendid apartments ; rolling in handsome carriages ; gazing on numerous servants in gaudy liveries ; and of repairing to London, and other fashionable scenes of resort ; all in a degree somewhat higher than that in which a calculating broker, after poring on her pedigree, summing up her property in hand, and computing, at the market price every item which is contingent or in reversion, would have pronounced her entitled to.

A few slight and obvious alterations would adapt the picture to the middle classes of society. But what do the terms imply as to the character of the man selected to be her husband? Probably nothing. His character is a matter which seldom enters into the consideration of the persons who use them ; unless it, at length, appears in the shape of an after-thought, or is awkwardly hitched into their remarks for the sake of decorum. If the terms imply any thing on this point, they mean no more than that he is not notoriously and scandalously addicted to vice. He may be covetous, he may be proud, he may be ambitious, he may be malignant, he may be devoid of Christian principles, practice, and belief; or, to say the very least, it may be totally unknown whether he does not fall, in every particular, under this description; and yet, in the language and in the opinion of the generality of both sexes, the match is excellent.

In like manner a diminution of power as to the supposed advantages already enumerated, though counterpoised by the acquisition of a companion eminent for his virtues, is supposed to constitute a bad match; and is universally lamented in polite meetings with real or affected concern. The good or bad fortune of a young man in the choice of a wife is estimated according to the same rules. From those who contract marriages, either chiefly, or in a considerable degree, through motives of interest or of ambition, it would be folly to expect previous solicitude respecting piety of heart. And it would be equal folly to expect that such marriages, however they may answer the purposes of interest or of ambition, should terminate otherwise than in wretchedness. Wealth may be secured; rank may be obtained: but if wealth and rank are to be main ingredients in the cup of matrimonial felicity, the pure and sweet wine will be exhausted at once, and nothing remain but bitter and corrosive dregs.

When attachments are free from the contamination of such unworthy motives, it by no means always follows that much attention is paid to intrinsic excellence of moral and religious character. Affection, quick-sighted in discerning, and diligent in scrutinizing, the minutest circumstances which contribute to shew whether it is met with reciprocal sincerity and ardor, is, in other respects purblind, and inconsiderate. It magnifies good qualities which exist; it seems to itself to perceive merits which, to other eyes, are invisible; it gives credit for all that it wishes to discover; it inquires not, where it fears a disappointment. It forgets that the spirit of the scriptural command " not to be yoked unequally with unbelievers," a command reiterated in other parts of holy writ, may justly be deemed to extend to all cases, in which there is reason to apprehend that religion is not the great operative principle in the mind of the man.

Yet on what grounds can a woman hope for the blessing of God on a marriage contracted without regard to his injunctions? What security can she have for happiness, as depending on the conduct of her husband, if the only foundation on which confidence can be safely reposed, be want-ing? And ought she not, in common prudence, to consider it as wanting, until she is thoroughly convinced of its existence? He, whose ruling principle is that of stedfast obedience to the laws of God, has a pledge to give, and it is a pledge worthy of being trusted, that he will discharge his duty to his fellow-creatures, according to the different relations in which he may be placed. Every other bond of confidence is brittle as a thread, and looks specious only to prove delusive.

A woman who receives for her husband a person of whose moral and religious character she knows no more than that it is outwardly decent, stakes her welfare upon a very hazardous experiment. She who marries a man not entitled even to that humble praise, in the hope of reclaiming him, stakes it on an experiment in which there is scarcely a chance of her success.

The prospect of passing a single month with an acquaint-ance, whose society we know to be unpleasing, is a pros-pect from which every mind recoils. Were the time of in-tercourse antecedently fixed to extend to a year, or to a longer period, our repugnance would be proportionally great. Were the term to reach to the death of one of the parties, the evil would appear in foresight scarcely to be endured. But farther; let it be supposed, not only that the parties were to be bound during their joint lives to the society of each other; but that in all circumstances their interests were to be inseparably blended together. And, in the next place, let it also be supposed that the two parties were not to engage in this association on terms of complete equality; but that one of them was necessarily to be placed as to various particulars, in a state of subordination to the other. What caution would be requisite in each of the parties, what especial caution would be requisite in the party destined to subordination, antecedently to such an engagement! How diversified, how strict, how persevering should be the inquiries of each respecting the other, and especially of the latter respecting the former! Unless the dispositions, the temper, the habits, the genuine character, and inmost principles were mutually known; what rational hope, what tolerable chance of happiness could subsist? And if happiness should not be the lot of the two associates, would not their disquietudes be proportionate to the close-ness of their union? Let this reasoning be transferred to the case of marriage.

As the choice of a husband is of the greatest consequence

to your happiness, be sure you make it with the utmost cir
cumspection.   Do not give way to a sudden sally of passion,
and then dignify it with the name of love.   Genuine love
is not founded in caprice; it is founded in nature, on ho
nourable views, on virtue, on similarity of tastes, and sympathy of souls.   If you have these sentiments, you will
never marry any one when you are not in that situation
which prudence suggests to be necessary to the happiness
of either of you.   What that competency may be, can only
be determined by your own tastes : if you have as much between you as to satisfy all your demands, it is sufficient.
Marriage may dispel the enchantment raised by external
beauty; but the virtues and graces that first warmed the
heart, may, and ought ever to remain.   The tumult of passion will necessarily subside; but it will be succeeded by
an endearment that affects the heart in a more equal, a more
sensible and tender manner.   Dr. Watts has some pretty verses
on the paucity of *happy Marriages* :—

Say, mighty Love, and teach my song,
To whom thy sweetest joys belong,
   And who the happy pairs,
Whose yielding hearts, and joining hands.
Find blessings twisted with their bands,
   To soften all their cares ?

Not the wild herd of nymphs and swains
That thoughtless fly into thy chains,
   As custom leads the way :
If there be bliss without design,
Ivies and oaks may grow and twine,
   And be as blest as they.

Not sordid souls of earthly mould,
Who, drawn by kindred charms of gold,
   To dull embraces move :
So two rich mountains of Peru
May rush to wealthy marriage too,
   And make a world of love.

Not the mad tribe that hell inspires
With wanton flames; those raging fires
   The purer bliss destroy :
On Ætna's top let furies wed,
And sheets of lightning dress the bed,
   T' improve the burning joy.

Nor the dull pairs whose marble forms
None of the melting passions warms,
   Can mingle hearts and hands ;
Logs of green wood that quench the coals
Are marry'd just like stoic souls,
   With osiers for their bands.

Not minds of melancholy strain,
Still silent, or that still complain,
   Can the dear bondage bless :
As well may heav'nly concerts spring
From two old lutes with ne'er a string,
   Or none besides the bass.

Nor can the soft enchantments hold
Two jarring souls of angry mould,
   The rugged and the keen:
Samson's young foxes might as well
In bonds of cheerful wedlock dwell,
   With firebrands ty'd between.

Nor let the cruel fetters bind
A gentle to a savage mind ;
   For love abhors the sight :
Loose the fierce tiger from the deer,
For native rage and native fear
   Rise and forbid delight.

Two kindred souls alone must meet,
'Tis friendship makes the bondage sweet,
   And feeds their mutual loves :
Bright Venus on her rolling throne
Is drawn by gentlest birds alone,
   And Cupid's yoke, the doves.

By way of contrast to the above, take the following beautiful verses actually written by the *Rev. Mr. Bishop*, to his
WIFE, a rare example of elegant and sincere affection. The
verses were accompanied by a ring.

    Thee, Bessy, with this Ring I wed,
    So sixteen years ago I said.
    Behold another Ring ; for what ?
    To wed the o'er again—why not?
    With that first Ring I married youth,
    Grace, beauty, innocence, and truth,
    Taste long admir'd, sense long rever'd,
    And all my Bessy then appear'd

If she, by merit, since disclos'd,
Prove twice the woman I suppos'd,
I plead that double merit now,
To justify a double vow.
Here, then, to-day, with faith as sure,
With ardour as intense and pure,
As when amidst the rites divine,
I took thy truth, and plighted mine,
To thee, sweet girl, my second Ring,
A token and a pledge I bring.
With this I wed, till death us part,
Thy riper virtues to my heart.
Those virtues which before untry'd
The wife has added to the bride;
Those virtues whose progressive claim,
Endearing wedlock's very name,
My soul enjoys, my song approves,
For conscience' sake, as well as love's.
For why? They shew me, hour by hour,
Honour's high thought, affection's pow'r,
Discretion's deed, sound judgment's *sentence*
And teach me all things but repentance.

BY THE SAME AUTHOR TO HIS LADY, WITH A KNIFE

A Knife, dear girl, cuts love, they say;
Mere modish love, perhaps, it may:
For any tool of any kind,
Can sep'rate what was never join'd.
The Knife that cuts our love in two,
Will have much tougher work to do,
Must cut your softness, worth, and spirit,
Down to vulgar size of merit:
To level your's with modern taste,
Must cut a world of sense to waste,
And from your single beauty's store,
Clip what would dizen out a score.
The self-same blade from me must sever
Sensation, judgment, sight, for ever,
All mem'ry of endearments past,
All hope of comforts long to last;
All that makes fifteen years with you
A summer, and a short one too;
All that affection feels and fears,
When hours without you seem like years,
Till that be done (and I'd as soon
Believe this Knife would clip the moon

Accept my present, undeterr'd,
And leave their proverbs to the herd :
If in a kiss, delicious treat,
Your lips acknowledge the receipt,
Love, fond of such substantial fare,
And proud to play the glutton there,
All thought of cutting will disdain,
Save only—cut and come again.

CHAPTER X.

DUTIES OF THE MARRIED STATE

To superintend the various branches of domestic management, or, as St. Paul briefly and emphatically expresses the same office, " to guide the house," is the indispensable duty of a married woman.   No mental endowments furnish an exemption from it ; no plea of improving pursuits and literary pleasures can excuse the neglect of it.   The task must be executed either by the master or the mistress of the house : and reason and scripture concur in assigning it unequivocally to the latter.

Custom, which in many instances presumes to decide in plain contradiction to these sovereign rules of life, has, in this point, so generally conformed to their determination, that a husband who should personally direct the proceedings of the housekeeper and the cook, and intrude into the petty arrangements of daily economy, would appear, in all eyes except his own, nearly as ridiculous as if he were to assume to himself the habiliments of his wife, or to occupy his mornings with her needles and work-bags.   It is true, nevertheless, that, in executing this office, a wife is to consult the wishes of her husband ; and in proportion to the magnitude of any particular points, to act the more studiously according to his ideas rather than her own.   The duty of obedience on her part extends to the province of guiding the house no less than to the other branches of her conduct. Are you then the mistress of a family ? Fulfil the charge for which you are responsible.   Attempt not to transfer your proper occupation to a favourite maid, however tried may be her fidelity and her skill.   To confide implicitly in servants, is the way to render them undeserving of confidence.   If they be already negligent or dishonest, your remissness encourages their faults, while it continues your own loss and inconvenience

If their integrity be unsullied, they are ignorant of the principles by which your expenses ought to be regulated; and will act for you on other principles, which, if you were conscious of them, you ought to disapprove. They know not the amount of your husband's income, nor of his debts, nor of his other incumbrances; nor, if they knew all these things, could they judge what part of his revenue may reasonably be expended in the departments with which they are concerned. They will not reflect that small degrees of waste and extravagance, when it would be easy to guard against them, are criminal; nor will they suspect the magnitude of the sum to which small degrees of waste and extravagance, frequently repeated, will accumulate in the course of the year. They will consider the credit of your character as intrusted to them; and will conceive, that they uphold it by profusion. The larger your family is, the greater will be the annual portion of your expenditure, which will by these means be thrown away. And if your ample fortune incline you to regard the sum as scarcely worth the little trouble which would have been required to prevent the loss; consider the extent of good which it might have accomplished, had it been employed in feeding the hungry and clothing the naked.

Be regular in requiring, and punctual in examining your weekly accounts. Be frugal without parsimony; save, that you may distribute. Study the comfort of all under your roof, even of the humblest inhabitant of the kitchen. Pinch not the inferior part of the family, to provide against the cost of a day of splendor. Consider the welfare of the servants of your own sex as particularly committed to you. Encourage them in religion, and be active in furnishing them with the means of instruction. Let their number be fully adequate to the work which they have to perform; but let it not be swelled either from a love of parade or from blind indulgence, to an extent which is needless.

In those ranks of life were the mind is not accustomed to continued reflection, idleness is a never-failing source of folly and of vice. Forget not to indulge them at fit seasons with visits to their friends; nor grudge the pains of contriving opportunities for the indulgence. Let not one tyrannize over another. In hearing complaints, be patient; in inquiring into faults, be candid; in reproving be temperate and unruffled. Let not your kindness to the meritorious terminate when they leave your house; but reward good conduct in them, and encourage it in others, by subsequent acts of benevolence adapted to their circumstances. Let it be your resolution, when called upon to describe the characters of servants who have quitted your family, to act conscientiously towards all the parties interested, neither aggravating nor disguising the truth. And never let any one of those whose qualifications are to be mentioned, nor of those who apply for the account, find you seduced from your purpose by partiality or by resentment.

There is sometimes seen in families an inmate, commonly a female relation of the master or of the mistress of the house, who, though admitted to live in the parlour, is, in truth, an humble dependent, received either from motives of charity or for the sake of being made useful in the conduct of domestic affairs, or of being a companion to her protectress when the latter is not otherwise engaged or amused.

Have you such an inmate? Let your behaviour to her be such as she ought to experience. Pretend not to call her friend, while you treat her as a drudge. If sickness, or infirmity, or a sudden pressure of occupation, disqualify you from personally attending in detail to the customary affairs of your household, avail yourself of her assistance. But seek it not from an indolent aversion to trouble, nor from a haughty wish to rid yourself of the employment. While you have recourse to it, receive it as an act of kindness, not as the constrained obedience of an upper servant. Teach the inferior parts of your family to respect her, by respecting her yourself. Remember the awkwardness of her situation, and consult her comfort.

Is she to look for friends in the kitchen, or in the house-keeper's room? You express surprise at the impropriety of the supposition. Is she to live an insulated being under your roof? Your benevolence revolts at the idea. Admit her then not merely to the formalities, but to the freedom and genuine satisfactions of intercourse. Tempt her not, by a reserved demeanour, perpetually reminding her of the obligations which she is unfortunate enough to owe you, to echo your opinions, to crouch to your humours, to act the part of a dissembler. If servile assiduities and fawning compliances be the means by which she is to ingratiate herself, blush for your proud and unfeeling heart. Is it the part of friendship, of liberal protection, to harass her with difficulties, to ensnare her sincerity, to establish her in the petty arts of cunning and adulation? Rather dismiss her with some pittance, however small, of bounty to search in obscurity for an honest maintenance, than retain her to learn hypocrisy and to teach you arrogance, to be corrupted and to corrupt.

In all the domestic expenses which are wholly, or in part,

regulated by your opinion, beware that, while you pay a decent regard to your husband's rank in society, you are not hurried into ostentation and prodigality by vanity lurking in your breast.   Examine your own motives to the bottom.

You are lavish, vain, proud, emulous, ambitious; you are defective in some of the first duties of a wife and of a Christian.   Instead of squandering, in extravagance and parade that property which ought partly to have been reserved in store for the future benefit of your offspring, and partly to have been liberally bestowed for the present advantage of those whom relationship or personal merit, or the general claim which distress has upon such as are capable of granting relief, entitles to your bounty; let it be your constant aim to obey the scriptural precepts of sobriety and moderation; let it be your delight to fulfil every office of unaffected benevolence.   Picture to yourself the difficulties, the calamities, the final ruin, in which tradesmen, with their wives and children, are frequently involved, even by the delay of payments due to them from families to which they have not dared to refuse credit.   Subject not yourself in the sight of God to the charge of being accessary to such miseries.

Guard by every becoming method of amiable representation and persuasion, if circumstances should make them necessary, and there is a prospect of their being taken in good part, the man to whom you are united from contributing to such miseries either by profusion or by inadvertence.   Is he careless as to the inspection of his affairs?   Endeavour to open his eyes to the dangers of neglect and procrastination.   Does he anticipate future, perhaps contingent, resources?   Gently awaken him to a conviction of his criminal imprudence.   Encourage him, if he stand in need of encouragement, in vigilant but not avaricious foresight; in the practice of enlarged and unwearied charity.

If your husband, accustomed to acquire money by professional exertions, should become too little inclined to impart freely that which he has laboriously earned; suggest to him that one of the inducements to labour, addressed to him by an apostle, is no other than this, " that he may have to give to him that needeth."   If his extensive intercourse with the world, familiarizing him to instances of merited or of pretended distress, have the effect of rendering him somewhat too suspicious of deceit, somewhat too severe towards those whose misfortunes are, in part at least, to be ascribed to themselves; remind him that " God is kind to the unthankful and the evil." Remind him that the gift which conscience may require to be withheld from the unwo thy, ought to be dedicated to the relief

of indigent desert. With him constantly and practically to
" remember the words of the Lord Jesus ; how he said, It is
more blessed to give than to receive."

Women, who have been raised by marriage to the possession
of rank and opulence unknown to them before, are frequently
the most ostentatious in their proceedings. Yet a moderate
share of penetration might have taught them to read, in the
example of others, the ill success of their own schemes to gain
respect by displaying their elevation. All such attempts sharp-
en the discernment and quicken the researches of envy ; and
draw from obscurity into public notice, the circumstances
which pride and pomp are labouring to bury in oblivion. The
want of the sedateness of character, which Christianity requires in all women, is in a married woman doubly reprehensible. If, now that you are entered into connubial life, you
disclose in your dress proofs of vanity and affectation, or
plunge headlong into the wild hurry of amusements ; the censure which you deserve is greater than it would be, were you
single.

Any approach towards those indelicate fashions in attire,
which levity and shamelessness occasionally introduce, would
for the same reason be even more blameable in you now than
heretofore. St. Paul, among various admonitions relating to
married women in particular, enforces on them the duty of
being " keepers at home." The precept, in its application to
modern times, may be considered as having a two-fold reference. It may respect short visits paid to acquaintances and
friends in the vicinity of your residence ; or excursions, which
require an absence of considerable duration. Facility of access and intercourse expose women, and not only those who
are fixed in towns, or within a small distance of towns, but most
of those also who live in the country, to the danger of acquiring a habit of continual visiting ; and the other habits which
St. Paul justly ascribes to those who have contracted the former : " They learn to be idle, wandering about from house to
house ; and not only idle, but tattlers also and busy-bodies,
speaking things which they ought not." The *wanderers* of
the present day could not have been more happily charac-
terized, had the apostle been witness of their proceedings. If,
week after week, the mornings be perpetually frittered away in
making calls, and the afternoons swallowed up by dining visits ;
what but idleness can be the consequence ? Domestic business
is interrupted ; vigilance as to family concerns is suspended ;
industry, reflection, mental and religious improvement, are deserted and forgotten. The mind grows listless ; home becomes

dull; the carriage is ordered afresh; and a remedy for the evil is sought from the very cause which produced it.

From being *idle* at home, the next step naturally is to be *tattlers and busy-bodies* abroad. In a succession of visits, all the news of the vicinity is collected; the character and conduct of each neighbouring family are scrutinized; neither age nor sex escapes the prying eye and inquisitive tongue of curiosity. Each *tattler*, anxious to distinguish herself by the dis play of superior knowledge and discernment, indulges unbounded license to her conjectures; seizes the flying report of the hour as an incontrovertible truth; and renders her narratives more interesting by embellishment and aggravation. And all, in revealing secrets, in judging with rashness, in censuring with satisfaction, in propagating slander, and in various other ways, *speak things which they ought not.* I shall not enlarge on the interruption of domestic habits and occupations, nor on the acquisition of an unsettled, a tattling, and a meddling spirit: evils which spring from the custom of *wandering* from place to place, no less than from that of *wandering from house to house ;"* and often display themselves in the former case on a wider scale and in stronger characters, than in the latter. But the loss of the power and opportunity of doing good, and the positive effects of a pernicious example, are points which must not be overlooked.

Home is the centre round which the influence of every married woman is accumulated. It is there that she will naturally be known and respected the most *;* it is there, at least, that she may be more known and more respected than she can be in any other place. It is there that the general character, the acknowledged property, and the established connexions of her husband, will contribute with more force than they can possess elsewhere, to give weight and impressiveness to all her proceedings. Home, therefore, is the place where the pattern which she exhibits in personal manners, in domestic arrangements, and in every branch of her private conduct, will be more carefully observed, and more willingly copied, by her neighbours in a rank of life similar to that which she occupies, than it would be in a situation where she was a little known and transitory visitant. Home too is the place where she will possess peculiar means of doing good among the humbler classes of society.

All the favourable circumstances already mentioned, which surround her there, add singular efficacy to her persuasions, to her recommendations, to her advice. Her habitual insight into local events and local necessities, and her acquaintance with the characters and the situations of individuals, enable her to adapt the relief which she affords to the merit and to the distress of the person assisted. They enable her, in the charitable expenditure of any specific sum, to accomplish purposes of greater and more durable utility than could have been attained in a place where she would not have enjoyed these advantages.

In the progress of matrimonial life it is scarcely possible but that the wife and the husband will discover faults in each other which they had not previously expected. The discovery is by no means a proof, in many cases it is not even a presumption, that deceit had originally been practised. Affection, like that Christian charity of whose nature it largely participates, in its early periods " hopeth all things, believeth all things." Time and experience, without necessarily detracting from its warmth, superadd judgment and observation. The characters of the parties united mutually expand; and disclose those little recesses which, even in dispositions most inclined to be open and undisguised, scarcely find opportunities of unfolding themselves antecedently to marriage. Intimate connexion and uninterrupted society reveal shades of error in opinion and in conduct, which, in the hurry of spirits and the dazzled state of mind peculiar to the season of growing attachment, escaped even the vigilant eye of solicitude. Or the fact unhappily may be, that in consequence of new scenes, new circumstances, new temptations, failings which did not exist when the matrimonial state commenced, may have been contracted since. The stream may have derived a debasing tincture from the region through which it has lately flowed. But the fault, whether it did or did not exist while the parties were single, is now discerned. What then is to be the consequence of the discovery ? Is affection to be repressed, is it to be permitted to grow languid, because the object or it now appears tinctured with some few additional defects ? I allude not to those flagrant desertions of moral and religious principle, those extremes of depravity, which are not unknown to the connubial state, and give a shock to the tenderest feelings of the heart. I speak of those common failings, which long and familiar intercourse gradually detects in every human character. Whether they are perceived by the husband in the wife or by the wife in the husband, to contribute by every becoming method to their removal is an act of duty strictly incumbent on the discoverer. It is more than an act of duty ; it is the first office of love. " Thou shalt not *hate* thy neighbour *in suffering sin upon him,*" is a precept, the disregard of

which is the most criminal in those persons, by whom the
warmest regard for the welfare of each other ought to be
displayed.

CHAPTER XI.

USEFUL HINTS TO MARRIED WOMEN.

CHEERFULNESS and good-humour, at all times necessary
and amiable qualities, should be more particularly sought by
married women. In a state of pregnancy, more than in any
other, the changes of bodily health seem to be almost wholly
under the immediate influence of the mind, and the mother
appears well or ill, according as she gives way to pleasing or
fretful emotions. During this important state of the body
every woman should be doubly attentive to preserve the utmost
sweetness and serenity of temper,—to dispel the glooms of
fear or melancholy,—to calm the rising gusts of anger,—and
to keep every other unruly passion or desire under the steady
control of mildness and reason. The joy of becoming a mother, and the anticipated pleasure of presenting a fond husband with the dearest pledge of mutual love, ought naturally
to increase her cheerfulness, and would certainly produce that
effect, were not those emotions too often checked by a false
alarm at the fancied danger of her situation. It is therefore of
the utmost importance to convince her that her terrors are
groundless ;—that pregnancy is not a state of infirmity or
danger, but affords the strongest presumption of health and
security ;—that the few instances she may have known of mis-
carriage or of death, were owing to the improper conduct of
the women themselves, besides being too inconsiderable to be
compared with the countless millions of persons in the like
condition, who enjoy both then and afterwards a greater degree of health than they ever before experienced ; and, lastly
that the changes which she feels in herself, and her quick per-
ceptions of uneasiness, are not symptoms of weakness, but the
consequences of an increased sensibility of her womb, and
timely warnings of the effect of indiscretion or intemperance.
    A late writer on this subject very justly observes, that, when
such an increase of sensibility takes place in a woman of a
very irritable frame and temper, it must certainly aggravate
her former complaints and weaknesses, and produce a variety
of feverish effects. She grows more impatient and fretful ;
her fears, as well as her angry passions, are more readily ex-

cited · the body necessarily suffers with the mind : debility emaciation, and many hectic symptoms, follow. But the only rational inference to be drawn from these facts is, that the feelings are more acute in a state of pregnancy : and that any previous indisposition, either of body or mind, now requires a more than ordinary degree of care and tenderness.

Though the chilling influence of fear, and the depressions of melancholy, are very injurious to the mother's health and to the growth of the *fœtus* in her womb; yet anger is a still more formidable enemy. It convulses the whole system, and forces the blood into the face and head with great impetuosity. The danger is increased by the usual fulness of the habit in pregnancy. When the blood runs high and rapid, a vessel may burst, and in such a part as to terminate, or bring into great peril, the existence of both the mother and the child. Cases often occur of the bursting of a blood-vessel in the brain, occasioned by a violent gust of passion. How much more likely is it to rupture those tender vessels that connect the mother and child ! Yet to the latter this is certain death. I knew a female who had the *aorta*, or great artery, so distended that it forced its way through the breast-bone, and rose externally to the size of a quart bottle. This extraordinary distension was chiefly owing to the violence of her temper. I have also met with a most shocking instance of a fighting woman, who, in the paroxysm of rage and revenge, brought forth a child, with all its bowels hanging out of its little body. There is no doubt but that passionate women are most subject to abortions, which are oftener owing to outward violence or internal tumult, than to any other cause. An accident of this sort is the more alarming, as the woman, who once miscarries, has the greatest reason ever after to dread the repetition of the same misfortune.

Cards, or any kind of gaming, at all times the worst of amusements, should be particularly avoided during pregnancy. The temper is then more liable to be ruffled by the changes of luck, and the mind to be fatigued by constant exertions of the judgment and memory. Old maids, are the only class of females, who may be allowed to spend some of their tedious hours in such absurd and such unhealthy pastimes.

Without entering into farther details, it will be easy for the sensible mother to apply the principle here laid down to every passion and propensity which may tend to excite painful emotions of the mind, and to impair in the same degree the health of the body.

The enjoyments of the table must be kept under the nice control of moderation. Any excess, or any deficiency

of proper supplies, will now be most severely felt.   The well-
being of both the mother and child will depend on her pursuing a happy medium between painful restraint or unnecessary self-denial, on the one hand, and the indulgence of a
depraved or intemperate appetite on the other.   But, as the
natural desire of aliment increases with the growth and increasing wants of the child, it will be proper to consider those variations as they appear in the different stages of pregnancy;
and to shew how far it may be also advisable to gratify the
involuntary, and often very wild and whimsical desires, which
are known by the name of *longings*.

All strong liquors, unripe fruits, and pastry should be avoided
as well as all sorts of food that are high-seasoned, inflammatory,
or hard of digestion.   If these are improper before marriage,
they must be doubly pernicious afterwards, when they may
not only injure the mother's health, but poison, infect, or im-
poverish the fountain of life and nutriment, whence her child
is to derive support.   Every female, therefore, will see the importance of guarding against bad habits, or the indulgence of
a vitiated taste at an early period ; that she may not have any
painful restraints to subject herself to when a mother, or be
then under the necessity of making any great change from
her former mode of living.

During a state of pregnancy all stiff stays and tightness of
dress should be studiously avoided.

We cannot conclude this chapter, without making some re
marks upon that prevalent complaint among pregnant women,
called *longing*.   As soon as a woman begins to consult her
caprice, instead of attending to nature, she is sure to be en
couraged in absurdity by old nurses, or female gossips, who
take a delight in amusing her credulity by the relation of
many wonderful and alarming injuries, said to have been done
to children, through the unsatisfied desires of their mothers.
Every fairy tale, however repugnant to common sense, gains
implicit belief; for reason dares not intrude into the regions
of fancy : and were a man bold enough to laugh at such fic-
t'ons, or to remonstrate with a pregnant woman on the danger
of giving way to any of her extravagant wishes, he would certainly be considered as a conceited fool, or an unfeeling monster.   Argument is lost, and ridicule has no force, where
people pretend to produce a host of facts in support of their
opinion.

Every woman, who brings into the world a marked child,
can immediately assign the cause : yet no mother was ever
able, before the birth, to say with what her child would be
marked ; and I believe it would be equally difficult afterwards,

without the aid of fancy, to discover in a flesh-mark any re
semblance to the object whence the impression had been
supposed to originate.

On examining various instances of flesh-marks, and other
dreadful events, said to be caused by disappointed *longings*, it
has appeared that most of them were the effects of obstructions, of pressure, or some external injury; and that none
could be fairly traced to the influence of imagination. Similar
accidents are observable in the brute species; and even in
plants, unconscious of their propagation or existence. It is
also well known, that several children are born with marks on
the skin, though their mothers never experienced any *longings*; and that, in other cases, where women had been refused
the indulgence of their *longings*, no effect was perceptible in
the child, though the mother's imagination had continued to
dwell on the subject for a considerable time.

The doctrine of imagination, like every thing founded in
absurdity, confutes itself by being carried too far. The same
power of marking or disfiguring the child is ascribed to the
sudden terrors and the ungratified cravings of pregnant women. The abettors of this doctrine are not even content with
a few specks or blemishes on the skin, but maintain that the
mother's imagination may take off a leg or an arm, or even
fracture every bone in the child's body. I have seen a child
born without a head ; but it was not alleged that the mother
had been present at the beheading of any person, or had ever
been frightened by the spectacle of a human body deprived of
its head. If shocking sights of this kind could have produced
such effects, how many headless babes had been born in
France during ROBESPIERRE's reign of terror!

In order to shew that the fancy, however agitated or strongly
impressed with the dread of any particular object, cannot
stamp its resemblance, or even the smallest feature of it on
the child in the womb, Doctor MOORE relates the following
story of a remarkable occurrence within the sphere of his own
knowledge :—

" A lady, who had great aversion to munkies, happened unfortunately, during the course of her pregnancy, to visit in a
family where one of those animals was the chief favourite. On
being shewed into a room, she seated herself on a chair, which
stood before a table upon which this favourite was already
placed : he, not naturally of a reserved disposition, and rendered more petulant and wanton by long indulgence, suddenly
jumped on the lady's shoulders. She screamed, and was ter
rified ; but on perceiving who had treated her with such indecent familiarity, she actually fainted ; and through the re-

maining course of her pregnancy, she had the most painful
conviction that her child would be deformed by some shocking feature, or perhaps the whole countenance of this odious
monkey.

" The pangs of labour did not overcome this impression, for
in the midst of her pains she often lamented the fate of her
unfortunate child, who was doomed through life to carry about
a human soul in the body of an ape. When the child was
born, she called to the midwife with a lamentable voice for a
sight of her unfortunate offspring, and was equally pleased and
surprised when she received a fine boy into her arms. After
having enjoyed for a few minutes all the rapture of this change
to ease and happiness from pain and misery, her pains returned, and the midwife informed her that there was another
child. ' Another !' exclaimed she, ' then it is as I have dreaded, and this *must* be the monkey after all.' She was, however,
once more happily undeceived ; the second was as fine a boy
as the first. I knew them both :—they grew to be stout
comely youths, without a trace of the monkey in either their
faces or dispositions."

Frightful objects, scenes of horror, or any other cause of a
sudden shock, cannot be considered a matter of indifference
during pregnancy ;—they should be carefully avoided, as they
have often caused abortions, or otherwise injured the health
l oth of the mother and child, though they cannot discolour
the skin, derange the limbs, or alter the shape of the latter.

CHAPTER XII.

MANAGEMENT OF INFANTS.

If the mother, during pregnancy, has not suffered any injury from accident, or from her own imprudence ; and if, after
the accession of labour, neither she nor the midwife has disturbed or impeded the efforts of nature ; the offspring of strong
and healthy parents is sure at the birth to be well-formed,
healthy, and vigorous. Any instances to the contrary are so
rare and extraordinary, as almost to leave some doubt of the
possibility of such an event : yet it appears from the best cal-
culations, that at least one half of the children born die before
they are twelve years old. Of the surviving half at that period, how many perish before they attain to maturity ! How
many others are stunted in their growth, distorted in their
figure, or too much enfeebled ever to enjoy the real sweets of
life ! What a train of ills seems to await the precious charge,

the moment it is taken out of the hands of nature! **But as most of these calamities are the consequences of mismanage ment or neglect, I shall endeavour to shew how they may be prevented by tender and rational attention.**

1. *The Benefits of fresh Air.*

The first want of a new-born infant is clearly manifested by its cries, not arising from any sense of pain, but from a stimulus or impulse to expand the lungs, and thereby open a free passage for the circulation of the blood, and for admission of air, so essential to the existence of every living creature. While the child lay in the womb, its lungs were in a collapsed or shrivelled state : it received all its supplies through the medium of the navel-string. But at its birth a very obvious change takes place. The pulsation or throbbing of this cord first ceases at the remotest part, and then, by slow degrees, nearer and nearer to the child, till the whole string becomes quite flaccid, all circulation being confined to the body of the infant. It is then that the cries of a healthy child are heard ; in consequence of which the air rushes into the lungs ; their tubes and cellular spaces are dilated ; the bosom heaves ; the cavity of the chest is enlarged ; and the blood flows with the utmost ease. But as the air passes out, the lungs again collapse, and the course of the blood receives a momentary check, till a fresh influx or inspiration of air, in concurrence with the action of the heart and arteries, renews the former salutary process, which never ceases during life.

The air, thus inhaled, after imparting its vital properties to the whole frame, takes up the perspirable matter constantly issuing from the interior surface of the lungs, and carries off, on its expulsion, a considerable part of the noxious and superfluous humours of the body. Its purity is, of course, destroyed ; and, in consequence of being frequently breathed, it becomes unfit for the purpose of respiration. In a confined place, therefore, it is not air we inhale, but our own effluvia ; and every other cause, which tends to waste or pollute the air, renders it in the same degree injurious to the strength and health of those who breathe it.

It should, therefore, be the first object **of** a pregnant woman's care, to secure, at least for the time of her lying-in, a wholesome situation. Instead of flying from the country to town, as many do, she should fly from town to the country. If her circumstances will not admit of this, she must fix her abode in as open and airy a street as she can, and at as great a distance as possible from noise, from tumult, and from those nuisances which contaminate the atmosphere of great cities Let her apartments be lofty and spacious, dry rather thar warm, and exposed to the sun's morning rays. I have already explained the importance of cleanliness, and of occasionally letting down the upper sashes of the bed-room windows ii fine weather, to admit fresh air, and to prevent fever. An attention to these points is not less necessary on the new-born infant's account, than on his mother's. Let not the first air he breathes be foul from confinement, too much rarefied by heat, or charged with any noxious exhalations. The mild tempe rature to which he has been used in the womb, renders it very proper to preserve for some time the same moderate degree of warmth in his new place of residence. But he is not, on that account, to be roasted before a great fire, or kept panting in steam and pollution.

If the room be kept properly ventilated and free from impurity, the infant will soon get hardy enough to be taken out into the open air, not only without the least danger, but with the greatest advantage, provided always that the season of the year, and the state of the weather, encourage such early experiments. A month spent within doors, is confinement long enough in almost every case; and the nursery is then to be frequently exchanged for green fields and sunny eminences. There will your child drink, as it were, the vital stream pure from its source; he will draw in at every breath fresh supplies of strength and alacrity; while the bracing action of the air on the surface of his body, will give the degree of firmness unattainable by any other means.

In the course of a few months, the state of the weather need not be much regarded; and its unfavourable changes, unless the heat or cold be intense, must not operate as a check on those daily excursions from the nursery. Our climate is very fickle; we shall suffer much from its rapid variations, if we are not freely exposed to them in early life; do not, therefore, sacrifice the future comfort and safety of the grown man, to mistaken tenderness for the infant. If your child be accustomed from the cradle to go out in all weathers, he will have nothing to fear from the bleak north or the sultry south, but will bear every change of season, of climate, and of at mosphere, not only without danger, but without pain or inconvenience.

Children should not be sent when very young, or indeed a any age, to crowded schools, the atmosphere of which is really a floating mass of putrid effluvia. The breath and perspiration of so many persons in a room, even supposing them all to be in good health, must waste and corrupt the air destroy its vital properties, and of course render it wholly unfit for the support of animal life. But should any one child happen to be diseased, all the rest are very likely to catch the infection. When I see a poor baby, before it can well walk, carried in a nurse's arms to school, I really feel stronger emotions of pity, and of alarm for its safety, than if I had seen it conveyed to a pest-house. In the latter place, children would be kept separate, and proper means would be used to prevent the spreading of contagion : in the former, all are thrown together, and there remain with relaxed lungs, open pores, and steaming bodies, so as to render it almost impossible for any to escape.

As thousands of children die every year the victims of diseases caught at schools, and as the health and constitutions of still greater numbers are irretrievably ruined by the confinement and the bad air of such places, parents must not be offended at the seeming harshness of my language in reprobating so absurd, so cruel, and so unnatural a practice. I know that as soon as children begin to run about, they require the most watchful care to prevent mischief. Will any mother urge this as a reason for being tired of them, and for confining, as it were in stocks, that restless activity which is wisely designed by nature to promote their growth and vigour? Will she, from a wish to save herself some trouble, or to gain time for other business infinitely less important, send her little babes to school, under the silly pretence of keeping them out of harm's way ? I hope what I have already said is sufficient to convince persons of common understanding, that they cannot be exposed to greater harm, than by being fixed to a seat in the midst of noxious steam for six or seven hours a day, which should be spent in the open air and cheerful exercise.

Should it be alleged, that children are sent young to school, from a becoming zeal for their early improvement, I need only reply, that learning, however desirable, is too dearly bought at the expense of the constitution. Besides, learning can never be acquired by such preposterous means. Confinement and bad air are not less injurious to the mind, than to the body ; and nothing so effectually prevents the growth of the intellectual faculties, as premature application. Sending a child to school in his nurse's arms, is the sure way to make him an idiot, or to give him an unconquerable disgust to books : the only book he should then look at, is the great volume of nature. This is legible at every age, and is as gratifying to a child as to a man : it abounds with the most delightful and most useful information : it is equally conducive to pleasure, health, and knowledge.

2. On Bathing.

An infant's skin is covered with a slippery glue, which soon dries, and forms a sort of scurf. This should be washed off very gently with a soft sponge and warm water, having a little soap dissolved in it. Nurses, in general, are as eager to remove every speck of it, as if it was the most offensive impurity, though it is perfectly harmless, and will easily come away in three or four washings, without the danger of hard rubbing, or the aid of improper, and sometimes very injurious, contrivances. Ointments, or greasy substances, cannot fail to fill up the little orifices of the pores, and to put a stop to insensible perspiration. Spirits of any kind are still worse, on account of their inflammatory effect. Even Galen's advice to sprinkle the child's body with salt, that the glutinous matter may be more effectually rubbed off, is at best unnecessary. I have no particular objection to the modern improvement on that hint, which consists in dissolving salt in the warm bath, with a view of giving it the agreeable stimulus, as well as the cleansing and bracing properties of sea-water : but I would not encourage any solicitude in this respect, as the easiest and simplest mode of proceeding will fully answer the desired end.

In the hardy ages of antiquity, we are told that the Germans used to plunge their new-born infants into the freezing waters of the Rhine, to inure them betimes to the severe cold of their native country. I need not take any pains to point out the danger of following such an example in our times, when mothers and nurses are too apt to run into the opposite extreme of unnerving effeminacy. In this, as in every thing else, the golden mean is the line of wisdom—the line to be pursued by rational affection. It would be extremely hazardous to dip the tender body of a child, reeking from the womb, in cold water, and to keep it there during the necessary operation of washing ; but the use of the cold bath may be safely brought about by degrees in five or six months after the birth, and will then be found not only one of the best means of promoting health and strength, but of preventing also many of the most distressing complaints to which children are subject. The following method I can confidently recommend, having had frequent opportunities of observing its salutary effects.

The temperature of the bath, proper for a new-born infant, should approach nearly that of the situation which he has just quitted. It is proper to acquaint those who may not have an instrument to ascertain the degree of heat, that absolute precision in that respect is by no means necessary ; their feelings will inform them with sufficient exactness when the water is rather warmer than new milk : a little solution of soap, as I before observed, is all that is wanted to increase its softness and its purifying effect. The operation of washing should be performed in a vessel large enough to allow room for the expansion of the infant's limbs, and for easily discovering any defect in its structure, or any accident which may have happened to it during labour : either may be often remedied by timely care, but may become incurable through delay or neglect. The child should not be kept in the bath longer than five or six minutes ; and the moment it is taken out, it should be wrapped up in a soft warm blanket, and there kept for a few minutes in a state of gentle motion.

I would not have any difference made, either in the temperature of the bath, or the time of the infant's continuance in it, for the first month. The uncleanness of young children renders frequent washing necessary. It should be the first object of attention in the morning, and the last at night ; but it should not be performed with a full stomach, even when the child receives all its supplies from the breast. This is the only caution which need be added to those already given concerning gentleness in the manner of washing, space enough in the bathing-vessel, and strict care to wipe the child dry, and wrap it warm the instant it is taken out of the bath, when exposure to cold would be doubly dangerous, from the natural delicacy of the infant, and from the immediately preceding warmth and the openness of the pores.

After the first month, the warmth of the water may be lessened, but almost imperceptibly, so as to guard against the risk of sudden changes, or too rash experiments. The mildness of the weather, and the evident increase of the child's strength, must be taken into consideration ; for, though cold water is very serviceable in bracing weak and relaxed habits, yet, if tried too soon, its stimulus on the surface may be too strong, and the powers of re-action within too weak, so that the worst consequences may follow. These will be prevented by a gradual diminution of the temperature of the water, and by close attention to its effects, when reduced nearer and still nearer to a state of coldness. If immersion in the bath be quickly followed by a glow all over the body, and a perceptible liveliness in the child, we may be sure that the water has not been too cold for his constitution, and that we have proceeded with due care. But should it produce chilness, evident languor, and depression, we must make the water a little warmer next time, and not venture upon the cold bath till we are encouraged by more favourable appearances.

Rain or river water is fitter for the purpose of bathing, than pump or spring water; though the latter, in case of necessity, may be used, after having been exposed for some hours to the sun or the atmosphere. The child must not be dipped when its body is hot, or its stomach full, and should be put only once under the water at each time of bathing. All the benefit, as before observed, depends upon the first shock, and the re-action of the system. In order to prevent a sudden and strong determination of the blood to the head, it is always advisable to dip the child with this part foremost, and to be as expeditious as possible in washing away all impurities. I have been already so particular in my directions to have the young bather instantly wiped dry, and wrapped up in a soft warm blanket, that I need not repeat them; but I must add another injunction, which is, not to put the child to bed, but to keep it for some time in gentle motion, and to accompany the whole process with lively singing. It is of far greater importance than most people may be aware of, to associate in early life the idea of pleasure and cheerfulness with so salutary an operation.

During the use of the lukewarm bath, the whole body is to be immersed in it every night as well as morning. But, when recourse is had to cold bathing, it must be used in the manner above prescribed in the morning only. At night, it will be enough to wash the lower parts; and even for this purpose a little warm water may be added to the cold in severe weather. Every danger will thus be avoided; every benefit will be secured; and the habit of personal cleanliness, being rendered familiar in childhood, will be retained through life, and will contribute very much to its duration and enjoyment.

3. On Children's Dress.

Much injury, and many deaths are the consequence of not attending to the clothing of infants. Excess is generally the fault to be avoided. The midwife takes alarm at the imperfect indentation of the bones on the crown of the head, and not only strives to press them closer and to brace them by means of fillets, but is careful to keep the head warmly covered, to prevent the poor baby, as she says, from *catching his death* by the exposure of those open parts to the air. Deformity is the least of the evils that attend such acts of astonishing infatuation. The delicate texture of the brain is peculiarly liable to be affected; and though neither convulsions nor any other perceptible complaint may immediately follow, yet a weakness of understanding, or a diminution of the mental powers is often the consequence, and defeats all the efforts of the best education afterwards.

The ossification, or growing hardness of the bones of a child, and particularly those of the scull, is incomplete in the womb, to favour the purposes of easy and safe delivery. In consequence of their softness and pliancy, they admit of being squeezed together, and even of lapping over without injury, so as to make the head conform to the shape and dimensions of the parts through which it is to be expelled. They will soon resume their proper place, if left to the kind management of nature, and not tampered with by the profane finger of a conceited midwife or a silly nurse.

As to the opening or imperfect indentation of the bones of the scull, it is owing to the same cause, and designed for the same important purpose, to facilitate the birth of the infant. The free action of the external air is then necessary to promote the firmness and compactness of those bones, and to make them press into each other, and form sutures for the perfect defence of the brain, not only against blows and bruises, but colds and defluxions. Warm and tight covering directly counteracts all these benignant intentions of nature, and renders the scull a very weak shield for the security of its precious contents.

The curious distinction made by Herodotus, in the field of battle, between the sculls of the Egyptians and the Persians, has often been quoted to illustrate and confirm this doctrine. That historian having visited the scene of action, where the slain of those two nations had been separated, says, that on examining their remains, he found the sculls of the Egyptians so firm that the largest stones could hardly crack them, while those of the Persians were so thin and weak as to be easily fractured by a small pebble. After stating the fact, he accounts for it by observing, that the Egyptians were accustomed from their infancy to go bareheaded; whereas the Persians, on the contrary, always wore thick tiaras. These were like tne heavy turbans which they still use, and which some travellers think the air of the country renders necessary. I believe with Rousseau, that the generality of mothers will pay more regard to the suggestion of such travellers than to the remark of the judicious historian, and will fancy the air of Persia to be universal.

In opposition, however, to silly conceits and prejudices, I must assure my fair readers, that there is no part of the human frame which suffers more from heat and pressure than the head, and none of course which ought to be kept cooler and less encumbered. A thin, light cap, slightly fastened with a bit of tape, should constitute the whole of an infant's head-dress, from the moment of its birth till the increased growth of the hair renders any other protection unnecessary As soon as nature supplies your child with this best of all cover ings, never think of any thing more, even when you take him out into the open air, unless rain or intense heat or cold should make the occasional use of a very light and easy hat advisable. I must also forbid the use of stay-bands to keep the poor infant's head as fixed and immoveable as if it were placed in a pillory. One would suppose that our heads were so badly secured by the Author of our being, that they would fall off, if they were not held fast by those pernicious contrivances. It is strange that women should be so blind to the importance of letting the head move freely in every direction, in order to facilitate the discharge of the fluid excretions voided at the mouth !

It is not necessary to enter into minute details respecting the other parts of an infant's dress. Any nurse of common sense and docility will easily catch the spirit of my former arguments on the subject, and will pay due regard to the following general direction, with the writer's very plain and sensible remarks. " Rational tenderness (says this author) shews itself in making the dress *light, simple,* and *loose.* By being as light as is consistent with due warmth, it will neither encumber the infant, nor cause any waste of his powers ;—in conse quence of its simplicity it will be readily and easily put on, so as to prevent many cries and tears, an object of infinite importance :—and its looseness will leave full room for moving and stretching those little limbs which have been long heaped together, and for the growth and expansion of the entire frame." I before desired the nurse to have always a soft warm blanket, in readiness to wrap up the infant on being taken out of the bath. In that wrapper the child should be kept for at least ten mi nutes, in gentle motion, and then dressed. A piece of fine flannel round the navel, a linen or cotton shirt, a flannel petticoat, and a linen or cotton robe, are soon put on ; and where fastenings are requisite, they should consist of tape, without the dangerous use of pins.

No part of an infant's dress should hang down above two or three inches lower than the feet. Long robes and long petticoats serve only to conceal the nurse's inattention to cleanliness, and are, even on that account, very improper, as well as cumbersome. The night clothes should be much lighter than those worn by day, from a due regard to the situation of the infant, who should at all times, either in bed or out, experience nearly the same degree of warmth. Every moisture or impurity, should be instantly removed, and as those parts of the dress which are next to the skin are constantly imbibing perspirable matter, they should be changed frequently. Indeed, the same clothes ought never to be kept on for many days together. Away with finery; but take care that the child is always clean and dry.

4. *On Suckling.*

Were I called upon to point out any one remedy for the greatest part, not only of the diseases, but of the vices also of society, I would declare it to be, the strict attention of mothers to the nursing and rearing of their children. "Would you have mankind return all to their natural duties," says the eloquent Rousseau, in one of his fine sallies of sentimental enthusiasm, "begin with mothers of families : you will be astonished at the change this will produce. Almost every kind of depravation flows successively from this source : the moral order of things is broken, and nature quite subverted in our hearts : home is less cheerful and engaging : the affecting sight of a rising family no more attaches the husband, nor attracts the eyes of the stranger : the mother is less truly respectable, whose children are not about her : families are no longer places of residence : habit no longer enforces the ties of blood : there are no fathers, nor mothers, children, brethren, nor sisters : they hardly know, how should they love, each other? Each cares for no one but himself; and when home affords only a melancholy solitude, it is natural to seek diversion elsewhere.

"But," continues he, "*should mothers again condescend to nurse their children,* manners would form themselves : the sentiments of nature would revive in our hearts : the state would be re-peopled : this principal point, this alone would re-unite every thing. A taste for the charms of a domestic life, is the best antidote against corruption of manners. The noise and bustle of children, which is generally thought troublesome, becomes hence agreeable : they render parents more necessary, more dear to each other, and strengthen the ties of conjugal affection. When a family is all lively and animated, domestic concerns afford the most delightful occupation to a woman, and the most agreeable amusement to a man. Hence, from the correction of this one abuse, will soon result a general reformation : nature will quickly re-assume all her rights. let wives but once again become mothers ; and the men will presently again become fathers and husbands."

To this sketch, drawn by the pencil of so great a master, I shall only add, that the happy consequences of such a reform would be no less striking in a medical than in a moral point of view. A stop would be put to the cruel ravages of death in early life. The long catalogue of infantile afflictions would almost become a blank, or contain nothing to excite alarm. Every child, invigorated by his mother's milk, would, like the young Hercules, have force sufficient to strangle in his cradle any serpents that might assail him. Occasional illness would be to him only part of a necessary course of discipline, to enure him by times to bear pain with manly fortitude. In short, health, strength, and beauty, would take place of puniness, deformity, and disease; society would be renovated; and man, instead of dwindling away, as he now does, by a gradual degeneracy, would soon rise to the original perfection of his nature.

If you entertain any doubt of the truth of what is here advanced, look at other parts of the animated creation, and your doubts will immediately vanish. Wild animals never degenerate : they bring forth and rear their young with undiminished strength. And why ? Because the females, obedient in every thing to the impulses of nature, nurse their offspring, and watch over them with the most tender solicitude, till they can provide for themselves. Not only the inhabitants of the howling wilderness, the she-wolf and the fell tigress, but even the monsters of the great deep, draw out the breast, and give suck to their young. Will woman then suffer herself to be stigmatized as the only unfeeling monster that can desert the issue of her own womb, and abandon it to the care of another ? Will she alone entail the curse of her unnatural conduct on her hapless posterity ?

But let me vindicate the female character from so foul a reproach. It is not so much the fault of the women, as of what is improperly called civilized society. In its ruder state, this never happened. It never happens now among savage nations. I have already mentioned some remarkable instances of their parental tenderness. The influence of so strong a principle can be weakened only by the prevalence of vice, and of artificial refinement. Wherever an innocent simplicity of manners prevails, the children are not brought up by proxy : the women are not satisfied to be mothers by halves, as an old writer expresses it,—to bring forth, and then to cast off their offspring. They think with him, that nothing can be more contrary to nature, that such an imperfect sort of mother, who, after having nourished in her womb, and with her blood, something which she did not see, refuses now her breast-milk to what she sees living, become a human creature, and imploring the assistance of its parent !

In the polished, or rather the depraved circles of social life, those sentiments are either unfelt, or disregarded. Women, enervated by luxury, allured by a false taste for mistaken pleasures, and encouraged by shameless example, are eager to get rid of their children as soon as born, in order to spend the time thus gained from the discharge of their duty in dissipation or indolence. Let not husbands be deceived : let them not expect attachment from wives, who, in neglecting to suckle their children, rend asunder the strongest ties in nature. Neither conjugal love, fidelity, modesty, chastity, nor any other virtue, can take deep root in the breast of a female that is callous to the feelings of a mother. I am aware of the little tricks that are so often played off by new-married women to keep up the show of a wish to nurse their children, while every engine is secretly employed to make the deluded husband conjure her to relinqush her design, for fear of the injury it might do her constitution. If she has not injured her health by vice, nursing will not lessen, but increase her strength ; and if any constitutional defect renders her wholly unfit for suckling her child, she ought to abstain from procreation. The woman who cannot discharge the duties of a mother, ought again and again to be told, that she has no right to become a wife.

In cases of accidental injury or disease, where it may be impossible for the mother, or highly improper on her part, to give the child the breast, she is to be pitied in being thus deprived of the greatest pleasure of life, the pleasure of feeding and of rearing her own offspring. But the number of those women who really *cannot* suckle is very small, compared with those who *will not*. The latter excite our indignation—not our pity : they stifle every emotion of tenderness : they are deaf to the voice of nature : they sacrifice the most important duty to vicious pursuits ; and madly barter joys that will please on every reflection, for such as never can bear to be recalled.

Little do those dissipated mothers think of what their poor infants are likely to suffer, when committed to the care of hirelings. Ought they not to consider, that the woman who parts with her own babe to suckle one of theirs, unless she is impelled by the keenest distress, gives a proof in the first instance of her not being a good mother? How then is it to be expected that she should become a good nurse? Even should she acquire, in time and from habit, a tender affection for her foster-child, ought not a mother of any sensibility to take alarm at the idea of having that child's love transferred from herself to a stranger? Indeed, the claims of the nurse who

does her duty faithfully, are greatly superior to those of the
parent who neglects her's. It was a saying of Scipio Africa-
nus, ' that he took her to be more his mother, who had nursed
him for two years, though she had not brought him forth,
than her who, after she had brought him into the world, deserted and abandoned him.' But I am still better pleased
with the anecdote related by Van Swieten, of a Queen of
France, who gave her son suck, and would not desist from so
doing even when she was taken ill of an intermitting fever. It
happened during one of the fits, that another matron gave her
breast to the thirsty and crying child; at which the queen was
so much displeased, that she thrust her finger into the child's
mouth, in order to excite a vomiting, being unwilling that
another should perform any part of a mother's office.

I shall not enlarge any farther on this subject. I hope I
have said enough to excite good mothers to the most assidu-
ous observance of their duty, and to warn others of the evils
inseparable from the neglect of it. Such as may resolve to
obey the dictates of nature and reason, will find the following directions of some use in the prosecution of so laudable
a purpose.

The mother, after delivery, should be indulged with a few
hours' sleep, to recover from the fatigue which she has lately
undergone, and to allow due time for the secretion of the milk,
before the infant is put to the breast. The child can suffer no
inconvenience from this delay. Being replete with blood and
juices, he has not the least occasion for any fresh supply of
nutriment, till the mother is prepared by necessary repose to
give him the grateful and spontaneous ' beverage.' Whatever
the form of the nipples may be, they should be washed with
a little warm milk and water, in order to remove the bitter
viscid substance, which is furnished round them to defend the
tender parts from excoriation. I would also advise the mother,
during the whole time of her nursing, to wash the nipples,
immediately after giving suck, in warm water, whenever this
can be conveniently procured; and, in case the supplies of the
nutritive fluid are very copious, or seem to exceed the infant's
wants, she may always press out a little of the milk before the
child is put again to the breast, as the first drops issuing from
the fountain at every treat are the most liable to sourness and
putrescency.

I need not urge a fond mother freely to give her child what
nature freely produces. The only check in this respect is not
to suffer the infant to sleep at the breast, or to suck till vomiting ensues. But any attempts to entice the baby to the
use of spoon-meat are still more improper. This is a common

practice, not only with hired nurses, but even with affectionate mothers, from a foolish, though prevalent, idea of lessening the demands on the breast, or of strengthening the child with additional nourishment. If the nurse be not irregular in her own manner of living, she need not fear having a plentiful supply for the infant; and she may rest assured that her milk is far better suited to his young stomach, and will afford a greater quantity of nutritious chyle, than any preparation which art can devise.

Another error no less prevalent, and more injurious than the former, is the idea that a woman, when nursing, cannot eat and drink too *heartily,* as it is termed, to support her own strength and that of the infant. On the contrary, the tainted stream of intemperance must enfeeble and disorder the child, while the nurse really lessens her own power of giving suck, and invites the attacks of a fever by her thoughtless indulgence. The cooling regimen before recommended must be strictly complied with for the first week after delivery; and though a more liberal diet may then be allowed, yet this allowance must not extend to gross meats or heating liquids. A pint of porter or ale twice a day for at least a fortnight more, will be quite sufficient, and animal food should be very sparingly used for a much longer period. Indeed, it would be happy for the children, as well as for their nurses, if the latter could confine themselves without any painful restraint, to the salutary varieties of a milk and vegetable diet.

It is a great mistake to suppose, that a nurse is better fitted for her office by living on animal substances : the very reverse is the truth. The milk of women who live wholly on vegetables, is more abundant in quantity, will keep longer, and is far sweeter and more wholesome than what is prepared from animal food, which, beside its inflammatory tendency, must subject the children to gripes and worms.

It has been just hinted that the breast-milk of a woman in good health is abundantly sufficient for an infant's support. Nothing else should enter his lips for at least three or four months after the birth. A little thin pap or panado may then be occasionally introduced, with a view of familiarizing it to the child's taste, and thereby lessening the difficulty and dan ger of a complete and sudden alteration at the time of weaning But no spices, no wine, no sugar, should at any time be mixed with his food or drink. These and the like contrivances of silly women to make an infant's spoon-meat what they call palatable and nourishing, are sure to vitiate his natural taste, to inflame his blood, and to fill the stomach with slime and acidities. Sugar, in particular, has another very bad effect ; its frequent use not only gives children a disrelish for wholesome simplicity, but entices them to swallow more than they otherwise would, or tnan they want, and thus makes gluttons of them even before they can be strictly said to eat.

Infants are commonly deprived of the breast too soon. What people call solid food is supposed to contribute more to their growth and health. But, in the first place, milk, though a fluid, is immediately converted into a solid substance in the stomach, where it is soon after digested, and then affords the best nutriment possible. It also appears contrary to nature to put solid substances into the mouth of a child, before it is furnished with teeth to chew them. I should, therefore, look upon the previous cutting of the teeth as the surest indication of the proper time for weaning children. I do not mean to lay this down as an invariable rule. The state of the nurse's health, as well as of the child's, should be duly considered. It seems only that the cutting of the teeth gives a sort of hint or the use to which they may be applied. It is farther remarkable that, during the continuance of this usually sharp and painful operation, children, as it were instinctively, carry every thing that is put into their hands up to their mouths. Give them on such occasions crusts of bread, pieces of biscuit, dried fruits, or fresh liquorice-root, which they may suck and chew. Corals, glass, and the like hard bodies, are very improper, as they will either bruise the gums and cause an inflammation, or make them hard and callous by continual rubbing, so as to render the cutting of the teeth still more difficult, and the pain more acute and lasting.

5. On Weaning and Nurses.

A few weeks before the intended time of weaning, that is to say, in the interval between the first symptoms of cutting the teeth and the appearance of at least four of them, spoon-meat should be given more frequently, and in greater quantity, reducing in the like degree the proportion of breast-milk, till the gradual increase of the one and diminution of the other render the change almost imperceptible. The best spoon-meat that I know consists of bread and milk, prepared in the following manner; first boiling the bread in water, afterwards pouring the water off, and then mixing with the bread a proper quantity of new milk unboiled. Milk used this way is more wholesome and nourishing than when boiled, and is less liable to occasion costiveness.

It is not necessary, however, to confine children, after they are weaned, to one particular sort of food. The bill of fare may be gradually enlarged with the child's growth, provided always that it consist of an innocent variety. He may have bread and milk at one time, bread pudding at another, and bread sliced in broth, or in the gravy of roast meat, diluted with water, now and then, till at length, his teeth being pro perly grown, and fit to chew meat itself, he may be allowed a little of it at dinner, with a due proportion of bread and of wholesome vegetables. But I must forbid, in the most posi tive manner, any artificial sweetening of his food, all spices or seasoning, except salt, all sorts of pastry, butter in every form, unripe fruits, and fermented liquors.

As I have great reliance on the discretion of good mothers, when well informed of their duty, I should be sorry to tire them by too many details, or to fetter them by unnecessary restraints; I shall therefore only add one caution more on this part of the subject, and that is, not to adopt the perni cious custom of giving food or drink to children during the night. Even in the course of the day, they should not be crammed every hour, and trained up in habits of early glut tony. Temperance is that sure preservative of health, which they cannot be taught to practise too soon. Let them eat freely at proper intervals; and the longer they are kept from the things already forbidden, the more rapidly will they thrive, and the greater number of diseases will they escape.

As I have admitted that cases may occur, in which it would be impossible or improper for a mother to suckle her own child, I shall suggest a few hints on the choice of a nurse, and the remaining duties of the parent. From what I have said of the admirable manner in which the milk of a woman newly delivered is adapted to the various wants of a child newly born, it will be easily inferred, that when the mother cannot discharge that important duty, a nurse who has just lain in ought to be preferred. Otherwise the milk will not have the purgative qualities proper to bring away any remains of the *meconium*, nor will it be exactly suited to the infant's weak powers of digestion. Inconveniencies always arise, the moment we oppose the intentions of nature. This is what obliges us to have recourse to the precarious aid of art. When there is a difference of more than a week in the time of delivery between the mother and the nurse, some opening medicine may be necessary to cleanse the first passages; a table-spoonful of whey or water, with the addition of a little honey, or raw sugar, will commonly answer the purpose. But the infant's stomach cannot be so easily reconciled to foreign sustenance, or made strong enough to digest the thick milk prepared for an older child.

On the other hand, many difficulties must attend the very expedient which I propose. It will not be easy, except in cities like London, where there are several lying-in hospitals, to get nurses newly delivered for new-born infants. Then, as the nurse cannot be removed to the child, the latter must be taken to the nurse, and must remain with her till she can go to the parent's house. If an exact coincidence as to the time of delivery be made the leading consideration, an improper person may be fixed upon from that circumstance alone, though unqualified in all other respects. Thus, as I before hinted, whatever course we take, when we deviate from nature, we shall find numberless perplexities and obstacles in our way.

Almost every body is a judge of the other requisites in a nurse, such as health, plenty of breast-milk, the thriving state of her own child, cleanliness, and good temper. This last quality, though of very great importance, is seldom inquired into. Parents are commonly satisfied with the healthy appearance of the nurse and her child, or with a midwife's favourable account of her milk ; and seem to forget that a good disposition is as essential as a good constitution. I do not say that an infant will suck in the vices of his nurse ; but he will certainly suffer from them. They are doubly injurious, in spoiling her milk, and lessening her tender care of the child that is at her mercy. The twin founders of the Roman empire were said to have been suckled by a she-wolf ; I should think it much more unlikely that an infant could be properly nursed by a passionate or ill-tempered woman.

The mother is not to suppose herself relieved from all trouble by the choice of a good nurse. The latter may give the child the breast; but she should be directed and zealously assisted by the former in the discharge of every other duty. This will render her labour easy, and her situation comfortable. She should also have every indulgence consistent with good sense and with the rules before laid down. She should not be debarred from the occasional company of her husband : a rigorous chastity, or a total abstinence from wedded joys, is often as hurtful to the nurse and child as immoderate gratification. It is by humouring her that you will engage her to humour you in the strict observance of all your reasonable injunctions.

6. On Children's Diet.

It is too common with mothers, throughout every period of childhood, to pervert the use of food, by giving it when it is not wanted, and consequently when it does mischief, not only in a physical, but in a moral view. To give food as an indulgence, in the way of reward, or to withhold it as a matter of punishment, are both injurious. Whether good or naughty, children equally require food, proper, both in quantity and quality, to sustain their health and growth. Their faults ought to be corrected by more rational means. The idea of making them suffer in their health and growth on account of them, will fill every considerate mind with horror. It is the project only of an impotent mind to attempt to correct the disposition by creating bodily sufferings, which are so prone to hurt the temper, even at an age when reason should counteract such an effect.

The eatables usually given to children in the way of rewards, and frequently by well-meaning but injudicious persons, to court their favour, are still worse than the punishments inflicted on them in the way of privations of food. Sugar-plums, sugar-candy, barley-sugar, sweetmeat tarts, most kinds of cakes, &c. &c., are very pernicious.

Till children begin to run about, the uniformity of their lives makes it probable, that the quantity of food they require in the day is nearly the same, and that it may be given to them at much the same stated times. By establishing a judicious regularity with regard to both, the danger of injury in these respects will be obviated.

This rule is to be understood as applying to infants at the breast, as well as after they are weaned. By allowing proper intervals between the times of giving children suck, the breast of the mother becomes duly replenished with milk, and the stomach of the infant properly emptied to receive a fresh supply.

The supposition that an infant wants food every time it cries, is a mere idle fancy. According to the usual practice of feeding children, they are more likely to cry from the uneasiness of an overloaded stomach. Even the mother's milk, the lightest of all food, will disagree with the child, if the administration of it is repeated improperly.

A very injurious practice is sometimes adopted by mothers, of suckling a child beyond the period when the milk can be proper for it. The reason for this is obvious, but it does not excuse the practice. A child is injured both physically and mentally by this unnatural protraction of a method of feeding and a kind of food, adapted only to the earliest stage of infancy. Suckling should not be continued after the cutting of the first teeth.

A child will sleep with an overloaded stomach, but it will not be the refreshing sleep of health. When the stomach is filled beyond the proper medium, it induces a similar kind of heaviness to that frequently arising from opiates and intoxicating liquors, and instead of awakening refreshed and lively, the child will be heavy and fretful.

As children begin to run about, the increase of their exercise will require an increase of their nourishment. But those who overload them with food at any time, in hopes of strengthening them, are extremely deceived. There is no prejudice equally fatal to such numbers of children.

Whatever unnecessary food a child receives, weakens instead of strengthening it. For when the stomach is over-filled its power of digestion is impaired; and food ill digested, is so far from yielding nourishment, that it only serves to debilitate the whole system, and to occasion a variety of diseases. Amongst these are obstructions, distortion of the body, rickets, scrofula, slow fevers, consumptions, and convulsion fits.

Another pernicious custom prevails with regard to the diet of children, when they begin to take other nourishment besides their mother's milk, viz., to give them such as their stomachs have not the power to digest; and to indulge them also in a mixture of such things at their meals as are hurtful to every body, and more especially to children, considering their feeble and delicate organs.

This injudicious indulgence is defended on the plea of its being necessary to accustom the stomachs of children to all kinds of food; but this idea is highly erroneous. Their stomachs must have time to acquire strength sufficient to enable them to digest varieties of food, and the filling them with indigestible things is not the way to give them strength.

Children can only acquire strength gradually with their proper growth, which will always be impeded if the stomach is disordered.

The food given to infants should be very simple, and easy of digestion. When they require something more solid than spoon-meats alone, they should have bread with them. Simple puddings, mild vegetables, and wholesome ripe fruits, eaten with bread, are also good for them. The giving them animal food is better deferred till their increased capability of taking exercise may permit it with the greater safety, and then care must be taken that the exercise is proportioned to this kind of food. The first use of it should be gradual, not exceeding two or three times in a week.

An exception should be made to these rules in the instances of scrofulous and rickety children, as much bread is always hurtful in these cases, and fruits are particularly pernicious.

Plain animal food is found to be the most suitable to their state.

The utmost care should be taken under all circumstances to procure good bread for children, as the great support of life. If the perverted habits of the present generation give them an indifference as to what bread they eat, or a vitiated taste for adulterated bread, they still owe it to their children, as a sacred duty, not to undermine their constitutions by this injurious composition.

The poor, and many also of the middling ranks of society, in large towns, are unhappily compelled to this species of infanticide, as it may almost be called, by being driven into towns to gain a subsistence; and thus, from the difficulty or doing otherwise, being obliged to take their bread of bakers, instead of making wholesome bread at home, as in former times, in more favourable situations. While these are to be pitied, what shall be said of those whose fortunes place them above this painful necessity? Let them at least rear their children on wholesome food, and with unsophistical habits, as the most unequivocal testimony of parental affection performing its duty towards its offspring.

Children ought not to be hurried in their eating, as it is of great importance they should acquire a habit of chewing their food well. They will derive from it the various advantages of being less likely to eat their food hot, of thus preparing what they eat properly for the stomach, instead of imposing upon it what is the real office of the teeth : and also that of checking them from eating too much. When food is not properly masticated, the stomach is longer before it feels satisfied; which is perhaps the most frequent, and certainly the most excusable cause of eating more than is fairly sufficient.

Thoughtless people will often, for their own amusement, give children morsels of high dishes, and sips of fermented liquors, to see whether they will relish them, or make faces at them. But trifling as this may seem, it would be better that it were never practised, for the sake of preserving the natural purity of their tastes as long as possible.

SPOON-MEATS FOR INFANTS.

Method of using Milk.—The best way of using milk is without skimming and without boiling. The cream is the most nutritious balsamic part of milk, and to deprive it of this is to render it less nourishing, and less easy of digestion, than in its pure state. In some particular cases skimmed milk may be preferable, but it may be adopted as a general rule, that new milk is the wholesomest and best. Where this stands any time before it is used, instead of taking off the cream, it should be mixed in with the milk.

Boiling milk, even very little, fixes it, and entirely alters its qualities. As a proof of this, it will not afterwards afford any cream, but merely a thin skin. In this state, it is hard of digestion, and of course liable to occasion obstructions. It is the most proper for food when raw, or only scalded.

Egg Pap.—Set a quart of good water on a clear, brisk fire; mix two full spoonfuls of fresh ground wheaten flour into a batter with the yolks of two or three new-laid eggs, well beaten, and a little cold water. When the water is ready to boil, but before it quite boils, stir in the batter, and keep stirring it till it is ready to boil, by which time it will be sufficiently thick. Take it off the fire, put in a little salt, pour it into a basin, and let it cool of itself till it become about as warm as milk from the cow.

If eggs cannot be procured, a small piece of butter may be added with the salt, and stirred in gently till well mixed, to prevent it oiling : but eggs are better.

This is a clean, sweet food, affords sound nourishment, and opens all the passages; breeds good blood and lively spirits; is pleasant to the palate, and grateful to the stomach. The common use of it purifies the blood and all the humours, prevents windy distempers and griping pain, both of the stomach and the bowels. From all the ingredients bearing a similitude to each other, no manifest quality violently prevails, so that it may justly challenge the first place amongst all spoon-meats or paps, and is the next food to breast-milk for children, indeed often much better, from the many diseases and the improper foods numbers of women are subject to or use. But no other ingredients should be added to this kind of food, such as sugar, spices, fruits, or the like, for then it will become of another nature and operation, and that for the worse.

It must be observed, that this kind of spoon-meat, and also all others, should be made rather thin than thick ; for in such foods the liquid elements ought to predominate, whether it be milk or water. For this reason all porridges and spoon-meats which are made thin, and quickly prepared, are sweeter, brisker on the palate, and easier of digestion, than those which are thick, and long in preparing.

Food should never be given to children more than milk-warm, and the proper way to cool it is by letting it stand uncovered to cool of itself; for much stirring alters the composition, and takes off the sweetness. Covering it down, too, keeps in the fumes that ought to go off, and by excluding the air, makes it less pure.

Flour Pap.—To two-thirds of new milk, after it has stood five or six hours from the time of milking, add one-third of river or spring water, and set it on a quick clear fire. Tem per some good wheaten flour into a batter, with either milk or water; and when the milk and water is near boiling, but before it actually does boil, pour in the batter, and stir it a little while. When it is again ready to boil, take it off, add a little salt, and let it stand to cool.

A good spoonful of flour is sufficient to thicken a pint of milk and water. This will make it about the thickness of common milk porridge, which is what will eat the sweetest and be the easiest of digestion.

This kind of food affords a firm substantial nourishment, neither binds nor loosens the body, but keeps it in proper order, and creates good blood, all which tend to produce brisk lively dispositions. Prepared thus, this pap is far more friendly to nature than in the common way of boiling, and may be constantly eaten with much better effect, and without ever tiring or cloying the stomach.

Oatmeal Pap.—Mix a pint of milk and water, in the proportion of two-thirds milk and one-third water, gradually with a full spoonful of oatmeal, or rather more if the pap is to be thick, though inclining to thin is best. Set it in a saucepan upon a quick clear fire, and when it begins to rise, or make a show of boiling, take it off, and pour it from one basin into another, backwards and forwards seven or eight times, which will bring out the fine flour of the oatmeal, and incorporate it with the milk. Then return it into the saucepan, set it upon the fire, and when it is again ready to boil, take it off, and let it stand in the saucepan a little to fine, for the husky part of the oatmeal will sink to the bottom. When settled, pour it off in a basin, add a little salt, and let it stand to cool. This is an excellent pap, very congenial to weak natures, affording a good firm nourishment, and easy of concoction.

Bread Pap.—Pour scalding water on some thin slices of good white bread, and let it stand uncovered till it cools, then drain off the water, bruise the bread fine, and mix with it as much new milk as will make a pap of a moderate thickness. It will be warm enough for use without setting it upon the fire.

It is common to put sugar into this pap, but this and almost all foods for children are better without it; and the taste will not require it, till habit makes it familiar

Water Gruel.—Take a spoonful and a half of fresh ground oatmeal, mix with it gradually a quart of river or spring water, and set it on a clear fire. When it is rising, or just ready to boil, take it off and pour it from one basin into another backwards and forwards five or six times : then set it on the fire again till it is ready to boil, but before it does boil take it off, and let it stand a little in the saucepan, that the coarse husks of the oatmeal may sink to the bottom. Then pour it out, add a little salt, and let it stand to cool.

When water gruel is made with grits, it must boil gently for some time. The longer it boils the more it will jelly. But moderation must be observed in this respect, for if it be very long boiled and very thick, it will be flat and heavy.

A mistaken idea very generally prevails that water gruel is not nourishing ; it is, on the contrary, a light, cleansing, nourishing food, good either in sickness or health, both for young and old.

Milk Porridge.—Make water gruel as above, and to two-thirds of gruel, when it has stood a little while to cool, add one-third of unboiled new milk. It may be eaten with or without salt.

Milk porridge is exceedingly cleansing, and easy of digestion, and may be given to the weakest stomach that is able to receive food.

Another Milk Porridge.—Stir a pint of water into three large spoonfuls of fresh oatmeal, let it stand till clear, and then pour off the water. Put a pint of fresh water to the oatmeal, stir it up well, and leave it till the next day. Strain off the liquor through a fine sieve, and set it in a saucepan on a clear and brisk fire. Add milk, in about half the quantity, gradually while it is warming, and when it is just ready to boil, take it off, pour it into a basin, and let it stand to cool. A little salt may be added. This, as well as the former porridge, is very light, and proper for weak stomachs.

To prepare Indian Arrow Root.—Put a dessert spoonful of the powdered root into a basin, and mix with it as much cold new milk as will make it into a paste. Pour on to this half a pint of milk scalding hot, stirring it briskly to keep it smooth. Set it on the fire till it is ready to boil, then take it off, pour it into a basin, and let it cool.

This may be made with water instead of milk, and some cold milk mixed with it afterwards. If the stomach be very weak it will be best without any milk.

Great care must be taken to get the genuine root, which makes a very nourishing excellent food for infants, or invalids.

Sago Jelly.—Soak a large spoonful of sago in cold water for an hour, then pour off the water, put a pint of fresh water to the sago, and stew it gently till it is reduced to about half the quantity. When done, pour it into a basin, and let it cool.

Sago with Milk.—Prepare a large spoonful of sago by soaking it in water as above, but instead of putting fresh water to it, put a pint and a half of new milk. Stew it gently till reduced to about half the quantity, then pour it into a basin, and let it cool.

Tapioca Jelly.—Wash two large spoonfuls of the large sort of tapioca in cold water, and then soak it in a pint and a half of water for four hours. Stew it gently in the same water till it is quite clear. Let it stand to cool after it is poured out of the saucepan, and use it either with or without the addition of a little new milk.

Barley Gruel.—Put two ounces of pearl barley, after it has been well washed, into a quart of water. Simmer it gently till reduced to a pint, then strain it through a sieve, and let it cool.

Rice Gruel.—Let two large spoonfuls of whole rice soak in cold water for an hour. Pour off the water, and put a pint and a quarter of new milk to the rice. Stew it gently till the rice is sufficiently tender to pulp it through a sieve, and then mix the pulp into the milk that the rice was stewed in. Simmer it over the fire for ten minutes, and if it appears too thick, add a little more milk very gradually, so as not to damp it from simmering. When done, pour it into a basin to cool.

Rice Milk—To four large spoonfuls of whole rice, washed very clean in cold water, add a quart of new milk, and stew them together very gently for three hours. Let it stand in a basin to cool before it is used.

Another way of making rice milk is, boiling the rice first in water, then pouring off the water, and boiling the rice with milk. But too much of the nutriment of the rice is thus lost, and both the boilings are bad.

Rice Milk the French Way.—After washing the rice well, set it over the fire for half an hour with a little water to break it. Put to it then, by a little at a time, some warm milk, till it is sufficiently done, and of a proper thickness. Let it do slowly. Season it with salt and some sugar.

For children the sugar had better be omitted.

Ground Rice Milk.—Mix a large spoonful of ground rice into a batter, with two or three spoonfuls of new milk. Set a pint of new milk on the fire, and when it is scalding hot, stir in the batter, and keep it on the fire till it thickens; but it must not boil. It should be stirred to prevent its burning. Cool it by letting it stand in a basin before it is eaten.

Millet Milk.—Wash three spoonfuls of millet seed in cold water, and put it into a quart of new milk. Stew it gently till it becomes moderately thick. Cool it by letting it stand in a basin till wanted for use.

The preparations which require some time in the doing, will also require the precaution of being stirred, to prevent their burning. But if they are done as directed, gently, and consequently set over the fire, not immediately upon it, a moderate stirring now and then will be sufficient.

DRINKS FOR CHILDREN.

If parents, and other persons who have the care of children, cannot reconcile themselves to the giving them the most salutary of all beverage, pure water, the following drinks will be found the best substitutes for it.

Milk and Water.—Put one-third of new milk to two thirds of river or spring water. This is best drank cold, but if it must be warmed, it should be by putting warm water to cold milk. It ought not to be made more than milk warm.

Whey.—Take a quart of new milk before it is cold, and put in as much runnet as will turn it to a clear whey. Let it stand till it turns properly, and pour it off through a cheese-cloth without pressing the curd, that the whey may be the purer. It may be drank cold, or just warmed by setting it before the fire for a little while.

If new milk cannot be procured, other milk must be warmed to the degree of new milk.

Pearl-barley Water.—Set an ounce of pearl-barley, with half a pint of water, upon the fire, till it is hot, to clean it. Pour off the water, and put a quart of fresh water to the pearl-barley. Let it simmer for an hour. If it appears to be too thick, add more water, but let it be warm, as any quantity of cold water would damp it too suddenly, and thus tend to spoil it.

Barley Water.—To a handful of common barley, well washed, add three pints of water. Let it simmer gently till of a proper thickness for use.

The longer barley boils the thinner the liquor becomes.

Both the above and the pearl-barley water may be used cold, or milk-warm.

Apple Water.—Slice two or three spirited ripe apples, according to the size of them, into a jug, and pour on them a quart of scalding hot water. Let this stand till cool or cold, and it will then be fit for use.

The apples should not be pared, as it takes off from the spirit of them.

Toast and Water.—Toast a moderate sized piece of white bread quite dry, and of a very dark brown colour; put it into a jug, and pump water upon it. Let it stand an hour before it is used. As all these preparations, both of spoon-meats and drinks, become flat and good for little by long standing, it is better to make only such quantities of them at a time, as will be soon used. When they are re-warmed, no more should be done at once than is just sufficient for the occasion, as repeated warming injures the nutritious quality of every thing.

It is better, when it can be avoided, not to set things on the fire to re-warm, but before the fire, or on the hob by the side of the fire. But care must be taken not to let them dry and scorch, as it makes them very strong and injurious. Some earthen-ware vessel should be used for this purpose, as less liable to produce this effect. A very good method of warming things is by setting them in a basin over boiling water, or by placing them in it.

7. *Exercise and Rest*

It has been justly observed, that children require no exercise for the first and second months after their birth, but a gentle motion, somewhat like that to which they had been accustomed in the mother's womb. A frequent change of posture, how ever, is advisable, lest by always laying them on the same side, or carrying them on the same arm, their soft limbs may be moulded into an improper shape. But violent agitations of any sort may do them much greater injury, by deranging the fine structure of the brain, and giving rise to the incurable evils of intellectual or nervous weakness.

Other parts of the body, as well as the brain, are exposed to great danger by tossing infants on high, or rapidly *dancing them,* as it is called, before their little limbs have gained some degree of firmness. A great deal of the spine is gristly, and the breast entirely so. Consider then what may be the effect of the grasp or strong pressure of your hands against those places, in order to prevent the child from falling. As he advances in age, his bones acquire solidity, and his whole body becomes able to endure a little shock. Brisk, lively, and frequent exercise, will then be of the greatest service to him ; and you run no risk of laying the foundations of any disease, or of destroying any part of that admirable symmetry of the human frame, on which health and beauty alike depend.

In the course of a few months, a well-nursed child, unfettered by any check on the free motion of his limbs, will be able to exercise himself, and to gather strength from every new effort. When you take him into the fields, which you should do every day in fine weather, let him roll upon the dry grass; and, when in the nursery, upon the carpet. He will soon learn the use of his legs, without the least possibility of making them crooked by the pressure of so light a body. When he begins to walk, you must help him a little in his first experiments: lead him about with the support of your hands, and then by the finger only, till you perceive he can do without your assistance. Go-carts and leading-strings not only retard the increase of a child's activity, and produce an awkwardness of gait very hard to be corrected afterwards, but often affect the chest, lungs, and bowels, in such a manner as to pave the way for habitual indigestion or costiveness, and for asthmatic or consumptive complaints.

Nothing can be more ridiculous than the numberless contrivances of mothers to teach their children to walk, as if it was a thing to be learned by their instruction; and to keep them propped up by wooden machines, or suspended by back-strings, as if their lives and limbs were to be endangered by the least tumble. They are too near the ground, and too light to hurt themselves by falling. Besides, the oftener they fall, the sooner they will learn, when down, to get up again; and the only way to make them sure-footed, is to accustom them betimes to trust more to the proper management of their own legs, than to any artificial support.

As to the best time for exercise during infancy, it admits of a very simple regulation. That sort of passive exercise, which consists of agreeable motion in a nurse's arms, must never be omitted after the use of the bath in the morning, and cannot be too often repeated in the course of the day. But when the child is able to take exercise himself, it will be easy to manage matters so as to let him have as much as he likes before meals, and never to rouse him into action upon a full stomach. If left to himself, or to nature, he will then be more inclined to stillness and repose.

The subject of rest requires some farther consideration. A healthy, thriving child sleeps more than two-thirds of his time for a few weeks after his birth. So strong a propensity must be indulged by day as well as by night; but, with judicious management, he will be gradually brought to want, and to enjoy repose by night only. This is evidently the order of nature; and such a habit, begun in childhood, and continued through life, will contribute more to its enjoyment and dura

tion, than any one maxim or rule of health ever yet laid down
by human wisdom.

Nurses, indeed, are too apt, for their own ease, or to gain
time for other concerns, to cherish the sleepy disposition of
infants, and to increase it by various things of a stupefactive
quality. All these are extremely pernicious. I would not
suffer opiates, under the name of cordials or carminatives, or
in any shape or form whatever, to be given to a child in
health. The only composing means, which art may at any
time be allowed to employ, are gentle motion and soft lulla-
bies. I very much approve of the little *cots* now in fashion,
which, being suspended by cords, are easily moved from side
to side, and promote the desired end, without the danger
which violent *rocking* was often attended with. Those swinging cots are in exact conformity to the suggestions of the best
medical writers, ancient and modern.

In England, as well as in most other parts of Europe,
cradles fixed upon wooden *rockers* have been in use from
time immemorial. No evil could arise from their continuance, while in the hands of careful and affectionate mothers ;
but, when left to the management of impatient nurses, or of
giddy boys and girls, the delicate texture of an infant's brain
would often be exposed to great danger. The agitation of a
cradle by such persons has been compared to the jolting of a
stage-coach basket; and I believe that a poor child would
suffer as much from the one as from the other, were he not a
little more confined in the former. Is it possible to conceive
a more shocking object than an ill-tempered nurse, who, in
stead of soothing the accidental uneasiness or indisposition to
sleep of her baby, when laid down to rest, is often worked up
to the highest pitch of rage ; and, in the excess of her folly
and brutality, endeavours, by loud, harsh threats, and the im-
petuous rattle of the cradle, to drown the infant's cries, and to
force him into slumber !—She may sometimes gain her point,
but never till the poor victim's strength is exhausted.

To guard against this evil, the transition from rocking
cradles to fixed bedsteads was not necessary. The gentle motion before described, at once so natural and so pleasing to
infants, may be given them with ease and safety in little
baskets suspended by cords, as used in the Highlands of Scot-
land, under the name of *creels,* or in the more elegant contrivances of *swinging cots,* which are now much in fashion.
I am sorry to see any of the latter surrounded with close curtains, which have almost as bad an effect as confining the infant in a room of the same dimensions. One green curtain
may be hung at some distance from his face, so as to inter-

cept the light in the daytime, but not to obstruct the free com
munication of air, or to reverberate the exhalations from his
lungs and body   Green window-blinds in the sleeping-room
will answer the same purpose.   Care should also be taken not
to expose infants, either in bed or out of bed, to an oblique
light, or they will become squint-eyed.   They should be kept
facing it, when up, and exactly the reverse, when laid down to
rest.   If the light come upon them from one side, their eyes
will take that direction, and thus they will get the habit of
looking crossways.

It is of still greater moment to pay strict attention to their
bedding.   Nothing can have a more relaxing tendency, or be
at the same time more unfavourable to cleanliness, than beds
and pillows stuffed with feathers.   These absorb and retain the
perspirable matter, as well as every other impurity, so that
the child who sleeps upon them must inhale the most noxious
vapour, while its action on the surface of his body must destroy
the energy of the skin, and render his whole frame, both
within and without, the ready receiver of disease.   Horse-hair
cushions and mattresses are far preferable; but if soft bran
were used instead of hair for the stuffing of children's beds
and pillows, these would more readily let any moisture pass
through them, would never be too much heated, and might
be frequently changed or renewed without any great trouble·
or expense.

CHAPTER XIII.

EDUCATION OF CHILDREN.

" Consider, thou who art a parent, the importance of thy
trust; the being thou hast produced it is thy duty to support

" Prepare him early with instruction, and season his mind
with the maxims of truth.

" So shall he rise like a cedar on the mountains; his head
shall be seen above the trees of the forest.

" The soil is thine own; let it not want cultivation · the
seed which thou sowest, that also shalt thou reap.

" Teach him obedience, and he shall bless thee; teach him
modesty, and he shall not be ashamed.   Teach him diligence,
and his wealth shall increase; teach him benevolence, and his
mind shall be exalted.

" Teach him science, and his life shall be useful; teach him
religion, and his life shall be happy."

The duties of a parent are so various and extensive, that the welfare and happiness of a nation depend in a great measure upon the proper and just performance of them. If the youth of both sexes are left unrestrained to follow their own inclinations, what can be expected, but that vice, intemperance, disloyalty, and anarchy, will follow such unpardonable neglect? You, then, who may soon have to undertake a charge of so much consequence, I earnestly entreat you to recollect, how much your own happiness, as well as that of your children, and of society in general, rests upon the careful discharge of those duties which the ties of nature render so interesting.

Though a constant and unremitting attention must be paid to children from the first dawn of reason, yet, if possible, it ought to be redoubled as they increase in years. Your own discretion must dictate to you the kind of education suitable to their situation, and fitted to their talents or inclination ; but, unless you can bestow on them a large fortune, the *more useful* that education the better. Young people, who are foolishly indulged, are in general the most useless beings in creation, and often the most ignorant. In the hour of misfortune, if they are deprived of their parents, and thrown upon the world, their own helplessness adds the most acute pangs to their distress, and they have the additional misery of finding themselves despised as well as neglected.

The period of infancy is generally suffered to slide away with little or no attention to the work of education. The child is supposed to be in a kind of irrational state, which will scarcely admit of moral discipline, and its parents seem to think only of its health and amusement. If it wants any thing its wish must be gratified ; if it cries, it is to be quieted by indulgence ; or if this cannot be, attempts are frequently made to cheat it into a belief that the desired object has suddenly vanished. If it has been hurt, the immediate cause of its misfortune, whether animate or inanimate, is not seldom to be beaten, and the child itself is encouraged to join in inflicting the punishment. Things proceed in this way nearly till the time when the child can talk, and often much longer ; and when this system is changed for another, still it gives way very slowly, and in many cases some remains of it may be discerned for years after the child is allowed to be capable of nstruction. What is the true character and tendency of this course of proceeding ? It unquestionably fosters those seeds of evil which abound in our nature. Is man naturally self-indulgent ? What then must be the effect of a studied system of indulgence ? Is he impatient, and passionate, and vindictive ? How greatly must these dispositions be cherished, by not only permitting but encouraging their gratification ! Is he disposed,

when in pursuit of favourite objects, to be little scrupulous
with respect to violations of plain-dealing and truth? The arti-
fices resorted to by nurses and female relations would almost
create such a disposition, were it not originally planted in his
bosom. With what eyes then must the Almighty look upon
such a course of proceeding! It would be trifling with my
readers to pursue this topic any farther.

But now we proceed to the important inquiry, what system
of management ought to be substituted in the place of that
which has been described? All persons who do not think that
a plea of necessity (a very unfounded plea, however, in the
present case), may be urged in favour of the practice of positive evil, must allow, that every thing should be avoided by
mothers and nurses which has a tendency to cherish and bring
into activity that evil nature, which it will not be denied that
we all bring into the world. It will be granted, therefore
that Nanny, or the cat, or the chair, are not to be *slapped*
because they happen to have displeased the child. But must
not we confine ourselves to mere abstinence from fostering
evils? Is it not visionary and chimerical to attempt to check
bad tempers and habits, and to lay a foundation for good
ones? Or if an attempt of this kind be not altogether hopeless,
is it not at least unnecessary to make it at so early a period,
when little success can be expected; and most advisable to
defer it till the reason of the child is further advanced, and its
ability to submit to discipline is greater? The Almighty
Creator very soon begins to unfold in man those intellectual
and moral faculties which are destined, when rightly employed, to qualify him for the highest services and enjoyments
through the ages of eternity.

In a few weeks after its birth, a child's reason begins to
dawn; and with the first dawn of reason ought to commence
the moral culture which may be best suited to counteract the
evils of its nature, and to prepare the way for that radical
change, that new birth promised in baptism, and the darling
object of the hopes of every parent who looks on the cove-
nants in that holy rite, not as forms, but as realities. Let me
appeal to every mother who delights to view her infant as it
lies in her lap, whether it does not soon begin to read " the
human face divine," to recognise her smile, and to shew itself
sensible of her affection in the little arts she employs to entertain it.

Does it not, in no long time, return that smile, and repay
her maternal caresses with looks and motions so expressive
that she cannot mistake their import? She will not doubt,
then, the importance of fostering in its bosom those benevo-

lent sympathies which delight her, by banishing from her nursery whatever is likely to counteract them. She will not tolerate in a nurse that selfish indifference to the wants of an infant, which sometimes leaves it to cry while she finishes her breakfast, or chats with a companion. Much less will she tolerate passionate snatches, and scolding names, and hard and impatient tones of voice, in the management of her child.

I may be pronounced fanciful, perhaps, but I certainly think it would be of importance to keep sour and ill-humoured faces out of a nursery, even though such faces were not commonly accompanied by corresponding conduct. I am persuaded that I have seen a very bad effect produced by a face of this kind on the countenance and mind of an infant. Is it not reasonable to suppose, that if an infant sympathizes with a smile, it may also sympathize with a scowl, and catch somewhat of the inward disposition which distorts the features of the nurse?

Thus begin the efforts of a parent to cherish all that is benevolent and affectionate in the bosom of a child; and to prevent the growth of every thing of an opposite nature. And who shall presume to assign limits to the importance of such efforts in the education of a being whose leading disposition, if it fulfil the will of its Maker, must, both through life and through all eternity, be *love?*

But parental cares soon extend. In a short time, impatience and selfishness shew themselves, and are accompanied by fretfulness, jealousy, anger, and envy. At so early a period does innate corruption display its powers, and call for the restraining hand of a parent! But how are these evils to be counteracted at an age when both the body and mind are so tender, and when neither arguments nor explanations can be understood? Undoubtedly great delicacy of treatment is required. The character of the child must be studied; and, if possible, such corrections of evils must be applied as will not deeply wound its feelings. It is surprising what female ingenuity, quickened by maternal tenderness, will achieve in this way.

Does a child, too young to listen to reason, want something it ought not to have? Its mother will suddenly turn its attention to another object, and thus prevent the rise of improper tempers, or arrest them in their course. Is it jealous of the attention paid to a brother? While she perseveres, perhaps, in shewing to the brother the kindness which has raised this jealousy, she will pour such a stream of affection on both the children as shall at once shew them how much each is the object of her love, and lead them by sympathy to feel a similar love for each other. This will be the best anti-dote to jealousy. But cases will arise, in which, with all her ingenuity, she will not be able to effect her purposes in this way. On such occasions, if the child is too young to under-stand reason and persuasion, she will as far as possible shorten and sweeten its trial, but without fostering bad dispositions in its bosom. If it is a little older, she will endeavour to turn the trial to good account, by holding up to it such Christian and filial motives as suit its capacity and character. These will be accompanied by such a description and exemplification, on the one hand, of the effects they ought to produce, and of the sunshine of soul to which they lead; and on the other, of the hatefulness of the faults in question, of the unhappiness which must attend the commission of it, and of the regret and bad consequences which must follow; as may, by God's help, prepare its tender mind for spiritual discrimination, and a spi-ritual taste (if I may so speak), and give its infant affections some bias on the side of God and duty.

But how, some parents may ask, how can this be effected at so tender an age? It seems to us impossible.—Believe me, much may be done, with very young children, by placing gra-dually before them, with cheerfulness and affection, and in a spirit suited to the occasion, religious truths, associated, as much as may be, with images pleasing to their minds. The appellations, God, and Jesus, should soon be made familiar to them; and the dwelling-place of these great Beings may be so pointed out and described; and their power and their holi-ness, and more especially their love, may be so set forth and brought home to the feelings, by little and simple illustrations, that, while the tender mind is imbued with the first rudiments of religious knowledge, reverence and affection for divine things shall, if God smile on the endeavour, be excited in the heart. But special care must be taken not to give fatiguing lectures, nor to make too powerful calls on the feelings. " Here a little and there a little," must be the parent's motto in conveying instruction at this age; and for that little, the seasons must be chosen, when the child is most likely to lend a willing ear; and the subject must always be dropped before it becomes tiresome, unless there be some very pressing call for its being continued; in which case, indeed, the occasion itself will generally make it interesting.

Very short and simple stories from Holy Writ may be em ployed with great advantage: as that of Jesus taking the little children in his arms, and blessing them; that of his restoring the widow's son to life; and many others. If these are told in a cheerful manner, and with such little appropriate touches as will present the scene to the imagination of the child, they will seldom fail to delight it, and will be called for again and again. When they are fixed in its memory, it is evident with what great advantage reference may be made to them when the parent finds occasion to have recourse to dissuasion, or reproof, or exhortation.

Some excellent advice to parents respecting the treatment of children is given in the *Prompter*, by Noah Webster. These hints should be inscribed in *letters of gold*, in every nursery, and are worthy the serious attention of all parents.

" Are you a parent? Then you have a hard task to be both the *friend* and the *master* of your children; and if you are not *both, you do not work it right*. Sometimes you are the fond, indulgent parent; nothing is too good for the darling; he may pout and strike, or kick over the tea-kettle, cups, and glasses; and you would moderately say, ' Why, Billy, how you behave! That is not pretty; I shall not love you for that.' At other times, you are in a pet, and the child by *accident* in mere play, or in attempting to drink, lets fall a tumbler, or a tea-cup; you fly at him, and fall on him like a mastiff, and cuff his ears, and shake him to a jelly. In the *first case,* you are the *weak silly dupe of* your child; in the *last*, you are the *ty-rant*, the *madman*: thus, *you do not work it right* Hear what the Prompter says; Never strike your child *in a passion;* never punish him for *accidental mischief;* never *fail* to punish for *obstinate disobedience*, or *wilful mischief:* and, a word to you in particular, when you have *real cause* to correct him, never cease till his temper gives way, and he becomes *really submissive*. A blow or two only raises his anger, and increases wilful obstinacy: if you quit them then, you do hurt rather than good; you make your child worse. But, if you continue to apply the rod, till his mind bends, and softens down into humble supplication, believe me, that child will rarely or never want a second correction: the Prompter has tried it in re-peated instances.

But, say some folks, the rod should be sparingly used. True; but, as most people use it, one correction only makes way for another, and frequent whippings harden the child, till they have no effect. Now, mind the Prompter; *two simple rules*, if observed, will prevent this: 1st. *Never punish a child when he does not deserve it;* 2d. *When he does deserve it, make the first punishment* EFFECTUAL. If you strike a child for *accidental* mischief, or for what he does *ignorantly* or in *good humour*, the child is not conscious he has done wrong; he is *grieved* at first. If such punishment is frequent, it excites indignation; he is angry with his parent, and thinks him cruel: then correction does more hurt than good.

I sincerely believe, that, nine times out of ten, the bad conduct of children is owing to parents, who father most of it upon Adam and the Devil.

Parents *then do not work it right.* They work it thus: a child wants an apple; and a child is governed by *appetite,* not by *reason.* The parent says *he must not have it;* but says it with a simple unmeaning tone of voice, that makes no impression on the child. The child cries for the apple; the parent is angry, and tells him he shall not have the apple: the child bawls, and perhaps strikes his little brother, or throws down a glass in anger: at last, the parent is tired with the noise, and, to appease the child, gives him the apple. *Does this parent work it right?* So far from it, that he loses the little authority he had over the child; the order of things is changed; the child is the *master;* and, when the child has been master a few months, you may as well break his *neck* as his *will.* A thousand lashes on a young *master's* back, will not do so much as one *decisive command,* before he becomes *master* of his parents.

Now, listen to my advice; the idea is *new:* A child does not regard so much *what* a parent says, as how he says it. A child looks at his parent's eye, when he speaks; and there he reads intuitively *what* his parent means, and *how much* he means. If a parent speaks with *an air of indifference without emphasis,* or looks another way when he speaks, the child pays little or no regard to what he says. (I speak of a young child over whom a parent has not yet established an authority.) But if a parent, when he commands a child to do or not to do, looks at him with the *eye of command,* and speaks with a tone and air of authority, the child is impressed with this *manner* of commanding, and will seldom venture to disobey. A steady uniform authority of this kind, which never varies from its purpose, which never gives way to the caprices or appetites of children, which carries every command *into effect,* will prevent the necessity of a rod. I am bold to say, that a parent, who has this steady authority, will never have occasion to correct a child of *common sensibility,* and *never but once a* child *of common obstinacy. This is the way every parent and master should work it.*

But the common practice is, for a parent to throw away his own authority, and become the slave of his children; and when the young *masters* grow headstrong, and commit all manner of mischief, then the parent complains of old Adam, original sin, and the Devil; and swears he'll drive the devil out, or he'll *know the reason why*. Then, for the *fist* and the *rod*."

Rules for the Management of Children.

The following rules will be found particularly useful in the management and care of children

RULE 1. *Let a parent be particularly on his guard against his faults and weaknesses when in the bosom of his family.*

The reverse is not seldom the case. The circumspection and restraint practised abroad, are often greatly relaxed at home. Here, liberties and self-indulgencies are thought more allowable; wrong tempers are not instantly repressed in the bosom, and are suffered to deform the countenance, and also sometimes to break out in unchristian tones, expressions, and conduct. We must all have observed this in others; and few of us, I conceive, are unconscious of having been sometimes taken by surprise on the entrance of a friend, of having felt that it was necessary to recal both the mind and the face to greater serenity and benignity, in order to receive him properly. Now can we seriously think, that a heart and a countenance unfit for our friend, was fit for our children, who surrounded us before his arrival?

Can we estimate the mischief which such moral deformity, placed before their eyes in the person of their father, may produce? Some one says, that no man is a hero before his valet-de-chambre. I will not stop to inquire what is becoming in a hero; but a Christian certainly ought, if possible, to be *more* a Christian before his family, where his influence is greatest, and the effects of his example the most important, than in any other situation. Juvenal has said, " maxima debetur pueris reverentia ;" though his view of education was only to prepare youth for an upright and able discharge of their common duties in this life, with little regard to God or eternity. How deep then ought his maxim to sink into the heart of a Christian, whose views are so much higher, and who is to educate beings called to perform all their duties as those who now sit in heavenly places, and are kings and priests unto God !

RULE 2. *Never make mere playthings of your children.*

Many fathers treat their little ones as if nothing was to be sought in their society but mutual amusement. All is good humour when they are together ; and therefore all is supposed to be right, though there be little besides folly and self-indulgence on one side, and improper liberties, caprice, self-will, or artifice on the other. In short, there seems to be a sort of conspiracy between the parties to indulge the natural man. The child is often even taught to be indecorous, and mischievous, and saucy, for the amusement of its parent. What excuse can be made for such a scene?

The poor child is greatly to be pitied; but really the parent, if we were to look no further, would appear to be a sort of monster, devoid of principle, of feeling, and of common sense. Follow him, however, to his serious occupations, and you may find him a useful and respectable man. What a shame, that he is insensible to the high destiny and unspeakable value of the little creature whom he is spoiling, for the sake of half an hour's foolish trifling! What would he say of any one who threw about his gold repeater as if it were a ball, or made marbles of his wife's jewels? And yet his own folly is infinitely greater. The creatures whom he is placing in such danger for his sport, are infinitely more precious than gold, which perisheth; and pearls and diamonds are worthless compared with them One would think that mere selfishness might restrain such absurdity, even in a man who did not extend his view beyond this world.

The time may come, when the evil fostered in the child will be a scourge to the parent, and when he will be made its victim, with the less regret from a recollection that these scenes of egregious folly had undermined that natural respect which would otherwise have been a check to ill conduct on the part of his child.—May parents, then, never relax with their children? must they always sustain the grave character of a tutor? Most certainly they may, and ought, frequently to relax with them, and even to take pains to make them happy: but they may combine this extremely well with a constant recollection of the immortal nature and high value of their children, for whom Christ died, and with a suitable behaviour towards them.

A father will soon learn, in such playful moments, " miscere utile dulci;" or, according to our English proverb, to " be merry and wise;" and he will rank such seasons among those which are most important for checking what is wrong in a child, fostering what is right, instilling good principles, infusing a just appreciation of things, and a taste for what is lovely and of good report. All the good seed sown on such occasions will be so combined with the child's pleasures and affections, as, with God's blessing, to take deep root in the soul, and promise a vigorous and permanent growth.

RULE 3. *In managing a child, let a parent always have the child's good rather than his own ease in view.*

In domestic education, *don't be so troublesome,* is perhaps the most common of all our complaints, when parents address their children. It is true, children ought not to be suffered to be troublesome, since both kindness and propriety forbid them to be so : but the tone of the complaint generally shews very clearly that the great grievance is, not that the child has those dispositions which make it troublesome, but that others, and particularly the complainant, are troubled. Thus the child soon discovers, that it is corrected rather for the ease of its parents and attendants, than for its own good ; and it has before it an example and a lesson of selfishness, which may do it as much harm as it receives benefit from the check given to a bad habit.

What ought to be done on such occasions? Undoubtedly the troublesome practice should be prevented ; but this should be done in a way to shew the child that the parent would willingly submit to trouble, to promote its good ; but that such dispositions as lead it to trouble others, are unchristian, and must be eradicated. The pleasure a christian will have in giving pleasure, and his pain in occasioning pain, must be pointed out, and proved and illustrated. As nothing is to be combated in children with more care and perseverance than selfishness, so nothing is to be more strictly guarded against in parental example.

The child is to be taught to make sacrifices cheerfully, and to deny himself, and take up his cross ; and the parent must be especially careful that his own example forward the learning of this difficult lesson. On occasions in which the admonition is " *don't be troublesome,*" would not " *don't be thoughtless,*" " *don't be violent,*" or " *don't be unkind,*" be often more appropriate ? Is it expedient very generally to use a mode of expression which points to the effect rather than the cause of a child's conduct; to the consequences produced to others, rather than the state of his own mind ?

RULE 4. *In correcting a fault, look to the heart rather than to the outward act.*

How common is it for parents to pursue the opposite course ! They are satisfied with condemning and preventing wrong conduct, without much attending to the temper of mind in which their animadversions are received, and the child is often left unhumbled and discontented, and in a state as displeasing to God as when it was committing the fault in question. This mode of proceeding appears to me essentially wrong, and productive of serious evil. It does not bring the child to repentance before God, and to peace with him. It directs its view to the maintenance of decency in externals, rather than to a jealous scrutiny of its motives and dispositions, and an earnest desire of reconciliation with its God, after having offended him.

Though these marks of true repentance cannot be expected at so early an age in their full extent, yet a broad foundation for them is often laid during the two or three first years of infancy. On the other hand, when we see a child scowl, or snatch up his shoulders, or pout or redden, on being blamed, can the rebellious and unbending spirit within be doubted? Is he humbled for his fault, and in a spirit to forsake it and seek forgiveness? Is there any putting off of the old man, and putting on of the new man? And yet, can it be denied that this is the only temper to which the promise of pardon is made? It is the temper in which adults must come to Christ for pardon and peace; and it is therefore the temper to which, from the very dawn of reason, we should endeavour to bring children.

In our endeavours to effect this great object, kind and mild and serene, but steady, perseverance is to be employed. There must be neither violence nor hurry. If the child is impatient, some constraint, if necessary, must be used to prevent ebullitions of passion or fretfulness, and time must be given for it to recover itself: then steady and unwearied, but calm and affectionate, addresses to its reason and feelings must be used, suited to its age and habits and natural disposition. The sagacity and ingenuity of the parent must be tasked to select the best topics, and handle them in the best manner, for the production of the desired effect. But, above all, his eye must be upon God for guidance and a blessing, and for putting his own mind in the frame best adapted to win upon the affections of the child, and impress his heart.

RULE 5. *Be on your guard against the little wiles and arti-fices which children will soon employ to obtain their ends.*

It is surprising how ingenious and adroit they will be in this way. They will endeavour to do, as a bit of play, something which they know to be wrong and forbidden; and to put you off by a laugh and a joke, when you require them to acknowledge that they have done wrong. These little tricks lead to much evil. They undermine sincerity and simplicity of character; and instead of being amused by them, as is often the case, a parent should carefully repress them. It is a good general rule with young folks, that nothing shall be said or done in joke, which would be naughty if in earnest.

More latitude may be allowed to those who are grown up: but children cannot discriminate between what is innocent in jokes, and what is not; and if they could, they have not sufficient steadiness of principle and self-command to confine themselves within the proper bounds, if suffered in their moments of gaiety to approach the brink of what is wrong. It is of the greatest possible importance to preserve the mind from the taint of cunning and deceit; and therefore we ought to be more anxious to avoid doing too little than too much, to secure this point. Simplicity and integrity of character, the great foundation of every thing good, depend upon it

RULE 6. *Do all you can to secure a consistency of system in the management of children.*

It is quite apparent how indispensable it is that the father and mother should at least not counteract each other. If they do not and cannot think alike on the subject of education, by mutual concessions and accommodations they should pursue a similar plan with their children. Grievous are the consequences when they proceed differently. The children presume to erect themselves into judges between their parents: they play off one against the other. Not only one parent sinks in their esteem, but they often lose respect for both, and are disobedient to both. Thus the fifth commandment is habitually broken; and bad principles and bad habits are as likely to be established by education in a young family, so circumstanced, as good ones.

Let me entreat parents to shun this fatal rock. If one of them is conscious that the other is best qualified for the work of education, let such parent be disposed to yield points as far as duty will allow, and to strengthen the hands of the other. And even that other, instead of presuming on superior ability in this line, and carrying matters with a high hand, and peremptorily insisting on points respecting which there may be a difference of opinion between them, should be as accommodating as can be made consistent with duty; and where a point cannot be yielded, still the necessary duty should be performed in a way as little grating and offensive to the parent who disapproves, as may be.

RULE 7. *Spend much time with your children; encourage them to be free before you; and carefully study their characters*

For what is education? It is co-operating with the Divine Spirit in forming the mind and changing the heart of an immortal being, weak and corrupt, averse to the change to be wrought in him, and whose nature is made up of various parts and differs greatly in different individuals. Is it possible to doubt, that what is above recommended must be necessary in this work? Can too great pains be taken where so much is at stake? Can success be rationally expected, unless great pains are taken, and your labours are enlightened and judicious? And can you flatter yourself that you take due pains, or that your labours will have a proper direction, if you give little time to your arduous task, and do not employ proper means for becoming well acquainted with the characters of your children?

It is wonderful that a parent can *hope* to be an effectual instrument under Divine grace, in leading his children from darkness to light, and from the power of Satan unto God, by proceeding in the way in which religious education is often conducted. Is it not generally true, that, even in religious families, more thought, and care, and time are employed in teaching children to read, than in teaching and persuading them, by God's help, to be real Christians? The father sees but little of those who are young, and much less than is desirable of such as are older. The first he considers as scarcely at all under his care; and though he probably gives some instructions to the latter, they are commonly such as are more calculated to enlarge their knowledge, and improve their understandings, than to regulate their dispositions, and make them new creatures.

His avocations often are such as to make it impossible for him to be a great deal with his children; but he generally might be much more with them than he is; and, when with them, might employ the time much more usefully, for the promotion of their best interests, than he does. It often happens that they are under a degree of restraint in his presence, which, added to the little time he spends with them, prevents his obtaining a deep insight into their characters: and, therefore, many evils either escape his notice, or he adopts some wrong mode of correcting them; and many a tender germ of good passes unobserved, and withers for want of his fostering care.

The mother is much more with her children, but generally, I think, not so much as she ought to be. This is the more to be lamented, because women are admirably fitted for training their offspring in the nurture and admonition of the Lord. They have a remarkably quick insight into character; and a warmth of affection, a tenderness and a delicacy, which win the affection of others, and enable them to correct faults without giving offence, and to present Christian principles and virtues to their children in their most amiable form. I believe that there has seldom been a man who had a good and amiable mother, that has not in after-life looked back on her instructions and example with reverence and delight. Cowper's admirable little poem, on viewing his mother's picture, touches the hearts of all of us, because it describes scenes and feelings dear to every virtuous mind; scenes and feelings of which many of us have partaken, and all wish to partake.

Every hour which a Christian mother spends with her children has balm on its wings. She contrives to make even their pastimes a moral lesson; and though she cannot (and it is not desirable that she should) make their regular lessons a pastime, yet she adapts them well to the abilities of her scholars, accommodates them well to times and circumstances, and divests them of whatever is oppressive and revolting.

CHAPTER XXII.

ATTENDANCE UPON THE SICK, AND MEDICAL RECEIPTS.

IN cases of illness which require the attention of medical men, an unskilful interference is both dangerous and presumptuous. But there are uneasy symptoms experienced more or less at times by all persons, not amounting to a decided disease, yet, if neglected, sure to end in such, that may generally be relieved by a proper diet, and attention to the state of the bowels; not only without risk, but even with greater advantage to the individual than by an application to a positive course of medicine.

The sensations of lassitude or weariness, stiffness or numbness, less activity than usual, less appetite, a load or heaviness at the stomach, some uneasiness in the head; a more profound degree of sleep, yet less composed and refreshing, than usual; less gaiety and liveliness, a slight oppression of the breast, a less regular pulse, a propensity to be cold, a disposition to perspire, or sometimes a suppression of a former disposition to perspire, are any of them symptomatic of a diseased state of the body, though not amounting to a decisive disease.

Under such circumstances persons are generally restless both in body and mind; do not know what to do with themselves; and often, for the sake of change, or on the supposition that their sensations proceed from lowness, they unhappily adopt the certain means of making them terminate in dangerous and often fatal diseases. They increase their quantity of animal food, leave off vegetables and fruit, drink freely of wine or other strong liquors, under an idea of strengthening the stomach and expelling wind, all which strengthen nothing but the disposition to disease, and expel only the degree of health yet remaining. The consequence of this mistaken management is, that all the evacuations are restrained, the humours causing and nourishing the diseases are not at all attempered nor diluted, and rendered proper for evacuation. On the contrary, they become more sharp and difficult to be discharged.

By judicious management it is practicable, if not entirely to prevent the disorders indicated by the above symptoms, to mitigate them so as to avert their danger. An early attention to the following points would seldom fail of this desirable effect.

1. To give up for the time all violent exercise or labour and take only a gentle easy degree of exercise.

2. To use very little or no solid food, and particularly to

abstain from all flesh, or flesh broth, eggs, and wine, or other strong liquors.

3. To drink plentifully, that is, at least three, or even four pints in a day, by small glasses at a time, at intervals of half an hour, one of the diluents given hereafter, which the French call *ptisans*. If these ptisans do not answer the purpose of keeping the bowels properly evacuated, stronger cathartics must be taken, or injections for the bowels, called lavements.

By pursuing these precautions the above symptoms of disease will be often removed without coming to any serious disorders; and, even where this is not the case, the disorder will be so lessened as to obviate any kind of danger from it.

When confirmed diseases occur, the only safe course is to resort to the most skilful medical advice that can be obtained. The poor will come at this the most readily in hospitals; those in better circumstances, by application to the most eminent of the medical profession. It is like employing an attorney, in the highest branches of the law, to call in advice that cannot challenge a full claim to the confidence that is to be reposed in it. Good advice and few medicines will much sooner effect a cure than all the medicines of the apothecary's shop, unskilfully administered. But the success of the best advice may be defeated, if the patient, and the friends of the patient, will not concur to render it effectual. If the patient is to indulge longings for improper diet, and the friends to gratify them, the advantage of the best advice may be defeated by one such imprudent measure. As what is here said applies equally to the cases of patients labouring under accidents which require surgical assistance, they must be considered as included in it.

General directions are all that a physician or surgeon can give respecting diet, and many other circumstances requiring attention in the attendance on a sick person. To expect more of them, is to expect them to undertake the office of a nurse. As much therefore must depend on good nursing to sick persons, and many mistakes that often prove fatal are committed by those about them, from ignorance and prejudice, a few rules to which they may always refer, at the intervals when they cannot refer to their medical director, may be useful on these occasions; more especially when the patient is so far recovered as to be released from medicines, and put under a proper regimen, with the use of gentle exercise, and such other regulations as a convalescent state requires. When labouring under acute disorders, or accidents, patients frequently suffer from the injudiciousness of those about them, in covering them up in bed with a load of clothes that heat and

debilitate them exceedingly, and in keeping them in bed, when
the occasion does require it, without even suffering them to
get up and have it new made, and by never allowing a breath
of fresh air to be admitted into the room.

The keeping patients quiet is of essential importance ; they
should not be talked to, nor should more persons than are absolutely necessary even be in the room.   Every thing should
be moved out of the room directly that can be offensive in it.
Sprinkling the room sometimes with vinegar will contribute
to keep it in a better state.   The windows should be opened
occasionally for a longer or a shorter time, according to the
weather and season of the year, without letting the air come
immediately upon the patient.   Waving the chamber-doo.
backward and forward for a few minutes, two or three times
in a day, ventilates the room without exposing the sick person
to chillness. Burning pastils in the room is also useful at times.

The linen, both of the bed and patient, should be changed
every day, or in two or three days, as circumstances admit
and require it.   A strict forbearance from giving sick persons
any nourishment but what is permitted by their medical attendant should be invariably observed. Above all things, both
sick persons and those about them must await the slow progress of recovery from disease or accidents with patience.   A
contrary conduct will only retard this desired event.   What
has been long undermining the stamina of health, which is
commonly the case with diseases,—or what has violently
shocked it, as accidents,—can only be slowly recovered.   Medicines will not operate like a charm; and, even when they are
the most efficacious, time must be required to recover from
the languid state to which persons are inevitably always reduced both by diseases and accidents.

When the period is arrived at which sick persons may be
said to be out of danger, a great deal of patience and care
will yet be required to prevent their relapsing.   The great
hazard of this will be averted by the persons who are recovering, on their own part, and their friends for them, being contented for some time with a very moderate share of food.   We
are not nourished in proportion to what we swallow, but to
what we digest.   Persons on the recovery, who eat moderately,
digest their food, and grow strong from it.   Those who eat
much do not digest it, and, instead of being nourished and
strengthened, wither away insensibly.

The few following rules comprise all that is most essenti▿
to be observed to perfect the cure of acute diseases or of accidents, and prevent their leaving behind them any impedi-
ments to health.

1. Let those who are recovering, as well as those who are actually sick, take very little nourishment at a time, and take it often.

2. Let them take but one sort of food at each meal, and not change their food too often.

3. Let them chew whatever solid food they eat very carefully.

4. Let them diminish their quantity of drink. The best drink for them, in general, is water, with a third or fourth part of white wine. Too great a quantity of liquids at this time prevents the stomach recovering its tone and strength, impairs digestion, keeps up weakness, increases the tendency to a swelling of the legs; sometimes even occasions a slow fever, and throws back the person recovering into a languid state.

5. Let them be in the air as much as they are able, whether on foot, in a carriage, or on horseback. This last exercise is the healthiest of all. It should be taken before the principal meal, which should be about noon: after it, riding is not good. Exercise taken before a meal strengthens the organs of digestion, which is promoted by it. If the exercise is taken soon after the meal, it impairs it.

6. As people in this state are seldom quite so well towards night, they should take very little food in the evening. Their sleep will be the less disturbed for this, and repair them the more and the sooner.

7. They should not remain in bed above seven or eight hours. If they feel fatigued by sitting up, let them lie down for half an hour, or longer, at a time, as they may find it necessary.

8. The swelling of the legs and ancles, which happens to most persons at this time, is not dangerous, and generally disappears of itself, if they live soberly and regularly, and take moderate exercise.

9. They should pay attention to the state of the bowels. It will not be necessary to apply to any artificial means of keeping them open every day, if they should not be regular; but they should not pass over the third day without doing this, if required, and should apply to them sooner, if they feel heated, puffed up, restless, or have any pains in the head. Either of the three following recipes may be resorted to.

10. They must not return to hard exercise, or to any laborious occupation, too soon. Some persons have never recovered their usual strength for want of this precaution.

Recipe, No. 1

Take a large pinch, between the thumb and fingers, of elder

flowers, put them into an earthenware jug, with two ounces of honey and an ounce and a half of good vinegar. Pour upon these three pints and a quarter of boiling water. Stir it about a little with a spoon, to mix and dissolve the honey: then cover up the jug, and, when the liquor is cold, strain it through a piece of linen.

Recipe, No 2.

Wash two ounces of whole barley very clean and well in hot water; then put it into five pints of cold water, and boil it till the barley opens. Towards the end of the boiling put in a drachm and a half of nitre; strain it through a linen cloth, and then add to it an ounce and a half of honey, and an ounce of vinegar.

Recipe, No. 3.

Take two pinches, between the fingers and thumb, of mallow leaves and flowers, and pour upon them a pint of boiling water. After standing some time, strain it, adding to it an ounce of honey. For want of mallows, which are preferable, leaves of mercury, pellitory of the wall, marsh-mallows, the greater mallows, lettuce, or spinach, may be used. Some few particular constitutions find none but lavements of warm water efficacious. Such persons should use no other, and the water should not be very hot.

The quantities given are for grown persons from eighteen to sixty. From the age of twelve to eighteen, two-thirds of the dose will generally be enough. From seven to twelve, half; and, under seven, it must be diminished in proportion to the age. An infant under a year should not take more than an eighth part. Some consideration must be paid to the constitution. Persons should observe whether they require a strong or weak dose.

Medical Receipts.

Cure for Consumption.

Gently boil in a stew-pan a pound of good honey; clean, scrape, and grate two large sticks of horse-radish; stir it into the honey. Let it boil for about five minutes, but it must be kept continually stirred. Two or three table-spoonfuls a day, according to the strength of the patient, some time persisted in, may do a great deal, even where there is a confirmed consumption of tne lungs. It is serviceable in all coughs where the lungs are affected.

Strengthening Pills.

Take soft extract of bark, and vitriolated iron, each a drachm. Make into pills.—In disorders arising from excessive debility, or relaxation of the solids, as the *chlorosis*, or green sickness, two of these pills may be taken three times a day.

Strengthening Fomentation.

Take, of oak bark, one ounce; granate peel, half an ounce; alum, two drachms; smiths' forge-water, three pints. Boil the water with the bark and peel to the consumption of one-third; then strain the remaining decoction, and dissolve in it the alum.—This astringent liquor is employed as an external fomentation to weak parts; it may also be used internally.

To cure Chilblains.

Apply a poultice of roasted onions hot; keep it on two or three days, if not cured sooner.

Hard Breasts.

Apply turnips roasted till soft, then mashed and mixed with a little oil of roses; change this twice a day, keeping the breast very warm with flannel.

Sore Breasts, and swelled.

Boil a handful of camomile and as much mallows in milk and water; foment with it between two flannels, as hot as can be borne, every twelve hours; it also dissolves any knot or swelling in any part.

Receipt for the Rheumatism.

Take of garlic two cloves, of ammoniac one drachm : blend them, by bruising, together; make them into two or three bolusses, with fair water, and swallow them, one at night, and one in the morning. Drink, while taking this medicine, sassafras tea, made very strong, so as to have the teapot filled with chips. This is generally found to banish the rheumatism, and even contractions of the joints, in a few times taking.

Remedy for the Hooping-Cough.

Take two ounces each of conserve of roses, raisins of the sun stoned, brown sugar-candy, and two pennyworth of spirits of sulphur; beat them up into a conserve, and take a tea-spoonful night and morning.

Stomach-Plaster for a Cough

Take an ounce each of bees' wax, Burgundy pitch, and rosin; melt them together in a pipkin, and stir in three quarters of an ounce of common turpentine, and half an ounce of oil of mace. Spread it on a piece of sheep's leather, grate some nutmeg over it, and apply it quite warm to the pit of the stomach.

Linseed Cough-Syrup.

Boil one ounce of linseed in a quart of water till half wasted; add six ounces of moist sugar, two ounces of sugar-candy, half an ounce of Spanish liquorice, and the juice of a large lemon. Let the whole slowly simmer together till it becomes of a syruppy consistence; when cold, put to it two table-spoonfuls of the best old rum.

Celandine.

The juice of celandine cures tetters and ring-worms, and is said to cure the itch.

A Remedy for the Piles.

Take a spoonful of the flour of brimstone in half a pint of milk every morning till cured.

A sure Preservation from the Tooth-Ache, and Defluxions on the Gums or Teeth.

After having washed your mouth with water, as cleanliness, and indeed health requires, you should every morning rinse the mouth with a tea-spoonful of lavender-water mixed with an equal quantity of warm or cold water, whichever you like best, to diminish its activity. This simple and innocent remedy is a certain preservative, the success of which has bee confirmed by long experience.

Cure for the Tooth-Ache.

An eminent apothecary, in the vicinity of this metropolis, has lately recommended, as an effectual cure for the tooth-ache, the following remedy, which he has been in the habit of using for many years; and, out of the number of cases, eight-tenths have succeeded; viz. to take three table-spoonfuls of brandy, adding to it one drachm of camphor, with thirty or forty drops of laudanum, and then dropping a little upon some lint, and applying it to the tooth affected, keeping the lint moistened for five minutes only on the tooth and gum.

Cure for the Gravel

Dissolve three drachms of prepared natron in a quart of cold soft water, and take half this quantity in the course of the day. Continue this medicine for a few days, and that painful complaint will be dislodged.—It may be taken at any hour, but it is best after a meal. It is said that the greatest martyrs to this disorder have been perfectly relieved by this simple remedy, which every person should remember, and note in a pocket-book, as few families are without some individual afflicted with gravel in a greater or less degree.

Putrid Fever.

A physician called to visit a youth ill with a typhus fever, had given him over, and his pulse was at 140; blood issued from his eyes, nose, and ears; his mouth and fauces were ulcerated, and the stench of his chamber was very great. At this time yeast was given in a spoon, diluted with warm water and coarse sugar; he presently found himself refreshed, grew more calm, and all the bad symptoms abated; the next day his pulse was fallen to 100, and he was so much recovered, that in a few days more he was perfectly well. A pail of fomenting yeast was put in the room, and he took from three to four table-spoonfuls of pure yeast in fourteen hours. It did not affect the bowels.

An infallible Receipt for the Bite of a mad Dog.

Take one ounce of the best dragon's blood; of Spanish brown, one ounce and a half; of *box-leaves*, dried, pounded, and sifted through a fine sieve, five ounces; mix these together, and take it in the following manner: to a man or a woman, in the morning fasting, one large table-spoonful in a little gruel, white-wine whey, or warm ale.—To children a quantity in proportion to their age.—Observe to refrain from any food for three hours after taking.

To a horse or cow, two spoonfuls in warm water, or mixed in butter.

To a hog, one spoonful and a half.

To a dog, one spoonful.

The above medicine should be taken, by each, three mornings successively, as soon after being bit as possible.

Hydrophobia.—(From Dr. Rees's Cyclopedia.)

We know of no instance of the complaint (canine madness) being *cured*, nor have we, in any instance, even attempted any thing of the kind; but we flatter ourselves that we have been successful in bringing forward a *preventive*. We claim not the discovery of this most valuable and truly important remedy; we only, by exertion, rescued it from oblivion, and, by a long course of well-conducted experiments, have established the certainty of its efficacy, that of more than ninety animals, as horses, sheep, swine, and dogs, one only has gone mad to whom this remedy was administered, and this failure did not occur under our own immediate inspection, so that it might have been wasted or brought up. This remedy, as prepared by us, is as follows :—Take, of the fresh leaves of the *box-tree*, two ounces; of the fresh leaves of rue, two ounces; of sage, half an ounce ; chop these fine, and boil in a pint of water to half a pint ; strain carefully, and press out the liquor very firmly; put back the ingredients into a pint of milk, and boil again to half a pint; strain as before; mix both liquors, which forms three doses for a human subject.—Double this quantity is proper for a cow or horse; two-thirds for a large dog, half for a middle-sized, and one-third for a small dog. Three doses are sufficient, given each subsequent morning, fasting; the quantity directed being that which forms these doses. As it sometimes produces strong effects on dogs, it may be proper to begin with a small dose, increasing it till the effects are evident, by the sickness, panting, and uneasiness of the dog. In the human subject, where this remedy appears equally efficacious, we have never witnessed any unpleasant effects. About forty human persons have taken this remedy, and in every instance has succeeded equally as with animals. That this remedy, therefore, has a *preventive* quality, is unquestionable, and now perfectly established; for there was not the smallest doubt of the animals mentioned either having been bitten, or of the dog being mad who bit them, as great pains were, in every instance, taken to ascertain these points.

The writer of the above article in Dr. Rees's Cyclopedia has attentively observed, during its whole progress, above two hundred cases of canine madness, and has dissected near one hundred bodies of dogs who died of th malady.

Head-Ache.

The juice of ground ivy snuffed up the nose is said to have cured those who have been thus afflicted for twelve years. Pillacochiæ will also give relief in the most obstinate and severe head-ache.

To cure Corns.

Bind on them a leaf of houseleek, after the feet have been soaked in warm water.

Receipt for a Cold.

Take a tea-cupful of linseed, a quarter of a pound of stick liquorice sliced, and a quarter of a pound of sun raisins; put them into two quarts of soft water, and let it simmer over a slow fire till it is nearly reduced to one quart; then strain it off, and add to it, while it is hot, a quarter of a pound of brown sugar-candy pounded.

Drink half a pint of it a little warmed at going to bed, and take a little in the morning, and at any time when the cough is troublesome. Add to every half-pint a large tea-spoonful of old rum, and the same quantity of the best white-wine vinegar, or lemon-juice. This receipt generally cures the worst of colds in two or three days, and, if taken in time, may be said to be almost an infallible remedy. It is a most sovereign and balsamic cordial for the lungs, without the opening qualities, which endanger fresh colds in going out. It has been known to cure colds, that have been almost settled in consumptions, in less than three weeks.

Tincture for the Teeth and Gums.

Mix six ounces of the tincture of Peruvian bark with half an ounce of sal ammoniac. Shake it well before using. Take a tea-spoonful, and hold it near the teeth; then, with a finger dipped in, rub the gums and teeth, which must afterwards be washed with warm water. This tincture cures the tooth-ach, preserves the teeth and gums, and makes them adhere to each other.

For chapped Hands.

Mix a quarter of a pound of unsalted hogs' lard, which has been washed in water, and then in rose-water, with the yolks of two new-laid eggs, and a large spoonful of honey. Add as much fine oatmeal, or almond paste, as will work it into a paste.

For chapped Lips.

Put a quarter of an ounce of benjamin, storax, and spermaceti, two pennyworth of alkanet-root, a juicy apple chopped, a bunch of black grapes bruised, a quarter of a pound of unsalted butter, and two ounces of bees' wax, into a new tin saucepan. Simmer gently till all is dissolved, and then strain it through a linen. When cold, melt it again, and pour into small pots or boxes; if to make cakes use the bottom of tea-cups.

For the Palsy, Rheumatism, &c

Take four ounces each of good fresh butter and common hard soap, a quartern of brandy, and ten ounces of the white part of leeks, torn or twisted off from the green, but not cut with a knife, or washed.   Put the butter into a pipkin, add the white of the leeks torn or broken small, set the pipkin in boiling water, stir the ingredients till all are well mixed and quite soft, and then put in soap thinly scraped.   When that also is well mixed, add the brandy by degrees, and continue stirring the whole till it becomes an ointment.   With this embrocation, every part where the disease prevails is to be well rubbed before a good fire, morning and night, till the skin is completely saturated.

For the Jaundice.

A quarter of an ounce of Venice soap, made into moderate-sized pills, with eighteen drops of the oil of aniseed; three of these pills to be taken night and morning.

Embrocation for the Hooping-Cough.

Mix well together half an ounce of spirit of hartshorn and an equal quantity of oil of amber; with which plentifully anoint the palms of the hands, the pit of the stomach, the soles of the feet, the arm-pits, and the back-bone, every morning and evening for one month : no water must come near the parts thus anointed, though the fingers and backs of the hands may be wiped with a damp cloth.   It should be rubbed in near the fire, and care must be taken to prevent taking cold.   It is best to make only the above quantity at a time ; because, by often opening the bottle, much of the virtue will be lost.   It should be kept in a glass-stopper bottle.

Balsamic Elixir for Cough and Consumption.

Take a pint of old rum, two ounces of balsam of Tolu, an ounce and a half of Strasburg turpentine, an ounce of powdered extract of Catechu (formerly called Japan earth), half an ounce of gum guaiacum, and half an ounce of balsam of copaiva. Mix them well together in a bottle ; and keep it near the fire, closely corked, for ten days, shaking it frequently during that time.   Afterwards let it stand two days to settle, and pour off the clear for use.   Half a pint of rum may be poured over the dregs ; and, being done in the same manner, for ten or twelve days, as the first, will produce more elixir, and equally good. The dose may be from fifty to a hundred or two hundred drops, according to the urgency of the case, taken twice or thrice a day in a wine-glass of water.

Cure for a Wen.

Put some salt and water into a saucepan, and boil it for four or five minutes; with which, while tolerably hot, bathe the entire surface of the wen, however large; and continue to do so, even after it is cold. Every time, before applying it, stir up the salt deposited at the bottom of the basin, and incorporate it afresh with the water. In this manner the wen must be rubbed well over, at least ten or twelve times every twenty-four hours; and, very often in less than a fortnight, a small discharge takes place, without any pain, which a gentle pressure soon assists to empty the whole contents. In particular instances, the application must be continued several weeks, or even months : but it is said always finally to prevail, where persisted in, without occasioning pain or inconvenience of any kind, there being not the smallest previous notice of the discharge.

Remedy for the Eyes, when the Rheum is most violent.

Take two ounces of hemlock, pounded, with a pinch of bay salt; as much bole ammoniac as will spread it on a cloth; lay it on the wrists, and renew it every twelve hours as long as there is occasion for it; if one eye only is affected, lay the bandage on the contrary wrist.—Then take one ounce each of red rose-water, tutty, and double-refined sugar powdered; shake them well, let them settle, and wash the eyes with the clear, with a fine soft rag. Then take a pint of sweet oil, and twelve ounces of yellow wax; put them on the fire in a new pipkin, stir the wax till melted; add half a pound of ceruse or white lead, and boil it half an hour : after which put in two ounces each of finely-powdered myrrh, olibanum, and mastich. Each article is to be separately prepared, and used in the same order as they are here mentioned, each being well mixed in before the next is added. Let the whole boil gently till it becomes blackish; and it must not only be stirred at the time it remains on the fire, but after it is taken off, and till it gets cold enough to work up with the hands, like dough, into rolls, for use. Great care is necessary to be taken that it is well mixed, and properly boiled. This salve is to be applied to the temples, and behind the ears; where it must remain till it grows moist, and falls off. It is not only thus excellent for the eyes, but makes a good plaster for many other purposes, and very proper for swellings or tumors. It speedily cures cuts, and heals al-

most any sore where much drawing is not necessary : as it
will retain all its virtues for a long time, it may be considered as one of the most generally useful of all family
salves

Cure for Dropsy.

Take sixteen large nutmegs, eleven spoonfuls of broom
ashes dried and burnt in an oven, an ounce and a half of
bruised mustard-seed, and a handful of scraped horse-radish ;
put the whole into a gallon of mountain wine, and let it
stand three or four days. A gill, or half a pint, according
to the urgency of the disease and strength of the patient, is
to be drunk every morning fasting, taking nothing else for
an hour or two after.

Lozenges of Marshmallows, for Coughs

Clean and scrape roots of marshmallows freshly taken out
of the earth ; boil them in pure water till they become quite
soft ; take them from their decoction ; beat them in a marble
mortar, to the consistence of a smooth paste, and place it at
the top of an inverted sieve, to obtain all the pulp which can
be forced through it with a wooden spoon.   Boil a pound and
a half of loaf-sugar in six or seven ounces of rose-water, to a
good solid consistence ; whisk it up, off the fire, with a quarter
of a pound of the marshmallow pulp : after which, place it
over a gentle heat, to dry up the moisture, stirring it all the
time ; and, when a good paste is formed, empty it on paper
brushed over with oil of sweet almonds, roll it out with a rolling-
pin, and cut into lozenges with a tin lozenge-cutter.   These
lozenges are adapted to sheathe and soften the acrimony by
which the cough is excited, and to promote expectoration.
For these purposes, a small lozenge must often be gradually
melted in the mouth.   Marshmallow lozenges are often made
by beating the roots to a pulp, pounding them with pulverized
sugar to a paste, rolling and cutting it out, and drying them
in the shade.

The compound lozenges of marshmallow, celebrated for
curing inveterate coughs, the asthma, and even consumption
of the lungs, are thus made : Take two ounces of the pulp of
boiled marshmallow roots ; three drachms each of white poppy
seeds, Florentine iris, liquorice, and powdered gum tragacanth.
Pound the white poppy seeds, iris, and liquorice, together,
and then add the powdered tragacanth.   Having boiled a pound
of loaf-sugar, dissolved in rose-water, to syrup of a good
consistence, mix into it, off the fire, first the pulp, and then
the powders to compose the paste : which must be rolled out

on oiled paper, and cut into lozenges, in the same manner as the former.

Remedy for St. Anthony's Fire.

Take equal parts of spirits of turpentine and highly rectified spirits of wine ; mix them well together, and anoint the face gently with a feather dipped in it immediately after shaking the bottle. This should be done often, always shaking the bottle, and taking care never to approach the eyes. It will frequently effect a cure in a day or two : though it seems at first to inflame it softens and heals.

Friar's Balsam.

Put four ounces of sarsaparilla cut in short pieces, two ounces of China root thinly sliced, and an ounce of Virginian snake-weed cut small, with one quart of spirits of wine, in a two-quart bottle. Set it in the sun, or any equal degree of heat; shake it two or three times a day, till the spirit be tinctured of a fine golden yellow. Then clear off the infusion into another bottle ; and put in eight ounces of gum guaiacum ; set it in the sun, or other similar heat, shaking it often, till all the gum be dissolved, except dregs, which will be in about ten or twelve days. It must be again cleared from the dregs ; and, having received an ounce of Peruvian balsam, be well shaken, and again placed in the sun for two days : after which, add an ounce of balm of Gilead, shake it together, and finally set it in the sun for fourteen days, when it will be fit for use.

For Stone and Gravel.

Cut off a large handful of the beards of leeks, and put them in a pipkin with two quarts of water : cover close up, and simmer till the liquor is reduced to a quart. Then pour it off ; and drink it every morning, noon, and evening, about the third part of a pint each time. Half the quantity, or less, may be sufficient for children, according to their respective ages, and the violence of the disease.

Emollient Gargle.

Take an ounce of marshmallow roots, and two or three figs ; boil them in a quart of water till near one half of it be consumed ; then strain out the liquor. If an ounce of honey, and half an ounce of *water of ammonia,* be added to the above, it will then be an exceedingly good *attenuating gargle.* This gargle is beneficial in fevers, where the tongue and fauces are rough and parched, to soften these parts, and promote the discharge of saliva.—The learned and accurate Sir John Pringle observes, that, in the inflammatory quinsey, or strangulation of the fauces, little benefit arises from the common gargles; that such as are of an acid nature do more harm than good, by contracting the emunctories of the saliva and mucus, and thickening those humours; that a decoction of figs in milk and water has a contrary effect, especially if some sal-ammoniac be added, by which the saliva is made thinner, and the glands brought to secrete more freely; a circumstance always conducive to the cure

Anodyne Balsam.

Take, of white Spanish soap, one ounce; opium, unprepared, two drachms; rectified spirits of wine, nine ounces. Digest them together in a gentle heat for three days: then strain off the liquor, and add to it three drachms of camphor. This balsam, as its title expresses, is intended to ease pain. It is of service in violent strains and rheumatic complaints, when not attended with inflammation. It must be rubbed with a warm hand on the part affected: or a linen rag moistened with it may be applied to the part, and renewed every third or fourth hour till the pain abates. If the opium is left out, this will resemble the soap liniment, or opodeldoc.

Anodyne Plaster.

Melt an ounce of adhesive plaster, and, when it is cooling, mix with it a drachm of powdered opium, and the same quantity of camphor, previously rubbed up with a little oil. This plaster generally gives ease in acute pains, especially of the nervous kind.

Compound Tincture of Bark.

Take, of Peruvian bark, two ounces; Seville orange-peel and cinnamon, of each half an ounce. Let the bark be powdered, and the other ingredients be bruised; then infuse the whole in a pint and a half of brandy, for five or six days, in a close vessel; afterwards strain off the tincture. This tincture is not only beneficial in intermitting fevers, but also in slow, nervous, and putrid kinds, especially towards their decline. The dose is from one drachm to three or four every fifth or sixth hour. It may be given in any suitable liquor, occasionally sharpened with a few drops of vitriolic acid.

Decoction of Bark

Take two ounces of the best bruised or powdered Peruvian bark, and put it into a pint and a half of boiling water, in a tin saucepan, with a cover, with some cinnamon and a little Seville orange peel. Boil it together for twenty minutes ; then take it off the fire, and let it stand till quite cold : afterwards strain it through flannel, put it up in small phials, and take four table-spoonfuls three times a day.

Another Way.

Boil an ounce of Peruvian bark, grossly powdered, in a pint and a half of water, to one pint; then strain the decoction. If a tea-spoonful of the *diluted acid of vitriol* be added to this medi-cine, it will render it both more agreeable and efficacious.

Compound Decoction of Bark.

Take of bark and Virginian snake-root, grossly powdered, each three drachms. Boil them in a pint of water to one half. To the strained liquor add an ounce and a half of aromatic water. —Sir John Pringle recommends this as a proper medicine towards the decline of malignant fevers, when the pulse is low, the voice weak, and the head affected with a stupor, but with little delirium.—The dose is four spoonfuls every fourth or sixth hour.

Compound Decoction of Chalk.

Take of the purest chalk, in powder, two ounces ; gum ara-bic, half an ounce ; water, three pints. Boil to one quart, and strain the decoction.—This is a proper drink in acute diseases, attended with or inclining to a looseness, and where acidities abound in the stomach or bowels. It is peculiarly proper for children when afflicted with sourness of the stomach, and for persons who are subject to the heartburn. It may be sweetened with sugar as it is used, and two or three ounces of simple cin-namon-water added to it.—An ounce of powdered chalk, mixed with two pints of water, will occasionally supply the place of this decoction, and also of the chalk mixture of the London pharmacopœia

Cure for the Convulsive Hiccup.

One drop of chemical oil of cinnamon on a lump of sugar, which must be kept in the mouth till dissolved, and then gently swallowed.

Laxative Absorbent Mixture.

Rub one drachm of magnesia alba in a mortar with ten or twelve grains of the best Turkey rhubarb, and add to them three ounces of common water : simple cinnamon-water, and syrup of sugar, of each one ounce.—As most diseases of infants are accompanied by acidities, this mixture may either be given with a view to correct these, or to open the body. A table-spoonful may be taken for a dose, and repeated three times a day. To a very young child half a spoonful will be sufficient. When the mixture is intended to purge, the dose may either be increased, or the quantity of rhubarb doubled.—This is one of the most generally useful medicines for children with which we are acquainted.

Asafœtida Pills.

Take, of asafœtida, half an ounce : simple syrup, as much as is necessary to form it into pills.—In hysteric complaints, four or five pills, of an ordinary size, may be taken twice or thrice a day. They may likewise be of service to persons afflicted with the asthma.—When it is necessary to keep the body open, a proper quantity of rhubarb, aloës, or jalap, may occasionally be added to the above mass.

Stomachic Pills.

Take extract of gentian, two drachms; powdered rhubarb and vitriolated kali, of each one drachm; oil of mint, thirty drops; simple syrup, a sufficient quantity.—Three or four of these pills may be taken twice a day, for invigorating the stomach, and keeping the body gently open.

Strengthening Pills.

Take soft extract of bark, and vitriolated iron, each a drachm. Make into pills.—In disorders arising from excessive debility, or relaxation of the solids, as the *chlorosis,* or green sickness, two of these pills may be taken three times a day.

Diachylon or Common Plaster.

Take, of common olive oil, six pints ; litharge, reduced to a fine powder, two pounds and a half. Boil the litharge and oil together over a gentle fire, continually stirring them, and keeping always about half a gallon of water in the vessel : after they have boiled about three hours, a little of the plaster may be taken out, and put into cold water, to try if it be of a proper consistence : when that is the case, the whole may be suffered to cool, and the water well pressed out of it with the hands.—This plaster is generally applied in slight wounds and excoriations of the skin. It keeps the part soft and warm, and defends it from the air, which is all that is necessary in such cases. Its principal use, however, is to serve as a basis for other plasters.

Blistering Plaster.

Take, of Venice turpentine, six ounces; yellow wax, two ounces; Spanish flies, in fine powder, three ounces; powdered mustard, one ounce. Melt the wax, and, while it is warm, add to it the turpentine, taking care not to evaporate it by too much heat. After the turpentine and wax are sufficiently incorporated, sprinkle in the powder, continually stirrring the mass till it be cold —Though this plaster is made in a variety or ways, one seldom meets with it of a proper consistence. When compounded with oils, and other greasy substances, its effects are blunted, and it is apt to run : while pitch and rosin render it too hard, and very inconvenient. When the blistering plaster is not at hand, its place may be supplied by mixing with any soft ointment a sufficient quantity of powdered flies; or by forming them into a paste with flour and vinegar.

Stomach-Plaster.

Take, of gum plaster, half a pound; camphorated oil, an ounce and a half; black pepper (or capsicum, where it can be had), one ounce. Melt the plaster, and mix with it the oil; then sprinkle in the pepper, previously reduced to a fine powder. An ounce or two of this plaster, spread upon soft leather, and applied to the region of the stomach, will be of service in flatulencies arising from hysteric and hypochondriac affections. A little of the expressed oil of mace, or a few drops of the essential oil of mint, may be rubbed upon it before it is applied.—This may supply the place of the anti-hysteric plaster.

Carminative Powder.

Take, of coriander-seed, half an ounce ; ginger, one drachm; nutmegs, half a drachm; fine sugar, a drachm and a half. Reduce them into powder for twelve doses.—This powder is employed for expelling flatulencies arising from indigestion, particularly those to which hysteric and hypochondriac persons are so liable. It may likewise be given in small quantities to children, in their food, when troubled with gripes.

Wood Strawberries for Stone and Gravel.

Fill a large bottle four parts in five with fresh-gathered wood strawberries, and as much Lisbon or loaf sugar as will make it pleasant: fill up with the best brandy; or, if good rum be easier obtained, that will do as well. When it has stood six weeks, it is ready for use. A glass of this cordial will give immediate ease in the severest fit, and a continuance will entirely

cure the patient.   Pour off the first infusion at the expiration
of six weeks, and the same strawberries will make a second
quantity; fill the bottle up with brandy or rum, let it stand
two months, and then strain it off by pressure of the fruit.

Stiffness of the Joints.

Beat quite thin the yolk of a new-laid egg; and add, by a
spoonful at a time, three ounces of pure water; agitating it
continually, that the egg and water may be united.   This is to
be applied to the contracted part, either cold or milk-warm,
rubbing it for a few minutes, three or four times a day.

The Nettle Rash.

A mixture of oil, vinegar, and spirits of wine, applied to the
skin, affords a temporary relief, with regard to the itching ; and
the following simple medicine will complete the cure :—Half a
drachm of calcined magnesia ; take five grains of it, three times
a day, in a glass of lime-water.

Pills for the Sick Head-Ache.

A drachm and a half of Castile soap ; forty grains of rhubarb,
in powder; oil of juniper, twenty drops; syrup of ginger,
enough to form the whole into twenty pills.   The dose is two
or three of these pills, to be taken occasionally.

For an habitual head-ache, arising from costiveness, take,
of soccotrine aloës, one drachm : precipitated sulphur of antimony, and filings of iron, each half a drachm ; and simple
syrup enough to make into 24 pills ; two to be taken night and
morning.

Camphorated, or Paregoric, Elixir.

Take, of flowers of benzoin, half an ounce ; opium, two
drachms.   Infuse in one pound of the volatile aromatic spirit
for four or five days, frequently shaking the bottle; afterwards
strain the elixir.—This is an agreeable and safe way of admi-
nistering opium.   It eases pain, allays tickling coughs, relieves
difficult breathing, and is useful in many disorders of children,
particularly the hooping-cough.   The dose to an adult is
from fifty to a hundred drops.

Acid Elixir of Vitriol.

Take, of the aromatic tincture, one pint ; vitriolic acid, three
ounces.   Mix them gradually, and, after the fæces have subsided, filter the elixir through paper in a glass funnel.—This is
one of the best medicines for hysteric and hypochondriac patients, afflicted with flatulencies arising from relaxation or de-

buity of the stomach and intestines. It will succeed where the most stomachic bitters have no effect. The dose is from thirty to forty drops in a glass of wine or water, or a cup of any bitter infusion, twice or thrice a day. It should be taken when the stomach is empty.

Tincture of Rhubarb.

Take, of rhubarb, two ounces and a half; lesser cardamom-seeds, half an ounce; brandy, two pints. Digest for a week, and strain the tincture. Those who choose to have a vinous tincture of rhubarb may infuse the above ingredients in a bottle of Lisbon wine, adding to it about two ounces of proof spirits. If half an ounce of gentian and a drachm of Virginian snake-root be added to the above ingredients, it will make the bitter tincture of rhubarb.—All these tinctures are designed as stomachics and corroborants as well as purgatives. In weakness of the stomach, indigestion, laxity of the intestines, fluxes colicky, and such-like complaints, they are frequently of great service. The dose is from half a spoonful to three or four spoonfuls, or more, according to the circumstances of the patient, and the purposes it is intended to answer.

Stomachic Elixir.

Take, of gentian root, two ounces; Curaçoa oranges, one ounce; Virginian snake-root, half an ounce. Let the ingredients be bruised, and infused for three or four days in two pints of French brandy; afterwards strain out the elixir.—This is an excellent stomach bitter. In flatulencies, indigestion, want of appetite, and such like complaints, a small glass of it may be taken twice a day. It likewise relieves the gout in the stomach, when taken in a large dose.

Infusion for the Palsy.

Take of horse-radish root shaved, mustard-seed bruised, each four ounces; outer rind of orange-peel, one ounce. Infuse them in two quarts of boiling water, in a close vessel, for twenty-four hours.—In paralytic complaints, a tea-cupful of this stimulating medicine may be taken three or four times a day. It excites the action of the solids, proves diuretic, and, if the patient be kept warm, promotes perspiration.—If two or three ounces of the dried leaves of marsh-trefoil be used instead of the mustard, it will make the antiscorbutic infusion.

English Hypocras.

To make English hypocras, or hippocras, for easing palpitations and tremours of the heart, removing fearful apprehensions, sudden frights and startings, warming a cold stomach, giving rest to wearied limbs, &c., proceed as follows :—Infuse, for a few hours, in about three quarts of good white wine, a pound and a half of loaf-sugar, an ounce of cinnamon, two or three tops of sweet marjoram, and a little long pepper, all slightly beaten in a mortar.   Let the liquor run through a fil-tering-bag, with a grain of musk ; add the juice of a large lemon; give it a gentle heat over the fire ; pour it on the spices again ; and, when it has stood three or four days, strain it through a filtering-bag, and bottle it for use.—This is an excellent cordial to refresh and enliven the spirits.   If a red colour be wished for, the hypocras may be made of any required hue, by substi-tuting red for white wine ; or adding juice of elder-berries, or mulberries, syrup of clove-gilliflowers, cochineal, &c.

Syrup for Coughs, Spitting of Blood, &c.

Take six ounces of comfrey-roots, and twelve handfuls of plantain-leaves ; cut and beat them well, strain out the juice, and with an equal weight of sugar boil it up to a syrup.

Dropsy.

Boil three handfuls of the tops of green broom in a gallon of spring water, and take off the scum as long as any continues to rise ; then, after letting it stand till cold, pour the broom and decoction together into an earthen jug, and keep it closely covered for use.   Take, night and morning, a large spoonful of unbruised mustard-seed ; and, immediately after swallowing it, drink half a pint of the broom-water.   This remedy ought to be continued for some months ; and it will seldom fail to prove effectual, when the disease is not in its last stage.

Cure for inflamed or sore Eyes.

Get some clay that has a blue vein, and separate the vein from the rest of the clay.   Wash it clean ; then soften, and work it into a sort of ointment, with strong white-wine vinegar. Spread it on a piece of linen ; cover it over with part of the same cloth, and bind it over the eyes every night, for a fort-night, on going to bed.   At the same time, the application being a repellent, a little gentle physic should be taken.   Nor-thamptonshire abounds with proper clay for the purpose.

This has been known to restore sight, and perform a cure after the persons afflicted had been for some time quite blind.

Balm of Gilead Oil.

Put loosely, into a bottle of any size, as many balm of Gilead flowers as will come up to a third part of its height ; then nearly fill up the bottle with good sweet oil ; shake it a little, occasionally, and let it infuse a day or two ; it is then fit for use. If closely stopped, it will keep for years, and will be the better for keeping. When about half used, the bottle may be again filled up with oil, and well shaken; and, in two or three days, it will be as good as at first. Cuts and bruises of the skin are completely cured in a few days, and sometimes in a few hours, by this oil. It is excellent for all green wounds, burns, bruises, scalds, &c.

Cures for the Cramp.

Bathe the parts afflicted every morning and evening with the powder of amber; and take inwardly, at the same time, on going to bed at night, for eight or ten nights together, half a spoonful, in from a gill to half a pint of white wine.—For sudden attacks of the cramp in the legs, relief may be instantly obtained by stretching out the limb affected, and elevating the heel as much as possible, till the toes bend backward toward the shin. This, also, may be considered as an infallible remedy, when only in the leg :—A hot brick, in a flannel bag, placed for the feet, at the bottom of the bed, all night; and friction with the hand, warm flannels, coarse cloths, or the flesh-brush, well applied, to restore the free circulation of the blood in the contracted part, are all recommended as efficacious expedients for relieving this terrible pain, as well as for preventing its return. In Italy, as an infallible cure, a new cork is cut in thin slices, and a narrow ribbon passed through the centre of them, and tied round the affected limb, laying the corks flat on the flesh : this, while thus worn, is said to prevent any return of the cramp.

Receipts for the Rheumatism.

Take of garlic two cloves, of ammoniac one drachm; blend them, by bruising, together; make them into two or three bolusses, with fair water; and swallow them one at night and one in the morning. Drink, while taking this medicine, sassafras tea, made very strong, so as to have the teapot filled with chips. This is generally found to banish the rheumatism, and even contractions of the joints, in a few times taking.

Negro Remedy for the Rheumatism.

Frequently rub the part affected with a mixture of Cayenne pepper and strong spirits.

To quench Thirst, where Drink is improper.

Pour vinegar into the palms of the hands, and snuff it up the nostrils, and wash the mouth with the same

Cure for the Ague.

Take thirty grains of snake-root; forty of wormwood; half an ounce of the best powder of Jesuits' bark; and half a pint of red Port wine. Put the whole into a bottle, and shake it well together. It should be taken in four equal quantities, the first thing in the morning, and the last thing at night, when the fit is quite over. The quantity should be made into eight parts for a child, and the bottle should always be well shaken before taking it.

This medicine should be continued some time after the ague and fever have left.

To stop Retching.

Swallow a tea-spoonful of Quincey's bitter stomach-tincture, sweetened with syrup of oranges or quinces.

Another Way.

Squeeze the juice of a lemon into a large cup, and mix with it just as much salt of tartar as will blunt the acid, and render it insipid. Take a spoonful, and repeat it till the retching ceases, and, if during the ebullition, so much the better. The same mixture, diluted with simple cinnamon-water, and taken every three hours, is good for fevers.

Pills for a Cough

Take, of Ruffus's pill, four scruples; storax pill, one scruple; tartar of vitriol in fine powder, and squills in powder, ten grains of each; chemical oil of camomile, ten drops; syrup of saffron, enough to make it up. Make into twenty-four pills, and take two or three every third night. On the intermediate days take a tea-spoonful of the following tincture every four hours, washing it down with three table-spoonfuls of the pectoral mixture.

Take conserve of roses and heps, each two ounces; pectoral syrup and syrup of violets, of each half an ounce; spermaceti, three drachms: oil of almonds, six drachms; confection of alkermes, half an ounce; genuine balm of Gilead, two drachms; true oil of cinnamon, six drops; acid elixir of vitriol, two drachms. Mix well together.

For the pectoral mixture, take febrifuge elixir, four ounces; pectoral decoction, a quart; balsamic syrup, three ounces; Mynsicht's elixir of vitriol, three drachms, or as much as will make it gratefully acid.

Stomach-Plaster for a Cough.

Take an ounce each of bees' wax, Burgundy pitch, and rosin; melt them together in a pipkin, and stir in three quarters of an ounce of common turpentine, and half an ounce of oil of mace. Spread it on a piece of sheep's leather, grate some nutmeg over, and apply it quite warm to the pit of the stomach.

A Powder for Shortness of Breath.

Take an ounce each of carraway-seeds and aniseeds, half an ounce of liquorice, a nutmeg, an ounce of prepared steel, and two ounces of double-refined sugar; reduce the whole to a fine powder, and take as much as will lie on a shilling every morning fasting, and the same quantity at five in the afternoon Exercise must be used while taking this medicine.

Remedy for the Hooping-Cough.

Take two ounces each of conserve of roses, raisins of the sun stoned, brown sugar-candy, and two pennyworth of spirits of sulphur; beat them up into a conserve, and take a tea-spoonful night and morning.

Electuary for Falling Fits, Hysterics, and St. Vitus's Dance.

Take six drachms of powdered Peruvian bark, two drachms of pulverized Virginian snake-root, and syrup of piony sufficient to make it up into a soft electuary. One drachm of this electuary, after due evacuations, should be given to grown persons, and a less dose to those who are younger, every morning and evening for three or four months, and then repeated for three or four days before the change and full of the moon.

Calamine Cerate.

Take of olive oil one pint; calamine prepared, and yellow wax, of each half a pound. Melt the wax with the oil; and, as soon as the mixture begins to thicken, mix with it the calamine, and stir the cerate until it be cold.—This composition is formed upon the plan of that which is commonly known by the name of *Turner's Cerate,* and which is an exceedingly good application in burns, and in cutaneous ulcerations and excoriations, from whatever cause.

Syrup of Angelica-Root for the Influenza, &c.

Boil down gently, for three hours, a handful of angelica-root, n a quart of water; then strain it off, and add liquid Narbonne or best virgin honey, sufficient to make it into a balsam or syrup; and take two tea-spoonfuls every night and morning, as well as several times in the day. If there be any hoarseness, or sore throat, add a few nitre drops.

Syrup for the Scurvy, King's Evil, Leprosy, and all Impurities of the Blood.

Boil together, in two gallons of soft water, over a slow fire, till one half is reduced, half a pound of angelica-roots sliced; four ounces each of the leaves of male speedwell or fluellen, the roots of comfrey and of fennel, both sliced; three ounces of Winter's bark; and two ounces of bark of elder. Strain off the decoction into an earthen pan, and let it stand all night to settle. In the morning, pour the liquor carefully off from the sediment; and dissolve, in the clear liquid, three pounds of treble-refined sugar, and two pounds of virgin honey; then simmer the whole into a thin syrup. Take a large tea-cupful night and morning; or, in some cases, morning, noon, and night; adding to each dose, at the time of taking it, a small tea-spoonful of Dr. Huxam's celebrated essence of antimony, which greatly heightens and improves the virtue of the former medicine.

Excellent Worm-Powder.

Take a quarter of an ounce each of rhubarb, wormseed, senna, and burnt hartshorn, all finely powdered, and well mixed together. The dose, for a child ten or twelve years of age, is as much as will lie on a shilling; to be taken in treacle, or any liquid, the last thing at night, or the first in the morning, for three nights or mornings successively. Though this will often prove sufficient, it may safely be repeated, whenever there seems the least necessity for it.

Remedy for the Gout.

Mix two ounces of finely-pounded gum guaiacum, with three quarts of the best rum, in a glass vessel; stir and shake it from time to time. When it has remained for ten days properly exposed to the sun, distil the liquor through cotton or strong blotting paper, and bottle the whole, corking it up tight. The more is made of it at a time the better, as it improves by keeping. The dose is a table-spoonful every morning fasting. The bottles should be corked as closely as possible; but should not be quite filled, lest the fermentation of the liquor should make them burst. This medicine must not be made with brandy, or any other spirit but good genuine rum.

Edinburgh Yellow Balsam.

Gather, on a dry day, a pound of elder-flowers, but let neither the stems nor green be in them, and mix them with four pounds of May butter, in a close well-glazed vessel. Put them in the sun by day, and near the fire by night. Keep them thus till the green broom blossoms; then get a pound of the blossom, and mix them well together. Keep it, as before directed, for five or six weeks; then warm it well, but do not boil it, and wring it all out in a cloth quite dry. It is good for inflammation, pain, or stitch, rubbing the part affected before the fire with a small bit of balsam. If taken inwardly, swallow five or six pills of it rolled in sugar.

German Styptic Powder.

Reduce to fine powder two drachms each of Peruvian bark and loaf-sugar, one drachm of cinnamon, and half a drachm or lapis hæmatites, or blood-stone. Take a tea-spoonful of it every hour, or oftener, according to the urgency of the case and its effects, in balm or camomile tea.

Cream for Consumption.

Boil, in three pints of water, till half-wasted, one ounce each of eringo root, pearl barley, sago, and rice; strain it off, put a table-spoonful of the mixture into a coffee-cup of boiling milk, so as to render it of the consistence of cream, and sweeten with loaf or Lisbon sugar to the taste.

Fox-Glove Juice, for Deafness.

Bruise, in a marble mortar, the flowers, leaves, and stalks, of fresh fox-glove; mix the juice with double the quantity of brandy, and keep it for use. The herb flowers in June, and the juice will thus keep good till the return of that season. The method of using it is, to drop one drop in the ear every night; and then moisten a bit of lint with a little of the juice put it also in the ear, and take it out next morning, till the cure be completed.

Decoction of Logwood, for the Flux.

Boil three ounces of the shavings or chips of logwood in four pints of water, till half the liquor is evaporated. Two or three ounces of simple cinnamon-water may be added to this decoction. In fluxes of the belly, where stronger astringents are improper, a tea-cupful of this may be taken with advantage three or four times a day.

Electuary for the Dysentery.

Take, of the Japonic confection, two ounces; Locatelli's balsam, one ounce; rhubarb, in powder, half an ounce; syrup of marshmallows, enough to make an electuary. This is a very safe and useful medicine for the purpose expressed in the tittle.   About the bulk of a nutmeg should be taken twice or thrice a day, as the symptoms and constitution may require.

Remedy for preventing Infectious Diseases in Hospitals, Prisons, &c.

Put some hot sand in a small pipkin, and place in it a tea-cup with half an ounce of strong vitriolic acid; when a little warm, add to it half an ounce of purified nitre-powder; stir the mixture with a slip of glass, or the small end of a tobacco-pipe. This should be repeated from time to time, the pipkin being set over a lamp.   This has so often been tried with success in infirmaries, gaols, &c., at land, and in hospital and other ships, that it is known to possess a specific power on putrid conta gion, gaol fevers, &c.

Conserve of Hedge Mustard, for the Cure of Asthma.

Beat, in a mortar, equal quantities of the leaves of hedge mustard and virgin honey, to make a thin conserve.   Italian honey is best for asthmatic persons, but any clean and pure kind of honey will generally prove effectual.   It may be taken at discretion, according to the state of the disease, and the benefit experienced.   Hedge mustard, both seed and herb, is considered as warm, dry, attenuating, opening, and expecto rant.   It is vulnerary, causes plentiful spitting, and makes the breathing easier.   Externally, it is recommended in occult can-cers, and hard swellings of the breast.

Cordial Electuary.

Boil a pint of the best honey; and, having carefully taken off all the scum, put into the clarified liquid a bundle of hyssop which has been well bruised previously to tying it up, and let them boil together till the honey tastes strongly of the hyssop. Then strain out the honey very hard, and put into it a quarter of an ounce each of powdered liquorice-root and aniseed, half that quantity of pulverized elecampane and angelica-roots, and one pennyweight each of pepper and ginger.   Let the whole boil together a short time, being well stirred all the while.   Then pour it into a gallipot, or small jar, and continue stirring till quite cold.   Keep it covered for use ; and whenever troubled with straightness at the stomach, or shortness of breath, take some of the electuary on a bruised stick of liquorice, which will very soon give relief.

Red Cabbage, dressed the Dutch Way, for Cold at the Breast.

Cut a red cabbage small, and boil it in water till tender: then drain it dry, put it in a stew-pan with some oil and butter, a small quantity of water and vinegar, an onion cut small, pepper and salt, and let it simmer till all the liquor is wasted. It may then be eaten at pleasure, either hot or cold, and is considered to be an excellent pectoral medicine, as well as a pleasant food.

Boluses for Rheumatism, and Contractions of the Joints.

Bruise four cloves of garlic with two drachms of gum ammoniac, and make them into six boluses with spring-water. Take one every morning and evening, drinking plentifully of strong sassafras tea, at least twice a day, while using this medicine.

Essence for Head-Ache, and other violent Pains.

Put two pounds of true French spirit of wine into a strong bottle, with two ounces of roche alum in very fine powder, four ounces of camphor cut very small, half an ounce of essence of lemon, and four ounces of strong volatile spirit of sal ammoniac. Stop the bottle close, and shake it three or four times a day for five or six days. The way to use it is to rub the hand with a little of it, and hold it hard on the part affected till it be quite dry. If the pain be not quite relieved, it must be repeated twice or three times. This essence, plentifully applied as above directed, will very often remove pains of almost all descriptions.

Analeptic Pills.

Mix twenty grains each of Dr. James's powder, Rufus's pill, and gum guaiacum, with any syrup, and liquorice powder or flour, to make the whole into twenty pills. Twenty grains of rhubarb may be put in, instead of Rufus's pill, if the small quantity of aloes therein contained should prove heating.

Linseed Cough-Syrup.

Boil one ounce of linseed in a quart of water, till half wasted; add six ounces of moist sugar, two ounces of sugar-candy, half an ounce of Spanish liquorice, and the juice of a large lemon. Let the whole slowly simmer together till it becomes of a syrupy consistence; when cold, put to it two table-spoonfuls of the best old rum.

Vegetable Syrup.

To four beer quarts of good rich sweet wort add half a pound of sassafras, an ounce of sarsaparilla, and four ounces of wild carrot. Boil them gently for three quarters of an hour, frequently putting the ingredients down with a ladle; then strain the same through a cloth. To each beer quart of this liquor put one pound and a half of thick treacle. Boil it gently for three quarters of an hour, skimming it all the time; put it into a pan, and cover it till cold; then bottle it for use. Be careful not to cork it too tight. A small tea-cupful should be taken night and morning, which must be persevered in some time ; a greater or less quantity may be taken, according to the state of the stomach.

The old Receipt for Daffy's Elixir.

Take elecampane-roots, sliced liquorice, coriander and anise seeds, senna, oriental guaiacum, and carraway-seeds, each two ounces, and one pound of raisins stoned. Infuse them four days in three quarts of aqua-vitæ, or white aniseed-water The largest dose is four spoonfuls, to be taken at night. One ounce of rhubarb, two ounces of manna, and one more of guaiacum, may be added.

SIMPLE RECIPES FOR STINGS, BITES, BURNS, SCALDS, AND SLIGHT WOUNDS.

Bees, wasps, hornets, gnats, harvest-bugs, bugs, vipers, and adders, are the principal animals of this country by whose sting or bite we are molested.

The sting of the animal must be taken out, if left in the wound.

The best applications to the wound are any of the following herbs, or some elder-flowers, bruised and laid upon the place. The herb robert, a species of geranium, or crane's bill, or chervil, or parsley. Spirits of hartshorn, applied directly, is often an effectual remedy for the stings or bites of these animals.

If there is much inflammation, flannels wrung out of a strong decoction of elder-flowers, and applied warm, afford the speediest relief. To this may be added a spoonful of spirits of hartshorn.

Or the part affected may be covered with a poultice, made of the crum of bread, milk, and honey.

Bathing the legs of a person stung, repeatedly, in warm water, will afford relief.

It will be prudent to retrench a little of the customary food, especially at night, and to drink an infusion of elder-flowers, with the addition of a little nitre.

Oil, if applied immediately after the sting, sometimes prevents the appearance of any swelling, and thence the pains attending it.

Pounded parsley is one of the most availing pplications in such accidents.

Burns or Scalds.

When a burn or scald is trifling, and occasions no blister it is sufficient to put a compress of several folds of soft linen upon it, dipped in cold water, and to renew it every quarter of an hour till the pain is entirely removed.

When a burn or scald blisters, a compress of fine linen, spread over with the pomatum given below, should be applied to it, and changed twice a day.

If the skin is burnt through, and the flesh under it injured, the same pomatum may be applied; but, instead of a compress of linen, it should be spread upon a piece of soft lint, to be applied exactly over it, and this covered with a slip of tne simple plaster, No. 1, given below, which any body may easily prepare; or No. 2, if that should be preferred.

For an extensive burn or scald, skilful advice should be immediately applied to, as it always endangers the life of the sufferer.

Pomatum.

Take an ounce of the ointment called nutritum, the whole yolk of a small egg, or the half of a large one, and mix them well together. The nutritum may be easily made by rubbing two drachms of ceruse (white lead), half an ounce of vinegar, and three ounces of common oil, well together.

If the ingredients for making nutritum are not at hand, to make the pomatum, one part of wax should be melted with eight parts of oil, and the yolk of an egg added to two ounces of this mixture.

A still more simple application, and sooner prepared, is to beat up an egg, white and yolk, with two spoonfuls of sweet oil, free from any rankness. When the pain of the burn and all its other symptoms have nearly subsided, it is sufficient to apply the plaster, No. 2.

Plaster, No. 1.

Melt four ounces of white wax; add to it, if made in winter, two spoonfuls of oil; if in summer, at most one, or it may be quite omitted. Dip into this slips of moderately thin linen, and let them dry; or spread it thin and evenly over them,

Plaster, No. 2

To half a 'pouna of oil of roses put a quarter of a pound

of red lead, and two ounces of vinegar. Boil them together nearly to the consistence of a plaster; then dissolve in the liquid three quarters of an ounce of yellow wax, and one drachm of camphire, stirring the whole about well. Take it off the fire, and spread it upon sheets or slips of paper of any size that may be most convenient.

Slight Wounds.

When simple wounds bleed much, lint dipped in vinegar or spirits of turpentine may be pressed upon the surface for a few minutes, and retained by a moderately tight bandage; but, if the blood spirts out in jets, it shews that an artery is wounded, and it must be held very firmly until a surgeon arrives. But when the blood seems to flow equally from every part of a wound, and there is no reason therefore to suppose that any considerable vessel is wounded, it may be permitted to bleed while the dressings are preparing. The edges of the wound are then to be gently pressed together, and retained by straps of sticking plaster, made as directed below.

These may remain on for three or four days, unless the sore becomes painful, or the matter smells offensive, in which case the straps of plaster must be taken off, the parts washed clean with warm water, and fresh slips of plaster applied, nicely adjusted to keep the wound together. The slips must be laid over the wound crossways, and reach several inches beyond each side of it, in order to hold the parts firmly together. By keeping the limb or part very still, abstaining from strong liquors, taking only light mild food, and keeping the bowels open, all simple wounds may be easily healed in this manner; but poultices, greasy salves, or filling the wound with lint, will have an opposite effect.

Even ragged or torn wounds may be drawn together and healed by sticking plaster, without any other salves or medicines.

A broken shin, or slight ruffling of the skin, may be covered with lint dipped in equal parts of vinegar and brandy, and left to stick on unless the place inflames, and then weak goulard is the best remedy.

Common cuts may be kept together by a strip of the sticking plaster, or with a piece of fine linen rag or thread bound round them.

The rag applied next to a cut, or wound of any kind, should be always of white linen; but calico, or coloured rags, will do quite as well for outward bandages.

Important wounds should always be put under the care of a skilful surgeon.

The Sticking Plaster.

Melt three ounces of diachylon with half an ounce of rosin, and, when cooled to about the thickness of treacle, spread it upon a piece of smooth soft linen.

Bruises.

Different external and internal remedies are applicable in contusions. When the accident has occurred in a slight degree, and there has been no general shock which might produce an internal soreness or contusion, external applications may be sufficient. They should consist of such things as are adapted, first, to attenuate and resolve the effused and stagnant blood, which shews itself in the blackness of the part affected soon after the contusion, changing successively brown, yellow, and grey, in proportion as the suffusion decreases, till at last the skin recovers its colour, the blood being gradually dissolved and taken in again by the vessels. Secondly, the medicines should be such as are qualified to restore the tone and to recover the strength of the affected vessels.

The best application is vinegar, diluted, if very sharp, with twice as much warm water. Folds of linen are to be dipped into this, and wrapped round the bruised part, or laid upon it as the nature of the place admits of. These folds must be remoistened every two hours on the first day.

Parsley, chervil, and houseleek-leaves, lightly pounded, have also been used with success : and they are preferable to vinegar when a wound is joined to a bruise. The poultice given below may also be used with advantage.

It is a common practice to apply spirituous liquors, such as brandy, and arquebusade water, on such occasions; but a long abuse ought not to be established by prescription. These liquids, which coagulate the blood instead of resolving it, are truly pernicious, notwithstanding they are sometimes used without any visible disadvantage, on very slight occasions.

It is a still more pernicious practice to apply greasy plasters to bruises, or those made of resins, gums, earths, &c. These are always hurtful, and many instances have occurred of slight bruises being aggravated into gangrenes by such plasters, which would have been well in three or four days by the economy of Nature, if left to herself.

Severe external contusions, or any internal ones, should be put under the care of medical skill.

Poultice.

Take four ounces of crums of bread, a pinch of elder flowers between the fingers and thumb, the same quantity of camomile and of St. John's wort. Boil them into a poultice in equal quantities of vinegar and water.

If fomentations should be thought preferable, take the same herbs, put them into a pint and a half of boiling water, and let them infuse some minutes. Add a pint of vinegar to this; let flannels or other woollen cloths be dipped into it, wrung out, and applied to the part affected.

A still better poultice may be prepared of linseed flour, and the dregs of ale or porter barrels, boiled slightly. It always keeps soft from the oiliness of the seeds, and the yesty deposit of the malt liquor is both cooling and sweetening.

Benumbed or frozen Limbs.

It sometimes happens in severe weather that persons much exposed to the cold have their hands and feet benumbed, or even quite frozen.

If a person thus pierced with the cold attempts to walk about, which seems a natural and obvious means to get warm, or still more if he attempts to warm the parts that have been frozen, his case proves irrecoverable. Intolerable pains are the consequence, which are soon followed by a dangerous mortification.

The only certain remedy in these cases is to convey the patient into some place where it does not freeze, but is very moderately warm, and there to apply snow, if it be at hand, continually to the parts affected. If snow is not to be had, they should be washed incessantly, but very gently (as all friction at this juncture would be dangerous), in ice-water, as the ice thaws in the room. By this application the patient will be sensible of a gradual return of feeling to the limbs, and that they begin to recover their motion. In this state he may safely be moved into a rather warmer place, and drink some cups of the infusion given below.

The danger of attempting to relieve such accidents by heat, and the good effects of cold water, are obvious from the commonest experience If apples, potatoes, meat, &c., when frozen, are put into cold water, they recover their former state; but if put into warm water, or a hot place, they become rotten, which is one kind of gangrene or mortification.

In very severe weather, when a person is exposed to the cold

long together, it often proves fatal, in consequence of its con
gealing the blood, and forcing it too thick up to the brain; so
that the patient dies of a kind of apoplexy, which is preceded
by drowsiness. A person must therefore use his utmost endeavours upon such an occasion to keep himself awake, as sleep,
if indulged, would prove his death.

The remedies for such a case are the same as for frozen
limbs. Persons have been revived by them, who had remained in the snow, or been exposed to the freezing air for five or
six days, and discovered no signs of life.

Infusion.

Pour three pints of boiling water upon a pinch and a half of
elder-flowers, taken between the fingers and the thumb. After standing some time, strain it, and dissolve in it three ounces
of honey.

Kibes or Chilblains.

These complaints are principally felt on the extreme parts,
arising from two causes: that the circulation being weaker at
the extremities than elsewhere, the effect of such causes as impair it must be the most felt there, and that these parts are
more exposed than any other to outward impressions.

The skin of the hands, as well as that of the whole body,
may be strengthened by the habit of washing or bathing in
cold water; and children who have been early inured to this
habit are seldom so much troubled with chilblains as others.

It would give children no pain, at the beginning of autumn,
to dip their hands in cold water, and keep them in it for
some moments; and, when this habit is once contracted, it will
be easy to continue it through the winter. They may also be
habituated to plunge their feet into cold water twice or thrice
a week; and this method, which might be less adapted for
grown persons, who have not been accustomed to it, cannot be
objectionable for such children as have, to whom it will be
generally useful and salutary. It will also be proper that
children should not bring their hands close to the fire, to avoid
the too speedy succession of heat and cold.

The most troublesome itching is assuaged by plunging the
hands into cold water. The effect of snow is still more speedy.
The hands should be gently and often rubbed with it for a
considerable time; they grow hot and very red for some moments, but entire ease quickly succeeds.

Persons who have extremely delicate and sensible skins do
not find the benefit of this application; it seems too active for
them. and affects the skin like a common blistering plaster.

When this is the case, or a child wants courage to go through it, or any other complaint exists which may be aggravated by this very cold application, some other must be substituted. One of the best is to wear gloves made of any smooth skin, day and night, without putting them off, which seldom fails to cure the disorder in some days. If it should fail, the hands may be gently fomented or moistened, several times a day, with some decoction rather more than warm, which should be both dissolving and emollient. Such is the decoction of scraped horse-radish, the efficacy of which is still further increased by adding a sixth part of vinegar. Another decoction is given below, which is of great efficacy, but it dies the hands yellow for a few days. As soon as the hands are taken out of these decoctions, they must be kept from the air by gloves.

When the disorder is removed by the use of these bathings, which make the skin supple and soft, it should be strengthened afterwards by washing it with a little camphorated brandy, diluted with an equal quantity of water.

Those who are troubled with obstinate chilblains should always be forbidden the use of strong liquors.

Decoction.

Put a pinch, between the fingers and thumb, both of the leaves of sow-bread, and the tops of camomile, into an earthen vessel, with half an ounce of soap, and the same of sal ammoniac, and pour upon them three pints of boiling water.

Whitlows.

As soon as the disorder is apparent, the finger affected is to be plunged into water a little more than warm, or the steam of boiling water may be applied to it; and, by doing one of these things almost constantly for the first day, the complaint has been often dispersed. But unfortunately it is generally supposed that such slight attacks can have only slight consequences, whence they are apt to be neglected till the disorder has increased considerably. In this state no time should be lost in resorting to skilful advice, as the danger of these small tumours is much greater than is usually supposed.

Thorns, Splinters, &c.

To run prickles or thorns, such as those of roses, thistles, chesnuts, &c., or little splinters of wood, bone, &c., into the hands, feet, or legs, is a very common accident, and, provided any such substance is immediately extracted, is seldom attended with any bad consequences. But, the more certainly to prevent any such, a compress of linen dipped in warm water may be applied to the part, or it may be bathed a little while in warm water.

If the thorn or splinter cannot be extracted directly, or if any part of it be left in, it causes an inflammation, and nothing but timely precaution will prevent its coming to an abscess. A plaster of shoemaker's wax spread upon leather draws these wounds remarkably well. When it is known that any part of it remains, an expert surgeon would open the place and take it out; but if it is unobserved, as will sometimes happen, when the substance is very small, till the inflammation begins, and no advice be at once procured, the steam of warm water should be applied to it first, and then a poultice of crum of bread and milk, with a few drops of Peruvian balsam.

It is absolutely necessary that the injured part should be kept in the easiest posture, and as still as possible.

If this does not soon succeed, good advice must be applied to without delay, as an accident of this kind neglected, or improperly treated, may be the occasion of losing a limb.

In this and all cases of inflammation, a forbearance from animal food and fermented liquors is always advisable.

Warts and Corns.

Warts may be safely destroyed by tying them closely round the bottom with a silk thread, or a strong flaxen thread waxed. Or they may be dried away by some moderately corroding application, such as the milky juice of fig-leaves, of chelidonium, (swallow wort), or of spurge. Warts may also be destroyed by rubbing them with the inside of bean-shells. But these corrosives can only be procured in summer; and persons who have very delicate thin skins should not use them, as they may occasion a painful swelling. Instead of them a little vinegar, impregnated with as much salt as it will dissolve, is very proper. A plaster may also be made of sal ammoniac and some galbanum, which, well kneaded together and applied, seldom fails of destroying them.

The most general or only cause of corns is shoes either too hard and stiff, or too small.

The cure consists in softening the corns by repeated washing and soaking the feet in pretty hot water ; then cutting the corn, when softened, with a sharp penknife, without wounding the flesh, and afterwards applying a leaf of houseleek, ground ivy, or purslain, dipped in vinegar, upon the place. Or, instead of these leaves, they may be dressed every day with a plaster of simple diachylon, or of gum ammoniacum softened in vinegar.

The increase or return of corns can only be prevented by avoiding the cause that produces them.

VARIOUS DIETS AND DRINKS FOR THE SICK.

Herb Tea.

Herb tea should always be made with a proper proportion of the herb. When the tea is of a proper strength, the herb should be taken out, as it becomes nauseous by long infusion. These teas are best used fresh.

Water-Gruel made in the quickest Manner.

Mix a spoonful of ground oatmeal very smooth with as much hot water as will just make it liquid, then pour upon it, gradually, a pint of boiling water, stirring it all the time to keep it smooth. Then pour it from one basin to another till it is cool enough to drink. Water-gruel is very smooth and good in this manner; and, from being prepared in a few minutes, may be particularly useful when gruel is wanted in a hurry, for assisting the operation of physic.

A cooling Drink, No. 1.

Wash and cleanse two ounces of whole barley in hot water, then boil it in five pints of water till the barley opens, with a quarter of an ounce of cream of tartar. Strain it, and add nothing more to it.

A cooling Drink, No. 2.

Bruise three ounces of the freshest sweet almonds and an ounce of gourd melon-seeds in a marble mortar, adding to them, by a little at a time, a pint of water, and then strain it through a piece of linen. Bruise the remainder of the almonds and seeds again, with another pint of water added as before; then strain it, and repeat this process a third time. After this, pour all the liquor upon the bruised mass, stir it well, and strain it off finally. Half an ounce of sugar may safely be bruised with the almonds and seeds at first, though some weakly persons think it too heating. Delicate persons may be allowed a little orange-water in it.

A Currant Drink.

Put a pound of the best ripe red currants, clean picked, into a stone bottle; then mix three spoonfuls of the newest purest ale yeast with six pints of hot water; pour this upon the currants; stop the bottle close till the liquor ferments; then give it as much vent as is necessary, keep it warm, and it will ferment for about three days. Taste it at the end of two days, to try whether it is become pleasant. As soon as it is, run it through a strainer, and bottle it off. It will be ready to drink in five or six days.

Flummery, or Sowins.

To two spoonfuls of oatmeal put a quart of water, and let it stand till it begins to be sour; then stir it up, put it into a saucepan, and set it over a quick fire. When it is quite hot and beginning to rise, brew it to and fro with the ladle, to keep it from boiling. Do this for five or six minutes, and then take it off the fire, for it is prepared to the proper degree.

This is sometimes eaten with milk, cream, or other mixtures; but those who eat it to open, cleanse, assist digestion, and remove offensive matter from the stomach, eat it with bread only, as it thus more powerfully removes obstructions of the breast, helps the natural heat, strengthens the stomach, cools the body, opens the passages, and creates a cheerful active disposition.

This gruel is particularly to be recommended in hot seasons and climates, as an excellent wholesome breakfast. It is also favourable in putrid disorders.

Boniclapper.

Boniclapper is milk which has stood till it has become of a pleasant sourish taste, and of a thick slippery substance. In very hot weather this will be in about twenty-four hours from the time of its being milked, but longer in proportion as the weather is colder. If put into vessels which have been used for milk to be soured in, it will change the sooner. It must always be new milk that is used for this purpose.

Boniclapper is an excellent food both for healthy and unhealthy, particularly for all who are troubled with any kind of stoppages; for it powerfully opens the breast and passages, is itself easy of digestion, and helps to digest all hard or sweeter foods. It also cools and cleanses the whole body, renders it brisk and lively, and is very efficacious in quenching thirst.

No sort of milk-meat or other spoon-meat is so proper and beneficial for consumptive and languishing people as this, eaten with bread only. For, however debilitated, this sort of food will be light and easy on the stomach, when new sweet creamy milk will not.

It may possibly be objected that this soured milk will not agree with the stomach, nor be pleasant to the palate. This may be true at first, for Nature seems to dislike changes although for the better. A little custom and use, however, will make it not only familiar, but pleasant, to the stomach and palate · and those who have neither patience nor wisdom to submit to a little inconvenience will never have an opportunity of knowing the true intrinsic virtue of any thing, nor its nature and operation. There is no reason in nature why people should dislike this soured food ; and most people desire it in some way or other, more especially such as have disordered stomachs and weak heats ; for the assistance of which, vinegar, verjuice, the juice of lemons and oranges, and many other sharp keen juices, have been ordered, and mixed with food, with evident advantage.

Beef Tea.

To half a pound of very nice lean juicy beef, sliced into small thin pieces, pour half a pint of boiling water. This tea may be used when cool enough to drink, without boiling ; or it may have one boil for about two minutes. A little salt may be added.

Animal Jelly.

Take shin of beef or knuckle of mutton, and to every pound of either allow a pint and a half of water ; or chicken, and allow a pound to a pint of water. Let this stew till the juices are fairly drawn from the meat, but no longer, as this would destroy their nutritious qualities, convert them to glue, and render them indigestible. A little salt should be added. When cold, take off all the fat, and use the jelly clear of the settlement at the bottom. Warm no more at a time than the patient is to take, as repeated warmings spoil it. The best way to warm it is to set the cup into boiling water. No two kinds of meat should be used together.

Jelly of Feet, or Shanks.

To three quarts of water allow two cow-heels, or three calf's feet, or five sheep's feet, or fifteen shanks of mutton. Let these stew no longer than to draw a good jelly, which, with these proportions, may be done without excessive doing. When cold, take off the fat, and clear it from the settlement at the bottom ; it may be cleared with whites of eggs, and run through a jelly-bag, or used without it at pleasure. Orange or lemon juice, or wine, and some sugar, may be added, as is suitable for the patient. Wines should never be given to invalids without the express permission of their medical attendant, as they are dangerous medicines, and do more harm than good, unless used with great discretion. Any kind of spirits should still less be given, as they are of a much more dangerous nature than wines.

Jelly of Hartshorn-Shavings, or Isinglass.

To a pint of water allow two ounces and a half of hartshorn-shavings, or an ounce and a half of islinglass. Stew them to a good jelly, without overdoing it. Clear and flavour it so above, as most approved for the patient.

Directions for broth will be found under the article Broth.

Orange jelly, imperial water, lemonade, orangeade, and orgeat, will be found under their respective heads.

Orange, Lemon, or Vinegar Whey.

Set as much milk upon the fire as is wanted for the occasion, and, when it is ready to boil, put in Seville orange or lemon-juice, or vinegar, enough to turn it to a clear whey. Let it stand some minutes, and then pour it off. If too acid, a little warm water may be added.

These all promote perspiration.

Cream-of-Tartar Whey.

To a pint of milk, when ready to boil, strew in gradually two tea-spoonfuls of cream of tartar, and keep stirring it till it is clear; then strain it.

This whey is very cooling, and is a powerful diuretic.

Mustard Whey.

To a pint of milk, when ready to boil, scatter in flour of mustard slowly, until it curdles. Let it stand two or three minutes, and then strain it off.

This whey warms the stomach, and promotes perspiration. It is good after much fatigue, and exposure to wet and cold, when the appetite is *not* craving for food.

Treacle Posset.

Add two table-spoonfuls of treacle to a pint of milk, when ready to boil, stirring it briskly over the fire until it curdles. Strain it off after standing two or three minutes.

This whey promotes perspiration and children take it readily.

Buttermilk.

New buttermilk is cooling and moist, the best remedy for a hot thirsty stomach, good for a hoarseness, excellent in con sumptioons, hectic fevers, ulcers of the kidneys, and the dry scurvy, and for constipated bodies. When stale and sour it is not so beneficial, but is then serviceable to such as are troubled with great perspirations.

Whey.

Whey is good for hot constitutions : it quenches thirst, pro-motes sleep, is the most relaxing and diluting of all drinks, even dissolving and carrying off salts; and is a powerful remedy in the hot scurvy.

Herb Porridge, No. 1.

Take elder-buds, nettle-tops, clivers, and water-cresses, or smallage ; and, in proportion to the quantity of these, mix a proper quantity of oatmeal and water, and set it upon the fire. When it is just ready to boil, put in the herbs, cut or uncut, as most approved ; and, when again ready to boil, ladle it to and fro, to keep it from boiling ; and it must never be suffered to boil.   Do this for seven or eight minutes; then take it off the fire, and let it stand a while.   It may be eaten either with the herbs, or strained, as preferred, and should not be eaten warmer than milk from the cow.   A little butter, salt, and bread, may be added when eaten.

Observation.

This is an excellent cleansing kind of porridge, far beyond what is commonly made.

Herb Porridge, No. 2.

Set some water and oatmeal on a quick fire, and, when it is scalding hot, put in a good quantity of spinach, corn salad, tops of pennyroyal, and mint cut small.   Let it stand on the fire till ready to boil, then ladle it up and down six or seven minutes.   Take it off the fire, and let it stand a little time, that the oatmeal may sink to the bottom.   Strain it, and add but-ter, salt, and bread.   When it is about milk-warm it will be fit to eat

Observation.

This is a most excellent porridge, pleasant to the palate and stomach, cleansing the passages by opening obstructions.   It also breeds good blood, thus enlivens the spirits, and makes the whole body active and easy

Garlic or Onion Porridge.

Stir some oatmeal and water together, set it upon the fire, and, when ready to boil, put in as much bruised garlic, or onion, as will make it strong or weak at pleasure.   Brew it to and fro with a ladle for five or six minutes, that it may not boil, Take it off, let it stand a little ; then add salt, butter, and bread, and eat it milk-warm.

Observations

This is a good, warming, cleansing, and opening porridge.
It must always be remembered that these porridges are never
to boil.

To make Diet-Drinks, by infusing Herbs, Grains, Seeds, &c.,
into Liquors.

The best way to make all sorts of herb-drinks is to gather
the herbs in their proper seasons.   Then dry them in the shade,
and put them into close paper bags.   When they are wanted
for use, take out the proper quantity, put it into a linen bag,
and hang the same in the beer or ale, while it is working or fermenting, for two, three, four, five, six, seven, or eight hours,
and then take it out.   Wormwood ought not to lie so long;
three or four hours will be sufficient for that.

In this manner, if the herbs are rightly gathered and ordered
as above, all their good, pure, balsamic virtues, will readily
infuse themselves into the beer, ale, wine, or other liquor, whatever it be, as the pure sweet quality in malt does into the warm
liquor in brewing, which is done effectually in one hour.   But
if malt, after it is put in, is suffered to remain six, eight, or ten
hours, before the liquor is drawn off, all the nauseous properties will be awakened, and overpower the good ones.   The
same is to be understood in infusing any sort of well-prepared
herbs ; and great care is therefore required, in all preparations,
that the pure qualities are neither evaporated nor overpowered;
for, then, whatever it is will soon tend to putrefaction, and
become nauseous, and loathsome to nature.

The beer, ale, or other liquor, into which these herbs are infused, must be unadulterated, or the benefit of these infusions
will be destroyed by its pernicious qualities.

There is nothing more prejudicial either to the health or intellectual faculties of mankind than the adulterating liquors. These
things, which, in their purest state, are of an equivocal character, and never to be trusted without caution, are thus converted
into decided poisons.

Wormwood Ale or Beer, another Way.

Take any quantity of wormwood, more or less, according
as the liquor is to be strong or weak.   Infuse it for half an
hour in the boiling hot wort ; then strain it out, and put the
wort to cool.

Wormwood drinks, prepared either this or the former way,
are good noble liquors, gentle, warming, assisting digestion,
and refining the blood, sending no gross fumes to the head.

The same method should be observed in making all sorts of drinks in which any strong bitter herbs are infused. It makes them pleasant and grateful both to the palate and stomach, and preserves all the physical virtues. Most bitter herbs naturally and powerfully open obstructions, if they are judiciously managed; whereas the usual way of making such drinks not only renders them unpleasant, but destroys all the medicinal virtues of the herbs.

All things have their good and bad qualities: thus fire, which is good to warm and comfort, will also burn, if not managed with discretion.

HINTS ON BATHING.

The bath, whether warm or cold, produces the most salutary effect on the absorbent vessels, which would otherwise reconduct the impurities of the skin through the pores, to the no small injury of health. To those in a perfect state of vigour, the frequent use of the bath is less necessary than to the infirm; as the healthy possess a greater power to resist impurities, by means of their unimpaired perspiration, the elasticity of their minute vessels, and the due consistence of their circulating fluids. The case is very different with the infirm, the delicate, and the aged. In these the slowness of circulation, the viscidity or clamminess of the fluids, the constant efforts of nature to propel the impurities towards the skin, combine to render the frequent washing of their bodies an essential requisite to their physical existence.

The *warm*, that is, the tepid or lukewarm bath, being about the temperature of the blood, between 96 and 98° of Fahrenheit, has usually been considered as apt to weaken and relax the body; but this is an ill-founded notion. It is only when its heat exceeds that of the human body, as in the *hot bath*, and *King's bath*, at Bath, (both of which are from 18 to 20 degrees higher than blood heat,) that the warm bath can produce a debilitating effect. Indeed, baths of the above immoderate heat ought not to be used in their natural state, that is, without reducing their temperature by cold water, except in particular cases, and under the immediate advice of a physician. On the contrary, the lukewarm or tepid bath, from 98 downwards to 85, is always safe, and so far from relaxing the tone of the solids, that it may justly be considered as one of the most powerful and universal restoratives with which we are acquainted. Instead of heating the body, it has a cooling effect; it diminishes the quickness of the pulse, and reduces it in a greater proportion, according as the pulse has been more quick and unnatural, and according to the length of time the bath is continued. Hence tepid baths are of eminent service where the body has been overheated, from whatever cause, whether after fatigue from travelling, or severe bodily exercise, or after violent exertion and perturbation of mind; as they allay the tempestuous and irregular movements of the body, and frequently, in the strictest sense, invigorate the system. By their softening, moistening, and tumefying power, they greatly contribute to the formation and growth of the bodies of young persons; and are of singular benefit to those in whom we perceive a tendency to arrive too early at the consistence of a settled age; so that the warm bath is particularly adapted to prolong the state of youth, and retard for some time the approach of full manhood. This effect the tepid baths produce in a manner exactly alike, in the coldest as well as in the hottest climates.

From what has been advanced, it will not be difficult to discover in what particular disorders the tepid bath may be of the greatest service, and the reason why it proves so eminently useful (particularly in a parched and rough state of the skin) in paralytic, spasmodic, hysteric, and insane cases, as well as in an acrimonious and corrupted state of the fluids, such as scorbutic and leprous eruptions, &c. One obvious effect of the habitual use of the bath, particularly the tepid, is, that it softens and renews the external integuments of the body. It considerably increases the pressure on the body from without: hence breathing, particularly on entering the bath, is frequently somewhat difficult, until the muscles have by practice become inured to a greater degree of resistance. Yet this effect, which in most instances is of small importance, requires the greatest precaution in some particular cases, as far as to prevent the use of the bath altogether; such, for instance, where there is danger of lacerating the internal vessels, when apoplexy, asthma, and the like, are apprehended.

Effects of the cold Bath.

Bathing in rivers, as well as in the sea, is effectual for every purpose of cleansing the body; it washes away impurities from the surface, opens the cutaneous vessels for a due perspiration, and increases the activity of the circulation of the blood. For these reasons it cannot be too much recommended, not only to the infirm and debilitated, under certain restrictions, but likewise to the healthy. The apprehension of bad consequences from the coldness of the water is in reality ill founded; for, besides that it produces a strengthening effect, by its astringent property, the cold sensation is not of itself hurtful. The same precaution, however, is requisite in the use of the cold as in that of the tepid bath ; for, after having overheated the body, especially in the hot days of summer, it may prove instantly fatal, by inducing a state of apoplexy. Hence the plethoric, or such as are of full habit, the asthmatic, and all those who perceive a great determination of the blood to the head, should be very circumspect in its use; for, although the consequences may not prove immediately fatal, yet the too great strain and pressure may easily burst some of the smaller blood-vessels in the head or breast, and thereby lay the foundation of an incurable disorder. To such as are of a sound and robust constitution, bathing may be rendered an agreeable exercise, by swimming against the stream ; for, as the fibres and vessels are thus compelled to resist the power of the undulating waves, the nerves are excited into action.

The general *properties* of the *cold bath* consist in its power of contracting the solid parts, and of inspissating the fluids. Any part of the body, which is exposed to the sudden contact of cold water, experiences at the same instant a degree of tension and contraction, and becomes narrower and smaller. Not only the blood-vessels, but likewise the small capillary tubes, are liable to this contraction and subsequent relaxation. What is vulgarly called *goose-skin* is a simple effort of the cutaneous fibres, a contraction of the orifices of the absorbent and exhalant vessels, occasioned by mental perturbation, spasms, or the effect of cold. Hence it happens that by the cold bath all the blood-vessels of the skin, and of the muscles in immediate contact with it, are so constricted and diminished, that at the time of this violent exertion they are unable to receive the usual quantity of blood. The smaller vessels of the skin are likewise closed, and press upon the humours contained in them, so as to prevent all perspiration. Thus all the fibres of the skin and muscles are brought into close contact ; and if the humours contained in these tubes had no other outlets, by which to discharge themselves, they would become thick or inspissated, and lose their natural warmth. Were this inspissation of the fluids really to take place, it would be attended with dangerous stagnations and obstructions. That it does not, however, produce these fatal effects, may be ascribed to the following cause. As soon as the pressure is made against the external vessels, the blood retreats from them, in search of places where it may find less resistance. All the great vessels within the body afford receptacles into which it now flows, till the principal arteries, and the veins of the intestines, being filled, extended, and enlarged, it rises to the heart. Although the effect consequent on the cold bath may

be considered as altogether mechanical, yet this simple operation is frequently productive of the most important and beneficial consequences. All other strengthening remedies operating, in general, only on the fluid parts of the body, require to
be previously dissolved by the fluids, blended with the mass of
the blood, and thereby conducted to the solid parts. The cold
bath, on the contrary, acts, almost instantaneously, on the solid
parts themselves, and produces its bracing effect before a
single drop of blood has been commuted. From which
remedy, therefore, is it most likely we should derive the desired
effect,—that which immediately answers the purpose, or that
which must pass through so many canals, and undergo so
many changes, before it arrives at the place where it is to
exert its efficacy?—The sudden changes arising from the application of the cold bath contribute in various ways to brace
the human body. The relaxed fibres of the skin and the muscles acquire more solidity and compactness from contraction.
Their elasticity is increased, and thus a considerable defect removed : the nerves are stimulated and incited to those powerful exertions, on which the ease, vigour, and habitual spright-
liness of the body so much depend. From that degree of irri-
tability which the nerves possess when in a debilitated state
arise all hysteric, spasmodic, and convulsive symptoms and
affections. These may be mitigated or removed by the cold
bath, because it greatly affects and alters the state of the
nerves; it shakes and animates them ; and, by its forcible
operation, overcomes their tendency to preternatural rigidity,
and other disagreeable sensations. Here, then, we have two
causes, which illustrate the excellent effects of this remedy :
there remains, however, a third, more important and powerful,
to be yet explained.

The blood, which by external pressure is driven into the
internal vessels, extends and enlarges them, without diminish-
ing that contractile force, or tendency, which is peculiar to
every artery. At the moment when the external pressure
ceases, all the internal vessels exert their powers of self-con-
traction more forcibly than usual, as they are more strongly
extended, and consequently enabled to exercise a greater
force. The blood, returned to the cutaneous and muscular
vessels, finds its reservoirs contracted and invigorated ; it flows
through muscles, the fibres of which have acquired greater
elasticity and power of assistance. It is accelerated in its new
motion by these improved fibres and veins, and the result of
the collective powers is a fresh impulse and rapidity given to
its circulation. Although, at the first immersion, the uniform
course of it is somewhat interrupted, this temporary stoppage

serves afterwards to re-establish and promote it. The blood can now penetrate with ease into the smallest capillary vessels; it can circulate freely through every part of the animal machine, without affecting or relaxing the solids.

" In the earliest ages of exercise, (said the late Dr. Currie, of Liverpool,) before profuse perspiration has dissipated the heat, and fatigue debilitated the living power, nothing is more safe, according to my experience, than the cold bath. This is so true, that I have for some years constantly directed infirm persons to use such a degree of exercise, before immersion, as may produce some increased action of the vascular system, with some increase of heat, and thus secure a force of re-action under the shock, which otherwise might not always take place. The popular opinion, that it is safest to go perfectly cool into the water, is founded on erroneous notions, and sometimes productive of injurious consequences. Thus persons heated, and beginning to perspire, often think it necessary to wait on the edge of the bath until they are perfectly cooled, and then, plunging into the water, feel a sudden chilliness that is alarming and dangerous. In such cases the injury is generally imputed to going into the water too warm, whereas, in truth, it arises from going in too cold.

" But, though it be perfectly safe to go into the cold bath in the earlier stages of exercise, nothing is more dangerous than this practice, after exercise has produced profuse perspiration, and terminated in languor and fatigue; because, in such circumstances, the heat is not only sinking rapidly, but the system parts more easily with the portion that remains."

These remarks are worthy of the learned Dr. Currie: at the same time, instead of advising any person to use the *cold bath after exercise,* I would certainly prefer the *tepid* or *lukewarm bath ;* both on account of the greater safety attending the use of it, and because it possesses nearly all the advantages of the cold bath, without being liable to so many strong objections Besides, the cold bath is altogether improper in a weak state of the lungs, in all complaints of the breast, in dropsies, in plethoric habits, and for very corpulent individuals; in all which cases the lukewarm bath may, if duly modified, produce effects highly beneficial.

The healthy and the vigorous, who resort to the cold bath, on account of its cleansing and bracing effects, may continue in it, with safety, for a considerable time. But, to strengthen and to give elasticity to the solid parts, every thing depends upon the sudden impression of the cold. This primary effect will be weakened, or frustrated, by remaining in the bath till the water feels warm, whereby the pressing or vibrating action on the nerves at length ceases. The most proper time of bathing is when the stomach is not employed in digestion; as in the morning or forenoon, or from three to four hours after dinner. The cold bath, between 65 and 32 of Fahrenheit, is not, strictly speaking, a dietetic remedy: its effects are not so much calculated for the healthy and robust as for the infirm and diseased, under particular circumstances. The external use of cold water is of singular benefit, when applied to individual parts of the body, where its use may be much longer continued without danger, and where we may accomplish the intended effects in a manner by compulsion and perseverance.

Of all parts of the body, the head receives most benefit from the effusion of cold water; this is a simple and effectual remedy against too great an impulse of the blood towards the head, where persons are threatened with apoplexy; in disorders of the brain and cranium; in wounds and other complaints, to which the head is subject. In these instances, its effects may be still farther improved by frigorific or cooling salts. The effusion of water upon the abdomen has likewise been employed with great advantage, in cases of obstinate costiveness, affording almost instantaneous relief, when internal remedies have produced no effect. This should not, however, induce any person to use that remedy indiscriminately, or without proper advice.

On the contrary, in all those cases where the cold bath might repel certain eruptive humours, which nature determines towards the surface of the body, it cannot be resorted to without danger.

Some think to fortify the body, by the use of the cold bath, against the vicissitudes of the weather; but it can be proved that children, who from their infancy have been bathed in cold water, are as much exposed to coughs and catarrhs as those who have not been habituated to this violent practice, provided they have not been mismanaged by effeminating indulgence. In general, all artificial plans of hardening and bracing the bodies of children are commendable only when the child shews no strong and lasting aversion to them.

It should be considered, that, as the cold bath powerfully contracts the fibres, by its frequent use it imparts to the juvenile body an unnatural degree of solidity and compactness, whereby it too early acquires the properties of an adult. The skin of such children as have been too frequently bathed is generally much drier and harder than it ought to be at their age.

The following rules for the use of the cold bath, in the cases where it may be of service, should be attended to :—

1st. Every cold bath applied to the whole body ought to be of short duration : all depends upon the first impression the cold makes on the skin and nerves, it being this impression which hardens us against the effects of rough and cold weather.

2d. The head should always be first wetted, either by immersion, or by pouring water on it, or the application of wet clothes, and then plunging over head into the bath.

3d. The immersion ought always to be sudden, not only because it is less felt than when we enter the bath slowly and timorously, but likewise because the effect of the first impression is uniform all over the body, and the blood in this manner is not driven from the lower to the upper parts. Hence the shower-bath possesses great advantages, as it pours the water suddenly upon the whole body, and thus, in the most perfect manner, fulfils the three rules above specified.

4th. The due temperature of the cold bath can be ascertained only as relative to individual cases ; for it extends from 33 to 56° of Fahrenheit, except in *partial bathings*, where, as has been already observed, the degree of cold may, and often ought to be, increased by ice, nitre, alum, salt, sal ammoniac, or other artificial means.

5th. Gentle exercise ought to precede the cold bath, to produce some re-actions of the vascular system in entering into it ; for neither complete rest nor violent exercise are proper, previous to the use of this remedy.

6th. The morning or forenoon is the most proper time for cold bathing, unless it be in a river ; in which the afternoon, or towards the evening, when the water has been warmed by the sun, and the dinner has been digested, is the most eligible period of the day :—a light breakfast will not be detrimental before using the bath.

7th. While in the water, we should not remain inactive, but move about, in order to promote the circulation of the blood from the centre of the body to the extremities.

8th. After immersion, the whole body ought to be wiped, as quickly as possible, with a dry and somewhat rough cloth. Moderate exercise out of doors, if convenient, is proper, and indeed necessary.

In the following general cases, we must absolutely refrain from the cold bath :—

1. In a general plethora, or full habit of body, and in the febrile disposition which attends it ; in hæmorrhages, or fluxes of blood ; and in every kind of inflammation.

2. In constipations or obstructions of the abdominal intestines.

3. In diseases of the breast, difficult breathing, and short and dry coughs

4. In an acrimonious state of the fluids, bad colour of the face, difficult healing of the flesh, and the true scurvy

5. In gouty and rheumatic paroxysms.

6. In cutaneous diseases.

7. In a state of pregnancy. And, lastly,

8. In a deformed or ill-shaped state of the body, except in some particular cases, to be determined by a physician.

Shower-Bath.

The best method of cold bathing is in the sea, or a river. Where, from necessity, it is done in the house, I recommend the SHOWER-BATH, for which a proper apparatus is to be had at the tin-men's. Where the saving of expense is an object, it may effectually be supplied by the following easy expedient: Fill a common watering-pot with cold water; let the patient sit down, undressed, upon a stool, which may be placed in a large tub; and let the hair, if not cut short, be spread over the shoulders as loosely as possible; then pour the water from the pot over the patient's head, face, neck, shoulders, and all parts of the body progressively down to the feet, till the whole has been thoroughly wetted. Let the patient then be rubbed dry, and take gentle exercise, as has been recommended, until the sensation of cold be succeeded by a gentle glow all over him. When we first resort to this kind of bath, it may be used gently, and with water having some degree of warmth, so as not to make the shock too great; but, as the patient becomes accustomed to it, the degree of cold may be increased, the water may be allowed to fall from a greater height, and the holes in the pot may be made larger, so as to make the shower heavier. A large sponge may, in some measure, be substituted for a watering-pot.

Although the shower-bath does not cover the surface of the body so universally as the cold bath, this circumstance is rather favourable than otherwise: those parts, which the water has not touched, feel the impression by sympathy as much as those in actual contact with it. Every drop of water becomes a partial bath in miniature, and thus a stronger impression is excited than in any other mode of bathing. The shower-bath indeed, upon the whole, possesses superior advantages to all others; viz.—

1. The sudden contact of the water, which in the common bath is only momentary, may here be prolonged, repeated, and made slow or quick, or modified at pleasure.

2. The head and breast, which are exposed to some inconvenience and danger in the common bath, are here at once secured by receiving the first shock of the water; the blood is consequently impelled to the lower parts of the body; and the

patient finds no obstruction in breathing, or undulations of blood towards the head.

3. The heavy pressure on the body occasioned by the weight of the water, and the free circulation of the blood in the parts touched by it, being for some time, at least, interrupted, make the usual way of bathing often more detrimental than useful. The SHOWER-BATH, on the contrary, descends in single drops, which are at once more stimulating and pleasant than the immersion into cold water; while it can be more readily procured, and more easily modified and adapted to the circumstances of the patient.

Dr. Hawes's Method of Restoring to Life drowned Persons.

THE greatest exertion should be used to take out the body before the lapse of one hour, and the resuscitative process should be immediately employed.

On taking bodies out of rivers, ponds, &c., the following cautions are to be used :—

1. Never to be held up by the heels.
2. Not to be rolled on casks, or other rough usage.
3. Avoid the use of salt in all cases of apparent death.

Particularly observe to do every thing with the utmost promptitude.

For the *drowned*, attend to the following directions :—

1. Convey the body, with the head raised, to the nearest convenient house.
2. Strip and dry the body :—clean the mouth and nostrils.
3. Young Children :—between two persons in a warm bed.
4. An Adult :—lay the body on a warm blanket, or bed; and, in cold weather, near the fire. In the warm season, air should be freely admitted.
5. It is to be gently rubbed with flannel, sprinkled with spirits; and a heated warming-pan, covered, lightly moved over the back and spine.
6. To restore Breathing :—Introduce the pipe of a pair of bellows (when no apparatus) into one nostril; close the mouth and the other nostril; then inflate the lungs, till the breast be a little raised; the mouth and nostrils must then be let free. Repeat this process till life appears.
7. Tobacco-smoke is to be thrown gently up the fundament, with a proper instrument; or the bowl of a pipe, covered so as to defend the mouth of the assistant.
8. The breast is to be fomented with hot spirits :—if no signs

of life appear, the warm bath ;—or hot bricks, &c., applied to the palms of the hands, and the soles of the feet.

9. Electricity, early employed by a medical assistant.

10. The breath is the principal thing to be attended to.

Intense Cold.

Rub the body with snow, ice, or cold water. Restore warmth, &c., by slow degrees ; and, after some time, if necessary, the plans to be employed for the resuscitation of drowned persons.

Suspension by the Cord.

A few ounces of blood may be taken from the jugular vein, and cupping-glasses may be applied to the head and neck : leeches also to the temples.—The other methods of treatment, the same as recommended for the apparently drowned.

Suffocation by noxious Vapours, or Lightning.

Cold water to be repeatedly thrown upon the face, &c., drying the body at intervals. If the body feels cold, employ gradual warmth, and the plans for the drowned.

Intoxication.

The body is to be laid on a bed, &c., to be removed. Obtain immediate medical assistance, as the modes of treatment must be varied according to the state of the patient.

The following *general observations* should be attended to :— On signs of returning life, the assistants are most earnestly advised to employ the restorative means with great caution, so as to nourish and revive the languid sign of life.

A tea-spoonful of warm water may be given, and, if swallowed and returned, warm wine, or diluted brandy. The patient should then be put into a warm bed ; and, if disposed to sleep, he will generally awake restored to health.

The plans above recommended are to be used for *three or four hours*. It is an absurd and vulgar opinion to suppose persons as irrecoverable, because life does not soon make its appearance.

Electricity and bleeding never to be employed, unless by the direction of the medical assistant.

CHAPTER XXVI

CONDUCT TO SERVANTS

————————There is an old poor man,
Who after me hath many a weary step
Limp'd in pure love :—Till he be first suffic'd,—
Oppress'd with two weak evils, age and hunger,—
I will not touch a bit.   *Shakespeare.*

A KIND and tender attention is due from the affluent to the deserving part of their fellow-creatures, though undistinguished by the accidental advantages of birth, rank, or fortune : to alleviate their sorrows, compassionate their distresses, and lighten their burden of woe, is a duty incumbent upon those who enjoy any of the above attractive and envied indulgences.

The Almighty, for wise and good purposes, has thought fit to place his children in very different situations ; but, at the time he has done so, he has likewise, by that invisible chain with which he has so uniformly and nicely connected all nature, made the one absolutely necessary to the happiness and convenience of the other. The great could not enjoy their riches without the assistance of the poor ; neither could the poor receive the reward of their labour, had there been no inequality of station. To consider those as disregarded by Providence, and unworthy our attention, who are placed in a state of servitude and dependence, would be the height of cruelty ; and not only unjust to our fellow-creatures, but an affront to that Being with whose favour they are undoubtedly honoured equally, or perhaps in a superior degree to ourselves.

A good and faithful servant is a treasure of inestimable value, a character truly respectable, and deserving of our utmost indulgence. I never knew any good and truly amiable, who treated their servants with unkindness and severity. Though indebted to their masters for support, their labours are an equivalent for the wages they receive. I may venture to say their wages are often unequal to their desert,—people sometimes not having it in their power to repay their honest endeavours to serve them with the liberality they deserve. But 'tis in every one's power to treat them with civility and kindness ; and to recollect that they have not only the same form, but the same desires, wants, and wishes, as themselves ; are liable to the same sorrows and infirmities, without the means of indulging the one or alleviating the other. How gratifying, how delightful, to a generous mind, to make a state of dependence and servitude as easy as possible to the worthy and industrious ! How much more delightful to be obeyed with the willing heart of affection than one driven to do so by the servile influence of fear ! How pleasant to be received, after any temporary absence from our own house, with the smiling countenance of a worthy domestic ; an eye lifted up with an humble, but grateful delight ; and a number of little attentions, which speak, in expressive silence, the sincerity of their attachment, and which add a number of additional comforts to our own home !

Though it would be highly improper for young people to associate with their servants, and to converse with them in the same unreserved manner as they would with an equal or a superior ; though it would bring them down on a level with their dependants, and would shew a want of judgment and knowledge of the world to make them the confidants of their secrets, which would give them an authority and freedom they otherwise would never dare to assume; it is equally reprehensible to treat them with contempt; to speak to them upon every occasion in the accents of austerity and harshness ; to suspect their honesty without just cause; or appear cold and insensible to their endeavours to please. Authority may be preserved without unkindness, and a proper distinction kept up without either pride, reserve, or coldness. When we consider that the good character of a servant is their only inheritance, it would be cruel and unjust to deprive them of that valuable portion through caprice or prejudice. That there are a number of bad people in all situations is a truth, however unpleasant, not to be denied : but it would be very hard for all to be suspected because some will err. In my opinion it is far better to be often deceived than to live under the perplexing influence of continual distrust. Many of the servants in genteel families have been reduced, perhaps, to their humiliating situations by the imprudence of their parents, or by many other unavoidable misfortunes, whose education may have been as liberal as theirs whom a reverse of fortune has reduced them to serve, and whose flattering prospects once promised them better days and far more exalted views ; who once knew what it was to have every indulgence at their own command, without any reason to apprehend being deprived of them. Surely, such blameless sufferers, whilst they submit to their change o fortune with cheerful humility, are entitled to our tenderest regard, and have a just claim upon our benevolence to make them feel as little inconvenience as possible from a state of dependence, to which, so uncertain is every thing on earth, it may one day be our turn to submit.

The meanest, the most despised, of human beings, may, if treated with cruelty and injustice, prove a dangerous enemy; or, on the contrary, rise so far superior to his present station, as to be a valuable and useful friend. Therefore, from motives of policy, as to worldly matters, as well as from all those of a more captivating and generous nature, it is far better to behave with an uniform steadiness of humanity to those you have it in your power to make happy or miserable, than to extort an unwilling compliance to any unreasonable commands with unfeeling and rigid severity.

I have often heard it observed, that, to know a person's real character, you must see them in their own family. To hear any one speak improperly to their servants, or to see them compelled to submit to their pride, caprice, or ill humour, must give the careful observer a mean opinion of their disposition. It calls in question, not only their want of knowledge, as to the duties of their station, but a want of good temper, which is a jewel of such value as should ever be preserved with care.—'Tis so becoming an ornament as never should for one hour be laid aside: it will make the plainest form agreeable, prove a prevailing advocate in procuring friends, and has been known to disarm the most resolute and determined enemy of their resentment. A person blest with an uniform sweetness of temper will ever be admired, respected, and beloved: it never can be seen in a more interesting point of view, or its sincerity and sweetness be more fully proved, than by its benign exertions to render dependants happy, and satisfied with their humble station. To be perpetually out of humour for every frivolous trifle, and to make others wretched for our capricious disappointments, serves to shew a weakness of understanding, and a total want of that considerate humanity which would scorn to lessen its own regrets at the expense of a fellow-creature, though that fellow-creature be a servant. The very name, if properly considered, should make every one desirous of proving themselves kind masters or indulgent mistresses.

Sir William Auburn's family lived in a most luxurious and fashionable style, till perpetual dissipation had so far reduced their fortune, as to oblige them to retire into the country, in order to save expenses. They had only one son and a daughter, who, from being accustomed to gaiety and extravagance, accompanied their parents with unwillingness and discontent Miss Auburn was naturally of a sweet and placid disposition, and very soon became perfectly conformable to their necessary change of life; but her brother Edmund found it impossible to reconcile himself, or humble his proud spirit to the degrading and mortifying alteration, notwithstanding his father and mother had endeavoured to convince him of the necessity to retrench, and expressed their sorrow for having, by their obstinate imprudence, made the change not only prudent, but unavoidable.

The house-steward was the only one in the family who had dared to acquaint Sir William with the deranged state of his finances; and, in the all-persuasive language of truth and friendly warmth, pointed out the danger of any longer deferring the plan of retiring. He was a good and venerable old man, who had held the same place under Sir William's father, and ever maintained a character free from reproach. Edmund, by some means or other, discovered that Godfrey had put these prudential notions into his father's head; and therefore took every opportunity to ridicule, tease, and mortify this worthy and faithful servant, who at length grew so weary of his situation, that he determined to leave his place. He had, fortunately, a few years before, a pretty estate, descended to him at the death of a distant relation, and had saved a considerable sum during the time he had lived in Sir William's family, exclusive of a very handsome legacy left him by a former master. When he informed Sir William and his lady of his intention to quit their service, they were much hurt and surprised, and even condescended to request that he would give up his design; and begged to know if he had met with any thing particularly disagreeable, that had determined him to leave them. Miss Auburn, who really loved the good man, burst into tears, and inquired how he could be so unkind as to think of leaving her father; adding, that she hoped she had never given him any offence, or any cause of complaint. ' For shame, Caroline!' exclaimed her brother, ' do not degrade yourself by asking such humiliating questions of a servant. What business have such people to be offended? If the old fellow thinks he can do better, let him go: I am persuaded we shall do as well without him: his old-fashioned honesty, and busy impertinence, have caused sufficient revolutions in this family. If he stays any longer, he may make still farther innovations; and by-and-by you and I must submit to be under his tuition, as my father has already been too much for our happiness.'—Sir William desired his son to be silent; and honest Godfrey thus addressed his master :—

'The cause of my leaving you, Sir, is now sufficiently explained, and that by the person who occasioned me to form the resolution, or it otherwise never should have been explained by me. I am too old to be insulted, and too honest to deceive a master, for whom I shall ever retain the sincerest respect. My heart is distressed at leaving this house, but go I must; I cannot join with others to betray him into misery, neither can I submit to connive at the vices of his son. My ever dear Miss Auburn, I love you as my child. I admire your virtues, and own your sweetness : if ever you want a friend, condescend to remember old Godfrey; it may one day be in his power to convince you that the humblest of your attendants may be a sincere friend.'

In a short time Godfrey left Sir William's service, to the great regret of all the family, except Edmund, who rejoiced that the saucy monitor was no longer present to talk of prudence or prevent pleasure.

In about six months Sir William grew weary of retirement, and Lady Auburn impatiently sighed for dissipation. Edmund availed himself of the proper moment, and wrought them to his purpose. They returned to London, entered with more avidity than ever into every fashionable and expensive amusement, nor did they stop their mad career till Lady Auburn had consented to give up her jointure, and the last acre was gone. Sir William fell a victim to repentance, vice, and shame: Edmund met with his proper reward, by being obliged to go out to one of our West-Indian settlements, with an ensign's commission. Lady Auburn retired with her daughter into the country, to live upon an annuity of about fifty pounds a year, which was generously settled upon her by the creditors during her life. The sweetness of Miss Auburn's temper did not forsake her in this change of situation; and though she foresaw that, at her mother's decease, she must be left destitute of support, she looked forwards with hope; and with composed resignation, and pious fortitude, submitted to this humiliating reverse of fortune; by doing which she taught her mother to bear her afflictions with less regret.

Not long after they were settled in a neat but humble cottage, within a few miles of the place in which they had once lived with so much splendour, they were told that a gentleman desired to speak with them, who had been shewn into their little parlour, by a girl (the only servant they kept). When Lady Auburn and her daughter entered the room, they were struck with pleasing astonishment at seeing Godfrey. The venerable old man arose respectfully on their entrance ; and, bursting into tears : 'Gracious God!' he exclaimed, 'why have I lived to this day, to see the grand-daughter of my ever dear and respected master reduced to a situation so beneath her rank, so unworthy her worth and sweetness?—And you, my good lady, it wrings my heart to see you in such a house as this!' Lady Auburn was affected, and welcomed the worthy creature, with tears of joy, to her humble habitation. Miss Auburn took him by the hand—' My good friend,' said she, with her accustomed composure, ' grieve not for us : we are not so wretched as you may suppose. We have still sufficient to procure us all the necessaries of life, and many of its comforts. We have reconciled ourselves entirely, my dear Godfrey, to the loss of its luxuries ;—it had been better for us had we never been trusted with them. Several ladies in the neighbourhood have been very kind in sending me work. I am now painting a set of trimmings for a friend, against the next birth-night, for which I shall be handsomely paid; we shall be quite rich! You shall stay with us some days, and be witness to our happiness.'—' I will live with you,' he cried, ' if you will give me leave (I can afford to pay for my board), and attend you as usual. I have not a relation in the world. I am rich ;—all I have shall be one day yours : it will be no contemptible fortune. I always foresaw what would happen, and have kept myself in readiness to fly to you in the hours of adversity. Excuse me, Miss Auburn ; you were ever the darling of my heart. Many hours' delight have you afforded your faithful Godfrey in your prattling infancy ; and your increasing virtues, as you grew up, created in my bosom a kind of parental fondness, which, at times, I have found it difficult to suppress and conceal, as it was my place to do. Your sweetness of temper, my dear young lady, your kind attentions to me in sickness or distress, won my heart, and determined me, long ago, to make you my heir. I have brought a hundred pounds for any present emergencies. My income, in future, shall be at your disposal : you must, however, still consider me only as your steward.' Miss Auburn threw herself into his arms. ' My guardian friend! my second parent! talk not of being our servant: you are our equal ; and, in generosity and goodness, far our superior.—Never, never will we be so cruel as to rob you of the fruits of your honest industry.'—' I shall die if I may not be permitted to attend you, my dear young lady,' cried Godfrey: ' I must never leave you more, unless you mean to destroy me ;—I will be your servant whilst I live.'—' Our friend you mean,' said lady Auburn ; ' as such, you shall live with me and Caroline. She shall attend you in your declining years : 'tis but a just return for your kindness to her in infancy, and your friendship to her almost unprotected and deserted youth.'—' What, then, is become of Mr. Rivers,

madam?' said honest Godfrey; (his cheek tinged with an in
dignant blush, and his eye again glistening with a tear)—'Surely
he has not forsaken you, my dear young lady :—if he has, I hope
you have forgotten him.' Miss Auburn left the room. Lady
Auburn, addressing her humble friend, informed him, that, from
the time the deranged state of sir William's affairs became publicly known, there had been a visible coldness in the parents of
Mr. Rivers ; and, from the time of his death, the young gentleman's visits had been prohibited, on pain of being disinherited.
The prohibition has been obeyed, but the lover remained constant, and sincerely lamented being obliged to give up his hopes;
but was determined, if Miss Auburn continued disengaged, to
prove the sincerity of his affection by a second offer of his hand.
—' Then she shall be happy! since her lover is deserving of
her, she shall be happy !' said Godfrey : ' it is in my power to
put her in possession of a fortune equal to that my master designed to give her, and it shall be done immediately ;—but she
must let me be her servant—'tis all the reward I wish.—Thank
God, I shall yet live to see her happy !'

It was with the greatest difficulty lady Auburn and her
daughter could prevail upon this worthy man to live with them
upon terms of equality; to sit down at table with them ; or to be
treated as a friend, instead of an humble dependant. At length
they gained their purpose ; but he never could conquer his diffident respect, to be present whenever any of the genteel families in the neighbourhood visited them. They soon removed
into a better and more commodious house : two servants were
added to the one who lived with them when Godfrey arrived at
the village. Miss Auburn soon had an opportunity of informing her lover of the sudden and unexpected change in her affairs. As the want of fortune was the only objection his parents made to his marrying the daughter of their former friend ;
that obstacle removed, their consent was soon obtained by the
impatient lover. Godfrey had the happiness of living with his
young lady, of being many years a witness to her felicity, and of
seeing her eldest daughter as lovely and good humoured as his
beloved Miss Auburn. He was not only respected and revered
for his virtues, whilst living; but lamented as a friend and pa-
ent, when summoned to receive the just reward of fidelity, generosity, and undissembled worth.

CHAPTER XXVII.

ADVICE TO SERVANTS, WITH EXAMPLES.

THE good servant rises early. She is quick and diligent at her work; and does it so willingly and cheerfully, and handily, that it seems a pleasure to her rather than a task.

She is strictly honest, so that she might safely be trusted with gold untold. Never, without leave, does she take for herself, or lend or give away, even the smallest thing belonging to her master or mistress, or any one else. She always speaks the truth. If she has done any mischief, or committed a fault, she confesses it at once, and hopes and endeavours not to do the like again.

Whatever she has the care of is kept in excellent order, and always in its proper place. She loses no time in seeking for the things which she uses: she knows exactly where she puts them; and she could find them almost in the dark. She takes pains to make things clean and neat, and to keep them so. She leaves not even a lumber-room in litter; and no passage, door-way, window, nor any hidden corner, dirty. She endeavours to be as careful of the property of her master and mistress as she is of her own; and as contriving about it. She thinks there would be almost as much dishonesty in wilfully wasting or abusing it, as in absolutely stealing it.

Her master and mistress have no fear nor suspicion about her when she is out of their sight. They know that she is as careful, as industrious, and as attentive to any directions which they have given her, as if they were standing by, and looking at her: nay, she is even more so; for one of her greatest fears is to offend her heavenly Master, who has strictly forbidden eye-service.

She always looks clean and tidy; even when dressed in a close bedgown, and a plain linen or cotton cap, she is doing dirty work. She is never seen going about the house with holes in her stockings, or slipshod shoes, or a tattered gown, or blowzy hair, or dirty hands. She makes, and mends, and puts on her clothes, in a very neat manner. She wears a stuff gown, or a dark-coloured cotton one, and a stuff petticoat. Her caps and bonnets are very neat and becoming; but without any lace or fancy-work, or other expensive ornaments. Her handkerchief is always tidily put on, and pinned close over her neck. Her dress on Sundays, and when she goes out, is the same as at other times, except that she is then particularly neat and clean, and has always on clothes that she has not yet worn in common.   She does not think much about her dress, or spend much time in putting it on.   To be modestly and neatly dressed, and to have on sufficient clothing to keep her healthy and strong, and able to do her work, is always her desire.

When she buys new clothes, she always considers whether they are of a reasonable price, and likely to last long ; and are proper for a person in her situation.

The good servant never desires to go to races, or feasts, or fairs, or any merrymakings ; never spends any time, or money, on silly books or songs; or in running after fortune-tellers ; or in buying lottery-tickets.   She never plays at cards : she does not want to get other people's money from them, and she does not want to lose her own.   A walk in her master's garden or in the fields, either by herself, or with sober company ; a visit to her friends ; or a good book to read ; are the amusements which she likes best.

She never invites or encourages any company to come and see her at her master's house, not even her own near relations, without first asking leave ; and she is not very forward in doing that, for fear she should be thought troublesome and encroaching : nor would she, on any account, give to any body the least scrap of her master's victuals, unless she were told that she might do it.

She is no tattler, nor busybody, nor talebearer, gossiping about from house to house, speaking things which she ought not.   She does not want to find out other people's secrets, or to tell those of the family in which she lives.   She would grieve very much if she thought that her master and mistress, or any of their family, looked upon her as a spy, or as an enemy, glad to take every little opportunity to speak ill of them, or to do them any unkindness.

Every morning, and every evening, she prays to the great God, to bless her, and her master and mistress, and all their family ; and daily reads some portion of the Holy Scriptures. She delights to follow her master and mistress, and their children, to the house of God.

She treasures up in her memory the texts in Scripture that teach a servant's duty.   She often reflects upon them, and repeats them to herself; and considers, very attentively, whether she does her best to practise them.   Especially, she remembers our blessed Lord's golden rule, of doing to others as we wish that they should do to us, and endeavours to do to her master and mistress as she would wish, if she had servants, that they should do to her.

Golden Rules for Servants.

1. **Engage** yourselves cautiously. Always prefer sober re-gular families, even if you could have higher wages, or less work to do, elsewhere.—It is, in general, safer and better, es-pecially for young persons first leaving home, to go into small families : they are there more under the kind care and notice of their masters and mistresses ; and less exposed to the bad example, and bad advice, of fellow-servants.

2. If you have been well brought up, and have good cha-racters, you will seldom be at a loss to find proper places in your own neighbourhood, and to hire yourselves in a private respectable way. But if ever you should be under the neces-sity of standing for hire at any statutes, or of making appli-cation at public register offices, be very careful not to engage yourselves to any persons, without inquiring (not of turned-off servants, but of people whom you can safely depend upon) what character, and what kind of families, they have ; nor without knowing of them what they will require of you ; and particularly whether they will allow you, on Sundays, regularly to attend the public worship of your God. Many young per-sons, for want of proper care and thought on such occasions, have got into sad places, and ruined themselves.

3. Do not go to London, or any other large city, in search of a place, unless you have kind and reputable friends there, with whom you can prudently stay till you meet with a pro-per situation. No safe and profitable places are to be met with in London, or any where else, without proper recom-mendations, and the assistance of friends.

4. When you are in a sober service, whether in town or country, be very careful not to indulge yourselves in a rambling fickle disposition ; nor suffer yourselves to be tempted away, for the sake of rather higher wages, or a little more liberty to do evil. Long and faithful service is very creditable. Ser-vants who frequently change their places get but a poor cha-racter, and few true friends ; and they seldom prosper in the world.

5. If indeed you are in situations, where, with your best en-deavours, you cannot obtain reasonable support, or live in any degree of peace or comfort ; and, above all, where your health, morals, or character, are in any danger ; you ought to change as soon as you have a proper opportunity. But beware of giving warning in a pet, merely because you are found fault with, or have not every little favour and indulgence you could wish. Put up with many inconveniences, and even hardships, rather

than foolishly throw yourselves out of a suitable place, or run the risk of hurting your character.

6. Many persons, who have left their places without proper thought, have come to shame and distress; and they would gladly have accepted of situations far worse than those which they once despised. You will no where meet with a place in which you will have every thing you desire ; unless you should be of so Christian a spirit, as to desire nothing but what God appoints for you. Remember that this world is, at best, but a state of trial.

7. Never desire or expect your masters or mistresses to give you a better character, to any persons who may apply to them about you, than they fully believe you deserve ; for, if they were to do so, they would break the laws of God, which absolutely forbid all lying and deceiving, and they would break the laws of their country. Every master or mistress, who gives a servant a false character, is liable to a penalty of *twenty pounds.*

8. If ever you should be out of place, and have no home to go to, be cautious where you lodge. Living in a disreputable house, even if you should behave, while you are there, in the most prudent manner, will hurt your character ; and will, most likely, prevent your getting into a good place.

9. Be diligent to understand your business, and to do it thoroughly. Keep at your work as long and as steadily as can fairly be expected from you. Your masters have agreed to pay you wages, and to provide you with food and lodging, and, perhaps, even with part of your clothing ; and, in return, you have engaged to give them all reasonable labour, and care, and pains. If you waste any part of your working time in absolute idleness, or in loitering about, or if you do your work in a negligent slovenly manner, you defraud your masters of what is due to them . you break your word; you rob them as much as if you were absolutely to take money out of their pockets. You are paid as if you did your best.

10. Be desirous to do more than is required or expected of you, and more than you positively engaged for, rather than less. In busy times, or when there is any sickness in your master's family, do not grudge a little extraordinary labour or fatigue. Willing and cheerful service is always very pleasing, especially on such occasions ; and it is seldom overlooked or forgotten, even by unkind masters and mistresses.

11. Rise early. This is a very necessary practice ; but, if you have been accustomed to slothfulness and over indulgence, you will find it a very difficult one. If, however, you persevere in it for some time, it will become easy to you, and even

pleasant : and you will wonder that you could ever have taken delight in wasting so much precious time in sluggishness; hurting your health and spirits ; robbing your masters of part of the labour which they pay you for ; and getting their ill word, and the ill word of almost every body that knows you. People may bring themselves, by habit, to wake and rise regularly at such an hour every morning.

12. Obey the orders which your masters or mistresses give you : obey them at once, and cheerfully ; always remembering that it is their duty to command, and yours to obey ; and that it is the great God himself who appoints to all persons their stations and their duties. Do every thing as exactly as possible, at the time and in the way which they desire, even if you should think your own time and way would be best. Surely it is the right of masters and mistresses to have their own work done at the time and in the manner they like : no doubt you will think so yourselves, if ever you should have servants of your own.

13 When your masters or mistresses find fault with you, or give you orders which do not quite suit your own fancies, do not answer pertly, or mutter to yourselves, or shew any anger or sullenness, even if you should think they reprove you more than is necessary, or use you unkindly.

14. Look at your masters and mistresses very respectfully whilst they are speaking to you : attend to what they say ; and, when they have done speaking, express, in a few civil words, your readiness to obey. Never rudely contradict them. When it seems proper for you to mention your own opinion or desire, or to complain of any grievance which you think might be redressed, do it in the most respectful manner you are able.

15. Be strictly honest. Never give, or lend, or take for yourselves, any thing, not even a rag, or the least scrap of victuals, that you are not allowed to have. Neither rob, cheat, nor in any way defraud your masters or mistresses yourselves ; nor see them robbed, cheated, or in any way defrauded, by other people, without informing them of it, and putting them upon their guard.

16. If you are commissioned to buy or sell any goods for them, do it honestly, faithfully, and to the best of your judgment. Try to make as good bargains for them as you would to for yourselves. Return the smallest change that is due to them, keeping back nothing for yourselves. See that every thing you buy or sell is of proper weight or measure ; and, as far as you can judge, of a proper quality for the price.

17. If the choice of shops be left to you, go to those whose owners have the best character and the best goods. For fear

that in buying or selling you should be tempted to wrong your masters or mistresses, or suspected of unjust dealings, receive no present from any shopkeepers, or other persons, with whom you have money matters to settle on your masters' or mistresses' account, except it be with the knowledge and consent of your masters or mistresses themselves. Refuse such presents civilly, but very steadily.

18. Never take for your own use any money with which you are intrusted; even if you should fully intend and expect to restore it before it is wanted, or even missed. Settle all money matters as soon as possible; and be exact in them, even to a farthing. If you can write, set down immediately every sum which you receive, and every sum which you pay, even before the money is well out of your hands.

19. Do every part of your work in its proper season. Keep every thing that you have the care of in order, and thoroughly clean. Take pleasure in making things last as long, and go as far, as you can; and in having them neat and handsome, with as little expense as possible. Keep in your memory an inventory of the things in your care; or, if they are numerous, have a written inventory of them: compare it with the things once or twice a year, or oftener; and endeavour to have it, now and then, properly examined by those whom you serve.

20. When an accident happens to any thing that you have the care of, fail not to mention it on the earliest opportunity; and, if you have been at all to blame, promise and endeavour to be more attentive in future.—Remember that it is doing a master and mistress as much injury to waste or neglect their property as to steal it.

21. Be particularly careful with respect to fire. Never set a lighted candle near a bed, or near window-curtains; or near any drawers or closets where there are papers or linen. Never leave linen airing by a fire, without being watched: or little children by themselves in a room where there is a fire, or let them at any time play with fire. Never take a lighted candle without a lanthorn into a stable or venture into a hayloft even with a lanthorn.

22. Leaving chimneys too long unswept, making too great a blaze in the fire-place, letting a candle burn, or a poker remain in the fire, when there is no person in the room, and carrying about the house a candle with a long snuff, should be carefully avoided; as should also every thing else that is at all likely to occasion any mischief by fire. When the light of a candle is necessary in going about the house, and especially to bed, it is safest to use a lanthorn, or a short candle in a large flat candle-stick, with snuffers, and an extinguisher

23. By the laws of our land, every servant, through whose carelessness or negligence a house, or outhouse, is set on fire, is liable to pay a penalty of *one hundred pounds;* and, if it be not immediately paid, to be sent to some house of correction for eighteen months, and there kept to hard labour.

24. Take no advantage of the absence of your masters and mistresses, or of their want of attention, to neglect their business, to disobey their orders in any respect, or to waste, or any way wilfully abuse, their property.

25. Never tell an untruth, or attempt to deceive any body. On no occasion, especially when you propose yourselves for hire, pretend that your health, or strength, or any of your qualifications, are greater than you really think they are. When you have been guilty of a fault, or met with an accident (which the most steady careful people will sometimes do), never deny it, even if you should expect to be much blamed, or made to suffer for it. How much better is it to be blamed or punished by men than to break God's holy law, and offend him! But, in general, to speak the truth constantly and steadily, is by far the best policy, as well as our absolute duty ; and, when it .s done in a civil prudent manner, it makes people respected and trusted.

26. To confess a fault before it is found out, and to do our best to make all due amends for it, is the behaviour of a true Christian. It is particularly pleasing in servants : and seldom fails to incline their masters and mistresses to shew them great favour and indulgence, and to put the utmost confidence in them.

27. Never pry into the affairs of the family in which you live. Especially never read any persons' letters, or other written papers, without their leave ; nor listen at doors, or any where else, to overhear private conversations. Resolve never to speak any ill of your master and mistress, and their family, unless it be absolutely necessary, in order to prevent some great mischief or ruin, either to yourselves or any one else ; and, even then, you must be very cautious what you say.

28. Tell no idle tales ; make no idle complaints ; not even to your dearest friends and companions. When you leave the family, say as little as possible to its disadvantage.

29. Never go out, except on your usual business, without leave ; and endeavour to return as soon as you are desired or expected. When you are sent on any errand, or other business, do not stay longer than is necessary: a quick return shews diligence and faithfulness.

30. Deliver every message to or from your master or mistress as soon, and as exactly, as you are able.

Examples of Good Servants.

1. The following epitaph, on a faithful female servant, is in the churchyard at Croydon, in Surry:—

In memory of URSULA SWINBOURN,
Who, after fulfilling her duty
In that station of life which her Creator had allotted her;
And by her faithful and affectionate conduct,
In a series of thirty-five years,
Rendering herself respected and beloved,
And her loss sincerely regretted
By the family she lived with;
Departed this life, the 5th of January, 1781 : aged 55.
Reader!
Let not her station in life
Prevent thy regarding her example;
But remember,
According to the number of talents given,
Will the increase be expected.

2. " The daughter of an old day-labourer (says a clergyman), residing in my parish, lived many years as a servant of all work with a tradesman in our county town. During the former part of her service, her wages were only forty shillings a year. They were advanced five shillings on her undertaking the whole washing and ironing without assistance; and for the last nine years her master gave her four pounds a year, which were her highest wages. An old female relation of her master's passed a good deal of her time with him; but her temper was so very bad that no one had made any great effort to please her before this young woman, whose constant and unwearied endeavour it was to bear with her frowardness, and to comply with her wishes. The old gentlewoman was at length so won by her assiduity, that she rewarded her with several small sums of money, to the amount of four or five guineas. On receiving the first guinea she determined not to spend any part of it, but to save it against a time of need, although her wages were still at the lowest rate. She even then contrived to add something to her treasure; till, at length, after her wages had been increased, she became mistress of twenty pounds.

Application was made to her for this sum, to be lent out on interest. But, when she was deliberating upon the proposal, it came into her mind that she ought rather to bestow it on her parents, who were then, through age, becoming infirm. She proposed to give them the whole sum at once; but her brother-in-law prudently advised her to send them only half of it, to buy them a cow, and to save the remainder for a future occasion, which she did. A short time after, her father was afflicted with a disorder, which brought him to such a state that he could expect no relief but from a surgical operation Even this a country surgeon had pronounced hopeless, a mortification having, in his opinion, already taken place. The affectionate daughter determined, nevertheless, to be at the expense of taking the advice of a surgeon from the infirmary, which was ten miles distant; and he was of a different opinion. I saw the operation performed. It succeeded, although the patient was then seventy years old : he is still living, and is now in his eighty-seventh year. The surgeon, for the operation and many attendances, required only ten guineas. This sum was thankfully paid him by the good daughter, being every shilling she possessed.

A few years after she had made this laudable use of her hard-earned savings, her master, intending to make his will, proposed to his executor and residuary legatee to bequeath fifty pounds to his old servant. The executor, dissatisfied with this bequest, reminded him of the strong proofs she had given of the strictest honesty ; and of her long and faithful services, not only in the house, but in the shop, by which she had helped him to gain, and had also preserved, much of his property. On these grounds, he persuaded her master to leave her a hundred pounds instead of fifty ; and to add to that sum the interest of three hundred pounds during her life, together with a quantity of household furniture. After his decease, the executor further requested her to take, as a present from him, any other article of furniture which she wished.

A few months after this, a farmer in comfortable circumstances, next neighbour to her aged parents, paid his addresses to her; and afterwards married her. In addition to all this, I have reason to hope that both she and her husband, as well as her aged parents, are pious persons ; and that her marriage has been the means of greatly promoting her spiritual welfare.

3. A Wiltshire young woman, Sarah ―― by name, left her home and kindred, to gain an honest maintenance ; and went into a clergyman's family, in the parish of Chelsea. She had a good natural disposition, improved by the precepts of Christianity. She did her work with cheerfulness. She was diligent, faithful, dutiful, and affectionate. She obeyed not with eye-service. Her conduct was approved, and she was esteemed by all.

In the summer of 1807, after she had been in the family some years, she fell sick, and had a fever. Her mistress anxiously tended her with a mother's care. In compliance with medical advice, a lodging was hired for her, in an airy part of the neighbourhood. A coach was considerately procured to take her thither. Pale as the water-lily, the sick young woman was slowly supported down stairs. She modestly expressed a wish to see her master, once more, before she went; adding her fear lest his engagements might prevent her from so doing. Her mistress, with kind concern, assured her that he stood at the gate, in order to see her safe into the carriage. At her coming out of the house, the clergyman stepped up, and kindly said, " Good morning to you, Sarah!—Come, come, I hope this fine weather will very soon recover you." The sight of her master, the sound of his voice, and the kindness of his words, together with the thoughts of her own illness, and the sad moment of parting, much affected her spirits: she turned away her head, and beheld her master's infant son, the child which she had fondled from its birth. For some days it had not been allowed to see her. It now looked in her face very earnestly, uttered a shrill cry of sudden joy, stretched forwards its little hands, and smiled. She would have spoken, but could not: she faltered, sobbed, leaned back on her female friend, and wept; then pointed to the coach with a sigh, and tottered into it.

CHAPTER XXVIII

ART OF COOKERY.

THE subject of Cookery is, in general, either despised by women as below their attention, or, when practically engaged in, it is with no other consideration than, in the good housewife's phrase, " to make the most of every thing," whether good, bad, or indifferent; or to contrive a thousand mischievous compositions, both savoury and sweet, to recommend their own ingenuity.

The injuries that result from these practices will appear in the course of this work. When these are fully considered, it can no longer be thought derogatory, but in the highest degree honourable, that a woman should study to avert them. If cookery has been worth studying as a sensual gratification, it is surely much more so as a means of securing one of the greatest of human blessings—good health.

The waste occasioned by provisions being dressed in a slovenly unskilful manner is another serious consideration. This not only makes a very material difference in the expenses of a family, but also an useless consumption of the various articles of food, that increases to the poor the difficulty of procuring a sufficiency of wholesome sustenance. It is of great import ance therefore on these accounts, as well as on that of health, that the mistress of a house should be competent to direct, or take an active part, in the culinary business of the family, according as the circumstances of it may require, instead of leaving it to the mercy of an ignorant or ill-informed cook. Nor is it of less consequence that the mistress of a family should attend to the purchase of the provisions, both for the sake of procuring them good, and of not being imposed upon in the purchase of them.

The various utensils used for the preparation and keeping of food are made either of metal, glass, pottery ware, or wood; each of which is better suited to some particular purposes than the others. Metallic utensils are quite unfit for many uses, and the knowledge of this is necessary to the preservation of health in general, and sometimes to the prevention of immediate dangerous consequences.

The metals commonly used in the construction of these vessels are silver, copper, brass, tin, iron, and lead. Silver is preferable to all the others, because it cannot be dissolved by any of the substances used as food. Brimstone unites with silver, and forms a thin brittle crust over it, that gives it the appearance of being tarnished, which may be accidentally taken with food; but this is not particularly unwholesome, nor is it liable to be taken often, nor in large quantities. The discolouring of silver spoons used with eggs arises from the brimstone contained in the egg.—Nitre or saltpetre has also a slight effect upon silver, but nitre and silver seldom remain long enough together in domestic uses to require any particular caution.

Copper and brass are both liable to be dissolved by vinegar, acid fruits, and pearl-ash. Such solutions are highly poisonous, and great caution should be used to prevent accidents of the kind. Vessels made of these metals are generally tinned, that is, lined with a thin coating of a mixed metal, containing both tin and lead. Neither acids, nor any thing containing pearl-ash, should ever be suffered to remain above an hour in vessels of this kind, as the tinning is dissolvable by acids, and the coating is seldom perfect over the surface of the copper or brass.

The utensils made of what is called block tin are constructed of iron plates coated with tin. This is equally liable to be dissolved as the tinning of copper or brass vessels; but iron is not an unwholesome substance, if even a portion of it should be dissolved and mixed with food. Iron is therefore one of the safest metals for the construction of culinary utensils; and the objection to its more extensive use only rests upon its liability to rust, so that it requires more cleansing, and soon decays. Some articles of food, such as quinces, orange-peel, artichokes, &c., are blackened by remaining in iron vessels, which therefore must not be used for them.

Leaden vessels are very unwholesome, and should never be used for milk or cream, if it be ever likely to stand till it become sour. They are unsafe also for the purpose of keeping salted meats.

The best kind of pottery ware is oriental china, because the glazing is a perfect glass, which cannot be dissolved, and the whole substance is so compact that no liquid can penetrate it. Many of the English pottery wares are badly glazed; and, as the glazing is made principally of lead, it is necessary to avoid putting vinegar, and other acids, into them. Acids and greasy substances penetrate into unglazed wares, excepting the strong stone ware; or into those of which the glazing is cracked, and hence give a bad flavour to any thing they are used for afterwards. They are quite unfit therefore for keeping pickles or salted meats. Glass vessels are infinitely preferable to any pottery ware but oriental china, and should be used whenever the occasion admits of it.

Wooden vessels are very proper for the keeping many articles of food, and should always be preferred to those lined with lead. If any substance has ever fermented or become putrid in a wooden cask or tub, it is sure to taint the vessel so as to make it liable to produce a similar effect upon any thing that may be put into it in future. It is useful to char the insides of these wooden vessels before they are used, by burning wood-shavings in them, so as to coat the insides with a crust of charcoal.

As whatever contaminates food in any way must be sure, from the repetition of its baneful effects, to injure the health, a due precaution with respect to culinary vessels is necessary, for its more certain preservation.

To choose Meats.

Venison.—If the fat be clear, bright, and thick, and the cleft part smooth and close, it is young; but if the cleft is wide and tough, it is old. To judge of its sweetness, run a very sharp narrow knife into the shoulder or haunch, and you will know by the scent. Few people like it when it has much of the *haut-gout.*

Beef.—If the flesh of the ox-beef is young, it will have a fine smooth open grain, be of a good red, and feel tender. The fat should look white rather than yellow; for, when that is of a deep colour, the meat is seldom good : beef fed by oil-cakes is in general so, and the flesh is flabby.   The grain of cow-beef is closer, and the fat whiter than that of ox-beef ; but the lean is not of so bright a red.   The grain of bull-beef is closer still, the fat hard and skinny, the lean of a deep red, and a stronger scent.   Ox-beef is the reverse.   Ox-beef is the richest and largest ; but in small families, and to some tastes, heifer-beef is better, if finely fed.   In old meat there is a streak of horn in the ribs of beef : the harder this is, the older ; and the flesh is not finely flavoured.

Veal.—The flesh of a bull-calf is firmest, but not so white; The fillet of the cow-calf is generally preferred for the udder. The whitest is not the most juicy, having been made so by frequent bleeding, and having had whiting to lick.   Choose the meat of which the kidney is well covered with white thick fat.   If the bloody vein in the shoulder looks blue, or of a bright red, it is newly killed ; but any other colour shews it stale.   The other parts should be dry and white ; if clammy or spotted, the meat is stale and bad.   The kidney turns first in the loin, and the suet will not then be firm.

Mutton.—Choose this by the fineness of its grain, good co-lour, and firm white fat.   It is not the better for being young ; if of a good breed and well fed, it is better for age : but this only holds with wether-mutton : the flesh of the ewe is paler, and the texture finer.   Ram-mutton is very strong flavoured ; the flesh is of a deep red, and the fat is spongy.

Lamb.—Observe the neck of a fore quarter : if the vein is blueish, it is fresh ; if it has a green or yellow cast, it is stale. In the hind quarter, if there is a faint smell under the kidney, and the knuckle is limp, the meat is stale.   If the eyes are sunk, the head is not fresh.   Grass-lamb comes into season in April or May, and continues till August.   House-lamb may be had in great towns almost all the year, but is in highest perfection in December and January.

Pork.—Pinch the lean, and, if young, it will break.   If the rind is tough, thick, and cannot easily be impressed by the finger, it is old.   A thin rind is a merit in all pork.   When fresh, the flesh will be smooth and cool ; if clammy, it is tainted. What is called measly pork is very unwholesome, and may be known by the fat being full of kernels, which in good pork is never the case.   Pork fed at still-houses does not answer for curing any way, the fat being spongy.   Dairy-fed pork is the best.

Bacon.—If the rind is thin, the fat firm, and of a red tinge, the lean tender, of a good colour, and adhering to the bone,

you may conclude it good, and not old.   If there are yellow
streaks in it, it is going, if not already rusty.

Hams.—Stick a sharp knife under the bone : if it comes
out with a pleasant smell, the ham is good ; but if the knife is
daubed, and has a bad scent, do not buy it.   Hams short in
the hough are best, and long-legged pigs are not to be chosen
for any preparation of pork.

Brawn.—The horny part of young brawn will feel moderately tender, and the flavour will be better; the rind of old
will be hard.

In every sort of provisions, the best of the kind goes far-
thest ; it cuts out with most advantage, and affords most nourishment.   Round of beef, fillet of veal, and leg of mutton, are
joints that bear a higher price ; but, as they have more solid
meat, they deserve the preference.   It is worth notice, however, that those joints which are inferior may be dressed as
palatably ; and being cheaper, they ought to be bought in turn ;
for, when they are weighed with the prime pieces, it makes the
price of these come lower.

In loins of meat, the long pipe that runs by the bone should
be taken out, as it is apt to taint; as also the kernels of beef.
Rumps and edge-bones of beef are often bruised by the blows
the drovers give the beasts, and the part that has been struck
always taints ; therefore do not purchase these joints, if bruised.

The shank-bones of mutton should be saved ; and, after soaking and brushing, may be added to give richness to gravies or
soups.   They are also particularly nourishing for sick persons.

When sirloins of beef, or loins of veal or mutton, come in,
part of the suet may be cut off for puddings, or to clarify.

Dripping will baste every thing as well as butter, exceed
fowls and game ; and, for kitchen pies, nothing else should be
used.

The fat of a neck or loin of mutton makes a far lighter pudding than suet.

Meat and vegetables that the frost has touched should be
soaked in cold water two or three hours before used, or more
if they are much iced.   Putting them into hot water, or to the
fire, till thawed, makes it impossible for any heat to dress them
properly afterwards.

In warm weather, meat should be examined well when it
comes in; and, if flies have touched it, the part must be cut off,
and then well washed.   In the height of summer it is a very
safe way to let meat that is to be salted lie an hour in very
cold water, rubbing well any part likely to have been fly-
blown: then wipe it quite dry, and have salt ready, and rub it

thoroughly in every part, throwing a handful over it besides. Turn it every day, and rub the pickle in, which will make it ready for the table in three or four days. If to be very much corned, wrap it in a well-floured cloth, after rubbing it with salt. This last method will corn fresh beef fit for the table the day it comes in, but it must be put into the pot when the water boils.

If the weather permit, meat eats much better for hanging two or three days before it is salted.

The water in which meat has been boiled makes an excellent soup for the poor, by adding to it vegetables, oatmeal, or peas.

Roast-beef bones, or shank bones of ham, make fine peas-soup; and should be boiled with the peas the day before eaten, that the fat may be taken off.

In some families great loss is sustained by the spoiling of meat. The best way to keep what is to be eaten unsalted is, as before directed, to examine it well, wipe it every day, and put some pieces of charcoal over it. If meat is brought from a distance in warm weather, the butcher should be ordered to cover it close, and bring it early in the morning; but even then, if it is kept on the road while he serves the customers who live nearest to him, it will very likely be fly-blown. This happens often in the country.

Wash all meat before you dress it: if for boiling, the colour will be better for soaking; but, if for roasting, dry it.

Boiling in a well-floured cloth will make meat white.

Particular care must be taken that the pot is well skimmed the *moment* it boils, otherwise the foulness will be dispersed over the meat. The more soups or broth are skimmed, the better and cleaner they will be.

The boiler and utensils should be kept delicately clean.

Put the meat into cold water, and flour it well first. Meat boiled quick will be hard; but care must be taken that in boiling slow it does not stop, or the meat will be underdone.

If the steam is kept in, the water will not lessen much; therefore, when you wish it to boil away, take off the cover of the soup-pot.

Vegetables should not be dressed with the meat, except carrots or parsnips with boiled beef.

As to the length of time required for roasting and boiling, the size of the joint must direct; as also the strength of the fire, the nearness of the meat to it, and, in boiling, the regular though slow progress it makes; for if the cook, when told to hinder the copper from boiling quick, lets it stop from boiling up at all, the usual time will not be sufficient, and the meat will be underdone.

Weigh the meat; and allow, for all solid joints, a quarter of an hour for every pound, and some minutes (from ten to twenty) over, according as the family like it done.

A ham of twenty pounds will take four hours and a half, and others in proportion.

A tongue, if dry, takes four hours slow boiling, and soaking: a tongue out of pickle, from two hours and a half to three hours, or more if very large: it must be judged, by feeling, whether it is very tender.

A leg of pork, or of lamb, takes the full allowance of twenty minutes, above a quarter of an hour to a pound.

In roasting, beef of ten pounds will take above two hours and a half; twenty pounds will take three hours and three quarters.

A neck of mutton will take an hour and a half, if kept at a proper distance. A chine of pork two hours.

The meat should be put at a good distance from the fire, and brought gradually near when the inner part becomes hot, which will prevent its being scorched while yet raw. Meat should be much basted; and, when nearly done, floured, to make it look frothed.

Veal and mutton should have a little paper put over the fat, to preserve it. If not fat enough to allow for basting, a little good dripping answers as well as butter.

The cook should be careful not to run the spit through the best parts; and should observe that it be well cleaned before and at the time of serving, or a black stain appears on the meat. In many joints the spit will pass into the bones, and run along them for some distance, so as not to injure the prime of the meat: and the cook should have leaden skewers to balance it with; for want of which, ignorant servants are often troubled at the time of serving.

In roasting meat it is a very good way to put a little salt and water into the dripping-pan, and baste for a little while with this, before using its own fat or dripping. When dry, dust it with flour, and baste as usual.

Salting meat before it is put to roast draws out the gravy: it should only be sprinkled when almost done.

Time, distance, basting often, and a clear fire of a proper size for what is required, are the first articles of a good cook's attention in roasting.

Old meats do not require so much dressing as young; not that they are ooner done, but they can be eaten with the gravy more in.

A piece of writing-paper should be twisted round the bone at the knuckle of a leg or shoulder of lamb, mutton, or venison, when roasted, before they are served.

When you wish fried things to look as well as possible, do them *twice* over with egg and crumbs. Bread that is not stale enough to grate quite fine will not look well. The fat you fry in must always be boiling hot the moment the meat, fish, &c., are put in, and kept so till finished : a small quantity never fries well.

To keep meat hot.—It is best to take it up when done, though the company may not be come : set the dish over a pan of boiling water; put a deep cover over it, so as not to touch the meat, and then throw a cloth over that. This way will not dry up the gravy.

To keep Venison.

Preserve the venison dry, wash it with milk and water very clean, and dry it with clean cloths till not the least damp remains ; then dust pounded ginger over every part, which is a good preventive against the fly. By thus managing and watching, it will hang a fortnight. When to be used, wash it with a little lukewarm water, and dry it. Pepper is likewise good to keep it.

To dress Venison.

A haunch of buck will take three hours and a half, or three quarters, roasting ; doe only three hours and a quarter. Venison should be rather under than over done.

Spread a sheet of white paper with butter, and put it over the fat, first sprinkling it with a little salt ; then lay a coarse paste on strong paper, and cover the haunch ; tie it with fine pack-thread, and set it at a distance from the fire, which must be a good one. Baste it often : ten minutes before serving take off the paste, draw the meat nearer the fire, and baste it with butter and a good deal of flour, to make it froth up well.

Gravy for it should be put into a boat, and not into the dish, (unless there is none in the venison), and made thus :—Cut off the fat from two or three pounds of a loin of old mutton, and set in steaks on a gridiron for a few minutes, just to brown one side ; put them into a saucepan with a quart of water, cover quite close for an hour, and simmer it gently ; then uncover it, and stew it till the gravy is reduced to a pint. Season with only salt.

Currant-jelly sauce must be served in a boat.

Formerly pap-sauce was eaten with venison, which, as some still like it, it may be necessary to direct. Grate white bread, and boil it with port wine, water, and a large stick of cinnamon ; and, when quite smooth, take out the cinnamon, and add sugar. Claret may be used for it.

Make the jelly-sauce thus :—Beat some currant-jelly and a spoonful or two of port wine, and set it over the fire till melted Where jelly runs short, put more wine, and a few lumps of sugar, to the jelly, and melt as above. Serve with French beans.

Haunch, Neck, and Shoulder of Venison.

Roast with paste, as directed above, and the same sauce.

To stew a Shoulder of Venison.

Let the meat hang till you judge proper to dress it : then take out the bone ; beat the meat with a rolling-pin; lay some slices of mutton-fat, that have lain a few hours in a little port wine, among it; sprinkle a little pepper and all-spice over it in fine powder ; roll it up tight, and tie it; set it in a stewpan that will only just hold it, with some mutton or beef gravy, not strong, half a pint of port wine, and some pepper and allspice ; simmer it close covered, and as slow as you can, for three or four hours. When quite tender, take off the tape, set the meat on a dish, and strain the gravy over it. Serve with currant-jelly sauce.

This is the best way to dress this joint, unless it is very fat, and then it should be roasted. The bone should be stewed with it.

Breast of Venison.

Do it as the shoulder, or make it into a small pasty.

Hashed Venison

Should be warmed with its own gravy, or some without seasoning, as before ; and only warmed through, not boiled. If there is no fat left, cut some slices of mutton-fat, set it on the fire with a little port-wine and sugar, simmer till dry, then put to the hash, and it will eat as well as the fat of the venison.

For Venison Pasty, look under the head PASTRY ; as likewise an excellent imitation.

To keep Beef.

The butcher should take out the kernels in the neck pieces, where the shoulder-clod is taken off, two from each round of beef: one in the middle, which is called the pope's eye ; the other from the flap : there is also one in the thick flank, in the middle of the fat. If these are not taken out, especially in the summer, salt will be of no use for keeping the meat sweet. There is another kernel between the rump and the edge-bone.

As the butchers seldom attend to this matter, the cook should take out the kernels, and then rub the salt well into such beef as is for boiling, and slightly sprinkle that which is for roasting.

The flesh of cattle that are killed when not perfectly cleared of food soon spoils. They should fast twenty-four hours in winter, aud double that time in summer, before being killed.

To salt Beef or Pork, for eating immediately.

The piece should not weigh more than five or six pounds : salt it very thoroughly just before you put it into the pot; take a coarse cloth, flour it well, put the meat in, and fold it up close. Put it into a pot of boiling water, and boil it as long as you would any other salt beef of the same size, and it will be as salt as if done four or five days.

Great attention is requisite in salting meat : and in the country, where large quantities are cured, this is of particular importance. Beef and pork should be well sprinkled, and a few hours afterwards hung to drain, before it is rubbed with the salt: which method, by cleansing the meat from the blood, serves to keep it from tasting strong. It should be turned every day; and, if wanted soon, should be rubbed as often. A salting tub or lead may be used, and a cover to fit close. Those who use a good deal of salt meat will find it answer well to boil up the pickle, skim it, and, when cold, pour it over meat that has been sprinkled and drained. Salt is so much increased in price, from the heavy duties, as to require great care in using it; and the brine ought not to be thrown away, as is the practice of some, after once using.

To salt Beef red.

Choose a piece of beef with as little bone as you can (the flank is most proper); sprinkle it, and let it drain a day; then rub it with common salt, saltpetre, and bay-salt, but only a small proportion of the saltpetre, and you may add a few grains of cochineal, all in fine powder. Rub the pickle every day into the meat for a week ; then only turn it.

It will be excellent in eight days. In sixteen drain it from the pickle, and let it be smoked at the oven-mouth when heated with wood, or send it to the baker's. A few days will smoke it.

A little of the coarsest sugar may be added to the salt.

It eats well, boiled tender with greens or carrots. If to be grated, as Dutch, then cut a *lean* bit, boil it till extremely tender; and, while hot, put it under a press. When cold, fold it in a sheet of paper, and it will keep in a dry place two or three months, ready for serving on bread and butter.

Beef à-la-mode.

Choose a piece of thick flank of a fine heifer or ox. Cut into long slices some fat bacon, but quite free from yellow; let each bit be near an inch thick : dip them into vinegar, and then into a seasoning ready prepared of salt, black pepper, allspice, and a clove, all in fine powder, with parsley, chives, thyme, savoury, and knotted marjoram, shred as small as possible, and well mixed. With a sharp knife make holes deep enough to let in the larding ; then rub the beef over with the seasoning, and bind it up tight with tape. Set it in a well-tinned pot over a fire, or rather a stove : three or four onions must be fried brown and put to the beef, with two or three carrots, one turnip, a head or two of celery, and a small quantity of water : let it simmer gently ten or twelve hours, or till extremely tender, turning the meat twice.

Put the gravy into a pan, remove the fat, keep the beef covered, then put them together, and add a glass of port wine. Take off the tape, and serve with the vegetables; or you may strain them off, and send them up cut into dice for garnish. Onions roasted, and then stewed with the gravy, are a great improvement. A tea-cupful of vinegar should be stewed with the beef.

To stew a Rump of Beef.

Wash it well, and season it high with pepper, Cayenne, salt, allspice, three cloves, and a blade of mace, all in fine powder; bind it up tight, and lay it into a pot that will just hold it. Fry three large onions sliced, and put them to it, with three carrots, two turnips, a shalot, four cloves, a blade of mace, and some celery. Cover the meat with good beef-broth, or weak gravy. Simmer it as gently as possible for several hours, till quite tender. Clear off the fat, and add to the gravy half a pint of port wine, a glass of vinegar, and a large spoonful of ketchup; simmer half an hour, and serve in a deep dish. Half a pint of table-beer may be added. The herbs to be used should be burnt, tarragon, parsley, thyme, basil, savoury, marjoram, penny-royal, knotted marjoram, and some chives if you can get them, but observe to proportion the quantities to the pungency of the several sorts : let there be a good handful altogether.

Garnish with carrots, turnips or truffles, and morels, or pickles of different colours, cut small, and laid in little heaps separate ; chopped parsley, chives, beet-root, &c. If, when done, the gravy is too much to fill the dish, take only a part to season for serving, but the less water the better ; and, to increase the richness, add a few beef-bones and shanks of mutton in stewing.

A spoonful or two of made mustard is a great improvement to the gravy.

Rump *roasted* is excellent; but in the country it is generally sold whole with the edgebone, or cut across instead of length-ways as in London, where one piece is for boiling, and the rump for stewing or roasting. This must be attended to, the whole being too large to dress together.

To press Beef.

Salt a bit of brisket, thin part of the flank, or the tops of the ribs, with salt and saltpetre, five days; then boil it gently till extremely tender: put it under a great weight, or in a cheese-press, till perfectly cold.

It eats excellently cold, and for sandwiches.

To collar Beef.

Choose the thin end of the flank of fine mellow beef, but not too fat; lay it into a dish with salt and saltpetre, turn and rub it every day for a week, and keep it cool. Then take out every bone and gristle, remove the skin of the inside part, and cover it thick with the following seasoning, cut small: a large handful of parsley, the same of sage, some thyme, marjoram, and pennyroyal, pepper, salt, and allspice. Roll the meat up as tight as possible, and bind it; then boil it gently for seven or eight hours. A cloth must be put round before the tape. Put the beef under a good weight while hot, without undoing it: the shape will then be oval. Part of a breast of veal, rolled in with the beef, looks and eats very well.

Beef-Steaks

Should be cut from a rump that has hung a few days. Broil them over a very clear or charcoal fire: put into the dish a lit-tle minced shalot, and a table-spoonful of ketchup, and rub a bit of butter on the steak the moment of serving. It should be turned often, that the gravy may not be drawn out on either side.

This dish requires to be eaten so hot and fresh-done, that it is not in perfection if served with any thing else. Pepper and salt should be added when taking it off the fire.

Round of Beef

Should be carefully salted, and wet with the pickle for eight or ten days. The bone should be cut out first, and the beef skewered and tied up, to make it quite round. It may be stuffed with parsley, if approved; in which case the holes to admit the parsley must be made with a sharp-pointed knife, and the parsley coarsely cut, and stuffed in tight. As soon as it boils it should be skimmed, and afterwards kept boiling very gently.

Rolled Beef, that equals Hare.

Take the inside of a large sirloin; soak it in a glass of port wine and a glass of vinegar mixed, for forty-eight hours; have ready a very fine stuffing, and bind it up tight. Roast it on a hanging-spit; and baste it with a glass of port wine, the same quantity of vinegar, and a tea-spoonful of pounded all-spice. Larding it improves the look and flavour: serve with a rich gravy in the dish; currant-jelly and melted butter in tureens.

To roast Tongue and Udder.

After cleaning the tongue well, salt it with common salt and saltpetre three days; then boil it, and likewise a fine young udder with some fat to it, till tolerably tender; then tie the thick part of one to the thin part of the other, and roast the tongue and udder together.

Serve them with good gravy, and currant-jelly sauce. A few cloves should be stuck in the udder. This is an excellent dish.

Some people like neats' tongues cured with the root, in which case they look much larger; but otherwise the root must be cut off close to the gullet, next to the tongue, but without taking away the fat under the tongue. The root must be soaked in salt and water, and extremely well cleaned, before it is dressed; and the tongue should be laid in salt for a day and a night before pickled.

To pickle Tongues for boiling.

Cut off the root, but leave a little of the kernel and fat. Sprinkle some salt, and let it drain from the slime till next day: then for each tongue mix a large spoonful of common salt, the same of coarse sugar, and about half as much of salt-petre; rub it well in, and do so every day. In a week add another heaped spoonful of salt. If rubbed every day, a tongue will be ready in a fortnight; but, if only turned in the pickle daily, it will keep four or five weeks without being too salt.

When you dry tongues, write the date on a parchment, and tie it on. Smoke them, or dry them plain, if you like best.

When it is to be dressed, boil it extremely tender; allow five hours; and, if done sooner, it is easily kept hot. The longer kept after drying, the higher it will be; if hard, it may require soaking three or four hours.

Another Way.—Clean as before ; for two tongues allow an ounce of saltpetre, and an ounce of sal-prunella ; rub them well. In two days after well rubbing, cover them with common salt, turn them every day for three weeks, then dry them, and rub over them bran, and smoke them. In ten days they will be fit to eat. Keep in a cool dry place.

Beef-heart.

Wash it carefully ; stuff as a hare ; and serve with rich gravy and currant-jelly sauce.

Hash with the same, and port wine.

Stewed Ox-cheek, plain.

Soak and cleanse a fine cheek the day before it is to be eaten ; put it into a stew-pot that will cover close, with three quarts of water ; simmer it after it has first boiled up and been well skimmed. In two hours put plenty of carrots, leeks, two or three turnips, a bunch of sweet herbs, some whole pepper, and four ounces of allspice. Skim it often ; when the meat is tender, take it out ; let the soup get cold, take off the cake of fat, and serve the soup separate, or with the meat.

It should be of a fine brown ; which might be done by burnt sugar, or by frying some onions quite brown with flour, and simmering them with it. This last way improves the flavour of all soups and gravies of the brown kind.

If vegetables are not approved in the soup, they may be taken out, and a small roll to be toasted, or bread fried, and added. Celery is a great addition, and should always be served. Where it is not to be got, the seed of it gives quite as good a flavour boiled in, and strained off.

Marrow-bones.

Cover the top with a floured cloth ; boil them, and serve with dry toast.

Tripe

May be served in a tureen, stewed with milk and onion till tender. Melted butter for sauce.

Or fry it in small bits dipped in batter.

Or stew the thin part, cut into bits, in gravy : thicken with flour and butter, and add a little ketchup.

Or fricassee it with white sauce.

Soused Tripe.

Boil the tripe, but not quite tender : then put it into salt and water, which must be changed every day till it is all used. When you dress the tripe, dip it into batter of flour and eggs, and fry it of a good brown.

Ox-feet, or Cow-heels,

May be dressed in various ways, and are very nutritious in all.

Boil them; and serve in a napkin, with melted butter, mustard, and a large spoonful of vinegar.

Or broil them very tender, and serve them as a brown fricassee: the liquor will do to make jelly sweet or relishing, and likewise to give richness to soups or gravies.

Or cut them into four parts, dip them into an egg, and then flour and fry them; and fry onions (if you like them) to serve round. Sauce as above.

Or bake them as for mock turtle.

Bubble and Squeak.

Boil, chop, and fry, with a little butter, pepper, and salt, some cabbage, and lay on it slices of underdone beef, lightly fried.

To keep Veal.

The first part that turns bad of a leg of veal is where the udder is skewered back. The skewer should be taken out, and both that and the part under it wiped every day, by which means it will keep good three or four days in hot weather. Take care to cut out the pipe that runs along the chine of a loin of veal, as you do of beef, to hinder it from tainting. The skirt of the breast of veal is likewise to be taken off; and the inside of the breast wiped and scraped, and sprinkled with a little salt.

Leg of Veal.

Let the fillet be cut large or small, as best suits the number of your company. Take out the bone, fill the space with a fine stuffing, and let it be skewered quite round; and send the large side uppermost. When half-roasted, if not before, put a paper over the fat; and take care to allow a sufficient time, and put it a good distance from the fire, as the meat is very solid; serve with melted butter poured over it.—You may pot some of it.

Knuckle of Veal.

As few people are fond of boiled veal, it may be well to leave the knuckle small, and take off some cutlets or collops before it be dressed; but, as the knuckle will keep longer than the fillet, it is best not to cut off the slices till wanted. Break the bones, to make it take less room; wash it well; and put it into a saucepan with three onions, a blade of mace or two, and a few pepper-corns; cover it with water, and simmer till quite ready.   In the mean time some macaroni should be boiled with it, if approved, or rice, or a little rich flour, to give it a small degree of thickness; but don't put too much.   Before it is served, add half a pint of milk and cream, and let it come up either with or without the meat.

Or fry the knuckle with sliced onion and butter to a good brown; and have ready peas, lettuce, onion, and a cucumber or two, stewed in a small quantity of water an hour; then add these to the veal; and stew it till the meat is tender enough to eat, but not overdone.   Throw in pepper, salt, and a bit of shred mint, and serve all together.

Shoulder of Veal.

Cut off the knuckle for a stew or gravy.   Roast the other part for stuffing: you may lard it.   Serve with melted butter.

The blade-bone, with a good deal of meat left on, eats ex-tremely well with mushroom or oyster sauce, or mushroom ketchup in butter.

Neck of Veal.

Cut off the scrag to boil, and cover it with onion-sauce.   It should be boiled in milk and water.   Parsley and butter may be served with it, instead of onion-sauce.

Or it may be stewed with whole rice, small onions, and pep-per-corns, with a very little water.

Or boiled, and eaten with bacon and greens.

The best end may be either roasted, broiled as steaks, or made into pies.

Breast of Veal.

Before roasted, if large, the two ends may be taken off and fried to stew, or the whole may be roasted.   Butter should be poured over it.

If any be left, cut the pieces into handsome sizes, put them into a stew-pan, and pour some broth over it; or, if you have no broth, a little water will do; add a bunch of herbs, a blade or two of mace, some pepper, and an anchovy; stew till the meat is tender, thicken with butter and flour, and add a little ketchup; or the whole breast may be stewed, after cutting off the two ends.

Serve the sweetbread whole upon it, which may either be stewed or parboiled, and then covered with crumbs, herbs, pepper, and salt, and browned in a Dutch oven.

If you have a few mushrooms, truffles, and morels, stew them with it, and serve.

Boiled breast of veal, smothered with onion-sauce, is an ex cellent dish, if not old nor too fat.

To roll a Breast of Veal.

Bone it, take off the thick skin and gristle, and beat the meat with a rolling-pin. Season it with herbs chopped very fine, mixed with salt, pepper, and mace. Lay some thick slices of fine ham ; or roll it into two or three calves' tongues of a fine red, boiled first an hour or two, and skinned. Bind it up tight in a cloth, and tape it. Set it over the fire to simmer, in a small quantity of water, till it is quite tender : this will take some hours. Lay it on the dresser, with a board and weight on it till quite cold.

Pigs' or calves' feet, boiled and taken from the bones, may be put in or round it. The different colours laid in layers look well when cut : and you may put in yolks of eggs boiled, beet-root, grated ham, and chopped parsley, in different parts.

Another Way.

When it is cold, take off the tape, and pour over it the liquor ; which must be boiled up twice a week, or it will not keep.

Minced Veal.

Cut cold veal as fine as possible, but do not chop it.—Put to it a very little lemon-peel shred, two grates of nutmeg, some salt, and four or five spoonfuls of either a little weak broth, milk, or water ; simmer these gently with the meat, but take care not to let it boil ; and add a bit of butter rubbed in flour. Put sippets of thin toasted bread, cut into a three-cornered shape, round the dish.

To pot Veal or Chicken with Ham.

Pound some cold veal or white of chicken, seasoned as directed in the last article, and put layers of it with layers of ham pounded, or rather shred ; press each down, and cover with butter.

Cutlets Maintenon.

Cut slices about three quarters of an inch thick, beat them with a rolling-pin, and wet them on both sides with egg ; dip them into a seasoning of bread-crumbs, parsley, thyme, knotted marjoram, pepper, salt, and a little nutmeg grated ; then put them into papers folded over, and broil them ; and have in a boat melted butter, with a little mushroom-ketchup.

Veal Collops.

Cut long thin collops; beat them well; and lay on them a bit of thin bacon of the same size, and spread forcemeat on that, seasoned high, and also a little garlic and Cayenne. Roll them up tight, about the size of two fingers, but not more than two or three inches long; put a very small skewer to fasten each firmly; rub egg over; fry them of a fine brown, and pour a rich brown gravy over.

Scotch Collops.

Cut veal into thin bits about three inches over, and rather round; beat with a rolling-pin, and grate a little nutmeg over them; dip into the yolk of an egg, and fry them in a little butter of a fine brown: pour the butter off; and have ready warm to pour upon them half a pint of gravy, a little bit of butter rubbed into a little flour, a yolk of egg, two large spoonfuls of cream, and a bit of salt. Don't boil the sauce, but stir it till of a fine thickness to serve with the collops.

To boil Calf's Head,

Clean it very nicely, and soak it in water, that it may look very white; take out the tongue to salt, and the brains to make a little dish. Boil the head extremely tender; then strew it over with crumbs and chopped parsley, and brown them; or, if liked better, leave one side plain. Bacon and greens are to be served to eat with it.

The brains must be boiled; and then mixed with melted butter, scalded sage chopped, pepper, and salt.

If any of the head is left, it may be hashed next day, and a few slices of bacon just warmed and put round.

Cold calf's head eats well if grilled.

To hash Calf's Head.

When half-boiled, cut off the meat in slices, half an inch thick, and two or three inches long: brown some butter, flour, and sliced onion, and throw in the slices with some good gravy, truffles, and morels; give it one boil, skim it well, and set it in a moderate heat to simmer till very tender.

Season with pepper, salt, and Cayenne, at first; and, ten minutes before serving, throw in some shred parsley, and a very small bit of tarragon and knotted marjoram, cut as fine as possible; just before you serve, add the squeeze of a lemon. Forcemeat-balls, and bits of bacon rolled round.

Mock Turtle.

Bespeak a calf's head with the skin on, cut it in half, and clean it well; then half-boil it, take all the meat off in square bits, break the bones of the head, and boil them in some veal and beef broth, to add to the richness. Fry some shalot in butter, and dredge in flour enough to thicken the gravy; stir this into the browning, and give it one or two boils; skim it carefully, and then put in the head; put in also a pint of Madeira wine, and simmer till the meat is quite tender. About ten minutes before you serve, put in some basil, tarragon, chives, parsley, Cayenne pepper, and salt, to your taste; also two spoonfuls of mushroom-ketchup, and one of soy. Squeeze the juice of a lemon into the tureen, and pour the soup upon it. Forcemeat-balls, and small eggs.

Calf's Liver.

Slice it, season with pepper and salt, and broil nicely; rub a bit of cold butter on it, and serve hot and hot.

Calf's Liver roasted.

Wash and wipe it; then cut a long hole in it, and stuff it with crumbs of bread, chopped anchovy, herbs, a good deal of fat bacon, onion, salt, pepper, a bit of butter, and an egg; sew the liver up; then lard it, or wrap it in a veal-cawl, and roast it.

Serve with a good brown gravy, and currant-jelly.

Sweetbreads.

Half-boil them, and stew them in a white gravy; add cream flour, butter, nutmeg, salt, and white pepper.

Or do them in brown sauce seasoned.

Or parboil them, and then cover them with crumbs, herbs, and seasoning, and brown them in a Dutch oven. Serve with butter, and mushroom-ketchup, or gravy.

Sweetbread Ragout.

Cut them about the size of a walnut, wash and dry them, then fry them of a fine brown; pour to them a good gravy, seasoned with salt, pepper, allspice, and either mushrooms or mushroom-ketchup: strain, and thicken with butter and a little flour. You may add truffles, morels, and mushrooms.

Kidney.

Chop veal-kidney, and some of the fat; likewise a little leek or onion, pepper, and salt; roll it up with an egg into balls, and fry them.

Calf's heart stuff and roast as a beef's heart: or sliced, make it into a pudding, as directed for steak or kidney pudding.

PORK, &c.

Bacon-hogs and porkers are differently **cut up.**

Hogs are kept to a larger size; the chine (or back-bone) is cut down on each side, the whole length, and is a prime **part** either boiled or roasted.

The sides of the hog are made into bacon, and the inside is cut out with very little meat to the bone. On eacn side there is a large spare-rib, which is usually divided into two, one sweet bone and a blade-bone. The bacon is the whole outside, and contains a fore-leg and a ham; which last is the hind leg; but, if left with the bacon, it is called a gammon. There are also griskins. Hogs' lard is the inner fat of the bacon hog.

Pickled pork is made of the flesh of the hog as well as bacon.

Porkers are not so old as hogs; their flesh is whiter, and less rich; but it is not so tender. It is divided into four quarters. The fore-quarter has the spring or fore-leg, the fore-loin or neck, the spare-rib, and griskin. The hind has the leg and the loin.

The feet of pork make various good dishes, and should be cut off before the legs are cured. Observe the same of the ears.

The bacon-hog is sometimes scalded to take off the hair, and sometimes singed. The porker is always scalded.

To roast a Leg of Pork.

Choose a small leg of fine young pork: cut a slit in the knuckle with a sharp knife; and fill the space with sage and onion chopped, and a little pepper and salt. When half-done, score the skin in slices, but do not cut deeper than the outer rind.

Apple-sauce and potatoes should be served to eat with it.

To boil a Leg of Pork.

Salt it eight or ten days: when it is to be dressed, weigh it: let it lie half an hour in cold water, to make it white: allow a quarter of an hour for every pound, and half an hour over, from the time it boils up: skim it as soon as it boils, and frequently after. Allow water enough. Save some of it, to make peas-soup. Some boil it in a very nice cloth, floured, which gives a very delicate look. It should be small, and of a fine grain.

Serve peas-pudding and turnips with it.

Loin and Neck of Pork.

Roast them. Cut the skin of the loin across, at distances of half an inch, with a sharp pen-knife.

Shoulders and Breasts of Pork.

Put them into pickle, or salt the shoulder as a leg: when very nice they may be roasted.

Rolled Neck of Pork.

Bone it; put a forcemeat of chopped sage, a very few crumbs of bread, salt, pepper, and two or three berries of allspice, over the inside; then roll the meat as tight as you can, and roast it slowly, and at a good distance at first.

Spring or Forehand of Pork.

Cut out the bone; sprinkle salt, pepper, and sage dried, over the inside; but first warm a little butter to baste it, and then flour it: roll the pork tight, and tie it; then roast by a hanging jack. About two hours will do it.

Spare-rib

Should be basted with a very little butter and a little flour, and then sprinkled with dried sage crumbled. Apple-sauce and potatoes for roasted pork.

Pork Griskin

Is usually very hard: the best way to prevent this is to put it into as much cold water as will cover it, and let it boil up; then instantly take it off, and put it into a Dutch oven; a very few minutes will do it. Remember to rub butter over it, and then flour it, before you put it to the fire.

Blade-bone of Pork

Is taken from the bacon-hog; the less meat left on it, in moderation, the better. It is to be broiled; and, when just done, pepper and salt it. Put to it a piece of butter, and a tea-spoonful of mustard; and serve it covered, quickly. This is a Somersetshire dish.

To dress Pork as Lamb.

Kill a young pig of four or five months old; cut up the fore quarter for roasting as you do lamb, and truss the shank close. The other parts will make delicate pickled pork; or steaks pies, &c.

Pork Steaks.

Cut them from a loin or neck, and of middling thickness; pepper and broil them, turning them often; when nearly done, put on salt, rub a bit of butter over, and serve the moment they are taken off the fire, a few at a time.

To pickle Pork.

The quantities proportioned to the middlings of a pretty large hog, the hams and shoulders being cut off.

Mix and pound fine four ounces of saltpetre, a pound of coarse sugar, an ounce of sal-prunella, and a little common salt; sprinkle the pork with salt, and drain it twenty-four hours: then rub with the above; pack the pieces tight in a small deep tub, filling up the spaces with common salt. Place large pebbles on the pork, to prevent it from swimming in the pickle which the salt will produce. If kept from air, it will continue very fine for two years.

Sausages.

Chop fat and lean pork together; season it with sage, pepper, and salt, and you may add two or three berries of allspice: *half fill* hog's guts that have been soaked and made extremely clean: or the meat may be kept in a very small pan closely covered; and so rolled and dusted with a very little flour before it is fried. Serve on stewed red cabbage; or mash potatoes put in a form, brown with salamander, and garnish with the above; they must be pricked with a fork before they are dressed, or they will burst.

An excellent Sausage to eat cold.

Season fat and lean pork with some salt, saltpetre, black pepper, and allspice, all in fine powder, and rub into the meat; the sixth day cut it small, and mix with it some shred shalot or garlic, as fine as possible. Have ready an ox-gut that has been scoured, salted, and soaked well, and fill it with the above stuffing; tie up the ends, and hang it to smoke as you would hams, but first wrap it in a fold or two of old muslin. It must be high-dried. Some eat it without boiling, but others like it boiled first. The skin should be tied in different places, so as to make each length about eight or nine inches long.

Spadbury's Oxford Sausages.

Chop a pound and a half of pork, and the same of veal, cleared of skin and sinews; add three quarters of a pound of beef-suet; mince and mix them; steep the crumb of a penny-loaf in water, and mix it with the meat, with also a little dried sage, pepper, and salt.

To scald a sucking Pig.

The moment the pig is killed, put it into cold water, for a few minutes; then rub it over with a little resin beaten extremely small, and put it into a pail of scalding water half a minute : take it out, lay it on a table, and pull off the hair as quickly as possible; if any part does not come off, put it in again. When quite clean, wash it well with warm water, and then in two or three cold waters, that no flavour of the resin may remain. Take off all the feet at the first joint; make a slit down the belly, and take out the entrails; put the liver, heart, and lights, to the feet. Wash the pig well in cold water, dry it thoroughly, and fold it in a wet cloth, to keep it from the air.

To roast a sucking Pig.

If you can get it wnen just killed, this is of great advantage. Let it be scalded, which the dealers usually do; then put some sage, crumbs of bread, salt, and pepper, into the belly, and sew it up. Observe to skewer the legs back, or the under part will not crisp.

Lay it to a brisk fire till thoroughly dry, then have ready some butter in a dry cloth, and rub the pig with it in every part. Dredge as much flour over as will possibly lie, and do not touch it again till ready to serve; then scrape off the flour very carefully with a blunt knife, rub it well with the buttered cloth, and take off the head while at the fire; take out the brains, and mix them with the gravy that comes from the pig. Then take it up; and, without withdrawing the spit, cut it down the back and belly, lay it into the dish, and chop the sage and bread quickly as fine as you can, and mix them with a large quantity of fine melted butter that has very little flour. Put the sauce into the dish after the pig has been split down the back, and garnish with the ears and the two jaws; take off the upper part of the head down to the snout.

In Devonshire it is served whole, if very small, the head only being cut off to garnish as above.

Pettitoes.

Boil them, the liver and the heart, in a small quantity of water, very gently; then cut the meat fine, and simmer it with a little of the water and the feet split, till the feet are quite tender; thicken with a bit of butter, a little flour, a spoonful of cream, and a little salt and pepper : give it a boil up, pour it over a few sippets of bread, and put the feet on the mince

To make excellent Meat of a Hog's Head.

Split the head, take out the brains, cut off the ears, and sprinkle it with common salt for a day; then drain it; salt it well with common salt and saltpetre three days; then lay the salt and head into a small quantity of water for two days.

Wash it, and boil it till all the bones will come out; remove them, and chop the head as quick as possible; but first skin the tongue, and take the skin carefully off the head, to put under and over. Season with pepper, salt, and a little mace, or allspice-berries. Put the skin into a small pan, press the cut head in, and put the other skin over; press it down. When cold it will turn out, and make a kind of brawn. If too fat, you may put a few bits of lean pork to be prepared the same way. Add salt and vinegar, and boil these with some of the liquor for a pickle to keep it.

To roast a Porker's Head.

Choose a fine young head, clean it well, and put bread and sage as for pig, sew it up tight, and on a string or hanging jack roast it as a pig, and serve with the same sauce.

To prepare Pig's Cheek for boiling.

Cut off the snout, and clean the head; divide it, and take out the eyes and the brains; sprinkle the head with salt, and let it drain twenty-four hours. Salt it with common salt and saltpetre: let it lie eight or ten days if to be dressed without stewing with peas, but less if to be dressed with peas; and it must be washed first, and then simmered till all is tender.

To Collar Pig's Head.

Scour the head and ears nicely; take off the hair and snout, and take out the eyes and the brains; lay it into water one night; then drain, salt it extremely well with common salt and saltpetre, and let it lie five days. Boil it enough to take out the bones; then lay it on a dresser, turning the thick end of one side of the head towards the thin end of the other, to make the roll of equal size; sprinkle it well with salt and white pepper, and roll it with the ears; and, if you approve, put the pig's feet round the outside when boned, or the thin parts of two cow-heels. Put it in a cloth, bind with a broad tape, and boil it till quite tender; then put a good weight upon it, and do not take off the covering till cold.

If you choose it to be more like brawn, salt it longer, and let the proportion of saltpetre be greater, and put in also some pieces of lean pork, and then cover it with cow-heel to look like the horn.

This may be kept either in or out of pickle of salt and water boiled, with vinegar; and is a very convenient thing to have in the house

If likely to spoil, slice and fry it either with or without batter

To dry Hog's Cheeks.

Cut out the snout, remove the brains, and split the head, taking off the upper bone, to make the chawl a good shape; rub it well with salt; next day take away the brine, and salt it again the following day; cover the head with half an ounce of saltpetre, two ounces of bay-salt, a little common salt, and four ounces of coarse sugar. Let the head be often turned; after ten days, smoke it for a week like bacon.

Jelly of Pig's Feet and Ears.

Clean and prepare as in the last article, then boil them in a very small quantity of water till every bone can be taken out, throw in half a handful of chopped sage, the same of parsley, and a seasoning of pepper, salt, and mace, in fine powder; simmer till the herbs are scalded, then pour the whole into a melon form.

Pig's Harslet.

Wash and dry some liver, sweetbreads, and fat and lean bits of pork, beating the latter with a rolling-pin, to make it tender; season with pepper, salt, sage, and a little onion shred fine; when mixed, put all into a cawl, and fasten it up tight with a needle and thread. Roast it on a hanging jack, or by a string.

Or serve in slices with parsley for a fry.

Serve with a sauce of port wine and water, and mustard, just boiled up, and put into the dish.

Mock Brawn.

Boil a pair of neat's feet very tender; take the meat off, and have ready the belly-piece of pork salted with common salt and saltpetre for a week. Boil this almost enough, take out any bones, and roll the feet and the pork together. Then roll it very tight with a strong cloth and coarse tape. Boil it till very tender, then hang it up in the cloth till cold; after which keep it in a sousing liquor, as is directed in the next article

Souse for Brawn, and for Pig's Feet and Ears.

Boil a quarter of a peck of wheat-bran, a sprig of bay, and a sprig of rosemary, in two gallons of water, with four ounces of salt in it, for half an hour. Strain it, and let it get cold

To make black Puddings.

The blood must be stirred with salt till cold. Put a quart of it, or rather more, to a quart of whole grits, to soak one night; and soak the crumb of a quartern loaf in rather more than two quarts of new milk made hot. In the mean time prepare the guts by washing, turning, and scraping with salt and water, and changing the water several times. Chop fine a little winter savoury and thyme, a good quantity of penny-royal, pepper and salt, a few cloves, some allspice, ginger and nutmeg; mix these with three pounds of beef-suet, and six eggs well beaten and strained; and then beat the bread, grits, &c., all up with the seasoning; when well mixed, have ready some hog's fat cut into large bits; and, as you fill the skins, put it in at proper distances. Tie in links only half-filled, and boil in a large kettle, pricking them as they swell, or they will burst. When boiled, lay them between clean cloths till cold, and hang them up in the kitchen. When to be used, scald them a few minutes in water, wipe and put them into a Dutch oven.

If there are not skins enough, put the stuffing into basins, and boil it covered with floured cloths, and slice and fry it when used.

To cure Hams.

Hang them a day or two, then sprinkle them with a little salt, and drain them another day; pound an ounce and a half of saltpetre, the same quantity of bay-salt, half an ounce of sal-prunella, and a pound of the coarsest sugar. Mix these well, and rub them into each ham every day for four days, and turn it. If a small one, turn it every day for three weeks; if a large one, a week longer, but do not rub after four days. Before you dry it, drain and cover with bran; smoke it ten days.

Another Way.—Choose the leg of a hog that is fat and well-fed, hang it as above; if large, put to it a pound of bay-salt, four ounces of saltpetre, a pound of the coarsest sugar, and a handful of common salt, all in fine powder, and rub it thoroughly. Lay the rind downwards, and cover the fleshy part with the salts. Baste it as often as you can with the pickle; the more the better. Keep it four weeks, turning it every day. Drain it, and throw bran over it; then hang it in a chimney where wood is burnt, and turn it sometimes for ten days.

Another Way.—When the weather will permit, hang the ham three days; mix an ounce of saltpetre with a quarter of a pound of bay-salt, the same quantity of common salt, and also of coarse sugar, and a quart of strong beer; boil them together, and pour them immediately upon the ham; turn it twice a day in the pickle for three weeks. An ounce of black pepper, and the same quantity of allspice, in fine powder, added to the above, will give still more flavour. Cover it with bran when wiped, and smoke it from three to four weeks, as you approve; the latter will make it harder, and give it more or the flavour of Westphalia.   Sew hams in hessings (that is, coarse wrappers), if to be smoked where there is a strong fire.

A Method of giving a still higher Flavour.—Sprinkle the ham with salt, after it has hung two or three days,—let it drain; make a pickle of a quart of strong beer, half a pound of trea-cle, an ounce of coriander-seeds, two ounces of juniper-berries an ounce of pepper, the same quantity of allspice, an ounce of saltpetre, half an ounce of sal-prunel, a handful of common salt, and a head of shalot, all pounded or cut fine.   Boil these all together a few minutes, and pour them over the ham: this quantity is for one of ten pounds.   Rub and turn it every day for a fortnight, then sew it up in a thin linen bag, and smoke it three weeks.   Take care to drain it from the pickle, and rub it in bran before drying.

A Pickle for Hams, Tongues, or Beef, to be boiled and skimmed between each Parcel of them.

To two gallons of spring-water put two pounds of coarse sugar, two pounds of bay and two pounds and a half of com-mon salt, and half a pound of saltpetre, in a deep earthen glazed pan that will hold four gallons, and with a cover that will fit close.   Keep the beef or hams as long as they will bear, before you put them into the pickle; and sprinkle them with coarse sugar in a pan, from which they must drain.   Rub the hams, &c., well with the pickle, and pack them in close; put-ting as much as the pan will hold, so that the pickle may cover them.   The pickle is not to be boiled at first.   A small ham may lie fourteen days, a large one three weeks; a tongue twelve days, and beef in proportion to its size.   They will eat well out of the pickle without drying.   When they are to be dried, let each piece be drained over the pan; and when it will drop no longer, take a clean sponge, and dry it thoroughly. Six or eight hours will smoke them, and there should be only a little saw-dust and wet straw burnt to do this; but, if put into a baker's chimney, sew them in coarse cloth, and hang them a week.

To dress Hams.

If long hung, put the ham into water a night, and let it lie either in a hole dug in the earth, or on damp stones sprinkled with water two or three days, to mellow; covering it with a heavy tub, to keep vermin from it.   Wash well, and put it into a boiler with plenty of water; let it simmer four, five, or six hours, according to the size.   When done enough, if before the time of serving, cover it with a clean cloth doubled, and keep the dish hot over boiling water   Take off the skin, and strew raspings over the ham. Garnish with carrot. Preserve the skin as whole as possible, to keep over the ham wnen cold, whicn will prevent its drying.

Excellent Bacon.

Diviae the hog, and take the chine out; it is common to remove the spare-ribs, but the bacon will be preserved better from being rusty if they are left in. Salt the bacon six days, then drain it from that first pickle: mix as much salt as you judge proper with eight ounces of bay-salt, three ounces of saltpetre, and a pound of coarse sugar, to each hog, but first cut off the hams. Rub the salts well in, and turn it every day for a month. Drain, and smoke it a few days; or dry without, by hanging in the kitchen, not near the fire.

The manner of curing Wiltshire Bacon.

Sprinkle each flitch with salt, and let the blood drain off for twenty four hours; then mix a pound and a half of coarse sugar, the same quantity of bay-salt, not quite so much as half a pound of saltpetre, and a pound of common salt, and rub this well on the bacon, turning it every day for a month; then hang it to dry, and afterwards smoke it ten days. This quantity of salts is sufficient for the whole hog.

MUTTON.

Take away the pipe that runs along the bone of the inside of a chine of mutton; and if to be kept a great time, rub the part close round the tail with salt, after first cutting out the kernel.

The kernel in the fat on the thick part of the leg should be taken out by the butcher, for it taints first there. The chine and rib-bones should be wiped every day, and the bloody part of the neck be cut off, to preserve it. The brisket changes first in the breast; and if it is to be kept, it is best to rub it with a little salt, should the weather be hot.

Every kernel should be taken out of all sorts of meat as soon as brought it; then wipe dry.

For roasting, it should hang as long as it will keep, the hind-quarter especially, but not so long as to taint; for whatever fashion may authorize, putrid juices ought not to be taken into the stomach.

Mutton for boiling will not look of a good colour if it has hung long.

Great care should be taken to preserve, by paper, the fat of what is roasted.

Leg of Mutton.

If roasted, serve with onion or currant-jelly sauce; if boiled, with caper-sauce and vegetables.

Neck of Mutton

Is particularly useful, as so many dishes may be made of it but it is not advantageous for the family. The bones should be cut short, which the butchers will not do unless particularly desired.

The best end of the neck may be boiled, and served with turnips, or roasted, or dressed in steaks, in pies, or harrico.

The scrags may be stewed in broth, or with a small quantity of water, some small onions, a few pepper-corns, and a little rice, and served together.

When a neck is to be boiled to look particularly nice, saw down the chine-bone, strip the ribs half way down, and chop off the ends of the bones about four inches. The skin should not be taken off till boiled, and then the fat will look the whiter

When there is more fat to the neck or loin of mutton, than it is agreeable to eat with the lean, it makes an uncommonly good suet-pudding, or crust for a meat pie, if cut very fine.

Shoulder of Mutton roasted.

Serve with onion sauce : the blade-bone may be broiled.

To dress Haunch of Mutton.

Keep it as long as it can be preserved sweet by the different modes ; let it be washed with warm milk and water, or vinegar, if necessary ; but when to be dressed, observe to wash it well, lest the outside should have a bad flavour from keeping. Put a paste of coarse flour on strong paper, and fold the haunch in ; set it a great distance from the fire, and allow proportionable time for the paste ; do not take it off till about thirty-five or forty minutes before serving, and then baste it continually Bring the haunch nearer to the fire before you take off the paste, and froth it up as you would venison.

A gravy must be made of a pound and a half of loin of old mutton, simmered in a pint of water to half, and no seasoning but salt : brown it with a little burnt sugar, and send it up in the dish ; but there should be a good deal of gravy in the meat ; for though long at the fire, the distance and covering will prevent its roasting out.

Serve with currant-jelly sauce.

To roast a Saddle of Mutton.

Let it be well kept first. Raise the skin, and then skewer it on again ; take it off a quarter of an hour before serving sprinkle it with some salt, baste it, and dredge it well with flour. The rump should be split, and skewered back on each side. The joint may be large or small according to the com-

pany : it is the most elegant if the latter.   Being broad, it re
quires a high and strong fire.

Harrico.

Take off some of the fat, and cut the middle or best end of
the neck into rather thin steaks; flour and fry them in their
own fat of a fine light brown, but not enough for eating. Then
put them into a dish while you fry the carrots, turnips, and
onions ; the carrots and turnips in dice, the onions sliced : but
they must only be warmed, not browned, or you need not fry
them.   Then lay the steaks at the bottom of a stew-pan, the
vegetables over them, and pour as much boiling water as will
iust cover them ; give one boil, skim well, and then set the
pan on the side of the fire to simmer gently till tender.   In
three or four hours skim them ; and add pepper, salt, and a
spoonful of ketchup.

To hash Mutton.

Cut thin slices of dressed mutton, fat and lean; flour them ;
have ready a little onion boiled in two or three spoonfuls of
water; add to it a little gravy and the meat seasoned, and
make it hot, but not to boil.   Serve in a covered dish.   Instead of onion, a clove, a spoonful of currant-jelly, and half a
glass of port wine, will give an agreeable flavour of venison,
if the meat be fine.

Pickle cucumber, or walnut, cut small, warm in it for change.

To boil Shoulder of Mutton with Oysters.

Hang it some days, then salt it well for two days ; bone it ;
and sprinkle it with pepper, and a bit of mace pounded :
lay some oysters over it, and roll the meat up tight and tie it.
Stew it in a small quantity of water, with an onion and a few
pepper-corns, till quite tender.

Have ready a little good gravy, and some oysters stewed in
it ; thicken this with flour and butter, and pour over the mutton when the tape is taken off.   The stew-pan should be kept
close covered.

Breast of Mutton.

Cut off the superfluous fat, and roast and serve the meat with
stewed cucumbers; or to eat cold, covered with chopped
parsley.   Or half-boil, and then grill it before the fire ; in which
case cover it with crumbs and herbs, and serve with caper-
sauce.   Or if boned, take off a good deal of the fat, and cover
it with bread, herbs, and seasoning ; then roll and boil ; and
serve with chopped walnuts or capers and butter.

Loin of Mutton

Roasted, if cut lengthways as a saddle, some think it cuts better. Or for steaks, pies, or broth.

To roll Loin of Mutton

Hang the mutton till tender; bone it, and lay a seasoning of pepper, allspice, mace, nutmeg, and a few cloves, all in fine powder, over it. Next day prepare a stuffing as for hare; beat the meat, and cover it with the stuffing; roll it up tight, and tie it. Half bake it in a slow oven; let it grow cold; take off the fat, and put the gravy into a stew-pan; flour the meat, and put it in likewise; stew it till almost ready; and add a glass of port wine, some ketchup, an anchovy, and a little lemon-pickle, half an hour before serving; serve it in the gravy, and with jelly sauce. A few fresh mushrooms are a great improvement; but if to eat like hare, do not use these, nor the lemon-pickle.

Mutton Ham.

Choose a fine-grained leg of wether-mutton, of twelve or fourteen pounds weight; let it be cut ham shape, and hang two days. Then put into a stewpan half a pound of bay-salt, the same of common salt, two ounces of saltpetre, and half a pound of a coarse sugar, all in powder; mix, and make it quite hot: then rub it well into the ham. Let it be turned in the liquor every day; at the end of four days put two ounces more of common salt; in twelve days take it out, dry it, and hang it up in wood-smoke, a week. It is to be used in slices, with stewed cabbage, mashed potatoes, or eggs.

Mutton Collops.

Take a loin of mutton that has been well hung; and cut from the part next the leg, some collops very thin. Take out the sinews. Season the collops with salt, pepper, and mace; and strew over them shred parsley, thyme, and two or three shalots: fry them in butter till half done; add half a pint of gravy, a little juice of lemon, and a piece of butter rubbed in flour; and simmer the whole very gently five minutes. They should be served immediately, or they will be hard.

Mutton Cutlets in the Portuguese way.

Cut the chops; and half fry them with sliced shalot or onion, chopped parsley, and two bay-leaves; season with pepper and salt; then lay a forcemeat on a piece of white paper, put the chop on it, and twist the paper up, leaving a hole for the end of the bones to go through. Broil on a gentle fire. Serve with sauce Robart; or, as the seasoning makes the cutlets high, a little gravy.

Mutton Steaks

Should be cut from a loin or neck that has hung : **if a neck,** the bones should not be long. They should be broiled **on a** clear fire, seasoned when half-done, and often turned ; take them up into a very hot dish, rub a bit of butter on each, and serve hot and hot the moment they are done.

Steaks of Mutton, or Lamb, and Cucumbers.

Quarter cucumbers, and lay them into a deep dish, sprinkle them with salt, and pour vinegar over them. Fry the chops of a fine brown, and put them into a stew-pan ; drain the cucumbers, and put over the steaks ; add some sliced onions, pepper, and salt ; pour hot water or weak broth on them ; stew and skim well.

Mutton Steaks, Maintenon.

Half-fry ; stew them, while hot, with herbs, crumbs, and seasoning ; put them in paper immediately, and finish on the gridiron. Be careful the paper does not catch ; rub a bit of butter on it first, to prevent that.

Mutton Sausages.

Take a pound of the rawest part of the leg of mutton that has been either roasted or boiled ; chop it extremely small, and season it with pepper, salt, mace, and nutmeg ; add to it six ounces of beef suet, some sweet herbs, two anchovies, and a pint of oysters, all chopped very small ; a quarter of a pound of grated bread, some of the anchovy liquor, and the yolks and whites of two eggs well beaten. Put it all, when well mixed, into a little pot ; and use it by rolling it into balls or sausage-shape, and frying. If approved, a *little* shalot may be added, or garlic, which is a great improvement.

To dress Mutton Rumps and Kidneys.

Stew six rumps in some good mutton gravy half an hour ; then take them up, and let them stand to cool. Clear the gravy from the fat, and put into it four ounces of boiled rice, an onion stuck with cloves, and a blade of mace ; boil them till the rice is thick. Wash the rumps with yolk of eggs well beaten ; and strew over them crumbs of bread, a little pepper and salt, chopped parsley and thyme, and grated lemon peel. Fry in butter of a fine brown. While the rumps are stewing, lard the kidneys, and put them to roast in a Dutch oven. When the rumps are fried, the grease must be drained before they are put on the dish, and, the pan being cleared likewise from the fat, warm the rice in it. Lay the latter on the dish ; the rumps put round on the rice, the narrow ends towards the middle, and the kidneys between.   Garnish with hard eggs cut in half, the white being left on ; or with different-coloured pickles.

LAMB.

Leg of Lamb

Should be boiled in a cloth, to look as white as possible. The loin fried in steaks and served round, garnished with dried or fried parsley ; spinach to eat with it : or dressed separately, or roasted.

Fore Quarter of Lamb.

Roast it either whole or in separate parts. If left to be cold, chopped parsley should be sprinkled over it. The neck and breast together are called a scoven.

Breast of Lamb, and Cucumbers.

Cut off the chine-bone from the breast, and set it on to stew with a pint of gravy.   When the bones would draw out, put it on the gridiron to grill ; and then lay it in a dish on cucumbers nicely stewed.

Shoulder of Lamb forced, with Sorrel Sauce.

Bone a shoulder of lamb, and fill it up with forcemeat ; bruise it two hours over a slow stove.   Take it up, glaze it; or it may be glazed only, and not braised.   Serve with sorrel-sauce under the lamb.

Lamb Steaks.

Fry them of a beautiful brown ; when served, throw over them a good quantity of crumbs of bread fried, and crimped parsley ; the receipt for doing which of a finer colour will be given under the head of *Vegetables*.

Mutton or lamb steaks, seasoned and broiled in buttered papers, either with crumbs and herbs, or without, are a gen eel dish, and eat well.

Sauce for them, called Sauce Robart, will be found in the list of *Sauces*.

Lamb Cutlets with Spinach.

Cut the steaks from the loin, and fry them : the spinach is to be stewed and put into the dish first, and then the cutlets round it.

Lamb's Head and Hinge.

This part is best from a house-lamb ; but any, if soaked in cold water, will be white.   Boil the head separately till very tender. Have ready the liver and lights three parts boiled and cut small : stew them in a little of the water in which they were boiled, season and thicken with flour and butter, and serve the mince round the head.

Lamb's Fry.

Serve it fried of a beautiful colour, and with a good deal of dried or fried parsley over it.

Lamb's Sweetbreads.

Blanch them, and put them a little while into cold water Then put them into a stewpan, with a ladleful of broth, some pepper and salt, a small bunch of small onions, and a blade of mace ; stir in a bit of butter and flour, and stew half an hour. Have ready two or three eggs well beaten in cream, with a little minced parsley and a few grates of nutmeg. Put in some boiled asparagus-tops to the other things. Don't let it boil after the cream is in, but make it hot, and stir it well all the while. Take great care it does not curdle. Young French beans or peas may be added, first boiled of a beautiful colour.

FISH.

Turbot, if good, should be thick, and the belly of a yellowish white ; if a blueish cast, or thin, they are bad. They are in season the greatest part of the summer.

Salmon.—If new, the flesh is of a fine red (the gills particularly), the scales bright, and the whole fish stiff. When just killed, there is a whiteness between the flakes, which gives great firmness; by keeping, this melts down, and the fish is more rich. The Thames salmon bears the highest price ; that caught in the Severn is next in goodness, and is even preferred by some. Small heads, and thick in the neck, are best.

Cod.—The gills should be very red : the fish should be very thick at the neck, the flesh white and firm, and the eyes fresh. When flabby they are not good. They are in season from the beginning of December till the end of April.

Skate.—If good, they are very white and thick. If too fresh they eat tough, but must not be kept above two days.

Herrings.—If good, their gills are of a fine red, and the eyes bright ; as is likewise the whole fish, which must be stiff and firm.

Soles.—If good, they are thick, and the belly is of a cream-colour ; if this is of a blueish cast and flabby, they are not fresh. They are in the market almost the whole year, but are in the highest perfection about midsummer.

Whitings.—The firmness of the body and fins is to be looked to as in herrings; their high season is during the three first months of the year, but they may be had a great part of it.

Mackarel.—Choose as whitings. Their season is May, June, and July. They are so tender a fish, that they carry and keep worse than any other.

Pike.—For freshness observe the above marks. The best are taken in rivers: they are a very dry fish, and are much in-debted to stuffing and sauce.

Carp live some time out of water, and may therefore get wasted; it ·is best to kill them as soon as caught, to prevent this. The same signs of freshness attend them as other fish.

Tench.—They are a fine-flavoured fresh-water fish, and should be killed and dressed as soon as caught.—When they are to be bought, examine whether the gills are red and hard to open, the eyes bright, and the body stiff. The tench has a slimy matter about it, the clearness and brightness of which shew freshness The season is July, August, and September.

Perch.—Take the general rules given to distinguish the freshness of other fish. They are not so delicate as carp and tench,

Smelts, if good, have a fine silvery hue, are very firm, and have a refreshing smell like cucumbers newly cut.—They are caught in the Thames and some other large rivers.

Mullets.—The sea are preferred to the river mullets, and the red to the gray. They should be very firm.—Their season is August.

Gudgeons.—They are chosen by the same rules as other fish. They are taken in running streams; come in about midsum-mer; and are to be had for five or six months.

Eels.—There is a greater difference in the goodness of eels than of any other fish. The true silver eel (so called from the bright colour of the belly) is caught in the Thames. The Dutch eels sold at Billingsgate are very bad; those taken in great floods are generally good, but in ponds they have usually a strong rank flavour. Except the middle of summer they are al-ways in season.

Lobsters.—If they have not been long taken the claws will have a strong motion when you put your finger on the eyes and press them The heaviest are the best, and it is preferable to boil them at home. When you buy them ready boiled, try whether their tails are stiff, and pull up with a spring: other-wise that part will be flabby. The cock-lobster is known by the narrow back part of his tail, and the two uppermost fins within it are stiff and hard; but those of the hen are soft, and the tail broader. The male, though generally smaller, has the highest flavour, the flesh is firmer, and the colour, when boiled, is a deeper red.

Crabs.—The heaviest are best, and those of a middling size are sweetest. If light they are watery: when in perfection the joints of the legs are stiff, and the body has a very agreeable smell. The eyes look dead and loose when stale.

Prawns and Shrimps.—When fresh they have a sweet flavour, are firm and stiff, and the colour is bright.—Shrimps are of the prawn kind, and may be judged by the same rules.

Oysters.—There are several kinds; the Pyfleet, Colchester, and Milford, are much the best. The native Milton are fine, being white and fat; but others may be made to possess both these qualities in some degree by proper feeding. When alive and strong, the shell closes on the knife. They should be eaten as opened, the flavour becoming poor otherwise. The rock oyster is largest, but usually has a coarse flavour if eaten raw.

Flounders.—They should be thick, firm, and have their eyes bright. They very soon become flabby and bad. They are both sea and river fish. The Thames produces the best.— They are in season from January to March, and from July to September.

Sprats.—Choose by the same rules as herrings.

Observations on dressing Fish.

If the fishmonger does not clean it, fish is seldom very nicely done; but those in great towns wash it beyond what is necessary for cleaning, and by perpetual watering diminish the flavour. When quite clean, if to be boiled, some salt and a little vinegar should be put into the water to give it firmness; but cod, whiting, and haddock, are far better if a little salted, and kept a day; and if not very hot weather they will be good two days.

Those who know how to purchase fish may, by taking more at a time than they want for one day, often get it cheap: and such kinds as will pot or pickle, or keep by being sprinkled with salt and hung up, or, by being fried, will serve for stewing the next day, may then be bought with advantage.

Fresh-water fish has often a muddy smell and taste; to take off which, soak it in strong salt and water after it is nicely cleaned; or, if of a size to bear it, scald it in the same; then dry and dress it.

The fish must be put into the water while cold, and set to

do very gently, or the outside will break before the inner part is done.

Crimp fish should be put into boiling water; and when it boils up, pour a little cold water in to check extreme heat, and simmer it a few minutes.

The fish-plate on which it is done may be drawn up to see if it be ready; it will leave the bone when it is.—It should then be immediately taken out of the water, or it will be woolly. The fish-plate should be set crossways over the kettle, to keep hot for serving; and a clean cloth over the fish to prevent its losing its colour.

Small fish nicely fried, covered with egg and crumbs, make a dish far more elegant than if served plain.— Great attention should be paid to garnishing fish: use plenty of horse-radish, parsley, and lemon.

When well done, and with very good sauce, fish is more attended to than almost any other dish. The liver and roe should be placed on the dish, so that the lady may see them, and help a part to every one.

If fish is to be fried or broiled, it must be wrapt in a nice cloth after it is well cleaned and washed.—When perfectly dry, wet with an egg if for frying, and sprinkle the finest crumbs of bread over it; if done a second time with the egg and bread, the fish will look much better: then having a thick-bottomed frying-pan on the fire, with a large quantity of lard or dripping boiling hot, plunge the fish into it, and let it fry middlingly quick, till the colour is a fine brown yellow, and it is judged ready. If it is done enough before it has obtained a proper degree of colour, the cook should draw the pan to the side of the fire, carefully take it up, and either place it on a large sieve turned upwards, and to be kept for that purpose only, or on the under side of a dish to drain; and if wanted very nice, a sheet or cap paper must be put to receive the fish, which should look a beautiful colour, and all the crumbs appear distinct; the fish being free from all grease. The same dripping, with a little fresh, will serve a second time. Butter gives a bad colour; oil fries of the finest colour for those who will allow the expense.

Garnish with a fringe of curled raw parsley, or parsley fried, which must be thus done: When washed and picked, throw it again into clean water: when the lard or dripping boils throw the parsley into it immediately from the water, and instantly it will be green and crisp, and must be taken up with a slice; this may be done after the fish is fried.

If fish is to be broiled, it must be seasoned, floured, and put on a gridiron that is very clean; which, when hot, should be rubbed with a bit of suet, to prevent the fish from sticking. It must be broiled on a very clear fire, that it may not taste smoky; and not too near, that it may not be scorched.

To keep Turbot.

If necessary, turbot will keep for two or three days, and be in as high perfection as at first, if lightly rubbed over with salt, and carefully hung in a cold place.

To boil Turbot.

The turbot-kettle must be of a proper size, and in the nicest order. Set the fish in cold water sufficient to cover it completely, throw a handful of salt and a glass of vinegar into it, and let it gradually boil; be very careful that there fall no blacks; but skim it well, and preserve the beauty of the colour.

Serve it garnished with a complete fringe of curled parsley, lemon, and horse-radish.

The sauce must be the finest lobster, and anchovy butter, and plain butter, served plentifully in separate tureens.

To boil Salmon.

Clean it carefully, boil it gently, and take it out of the water as soon as done. Let the water be warm if the fish be split. It underdone it is very unwholesome.

Shrimp or anchovy sauce.

To broil Salmon.

Cut slices an inch thick, and season with pepper and salt; lay each slice in half a sheet of white paper, well buttered, twist the ends of the paper, and broil the slices over a slow fire six or eight minutes. Serve in the paper with anchovy-sauce.

To pickle Salmon.

Boil as before directed, take the fish out, and boil the liquor with bay-leaves, pepper-corns, and salt; add vinegar, when cold, and pour it over the fish.

COD.

Some people boil the cod whole; but a large head and shoulders contain all the fish that is proper to help, the thinner parts being overdone and tasteless before the thick are ready. But the whole fish may be purchased at times more reasonably; and the lower half, if sprinkled and hung up, will be in high perfection one or two days. Or it may be made salter, and served with egg-sauce, potatoes, and parsnips.

Cod when small is usually very cheap. If boiled quite

fresh it is watery; but eats excellently if salted and hung up for a day, to give it firmness, then stuffed, and broiled, or boiled.

Cod's Head and Shoulders

Will eat much finer by having a little salt rubbed down the bone, and along the thick part, even if it be eaten the same day

Tie it up, and put it on the fire in cold water which will completely cover it: throw a handful of salt into it. Great care must be taken to serve it without the smallest speck of black or scum. Garnish with a large quantity of double parsley, lemon, horse-radish, and the milt, roe, and liver, and fried smelts, if approved. If with smelts, be careful that no water hangs about the fish ; or the beauty of the smelts will be taken off, as well as their flavour.

Serve with plenty of oyster or shrimp sauce, and anchovy and butter.

Crimp Cod.

Boil, broil, or fry.

To dress Salt Cod.

Soak and clean the piece you mean to dress, then lay it all night in water, with a glass of vinegar. Boil it enough, then break it into flakes on the dish ; pour over it parsnips boiled, beaten in a mortar, and then boil up with cream and a large piece of butter rubbed with a bit of flour. It may be served as above with egg-sauce instead of the parsnip, and the root sent up whole; or the fish may be boiled and sent up without flaking, and sauces as above.

Thornback and Skate

Should be hung one day at least before they are dressed ; and may be served either boiled, or fried in crumbs, being first dipped in egg.

Crimp Skate.

Boil and send up in a napkin; or fry as above.

Maids

Should likewise be hung up one day at least. They may be broiled or fried : or, if a tolerable size, the middle may be boiled and the fins fried. They should be dipped in egg, and covered with crumbs

Boiled Carp.

Serve in a napkin, and with the sauce which you will find directed for it under the article Stewed Carp.

Stewed Carp

Scale and clean, take care of the roe, &c. Lay the fish in a stew-pan, with a rich beef-gravy, an onion, eight cloves, a dessert-spoonful of Jamaica pepper, the same of black, a fourth part of the quantity of gravy or port (cider may do); simmer close-covered; when nearly done add two anchovies chopped fine, a dessert-spoonful of made mustard, and some fine walnut ketchup, a bit of butter rolled in flour: shake it, and let the gravy boil a few minutes. Serve with sippets of fried bread, the roe fried, and a good deal of horse-radish and lemon.

Baked Carp.

Clean a large carp; put a stuffing as for soles, dressed in the Portuguese way. Sew it up; brush it all over with yolk of egg, and put plenty of crumbs; then drop oiled butter to baste them; place the carp in a deep earthen dish, a pint of stock (or, if fast-day, fish-stock), a few sliced onions, some bay-leaves, a faggot of herbs (such as basil, thyme, parsley, and both sorts of marjoram), half a pint of port wine, and six anchovies. Cover over the pan, and bake it an hour. Let it be done before it is wanted. Pour the liquor from it, and keep the fish hot while you heat up the liquor with a good piece of butter rolled in flour, a tea-spoonful of mustard, a little Cayenne, and a spoonful of soy. Serve the fish on the dish, garnished with lemon and parsley, and horse-radish, and put the gravy into the sauce-tureen.

Perch and Tench.

Put them into cold water, boil them carefully, and serve with melted butter and soy. Perch are a most delicate fish. They may be either fried or stewed, but in stewing they do not preserve so good a flavour.

To fry Trout and Grayline.

Scale, gut, and well wash; then dry them, and lay them separately on a board before the fire, after dusting some flour over them. Fry them of a fine colour with fresh dripping; serve with crimp parsley and plain butter.

Perch and *Tench* may be done the same way.

MACKAREL.

Boil, and serve with butter and fennel.

To broil them, split, and sprinkle with herbs, pepper, and salt; or stuff with the same, crumbs, and chopped fennel.

Collared, as Eel, page 424.

Potted ; clean, season, and bake them in a pan with spice, bay-leaves, and some butter ; when cold, lay them in a potting pot, and cover with butter.

Pickled ; boil them, then boil some of the liquor, a few pepper-corns, bay-leaves, and some vinegar ; when cold, pour it over them.

Caveach.

Clean and divide your mackarel ; then cut each side into three, or, leaving them undivided, cut each side into five or six pieces. To six large mackarel take near an ounce of pepper two nutmegs, a little mace, four cloves, and a handful of salt, all in the finest powder ; mix, and, making holes in each bit of fish, thrust the seasoning into them, rub each piece with some of it ; then fry them brown in oil ; let them stand till cold, then put them into a stone jar, and cover with vinegar ; if to keep long, pour oil on the top. Thus done, they may be preserved for months.

Red Mullet.

It is called the Sea-Woodcock. Clean, but leave the inside, fold in oiled paper, and gently bake in a small dish. Make a sauce of the liquor that comes from the fish, with a piece of butter, a little flour, a little essence of anchovy, and a glass of sherry. Give it a boil ; and serve in a boat, and the fish in the paper cases.

To bake Pike.

Scale it, and open as near the throat as you can, then stuff it with the following ; grated bread, herbs, anchovies, oysters, suet, salt, pepper, mace, half a pint of cream, four yolks of eggs ; mix all over the fire till it thickens, then put it into the fish, and sew it up ; butter should be put over it in little bits ; bake it. Serve sauce of gravy, butter, and anchovy. Note : if, in helping a pike, the back and belly are slit up, and each slice gently drawn downwards, there will be fewer bones given.

HADDOCK.

To dry Haddock.

Choose them of two or three pounds' weight : take out the gills, eyes, and entrails, and remove the blood from the backbone. Wipe them dry, and put some salt into the bodies and eyes. Lay them on a board for a night ; then hang them up in a dry place, and after three or four days they will be fit to eat : skin and rub them with egg, and strew crumbs over them. Lay them before the fire, and baste with butter until brown enough. Serve with egg-sauce.

Whitings, if large, are excellent this way; and it will prove an accommodation in the country, where there is no regular supply of fish.

Stuffing for Pike, Haddock, and small Cod.

Take equal parts of fat bacon, beef-suet, and fresh butter, some parsley, thyme, and savoury; a little onion, and a few leaves of scented marjoram, shred fine; an anchovy or two; a little salt and nutmeg, and some pepper. Oysters will be an improvement with or without anchovies; add crumbs, and an egg to bind.

SOLES.

If boiled, they must be served with great care to look perfectly white, and should be much covered with parsley.

If fried, dip in egg, and cover them with fine crumbs o bread; set on a frying-pan that is just large enough, and put into it a large quantity of fresh lard or dripping, boil it, and immediately slip the fish into it; do them of a fine brown. See to fry, page 421.

Soles that have been fried eat good cold with oil, vinegar, salt, and mustard.

Stewed Soles.

Take two or three soles, divide them from the back-bone, and take off the head, fins, and tail. Sprinkle the inside with salt, roll them up tight from the tail-end upwards, and fasten with small skewers. If large or middling, put half a fish in each roll; small do not answer. Dip them into yolks of eggs, and cover them with crumbs. Do the egg over them again, and then put more crumbs; and fry them a beautiful colour in lard, or for fast-day in clarified butter.

To fry Smelts.

They should not be washed more than is necessary to clean them. Dry them in a cloth; then lightly flour them, but shake it off. Dip them into plenty of egg, then into bread-crumbs grated fine, and plunge them into a good pan of *boiling* lard; let them continue gently boiling, and a few minutes will make them a bright yellow brown. Take care not to take off the light roughness of the crumbs, or their beauty will be lost.

Spitchcock Eels.

Take one or two large eels, leave the skin on, cut them into pieces of three inches long, open them on the belly side, and clean them nicely: wipe them dry, and then wet them with beaten egg, and strew over en both sides chopped parsley pepper, salt, a very little sage, and a bit of mace pounded fine, and mixed with the seasoning. Rub the gridiron with a bit of suet, and broil the fish of a fine colour.

Serve with anchovy and butter for sauce.

Fried Eels.

If small, they should be curled round and fried, being first dipped into egg and crumbs of bread.

Boiled Eels.

The small ones are best; do them in a small quantity of water, with a good deal of parsley, which should be served up with them and the liquor.

Serve chopped parsley and butter for sauce.

To stew Lamprey as at Worcester.

After cleaning the fish carefully, remove the cartilage which runs down the back, and season with a small quantity of cloves, mace, nutmeg, pepper, and allspice; put it into a small stew-pot, with very strong beef-gravy, port, and an equal quantity of Madeira or sherry.

It must be covered close; stew till tender, then take out the lamprey and keep hot, while you boil up the liquor with two or three anchovies chopped, and some flour and butter; strain the gravy through a sieve, and add lemon-juice and some made mustard. Serve with sippets of bread and horse-radish.

Eels, done the same way, are a good deal like the lamprey. When there is spawn, it must be fried and put round.

Note. Cider will do in common instead of white wine.

FLOUNDERS.

Let them be rubbed with salt inside and out, and lie two hours to give them some firmness. Dip them into egg, cover with crumbs, and fry them.

Water Souchy.

Stew two or three flounders, some parsley-leaves and roots, thirty pepper-corns, and a quart of water, till the fish are boiled to pieces; pulp them through a sieve. Set over the fire the pulped fish, the liquor that boiled them, some perch, tench, or flounders, and some fresh leaves and roots of parsley; simmer all till done enough, then serve in a deep dish. Slices of bread and butter are to be sent to table, to eat with the souchy

HERRINGS AND SPRATS.

To smoke Herrings.

Clean and lay them in salt and a little saltpetre one night, then hang them on a stick, through the eyes, in a row. Have ready an old cask, in which put some sawdust, and in the midst of it a heater red hot; fix the stick over the smoke, and let 'hem remain twenty-four hours.

Fried Herrings.

Serve them of a light brown, with onions sliced and fried.

Broiled Herrings.

Flour them first, and do of a good colour: plain butter for sauce.

To dress Red Herrings.

Choose those that are large and moist, cut them open, and pour some boiling small-beer over them to soak half an hour; drain them dry, and make them just hot through before the fire, then rub some cold butter over them and serve. Egg-sauce, or buttered eggs, and mashed potatoes, should be sent up with them.

Baked Herrings and Sprats.

Wash and drain without wiping them; season with allspice in fine powder, salt, and a few whole cloves; lay them in a pan with plenty of black pepper, an onion, and a few bay-leaves Add half vinegar and half small beer, enough to cover them. Put paper over the pan, and bake in a slow oven. If you like, throw saltpetre over them the night before, to make them look red. Gut, but do not open them.

Sprats,

When cleaned, should be fastened in rows by a skewer run through the heads, and then broiled, and served hot and hot.

LOBSTERS AND SHRIMPS.
To Pot Lobsters.

Half-boil them, pick out the meat, cut it into small bits, season with mace, white pepper, nutmeg, and salt, press close into a pot, and cover with butter; bake half an hour; put the spawn in. When cold take the lobster out, and put it into the pots with a little of the butter. Beat the other butter in a mortar with some of the spawn; then mix that coloured butter with as much as will be sufficient to cover the pots, and strain it. Cayenne may be added, if approved.

Another way to Pot Lobsters.

Take out the meat as whole as you can; split the tail and

remove the gut; if the inside be not watery, add that. Season
with mace, nutmeg, white pepper, salt, and a clove or two, in
the finest powder. Lay a little fine butter at the bottom of
the pan, and the lobster smooth over it, with bay-leaves between; cover it with butter, and bake gently. When done
pour the whole on the bottom of a sieve; and with a fork lay
the pieces into potting-pots, some of each sort, with the seasoning about it. When cold, pour clarified butter over, but not
hot. It will be good next day; or highly seasoned, and thick-
covered with butter, will keep some time.

Potted lobster may be used cold, or as a fricassee, with a
cream-sauce: it then looks very nicely and eats excellently,
especially if there is spawn.

Mackarel, Herrings, and *Trout,* are good potted as above.

To pot Shrimps.

When boiled, take them out of the skins, and season them
with salt, white pepper, and a very little mace and cloves.
Press them into a pot, set it in the oven ten minutes, and when
cold put butter.

CRABS.
Hot Crab.

Pick the meat out of a crab, clear the shell from the head,
then put the meat with a little nutmeg, salt, pepper, a bit of
butter, crumbs of bread, and three spoonfuls of vinegar, into
the shell again, and set it before the fire. You may brown it
with a salamander.

Dry toast should be served to eat it upon.

Dressed Crab cold.

Empty the shells, and mix the flesh with oil, vinegar, salt,
and a little white pepper and Cayenne: then put the mixture
into the large shell, and serve. Very little oil is necessary.

OYSTERS.
To feed Oysters.

Put them into water, and wash them with a birch besom til
quite clean; then lay them bottom-downwards into a pan,
sprinkle with flour or oatmeal and salt, and cover with water
Do the same every day, and they will fatten. The water
should be pretty salt.

To stew Oysters.

Open, and separate the liquor from them, then wash them
from the grit, strain the liquor, and put with the oysters a bit of

mace and lemon-peel, and a few white pepper-corns. Simmer them very gently, and put some cream, and a little flour and butter.

Serve with sippets.

To scallop Oysters.

Put them with crumbs of bread, pepper, salt, nutmeg, and a bit of butter, into scallop-shells, or saucers, and bake before the fire in a Dutch oven.

POULTRY, GAME, &c.

A Turkey Cock.—If young, it has a smooth black leg, with a short spur. The eyes full and bright, if fresh, and the feet supple and moist. If stale, the eyes will be sunk, and the feet dry

Hen-turkey is known by the same rules : but if old, her legs will be red and rough.

Fowls.—If a cock is young, his spurs will be short; but take care to see they have not been cut or pared, which is a trick often practised. If fresh, the vent will be close and dark. Pullets are best just before they begin to lay, and yet are full of egg : if old hens, their combs and legs will be rough ; if young, they will be smooth. A good capon has a thick belly and a large rump : there is a particular fat at his breast, and the comb is very pale. Black-legged fowls are most moist, if for roasting.

Geese.—The bill and feet of a young one will be yellow, and there will be but few hairs upon them ; if old, they will be red : if fresh, the feet will be pliable ; if stale, dry and stiff. Geese are called green till three or four months old. Green geese should be scalded : a stubble-goose should be picked dry.

Ducks.—Choose them by the same rules, of having supple feet, and by their being hard and thick on the breast and belly. The feet of a tame duck are thick, and inclining to dusky yellow ; a wild one has the feet reddish, and smaller than the tame. They should be picked dry. Ducklings must be scalded.

Pigeons should be very fresh ; when they look flabby about the vent, and this part is discoloured, they are stale. The feet should be supple; if old, the feet are harsh. The tame ones are larger than the wild, and are thought best by some persons ; they should be fat and tender ; but many are deceived in their size, because a full crop is as large as the whole body of a small pigeon.

The wood pigeon is large, and the flesh dark-coloured : if properly kept, and not over-roasted, the flavour is equal to teal. Serve with a good gravy.

Plovers.—Choose those that feel hard at the vent, which shews they are fat. In other respects, choose them by the same mark as other fowl. When stale, the feet are dry. They will keep sweet a long time. There are three sorts; the **grey,** green, and bastard plover or lapwing.

Hare or Rabbit.—If the claws are blunt and rugged, the ears dry and tough, and the haunch thick, it is old; but if the claws are smooth and sharp, the ears easily tear, and the cleft in the lip is not much spread, it is young. If fresh and newly killed, the body will be stiff, and in hares the flesh pale. But they keep a good while by proper care; and are best when rather beginning to turn, if the inside is preserved from being musty. To know a real leveret, you should look for a knob or small bone near the foot on its fore leg: if there is none, it is a hare.

Partridges.—They are in season in autumn. If young, the bill is of a dark colour, and the legs yellowish; if fresh, the vent will be firm; but this part will look greenish if stale.

Pheasants.—The cock bird is accounted best, except when the hen is with egg. If young, he has short, blunt, or round spurs; but if old, they are long and sharp.

All poultry should be very carefully picked, every plug removed, and the hair nicely singed with white paper.

The cook must be careful in drawing poultry of all sorts, not to break the gall-bag, for no washing will take off the bitter where it has touched.

In dressing wild fowl, be careful to keep a clear brisk fire Let them be done of a fine yellow brown, but leave the gravy in : the fine flavour is lost if done too much.

Tame fowls require more roasting, and are longer in heating through than others. All sorts should be continually basted; that they may be served with a froth, and appear of a fine colour.

A large fowl will take three quarters of an hour; a middling one half an hour; and a very small one, or a chicken, twenty minutes. The fire must be very quick and clear before any fowls are put down. A capon will take from half an hour to thirty-five minutes; a goose an hour; wild ducks a quarter of an hour; pheasants twenty minutes; a small turkey stuffed, an hour and a quarter; turkey-poults, twenty minutes; grouse, a quarter of an hour; quails, ten minutes; and partridges, from twenty to twenty-five minutes. A hare will take near an hour, and the hind part requires most heat.

Pigs and geese require a brisk fire and quick turning. Hares and rabbits must be well attended to; and the extremities brought to the quick part of the fire. to be done equally with the backs.

To boil Turkey.

Make a stuffing of bread, herbs, salt, pepper, nutmeg, lemon-peel, a few oysters or an anchovy, a bit of butter, some suet, and an egg : put this into the crop, fasten up the skin, and boil the turkey in a floured cloth to make it very white. Have ready a fine oyster-sauce made rich with butter, a little cream, and a spoonful of soy, if approved; and pour it over the bird : or liver and lemon-sauce. Hen birds are best for boiling, and should be young.

To roast Turkey.

The sinews of the leg should be drawn, whichever way it is dressed. The head should be twisted under the wing; and in drawing it, take care not to tear the liver, nor let the gall touch it.

Put a stuffing of sausage-meat; or if sausages are to be served in the dish, a bread-stuffing. As this makes a large addition to the size of the bird, observe that the heat of the fire is constantly to that part ; for the breast is often not done enough. A little strip of paper should be put on the bone, to hinder it from scorching while the other parts roast. Baste well, and froth it up. Serve with gravy in the dish, and plenty of bread-sauce in a sauce-tureen. Add a few crumbs, and a beaten egg, to the stuffing of sausage-meat.

To boil Fowl.

For boiling, choose those that are not black-legged. Pick them nicely, singe, wash, and truss them. Flour them, and put them into boiling water.—See time of dressing, page 428.

Serve with parsley and butter; oyster, lemon, liver, or celery sauce.

If for dinner, ham, tongue, or bacon, is usually served to eat with them ; as likewise greens.

Fowls roasted.

Serve with egg-sauce, bread-sauce, or garnished with sausages or scalded parsley.

A large barn-door fowl, well hung, should be stuffed in the crop with sausage-meat; and served with gravy in the dish, and with bread-sauce.

The head should be turned under the wing as a turkey.

Fowls broiled.

Split them down the back ; pepper, salt, and broil. Serve with mushroom-sauce.

Another way.—Cut a large fowl into four quarters, put them on a bird-spit, and tie that on another spit, and half roast; or half roast the whole fowl, and finish either on the gridiron, which will make it less dry than if wholly broiled. The fowl that is not cut before roasted, must be split down the back after.

To force Fowl, &c.

Is to stuff any part with force-meat, and it is put usually between the skin and flesh.

Fricassee of Chickens.

Boil rather more than half, in a small quantity of water: let them cool; then cut up; and put to simmer in a little gravy made of the liquor they were boiled in, and a bit of veal or mutton, onion, mace, and lemon-peel, some white pepper, and a bunch of sweet herbs. When quite tender, keep them hot while you thicken the sauce in the following manner: Strain it off, and put it back into the saucepan with a little salt, a scrape of nutmeg, and a bit of flour and butter; give it one boil; and when you are going to serve, beat up the yolk of an egg, add half a pint of cream, and stir them over the fire, but don't let it boil. It will be quite as good without the egg.

The gravy may be made (without any other meat) of the necks, feet, small wing-bones, gizzards, and livers; which are called the trimmings of the fowls.

To pull Chickens.

Take off the skin, and pull the flesh off the bones of a cold fowl, in as large pieces as you can: dredge it with flour, and fry it of a nice brown in butter. Drain the butter from it; and then simmer the flesh in a good gravy well seasoned, and thickened with a little flour and butter. Add the juice of half a lemon.

Another way.—Cut off the legs, and the whole back, of a dressed chicken; if under-done, the better. Pull all the white part into little flakes free from skin; toss it up with a little cream thickened with a piece of butter mixed with flour, half a blade of mace in powder, white pepper, salt, and a squeeze of lemon. Cut off the neck-end of the chicken; and broil the back and sidesmen in one piece, and the two legs seasoned Put the hash in the middle, with the back on it; and the two legs at the end.

Chicken Currie.

Cut up the chickens raw, slice onions, and fry both in butter with great care, of a fine light brown, or if you use chicken

that have been dressed, fry only the onions. Lay the joints,
cut into two or three pieces each, into a stew-pan; with a veal
or mutton gravy, and a clove or two of garlic. Simmer till
the chicken is quite tender. Half an hour before you serve it,
rub smooth a spoonful or two of currie-powder, a spoonful of
flour, and an ounce of butter; and add this, with four large
spoonfuls of cream, to the stew. Salt to your taste. *When
serving*, squeeze in a little lemon.

Slices of under-done veal, or rabbit, turkey, &c. make excellent currie. A dish of rice boiled dry must be served.

Another, more easily made.—Cut up a chicken or young
rabbit; if chicken, take off the skin. Roll each piece in a
mixture of a large spoonful of flour, and half an ounce of
currie-powder. Slice two or three onions ; and fry them in
butter, of a light brown : then add the meat, and fry altogether
till the meat begins to brown. Put it all into a stew-pan, and
pour boiling water enough just to cover it. Simmer very
gently two or three hours. If too thick, put more water half
an hour before serving.

If the meat has been dressed before, a little broth will be
better than water : but the currie is richer when made of fresh
meat.

Ducks roasted.

Serve with a fine gravy : and stuff one with sage and onion,
a dessert-spoonful of crumbs, a bit of butter, and pepper and
salt ; let the other be unseasoned.

To hash Ducks.

Cut a cold duck into joints ; and warm it, without boiling,
in gravy, and a glass of port wine.

To roast Goose.

After it is picked, the plugs of the feathers pulled out, and
the hairs carefully singed, let it be well washed and dried,
and a seasoning put in of onion, sage, and pepper and salt.
Fasten it tight at the neck and rump, and then roast. Put it
first at a distance from the fire, and by degrees draw it nearer.
A slip of paper should be skewered on the breast-bone. Baste
it very well. When the breast is rising, take off the paper ;
and be careful to serve it before the breast falls, or it will be
spoiled by coming flatted to table. Let a good gravy be sent
in the dish.

Gravy and apple-sauce : gooseberry-sauce for a green goose

To stew Giblets.

Do them as will be directed for giblet-pie (under the head

Pies); season them with salt and pepper, and a very small piece of mace. Before serving, give them one boil with a cup of cream, and a piece of butter rubbed in a tea-spoonful of flour.

Pigeons.

May be dressed in so many ways, that they are very useful. The good flavour of them depends very much on their being cropped and drawn as soon as killed. No other bird requires so much washing.

Pigeons left from dinner the day before may be stewed, or made into a pie; in either case, care must be taken not to over-do them, which will make them stringy. They need only be heated up in gravy made ready; and force-meat balls may be fried and added, instead of putting a stuffing into them. If for a pie, let beef-steaks be stewed in a little water, and put cold under them, and cover each pigeon with a piece of fat bacon, to keep them moist.

Season as usual, and put eggs.

To broil Pigeons.

After cleaning, split the backs, pepper and salt them, and broil them very nicely; pour over them either stewed or pickled mushrooms in melted butter, and serve as hot as possible.

Roast Pigeons

Should be stuffed with parsley, either cut or whole; and seasoned within. Serve with parsley and butter. Peas or asparagus should be dressed to eat with them.

Larks, and other small Birds.

Draw, and spit them on a bird-spit; tie this on another spit, and roast them. Baste gently with butter, and strew bread-crumbs upon them till half done : brown, and serve with fried crumbs round.

To keep Game, &c.

Game ought not to be thrown away even when it has been kept a very long time , for when it seems to be spoiled it may often be made fit for eating, by nicely cleaning it, and washing with vinegar and water. If there is danger of birds not keeping, draw, crop, and pick them , then wash in two or three waters, and rub them with salt. Have ready a large saucepan of boiling water, and plunge them into it one by one; drawing them up and down by the legs, that the water may pass through them. Let them stay five or six minutes in ; then hang them up in a cold place. When drained, pepper and salt the insides well Before roasting, wash them well.

The most delicate birds, even grouse, may be preserved thus. Those that live by suction cannot be done this way, as they are never drawn; and perhaps the heat might make them worse, as the water could not pass through them; but they bear being high.

Lumps of charcoal put about birds and meat will preserve them from taint, and restore what is spoiling.

Pheasants and Partridges.

Roast them as turkey; and serve with a fine gravy (into which put a very small bit of garlic), and bread-sauce. When cold, they may be made into excellent patties, but their flavour should not be overpowered by lemon.

A very cheap way of potting Birds.

Prepare them as directed in the last receipt; and when baked and grown cold, cut them into proper pieces for helping, pack them close into a large potting-pan, and (if possible) leave no spaces to receive the butter. Cover them with butter, and one-third part less will be wanted than when the birds are done whole.

The butter that has covered potted things will serve for basting, or for paste for meat pies.

To clarify Butter for potted Things.

Put it into a sauce-boat, and set that over the fire in a stew-pan that has a little water in it. When melted, take care not to pour the milky parts over the potted things: they will sink to the bottom.

To pot Moor-Game.

Pick, singe, and wash the birds nicely: then dry them; and season, inside and out, pretty high, with pepper, mace, nutmeg, allspice, and salt. Pack them in as small a pot as will hold them, cover them with butter, and bake in a very slow oven. When cold, take off the butter, dry them from the gravy, and put one bird into each pot, which should just fit. Add as much more butter as will cover them, but take care that it does not oil. The best way to melt it is, by warming it in a basin set in a bowl of hot water.

Grouse.

Roast them like fowls, but the head is to be twisted under the wing. They must not be over-done. Serve with a rich gravy in the dish, and bread-sauce. Then sauce for wild-fowl, as will be described hereafter under the head of *Sauces,* may be used instead of common gravy.

To roast Wild Fowl.

The flavour is best preserved without stuffing.   Put pepper salt, and a piece of butter, into each.

Wild fowl require much less dressing than tame; they should be served of a fine colour, and well frothed up.   A rich brown gravy should be sent in the dish ; and when the breast is cut into slices, before taking off the bone, a squeeze of lemon, with pepper and salt, is a great improvement to the flavour.

To take off the fishy taste which wild fowl sometimes have, put an onion, salt, and hot water, into the dripping-pan, and baste them for the first ten minutes with this; then take away the pan, and baste constantly with butter.

Wild Ducks, Teal, Widgeon, Dun-birds, &c.,

Should be taken up with the gravy in   Baste them with butter; and sprinkle a little salt before they are taken up, put a good gravy upon them, and serve with shalot-sauce, in a boat.

Woodcocks, Snipes, and Quails,

Keep good several days.   Roast them without drawing, and serve on toast.   Butter only should be eaten with them, as gravy takes off from the fine flavour.   The thigh and back are esteemed the most.

Ruffs and Reeves

Are skewered as quails ; put bars of bacon over them, and roast them about ten minutes.   Serve with a good gravy in the dish.

To dress Plovers.

Roast the *green* ones in the same way as woodcocks and quails (see above), without drawing ; and serve on a toast. *Grey* plovers may be either roasted, or stewed with gravy, herbs, and spice.

Plovers' Eggs

Are a nice and fashionable dish.   Boil them ten minutes, and serve either hot or cold on a napkin.

To roast Ortolans.

Pick and singe, but do not draw them.   Tie on a bird-spit, and roast them.   Some persons like bacon in slices tied between them, but the taste of it spoils the flavour of the ortolan. Cover them with crumbs of bread.

Hares,

If properly taken care of will keep a great time, and even when

the cook fancies them past eating, may be in the highest perfection ; which if eaten when fresh-killed they are not. As they
are usually paunched in the field, the cook cannot prevent
this ; but the hare keeps longer, and eats much better, if not
opened for four or five days, or according to the weather.

If paunched, as soon as a hare comes in it should be wiped
quite dry, the heart and liver taken out, and the liver scalded
to keep for the stuffing. Repeat this wiping every day ; mix
pepper and ginger, and rub on the inside ; and put a large
piece of charcoal into it. If the spice is applied early, it will
prevent that musty taste which long keeping in the damp
occasions, and which also affects the stuffing.

An old hare should be kept as long as possible, if to be
roasted. It must also be well soaked.

To roast Hare.

After it is skinned, let it be extremely well washed, and then
soaked an hour or two in water ; and if old, lard it ; which will
make it tender, as also will letting it lie in vinegar.

If however, it is put into vinegar, it should be exceedingly
well-washed in water afterwards. Put a large relishing stuffing
into the belly, and then sew it up. Baste it well with milk till
half-done, and afterwards with butter. If the blood has settled
in the neck, soaking the part in warm water, and putting it to
the fire warm, will remove it ; especially if you also nick the
skin here and there with a small knife to let it out. The hare
should be kept at a distance from the fire at first. Serve with
a fine froth, rich gravy, melted butter, and currant-jelly sauce ;
the gravy in the dish. For stuffing use the liver, an anchovy,
some fat bacon, a little suet, herbs, pepper, salt, nutmeg, a
little onion, crumbs of bread, and an egg to bind it all.

The ears must be nicely cleaned and singed. They are
reckoned a dainty.

To jug an old Hare.

After cleaning and skinning, cut it up : and season it with
pepper, salt, allspice, pounded mace, and a little nutmeg. Put
it into a jar with an onion, a clove or two, a bunch of sweet
herbs, a piece of coarse beef, and the carcase-bones over all.
Tie the jar down with a bladder, and leather or strong paper ;
and put it into a saucepan of water up to the neck, but no
higher. Keep the water boiling five hours. When it is to
be served, boil the gravy up with a piece of butter and flour ;
and if the meat gets cold, warm it in this, but not to boil.

Broiled and hashed Hare.

The flavour of broiled hare is particularly fine; the legs or wings must be seasoned first; rub with cold butter, and serve very hot.

The other parts, warmed with gravy, and a little stuffing, may be served separately.

To pot Hare,

For which an old one does well, as likewise for soup and pie.

After seasoning it, bake it with butter. When cold, take the meat from the bones, and beat it in a mortar. If not high enough, add salt, mace, pepper, and a piece of the finest fresh butter melted in a spoonful or two of the gravy that came from the hare. When well mixed, put it into small pots, and cover with butter. The legs and back should be baked at the bottom of the jar, to keep them moist, and the bones be put over them.

Rabbits.

May be eaten various ways, as follows.

Roasted with stuffing and gravy, like hare, or without stuffing; with sauce of the liver and parsley chopped in melted butter, pepper, and salt; or larded.

Boiled, and smothered with onion-sauce; the butter to be melted with milk instead of water.

Fried in joints, with dried or fried parsley. The same liver-sauce, this way also.

Fricasseed, as before directed for chickens.

In a pie, as chicken, with forcemeat, &c. In this way they are excellent when young.

Potted.

GRAVIES AND SAUCES

Beef Gravy.

To make beef gravy, take a piece of the chuck, or neck, and cut it into small pieces; then strew some flour over it, mix it well with the meat, and put it into the saucepan, with as much water as will cover it, an onion, a little allspice, a little pepper and some salt. Cover it close, and when it boils take off the scum, then throw in a hard crust of bread, or some raspings and let it stew till the gravy is rich and good; then strain it off, and pour it into your sauce-boat.

A very rich Gravy.

Take a piece of lean beef, a piece of veal, and a piece of mutton, and cut them into small bits; then take a large saucepan with a cover, lay your beef at the bottom, then your mutton, then a very little piece of bacon, a slice or two of carrot, some mace, cloves, whole black and white pepper, a large onion cut in slices, a bunch of sweet herbs, and then lay on your veal. Cover it close, and set it over a slow fire for six or seven minutes, and shake the saucepan often. Then dust some flour into it, and pour in boiling water till the meat is something more than covered. Cover your saucepan close, and let it stew till it is rich and good. Then season it to your taste with salt, and strain it off.—This gravy will be so good as to answer most purposes.

Brown Gravy.

Put a piece of butter, about the size of a hen's egg, into a saucepan, and when it is melted shake in a little flour, and let it be brown. Then by degrees stir in the following ingredients : half a pint of water, and the same quantity of ale or small beer, that is not bitter; an onion, and a piece of lemon-peel cut small, three cloves, a blade of mace, some whole pepper, a spoonful of mushroom pickle, the same quantity of ketchup, and an anchovy. Let the whole boil together quarter of an hour, then strain it, and it will be good sauce for various dishes.

Sauce for any Kind of Roast Meat.

Take an anchovy, wash it clean, and put to it a glass of red wine, some gravy, a shalot cut small, and a little juice of lemon. Stew these together, strain it off, and mix it with the gravy that runs from the meat.

A White Sauce.

Put some good meat broth into a stew-pan, with a good piece of crumb of bread, a bunch of parsley, shalots, thyme, laurel, basil, a clove, a little grated nutmeg, some whole mushrooms, a glass of white wine, salt, and pepper. Let the whole boil till half is consumed, then strain it through a sieve; and when you are ready to use it, put in the yolks of three eggs, beat up with some cream, and thicken it over the fire, taking care that the eggs do not curdle. This sauce may be used with all sorts of meat or fish that is done white.

Sauce for most Kinds of Fish.

Take some mutton or veal gravy, and put to it a little of the liquor that drains from your fish. Put it into a saucepan, with an onion, an anchovy, a spoonful of ketchup, and a glass of white wine. Thicken it with a lump of butter rolled in flour, and a spoonful of cream. If you have oysters, cockles, or shrimps, put them in after you take it off the fire · but it will be exceeding good without. If you have no cream, instead of white wine you must use red.

Egg Sauce.

Boil two eggs till they are hard : first chop the whites, then the yolks, but neither of them very fine, and put them together Then put them into a quarter of a pound of good melted but-'er, and stir them well together.

Bread Sauce.

Cut a large piece of crumb from a stale loaf, and put it into a saucepan, with half a pint of water, an onion, a blade of mace, and a few pepper-corns in a bit of cloth. Boil them a few minutes, then take out the onion and spice, mash the bread very smooth, and add to it a piece of butter and a little salt.

Anchovy Sauce.

Take an anchovy, and put it into half a pint of gravy, with a quarter of a pound of butter rolled in a little flour, and stir all together till it boils. You may add, at your discretion, a little lemon-juice, ketchup, red wine, or walnut-liquor.

Shrimp Sauce.

Wash half a pint of shrimps very clean, and put them into a stew-pan, with a spoonful of anchovy liquor, and half a pound of butter melted thick. Boil it up for five minutes, and squeeze in half a lemon. Toss it up, and pour it into your sauce-boat.

Oyster Sauce.

When the oysters are opened, preserve the liquor, and strain it through a fine sieve. Wash the oysters very clean, and take off the beards. Put them into a stew-pan, and pour the liquor over them. Then add a large spoonful of anchovy liquor, half a lemon, and two blades of mace, and thicken it with butter rolled in flour. Put in half a pound of butter, and boil it up till the butter is melted. Then take out the mace and lemon, and squeeze the lemon-juice into the sauce. Let it boil, stirring it all the time, and put it into your sauce-boat.

To melt Butter.

Keep a plated or tin saucepan for the purpose only of melting butter. Put a little water at the bottom, and a dust of flour. Shake them together, and cut the butter in slices. As it melts shake it one way ; let it boil up, and it will be smooth and thick.

Caper Sauce.

Take some capers, chop half of them very fine, and put the rest in whole. Chop also some parsley, with a little grated bread, and some salt ; put them into butter melted very smooth, let them boil up, and then pour it into your sauce-boat.

Lemon Sauce for boiled Fowls.

Take a lemon, and pare off the rind, then cut it into slices, take the kernels out, and cut it into small square bits ; blanch the liver of the fowl, and chop it fine ; mix the lemon and liver together in a boat, pour on some hot melted butter, and stir it up.

Gooseberry Sauce.

Put some coddled gooseberries, a little juice of sorrel, and a little ginger, into some melted butter.

Fennel Sauce.

Boil a bunch of fennel and parsley, chop it very small, and stir it into some melted butter.

Mint Sauce.

Wash your mint perfectly clean from grit or dirt, then chop it very fine, and put to it vinegar and sugar.

To Crisp Parsley.

When you have picked and washed your parsley quite clean, put it into a Dutch oven, or on a sheet of paper. Set it at a moderate distance from the fire, and keep turning it till it is quite crisp. Lay little bits of butter on it, but not to make it greasy. This is a much better method than that of frying.

Sauce for Wild Ducks, Teal, &c.

Take a proper quantity of veal gravy, with some pepper and salt ; squeeze in the juice of two Seville oranges, and add a little red wine ; let the red wine boil some time in the gravy.

Forcemeat Balls.

Take half a pound of veal, and half a pound of suet cut fine, and beat them in a marble mortar, or wooden bowl ; shred a few sweet-herbs fine, a little mace dried, a small nutmeg grated, a little lemon-peel cut very fine, some pepper and salt, and the yolks of two eggs. Mix all these well together, then roll some of it in small round balls, and some in long pieces. Roll them in flour, and fry them of a nice brown. If they are for the use of white sauce, instead of frying, put a little water into a saucepan, and, when it boils, put them in, and a few minutes will do them.

VEGETABLES.

In dressing these articles, tne greates attenaon must be paid to cleanliness. They are, particularly at some times of the year, subject to dust, dirt, and insects, so that if they are not properly cleansed, they will be unsatisfactory to those for whom they are provided, and disreputable to the cook. To avoid this, be careful first to pick off all the outside leaves, then wash them well in several waters, and let them lie some time in a pan of clean water before you dress them. Be sure your saucepan is thoroughly clean, and boil them by themselves in plenty of water. They should always be brought crisp to table, which will be effected by being careful not to boil them too much. Such are the general observations necessary to be attended to in dressing of Vegetables and Roots. We shall now proceed to particulars, beginning with

Asparagus.

Scrape all the stalks very carefully till they look white, then cut them all even alike, and throw them into a pan of clean water, and have ready a stew-pan with boiling water. Put some salt in, and tie the asparagus in little bunches, put them in, and when they are a little tender, take them up. If you boil them too much, they will lose both their colour and taste. Cut the round off a small loaf, about half an inch thick, and toast it brown on both sides: then dip it into the liquor the asparagus was boiled in, and lay it in your dish. Pour a little melted butter over your toast, then lay your asparagus on the toast all round your dish, with the heads inwards, and send it to table, with melted butter in a basin. Some pour melted butter over them ; but this is injudicious, as it makes the handling them very disagreeable.

Artichokes.

Twist off the stalks, then put them into cold water and wasn them well. When the water boils, put them in with their tops downwards, that all the dust and sand may boil out. About an hour and a half, or two hours, will do them. Serve them up with melted butter in cups.

Brocoli.

Carefully strip off the little branches till you come to the top one, and then with a knife peel off the hard outside skin that is on the stalks and little branches, and throw them into water. Have ready a stewpan of water, throw in a ittle salt, and when it boils put in your brocoli. When the stalks are tender it is enough. Put in a piece of toasted bread, soaked in the water the brocoli was boiled in, at the bottom of your dish, and put your brocoli on the top of it, as you do asparagus. Send them up to table laid in bunches, with butter in a boat

Cauliflowers.

Take off the green part, then cut the flowers into four parts, and lay them in water for an hour. Then have some milk and water boiling, put in the cauliflowers and be sure to skim the saucepan well. When the stalks feel tender, take up the flowers carefully, and put them in a cullender to drain. Then put a spoonful of water into a stewpan, with a little dust of flour, about a quarter of a pound of butter, a little pepper and salt, and shake it round till the butter is melted, and the whole well mixed together. Then take half the cauliflower, and cut it as you would for pickling. Lay it into the stewpan, turn it, and shake the pan round for about ten minutes, which will be a sufficient time to do it properly. Lay the stewed in the middle of your plate, the boiled round it, and pour over it the butter in which the one half was stewed. This is a delicate mode of dressing cauliflowers.—But the usual way is as follows:—Cut the stalks off, leave a little green on, and boil them in spring water and salt for about fifteen minutes. Then take them out, drain them, and send them whole to table, with melted butter in a sauce-boat.

Green Peas.

Let your peas be shelled as short a time as you can before they are dressed, as otherwise they will lose a great part of their sweetness. Put them into boiling water, with a little salt, and a lump of loaf sugar: and when they begin to dent in the middle, they are enough. Put them into a sieve, drain the water clear from them, and pour them into your dish. Put in them a good lump of butter, and stir them about with a spoon till it is thoroughly melted. Mix with them likewise a little pepper and salt. Boil a small bunch of mint by itself, chop it fine, and lay it in lumps round the edge of your dish. Melted butter is sometimes preferred to mixing it with the peas.

Windsor Beans.

These must be boiled in plenty of water, with a good quantity of salt in it; and when they feel tender, are enough. Boil and chop some parsley, put it into good melted butter, and serve them up with boiled bacon, and the butter and parsley in a boat.   Remember never to boil them with bacon, as that will greatly discolour them.

Kidney Beans.

First carefully string them, then slit them down the middle, and cut them across.   Put them into salt and water, and when the water boils in your saucepan, put them in with a little salt. They will be soon done, which may be known by their feeling tender.   Drain the water clear from them, lay them in a plate, and send them up with butter in a sauce-boat.

Spinach.

Be careful to pick it exceeding clean, then wash it in five or six waters, put it into a saucepan that will just hold it, without water, throw a little salt over it, and cover it close.   Put your saucepan on a clear quick fire, and when you find the spinach shrunk and fallen to the bottom, and the liquor that comes out boils up, it is done ; then put it into a clean sieve to drain, and just give it a gentle squeeze.   Lay it on a plate, and send it to table, with melted butter in a boat.

Cabbages.

After you have taken off the outer leaves, and well washed them, quarter them, and boil them in plenty of water, with a handful of salt.   When they are tender, drain them on a sieve, but do not press them.   Savoys and greens must be boiled in the same manner, but always by themselves, by which means they will eat crisp, and be of a good colour.

Turnips.

These may be boiled in the same pot with your meat, and, indeed, will eat best if so done.   When they are enough, take them out, put them into a pan, mash them with butter, pepper, and a little salt, and in that state send them to table.

Another method of boiling turnips is this : When you have pared them, cut them into little square pieces, then put them into a saucepan, and just cover them with water.   As soon as they are enough, take them off the fire, and put them into a sieve to drain.   Then put them into a saucepan, with a good piece of butter, stir them over the fire a few minutes, put them into your dish, and serve them up.

Carrots.

Scrape your carrots very clean, put them into the pot, and when they are enough, take them out, and rub them in a clean cloth.   Then slice them into a plate, and pour some melted butter over them. If they are young, half an hour will sufficiently boil them.

Parsneps.

These must be boiled in plenty of water, and when they are soft, which you may know by running a fork into them, take them up. Scrape them all fine with a knife, throw away all the sticky part, and send them to table, with melted butter in a sauce-boat.

Potatoes.

These must be boiled in so small a quantity of water as will be just sufficient to keep the saucepan from burning. Keep them close covered, and as soon as the skins begin to crack, they are enough. Having drained out all the water, let them remain in the saucepan covered for two or three minutes; then peel them, lay them in a plate, and pour some melted butter over them. Or when you have peeled them, you may do thus: lay them on a gridiron till they are of a fine brown, and send them to table. It is the custom of many to peel the potatoes before they are boiled; and in that case they are more dry and mealy.

Potatoes Scolloped.

Having boiled your potatoes, beat them fine in a bowl, with some cream, a large piece of butter, and a little salt. Put them into scollop shells, make them smooth on the top, score them with a knife, and lay thin slices of butter on the tops of them. Then put them into a Dutch oven to brown before the fire. This makes a pretty dish for a light supper.

PUDDINGS.

Some previous and general observations are necessary; the most material of which are, first, that your cloth be thoroughly clean, and before you put your pudding into it, dip it into boiling water, strew some flour over it, and then give it a shake. If it is a bread pudding, tie it loose; but if a batter pudding, close; and never put your pudding in till the water boils. All bread and custard puddings that are baked, require time and a moderate oven; but batter and rice puddings, a quick oven. Before you put your pudding into the dish for baking, be careful always to moisten the bottom and sides with butter.

BOILED PUDDINGS.

Bread Pudding.

Take the crumb of a small loaf, cut it into very thin slices, put it into a quart of milk, and set over a chafing-dish of coals, till the bread has soaked up all the milk. Then put in a piece of butter, stir it round, and let it stand till it is cold. Or you may boil your milk, and pour it over the bread, and cover it up close, which will equally answer the same purpose. Then take the yolks of six eggs, the whites of three, and beat them up with a little rose water and nutmeg, and a little salt and sugar. Mix all well together, and put it into your cloth, tie it loose to give it room to swell, and boil it an hour. When done, put it into your dish, pour melted butter over it, and serve it to table.

Batter Pudding.

Take a quart of milk, beat up the yolks of six eggs, and the whites of three, and mix them with a quarter of a pint of milk. Then take six spoonfuls of flour, a tea-spoonful of salt, and one of ginger. Put to these the remainder of the milk, mix all well together, put it into your cloth, and boil it an hour and a quarter. Pour melted butter over it when you serve it up.

A batter pudding may be made without eggs; in which case proceed thus; take a quart of milk, mix six spoonfuls of flour with a little of the milk first, a tea-spoonful of salt, two of beaten ginger, and two of the tincture of saffron. Then mix all together, and boil it an hour.

Custard Pudding.

Put a piece of cinnamon into a pint of thick cream, boil it, and add a quarter of a pound of sugar. When cold, put in the yolks of five eggs well beaten : stir this over the fire till it is pretty thick, but be careful it does not boil. When quite cold, butter a cloth well, dust it with flour, tie the custard in it very close, and boil it three quarters of an hour. When you take it up, put it into a basin to cool a little ; untie the cloth, lay the dish on the basin, and turn it carefully out. Grate over it a little sugar, and serve it up with melted butter and a little wine in a boat

Quaking Pudding.

Take a quart of cream, boil it, and let it stand till almost cold : then beat up four eggs very fine, with a spoonful and a half of flour : mix them well with your cream ; add sugar and nutmeg to your palate. Tie it up close in a cloth well buttered. Let it boil an hour, and then turn it carefully out. Pour over it melted butter.

Sago Pudding.

Boil two ounces of sago in a pint of milk till tender　When

cold, add five eggs, two Naples biscuits, a little brandy, and sugar to the taste. Boil it in a basin, and serve it up with melted butter, a little wine, and sugar.

Marrow Pudding.

Grate a small loaf into crumbs, and pour on them a pint of boiling hot cream. Cut a pound of beef marrow very thin, beat up four eggs well, and then add a glass of brandy, with sugar and nutmeg to your taste. Mix them all well together, and boil it three quarters of an hour. Cut two ounces of citron into very thin bits, and when you dish up your pudding, stick them all over it.

Biscuit Pudding.

Pour a pint of boiling milk or cream over six penny Naples biscuits grated, and cover it close. When cold, add the yolks of four eggs, the whites of two, some nutmeg, a little brandy, half a spoonful of flour, and some sugar. Boil it an hour in a china bason, and serve it up with melted butter, wine, and sugar.

Almond Pudding.

Take a pound of sweet almonds, and beat them as fine as possible, with three spoonfuls of rose-water, and a gill of sack or white wine. Mix in half a pound of fresh butter melted, with the yolks of five eggs, and two whites, a quart of cream, a quarter of a pound of sugar, half a nutmeg grated, one spoonful of flour, and three spoonfuls of crumbs of bread. Mix all together, and boil it. Half an hour will do it.

Tansey Pudding.

Put as much boiling cream to four Naples biscuits grated as will wet them, beat them with the yolks of four eggs. Have ready a few chopped tansey leaves, with as much spinach as will make it a pretty green. Be careful not to put too much tansey in, because it will make it bitter. Mix all together when the cream is cold, with a little sugar, and set it over a slow fire till it grows thick; then take it off, and when cold, put it in a cloth, well buttered and floured; tie it up close, and let it boil three quarters of an hour; then take it up in a basin, and let it stand one quarter, turn it carefully out, and put white-wine sauce round it.

Hunting Pudding.

Mix eight eggs beat up fine with a pint of good cream, and a pound of flour. Beat them well together, and put to them a pound of beef suet finely chopped, a pound of currants well cleaned, half a pound of jar-raisins stoned and chopped small, two ounces of candied orange cut small, the same of candied citron, a quarter of a pound of powdered sugar, and a large nutmeg grated. Mix all together with half a gill of brandy; put it into a cloth, and boil it four hours. Be sure to put it in when the water boils, and keep it boiling all the time. When done, turn it into a dish, and strew over it powdered sugar.

Steak Pudding.

Make a good crust, with flour and suet shred fine, and mix it up with cold water; season it with a little salt, and make it pretty stiff. Take either beef or mutton steaks, season them well with pepper and salt, and make it up as you would an apple pudding; tie it in a cloth, and put it in when the water boils. If a small pudding, it will take three hours; if a large one, five hours.

Plum Pudding.

Cut a pound of suet into small pieces, but not too fine, a pound of currants washed clean, a pound of raisins stoned, eight yolks of eggs, and four whites, half a nutmeg grated, a tea-spoonful of beaten ginger, a pound of flour, and a pint of milk. Beat the eggs first, then put to them half the milk, and beat them together; and by degrees stir in the flour, then the suet, spice, and fruit, and as much milk as will mix it well together, very thick. It will take four hours boiling. When done, turn it into your dish, and strew over it grated sugar.

Hasty Pudding.

Put four bay-leaves into a quart of milk, and set it on the fire to boil. Then beat up the yolks of two eggs with a little salt. Take two or three spoonfuls of milk, and beat up with your eggs; take out the bay-leaves, and stir up the remainder of the milk. Then, with a wooden spoon in one hand, and flour in the other, stir it in till it is of a good thickness, but not too thick. Let it boil, and keep it stirring; then pour it into a dish, and stick pieces of butter in different places. Remember, before you stir in the flour, to take out the bay-leaves.

Suet Pudding.

Take six spoonfuls of flour, a pound of suet shred small, four eggs, a spoonful of beaten ginger, a tea-spoonful of salt, and a quart of milk. Mix the eggs and flour with a pint of the milk very thick, and with the seasoning mix in the rest of the milk with the suet. Let your batter be pretty thick, and boil it two hours.

Apple Pudding.

Having made a puff paste, roll it near half an inch thick, and fill the crust with apples pared and cored. Grate in a little peel, and, in the winter, a little lemon-juice, (as it quickens the apples,) put in some sugar, close the crust, and tie it in a cloth. A small pudding will take two hours boiling, and a large one three or four.

Apple Dumplings.

When you have pared your apples, take out the core with the apple corer, and fill up the hole with quince, orange-marmalade, or sugar, as may best suit you. Then take a piece of paste, make a hole in it, lay in your apple, put another piece of paste in the same form over it, and close it up round the side of the apple. Put them into boiling water, and about three quarters of an hour will do them. Serve them up with melted butter poured over them.

Suet Dumplings.

Take a pint of milk, four eggs, a pound of suet, a little salt and nutmeg, two tea-spoonfuls of ginger, and such a quantity of flour as will make it into a light paste. When the water boils, make the paste into dumplings, and roll them in a little flour. Then put them into the water, and move them gently to prevent their sticking. A little more than half an hour will boil them.

Raspberry Dumplings.

Make a good puff paste, and roll it. Spread over it raspberry jam, roll it into dumplings, and boil them an hour. Pour melted butter into the dish, and strew over them grated sugar.

Yeast Dumplings.

Make a light dough with flour, water, yeast, and salt, as for bread, cover it with a cloth, and set it before the fire for half an hour. Then have a saucepan of water on the fire, and when it boils, take the dough, and make it into round balls, as big as a large hen's egg. Then flatten them with your hand, put them into the boiling water, and a few minutes will do them. Take care that they do not fall to the bottom of the pot or saucepan, as in that case they will be heavy: and be sure to keep the water boiling all the time. When they are enough, take them up, and put them in your dish, with melted butter in a boat.

Potatoe Puddings.

Boil half a pound of potatoes till they are soft, then peel

them, mash them with the back of a spoon, and rub them through a sieve to have them fine and smooth. Then take half a pound of fresh butter melted, half a pound of fine sugar, and beat them well together till they are quite smooth. Beat up six eggs, whites as well as yolks, and stir them in with a glass of sack or brandy. Pour it into your cloth, tie it up, and about half an hour will do it. When you take it out, melt some butter, put into it a glass of wine sweetened with sugar, and pour it over your pudding.

BAKED PUDDINGS.

Vermicelli Pudding.

Take four ounces of vermicelli, and boil it in a pint of new milk till it is soft, with a stick or two of cinnamon. Then put in half a pint of thick cream, a quarter of a pound of butter, the like quantity of sugar, and the yolks of four eggs beaten fine. Bake it without paste in an earthen dish.

Sweetmeat Pudding.

Cover your dish with a thin puff paste, and then take can died orange or lemon-peel, and citron, of each an ounce. Slice them thin, and lay them all over the bottom of the dish. Then beat up eight yolks of eggs, and two whites, and put to them half a pound of sugar, and half a pound of melted butter. Mix the whole well together, put it on the sweetmeats, and send it to a moderately heated oven. About an hour will do it.

Orange Pudding.

Boil the rind of a Seville orange very soft, then beat it in a marble mortar with the juice, and put to it two Naples biscuits grated very fine, a quarter of a pound of sugar, half a pound of butter, and the yolks of six eggs. Mix them well together, lay a good puff paste round the edge of your dish, and bake it an hour in a gentle oven.

Lemon Pudding.

Take three lemons, cut the rinds off very thin, and boil them in three quarts of water till they are tender. Then pound them very fine in a mortar, and have ready a quarter of a pound of Naples biscuits boiled up in a quart of milk or cream. Mix them and the lemon rind with it, and beat up twelve yolks and six whites of eggs very fine. Melt a quarter of a pound of fresh butter, and put in half a pound of sugar, and a little orange-flower water. Mix all well together, put it over the fire, keep it stirring till it is thick, and then squeeze in the juice of half a lemon. Put puff paste round your dish, then pour in your pudding, cut some candied sweetmeats and strew over it, and bake it three quarters of an hour.

Almond Pudding.

Take a little more than three ounces of the crumb of white bread sliced, or grated, and steep it in a pint and a half of cream. Then beat half a pint of blanched almonds very fine till they are like a paste, with a little orange-flower water Beat up the yolks of eight eggs, and the whites of four. Mix all well together, put in a quarter of a pound of white sugar and stir in about a quarter of a pound of melted butter. Put it over the fire, and keep stirring it till it is thick. Lay a sheet of puff paste at the bottom of your dish, and pour in the ingredients. Half an hour will bake it.

Rice Pudding.

Boil four ounces of ground rice till it is soft, then beat up the yolks of four eggs, and put to them a pint of cream, four ounces of sugar, and a quarter of a pound of butter. Mix them well together, and either boil or bake it.

Millet Pudding.

Wash and pick clean half a pound of millet-seed, put it into half a pound of sugar, a whole nutmeg grated, and three quarts of milk, and break in half a pound of fresh butter. Butter your dish, pour it in, and send it to the oven.

Cowslip Pudding.

Cut and pound small the flowers of a peck of cowslips, with half a pound of Naples biscuits grated, and three pints of cream. Boil them a little, then take them off the fire, and beat up sixteen eggs, with a little cream and rose-water. Sweeten to your palate. Mix it all well together, butter a dish, and pour it in. Bake it, and when it is enough, throw fine sugar over it, and serve it up.

Apple Pudding.

Pare twelve large apples, and take out the cores. Put them into a saucepan, with four or five spoonfuls of water, and boil them till they are soft and thick. Then beat them well, stir in a pound of loaf sugar, the juice of three lemons, and the peels of two, cut thin and beat fine in a mortar, and the yolks of eight eggs. Mix all well together, and bake it in a slack oven When done, strew over it a little fine sugar.

Yorkshire Pudding.

Take four large spoonfuls of flour, and beat it up well with four eggs and a little salt. Then put to them three pints of milk, and mix them well together. Butter a dripping-pan set under beef, mutton, or a loin of veal. When the meat is about half roasted, put in your pudding, and let the fat drip on it. When it is brown at top, cut it into square pieces, and turn it over ; and when the underside is browned also, send it to table on a dish.

PIES.

One very material consideration must be, that the heat of the oven is duly proportioned to the nature of the article to be baked. Light paste requires a moderate oven ; if it is too quick, the crust cannot rise, and will therefore be burnt; and if too slow, will be soddened, and want that delicate light brown it ought to have. Raised pies must have a quick oven, and be well closed up, or they will sink in their sides, and lose their proper shape. Tarts that are iced, should be baked in a slow oven, or the icing will become brown before the paste is properly baked.

Puff Paste must be made thus : Take a quarter of a peck of flour, and rub it into a pound of butter very fine. Make it up into a light paste, with cold water, just stiff enough to work it up. Then roll it out about as thick as a crown piece ; put a layer of butter all over, then sprinkle on a little flour, double it up, and roll it out again. Double and roll it, with layers of butter, three times, and it will be properly fit for use.

Short Crust. Put six ounces of butter to eight of flour, and work them well together; then mix it up with as little water as possible, so as to have a stiffish paste; and roll it out thin for use.

A good Paste for large Pies. Take a peck of flour, put to it three eggs; then put in half a pound of suet, and a pound and a half of butter and suet, and as much water as will make it a good light crust. Work it up well, and roll it out

A standing Crust for great Pies. Take a peck of flour and six pounds of butter boiled in a gallon of water ; skim it off into the flour, and as little of the liquor as you can. Work it up well into a paste, and then pull it into pieces till it is cold. Then make it up into what form you please.

Paste for Tarts. Put an ounce of loaf-sugar, beaten and sifted, to one pound of fine flour. Make it into a stiff paste, with a gill of boiling cream, and three ounces of butter. Work it well, and roll it very thin.

Paste for Custards. To half a pound of flour, put six

ounces of butter, the yolks of two eggs, and three spoonfuls of cream. Mix them together, and let them stand a quarter of an hour: then work it up and down, and roll it out very thin

MEAT PIES.

Beefsteak Pie.

Take some rump steaks, and beat them with a rolling pin; then season them with pepper and salt to your palate. Make a good crust, lay in your steaks, and then pour in as much water as will half fill the dish. Put on the crust, send it to the oven, and let it be well baked.

Mutton Pie.

Take off the skin and outside fat of a loin of mutton, then cut it into steaks, and season them well with pepper and salt. Set them into your dish, and pour in as much water as will cover them. Then put on your crust and let it be well baked.

Veal Pie.

Cut a breast of veal into pieces, season them with pepper and salt, and lay them in your dish. Boil six or eight eggs hard, take the yolks only, and put them into different places in the pie; then pour in as much water as will nearly fill the dish, put on the lid, and bake it well. A lamb pie may be done in the same manner.

Venison Pasty.

Take a neck and breast of venison, bone them, and season them well with pepper and salt; pot them into a deep pan, with the best part of a neck of mutton sliced and laid over them; pour in a glass of red wine, put a coarse paste over it, and bake it two hours in an oven; then lay the venison in a dish, pour the gravy over it, and put one pound of butter over it; make a good puff paste, and lay it near half an inch thick round the edge of the dish; roll out the lid, which must be a little thicker than the paste on the edge of the dish, and lay it on; then roll out another lid pretty thin, and cut in flowers, leaves, or whatever form you please, and lay it on the lid. If you do not want it, it will keep in the pot it was baked in eight or ten days; but let the crust be kept on, that the air may not get to it. A breast and shoulder of venison is the most proper for pasty.

Sweetbread Pie.

Lay a puff paste, half an inch thick, at the bottom of a deep dish, and put force-meat round the sides. Cut some sweetbreads in pieces, three or four, according to the size the pie is intended to be made ; lay them in first, then some cockscombs, a few truffles and morels, some asparagus tops, and fresh mush-rooms, yolks of eggs boiled hard, and force-meat balls ; season with pepper and salt. Almost fill the pie with water, cover it, and bake it two hours. When it comes from the oven, pour in some rich veal gravy, thickened with a very little cream and flour.

Cheshire Pork Pie.

Take the skin off a loin of pork, and cut it into steaks. Sea-son them with pepper, salt, and nutmeg, and make a good crust. Put into your dish a layer of pork, then a layer of pip-pins, pared and cored, and sugar sufficient to sweeten it   Then place another layer of pork, and put in half a pint of white wine. Lay some butter on the top, close your pie, and send it to the oven. If your pie is large, you must put in a pint of white wine.

PIES MADE OF POULTRY, &c.

A plain Goose Pie.

Quarter your goose, season it well with pepper and salt, and lay it in a raised crust. Cut half a pound of butter into pieces, and put it in different places on the top ; then lay on the lid, and send it to an oven moderately heated.

Giblet Pie.

Clean two pair of giblets well, and put all but the livers into a saucepan, with two quarts of water, twenty corns of whole pepper, three blades of mace, a bunch of sweet herbs, and a large onion. Cover them close, and let them stew very gently till they are tender. Have a good crust ready, cover your dish, lay at the bottom a fine rump steak seasoned with pepper and salt, put in your giblets with the livers, and strain the liquor they were stewed in ; then season it with salt, and pour it into your pie. Put on the lid, and bake it an hour and a half.

Pigeon Pie.

Pick and clean your pigeons very nicely, and then season them with pepper and salt ; or put some good force-meat, or butter, pepper, and salt, into each of their bellies. Then cover your dish with a puff paste crust, lay in your pigeons, and put between them the necks, gizzards, livers, pinions, and hearts, with the yolk of a hard egg, and a beef steak in the middle. Put as much water as will nearly fill the dish, lay on the top crust, and bake it well.

Chicken Pie.

Season your chickens with pepper, salt, and mace. Put a piece of butter into each of them, and lay them in the dish with their breasts upwards. Lay a thin slice of bacon over them, which will give them an agreeable flavour. Then put in a pint of strong gravy, and make a good puff paste. Put on the lid, and bake it in a moderately heated oven.

FRUIT PIES

Apple Pie.

Make a good puff-paste crust, and put it round the edge of your dish. Pare and quarter your apples, and take out the cores. Then lay a thick row of apples, and put in half the sugar you intend to use for your pie. Mince a little lemon-peel fine, spread it over the sugar and apples, squeeze in a little juice of a lemon; then scatter a few cloves over it, and lay on the rest of your apples and sugar, with another small squeeze of the juice of a lemon. Boil the parings of the apples and cores in some water, with a blade of mace, till the flavour is extracted; strain it, put in a little sugar, and boil it till it is reduced to a small quantity: then pour it into your pie, put on your crust, and send it to the oven. You may add to the apples a little quince or marmalade, which will greatly enrich the flavour. When the pie comes from the oven, beat up the yolks of two eggs, with half a pint of cream, and a little nutmeg and sugar. Put it over a slow fire, and keep stirring it till near boiling; then take off the lid of the pie, and pour it in. Cut the crust into small three-corner pieces, and stick them about the pie. A pear pie must be done in the same manner, only the quince and marmalade must be omitted.

Apple Tart.

Scald eight or ten large codlings, let them stand till they are cold, and then take off the skins. Beat the pulp as fine as possible with a spoon: then mix the yolks of six eggs, some grated nutmeg, and sweeten it to your taste. Melt some good fresh butter, and beat it till it is of the consistence of fine thick cream. Then make a puff paste, and cover a thin patty-pan with it; pour in the ingredients, but do not cover it with the paste. When you have baked it a quarter of an hour, slip it out of the patty-pan on a dish, and strew over it some sugar finely beaten and sifted.

Cherry Pie.

Having made a good crust, lay a little of it round the sides ot your dish, and strew some sugar at the bottom. Then lay in your fruit, and some sugar at the top. Put on your lid, and bake it in a slack oven. If you mix some currants with the cherries, it will be a considerable addition. A plum or gooseberry pie may be made in the same manner.

Mince Pies.

Take two or three calf's feet, boil them as you would do for eating, and take out the large bones; shred them very fine, put to them double their weight of beef suet, shred fine, and about a pound of currants well cleaned, a quarter of a pound of candied orange and citron cut in small pieces, half a pound of sugar, a little salt, a quarter of an ounce of mace, and a large nutmeg; beat the latter together, put in a little juice of lemon or verjuice to your taste, a glass of mountain wine or sack, which you please: so mix all together. Bake them in puff paste.

Mince Pies, another way.

Take a pound of beef, a pound of apples, two pounds of suet, two pounds of sugar, two pounds of currants, one pound of candied lemon, or orange peel, a quarter of a pound of citron, an ounce of fine spices, mixed together; half an ounce of salt, and six rinds of lemons shred fine. Let the whole of these ingredients be well mixed, adding brandy and wine sufficient to your palate.

Egg Pies.

Take and boil half a dozen eggs, half a dozen apples, and a pound and a half of beef suet, a pound of currants, and shred them; then season it with mace, nutmeg, and sugar, to your taste, a spoonful or two of brandy, and sweetmeats, if you please.

FISH PIES.

Eel Pie.

When you have skinned, gutted, and washed your eels very clean, cut them into pieces about an inch and a half long Season them with pepper, salt, and a little dried sage rubbed small. Put them into your dish, with as much water as will just cover them. Make a good puff paste, lay on the lid, and send your pie to the oven, which must be quick, but not so as to burn the crust.

Herring Pie.

Having scaled, gutted, and washed your herrings clean, cut off their heads, fins, and tails. Make a good crust, cover your dish, and season your herrings with beaten mace, pepper and salt. Put a little butter in the bottom of your dish, and then the herrings. Over these put some apples and onions sliced very thin. Put some butter on the top, then pour in a little water, lay on the lid, send it to the oven, and let it be well baked.

Carp Pie.

Scrape off the scales, and then gut and wash a large carp clean. Take an eel, and boil it till it is almost tender; pick off all the meat, and mince it fine, with an equal quantity or crumbs of bread, a few sweet herbs, lemon-peel cut fine, a little pepper, salt, and grated nutmeg, an anchovy, half a pint of oysters parboiled and chopped fine, and the yolks of three hard eggs cut small. Roll it up with a quarter of a pound or butter, and fill the belly of the carp. Make a good crust, cover the dish, and lay in your fish. Serve the liquor you boiled your eel in, put into it the eel bones, and boil them with a little mace, whole pepper, an onion, some sweet herbs, and an anchovy. Boil it till reduced to about half a pint, then strain it, and add to it about a quarter of a pint of white wine, and a piece of butter about the size of a hen's egg mixed in a very little flour. Boil it up, and pour it into your pie. Put on the lid and bake it an hour in a quick oven.

Tench Pie

Put a layer of butter at the bottom of your dish, and grate in some nutmeg, with pepper, salt, and mace. Then lay in your tench, cover them with some butter, and pour in some red wine with a little water. Then put on the lid; and when it comes from the oven, pour in melted butter mixed with some good rich gravy.

Trout Pie.

Take a brace of trout, and lard them with eels; raise the crust, and put a layer of fresh butter at the bottom. Then make a force-meat of trout, mushrooms, truffles, morels, chives, and fresh butter. Season them with salt, pepper, and spice; mix these up with the yolks of two eggs; stuff the trout with it, lay them in the dish, cover them with butter, put on the lid, and send it to the oven. Have some good fish gravy ready, and when the pie is done, raise the crust and pour it in.

Salmon Pie.

When you have made a good crust, take a piece of fresh salmon, well cleansed, and season it with salt, mace, and nutmeg. Put a piece of butter at the bottom of your dish, and then lay in the salmon. Melt butter in proportion to the size of your pie, and then take a lobster, boil it, pick out all the flesh, chop it small, bruise the body, and mix it well with the butter. Pour it over your salmon, put on the lid, and let it be well baked.

PANCAKES AND FRITTERS

Take care that your pan be thoroughly clean, that you fry them in nice sweet lard, or fresh butter, of a light brown colour, and that the grease is thoroughly drained from them before you carry them to table.

Pancakes.

Beat six or eight eggs well together, leaving out half the whites, and stir them into a quart of milk. Mix your flour first with a little of the milk, and then add the rest by degrees. Put in two spoonfuls of beaten ginger, a glass of brandy, and a little salt, and stir all well together. Put a piece of butter into your frying pan, and then pour in a ladle full of batter, which will make a pancake, moving the pan round, that the batter may spread all over it. Shake the pan, and when you think one side is enough, turn it, and when both sides are done, lay it in a dish before the fire; and in like manner do the rest. Before you take them out of the pan, raise it a little, that they may drain, and be quite clear of grease. When you send them to table, strew a little sugar over them.

Cream Pancakes.

Mix the yolks of two eggs with half a pint of cream, two ounces of sugar, and a little beaten cinnamon, mace, and nutmeg. Rub your pan with lard, and fry them as thin as possible. Grate over them some fine sugar.

Rice Pancakes.

Take three spoonfuls of flour of rice, and a quart of cream. Set it on a slow fire, and keep stirring it till it is as thick as pap. Pour into it half a pound of butter, and a nutmeg grated. Then pour it into an earthen pan, and when it is cold, stir in three or four spoonfuls of flour, a little salt, some sugar, and nine eggs well beaten. Mix all well together, and fry them nicely. When cream is not to be had, you must use new milk, but in that case you must add a spoonful more of flour of rice.

Plain Fritters.

Grate the crumb of a penny loaf, and put it into a pint o. milk; mix it very smooth, and, when cold, add the yolks of five eggs, three ounces of sifted sugar, and some grated nutmeg. Fry them in hog's lard, and when done, pour melted butter, wine, and sugar, into the dish.

Custard Fritters.

Beat up the yolks of eight eggs with one spoonful of flour, half a nutmeg, a little salt, and a glass of brandy ; add a pint of cream, sweeten it, and bake it in a small dish. When cold, cut it into quarters, and dip them in batter made of half a pint of cream, a quarter of a pint of milk, four eggs, a little flour, and a little ginger grated. Fry them in a good lard or dripping, and when done, strew over them some grated sugar.

Apple Fritters.

Take some of the largest apples you can get, pare and core them, and then cut them into round slices. Take half a pint of ale and two eggs, and beat in as much flour as will make it rather thicker than a common pudding, with nutmeg and sugar to your taste. Let it stand three or four minutes to rise. Dip your slices of apple into the batter, fry them crisp, and serve them up with sugar grated over them, and wine sauce in a boat.

Fritters Royal.

Put a quart of new milk into a saucepan, and when it begins to boil, pour in a pint of sack, or wine. Then take it off, let it stand five or six minutes, skim off the curd, and put it into a bason. Beat it up well with six eggs, and season it with nutmeg. Then beat it with a whisk, and add flour sufficient to give it the usual thickness of batter ; put in some sugar, and fry them quick.

Strawberry Fritters.

Make a batter with flour, a spoonful of sweet oil, another of white wine, a little rasped lemon-peel, and the whites of two or three eggs ; make it pretty soft, just fit to drop with a spoon. Mix some large strawberries with it, and drop them with a spoon into the hot fritters. When of a good colour, take them out, and drain them on a sieve. When done, strew some sugar over them, or glaze them, and send them to table.

TARTS AND PUFFS.

If you use tin patties to bake in, butter the bottoms, and then put on a very thin bit of crust, otherwise you will not be able to take them out; but if you bake them in glass or china, you need only use an upper crust. Put some fine sugar at the bottom, then lay in your fruit, strew more sugar on the top, cover them, and bake them in a slack oven. Currants and raspberries make an exceeding good tart, and require little baking.

Apples and pears intended for tarts, must be managed tnus : cut them into quarters, and take out the cores, then cut the quarters across, and put them into a saucepan, with as much water as will barely cover them, and let them simmer on a slow fire til' the fruit is tender. Put a good piece of lemon-peel into the water with the fruit, and then have your patties ready. Lay fine sugar at the bottom, then your fruit, and a little sugar at top. Pour over each tart one tea-spoonful of lemon-juice, and three of the liquor they were boiled in, then put on your lid, and bake them in a slack oven. Apricot tarts may be made in the same manner, only that you must not put in any lemon-juice.

Preserved fruit requires very little baking, and that which is very high preserved, should not be baked at all. In this case, the crust should be first baked upon a tin the size of the intended tart : cut it with a marking iron, and when cold, take it off, and lay it on the fruit.

Raspberry Tarts.

Roll out some thin puff paste, and lay it in a patty-pan ; then put in some raspberries, and strew over them some very fine sugar. Put on the lid, and bake it. Then cut it open, and put in half a pint of cream, the yolks of two or three eggs well beaten, and a little sugar. Give it another heat in the oven, and it will be fit for use.

Rhubarb Tarts.

Take the stalks of rhubarb that grow in a garden, peel them, and cut them into small pieces. Then do it in every respect the same as a gooseberry tart.

Marrow Tarts

To a quart of cream, put the yolks of twelve eggs, half a pound of sugar, some beaten mace and cinnamon, a little salt, and some sack ; set it on the fire with half a pound of biscuits, as much marrow, a little orange and lemon peel; stir it till it becomes thick, and when it is cold put it into pans with puff paste, then bake it gently in a slow oven.

Sweetmeat Tarts.

Make a little shell-paste, roll it, and line your tins ; prick them in the inside, and so bake them. When you serve them up, put in any sort of sweetmeats. You may have a different sort every day by keeping the shells ready baked by you.

Orange Tarts.

Take two or three Seville oranges, and boil them, shift them in the boiling to take out the bitterness, cut them in two, take out the pippins, and cut them in slices. They must be baked in crisp paste. When you fill the patty-pans, lay in a layer of oranges and a layer of sugar, (a pound will sweeten a dozen of small tins, if you do not put in too much orange,) bake them in a slow oven, and ice them over.

Sugar Puffs.

Beat up the whites of ten eggs till they rise to a high froth, and then put them into a marble mortar, with as much double refined sugar as will make it thick. Then rub it well round the mortar, put in a few carraway seeds, and take a sheet of wafers, and lay it on as broad as a sixpence, and as high as you can. Put them into a moderately-heated oven for about a quarter of an hour, and they will have a very white and delicate appearance.

Almond Puffs.

Take two ounces of sweet almonds, blanch them, and beat them very fine with orange-flower water. Beat up the whites of three eggs to a very high froth, and then strew in a little sifted sugar. Mix your almonds with the sugar and eggs, and then add more sugar till it is as thick as paste. Lay it in cakes, and bake them in a slack oven on paper.

Wafers.

Take a spoonful of orange-flower water, two spoonfuls of flour, two of sugar, and the same of milk. Beat them well together for half an hour; then make your wafer-tongs hot, and pour a little of your batter in to cover your irons. Bake them on a stove fire, and as they are baking, roll them round a stick like a spigot. When they are cold, they will be very crisp, and are proper to be eaten either with jellies or tea.

CHEESECAKES AND CUSTARDS.

The shorter time any cheesecakes are made before put into the oven, the better; but more particularly almond or lemon cheesecakes, as standing long will make them grow oily, and give them a disagreeable appearance. Particular attention must likewise be paid to the heat of the oven, which must be moderate; for if it is too hot, they will be scorched, and consequently their beauty spoiled; and if too slack, they will look black and heavy.

Common Cheesecakes

Put a spoonful of rennet into a quart of new milk, and set it near the fire. When the milk is blood warm, and broken, drain the curd through a coarse sieve. Now and then break the curd gently with your fingers, and rub into it a quarter of a pound of butter, the same quantity of sugar, a nutmeg, and two Naples biscuits grated, the yolks of four eggs and the white of one, with an ounce of almonds, well beaten, with two spoonfuls of rose-water, and the same of sack. Then clean and wash six ounces of currants, and put them into the curd. Mix all well together, fill your patty-pans, and send them to a moderate oven.

Bread Cheesecakes.

Slice a penny loaf as thin as possible, then pour on it a pint of boiling cream, and let it stand two hours. Then take eight eggs, half a pound of butter, and a nutmeg grated. Beat them well together, and mix them into the cream and bread, with half a pound of currants well washed and dried, and a spoonful of white wine or brandy. Bake them in patty-pans, or raised crusts.

Almond Cheesecakes.

Take four ounces of almonds, blanch them, and beat them with a little orange-flower water; add the yolks of eight eggs, the rind of a large lemon grated, half a pound of melted butter, and sugar to your taste; lay a thin puff paste at the bottom of your tins, and little slips across. Add about half a dozen bitter almonds.

———

In making of Custards, the greatest care must be taken that your pan be well tinned; and always remember to put a spoonful of water into it, to prevent your ingredients sticking to the bottom.

Plain Custards.

Put a quart of good cream over a slow fire, with a little cinnamon, and four ounces of sugar. When it has boiled, take it off the fire, beat the yolks of eight eggs, and put to them a spoonful of orange-flower water, to prevent the cream from cracking. Stir them in by degrees as your cream cools, put the pan over a very slow fire, stir it carefully one way till it is almost boiling, and then pour it into cups.

Baked Custards.

Boil a pint of cream with some mace and cinnamon, and when it is cold, take four yolks and two whites of eggs, a little rose and orange-flower water and sack, and nutmeg and sugar to your palate. Mix them well together, and bake it in cups.

Almond Custards.

Take a quarter of a pound of almonds, blanch and beat them very fine, and then put them into a pint of cream, with two spoonfuls of rose-water. Sweeten to your palate, beat up the yolks of four eggs very fine, and put it in. Stir all together one way over the fire till it is thick, and then pour it into cups.

Orange Custards.

Boil very tender the rind of half a Seville orange, and then beat it in a mortar till it is very fine. Put to it a spoonful of the best brandy, the juice of a Seville orange, four ounces of loaf sugar, and the yolks of four eggs. Beat them all well together for ten minutes, and then pour in by degrees a pint of boiling cream. Keep beating them till they are cold, then put them in custard-cups, and set them in a dish of hot water. Let them stand till they are set, then take them out, and stick preserved orange on the top. These, like the former, may be served up either hot or cold.

Beest Custards.

Set a pint of beest over the fire, with a little cinnamon, and three bay-leaves, and let it be boiling hot. Then take it off, and have ready mixed a spoonful of flour, and the same of thick cream. Pour the hot beest upon it by degrees, mix it well together and sweeten it to your taste. You may bake it either in crusts or cups.

CAKES AND BISCUITS.

One very material matter to be attended to in making these articles is, that all your ingredients are ready at the time you are going to make them, and that you do not leave them till your business is done; but be particularly observant with respect to the eggs when beaten up, which, if left at any time, must be again beaten, and by that means your cake will not be so light as it otherwise would and ought to be. If you use butter to your cakes, be careful in beating it to a fine cream before you mix the sugar with it. Cakes made with rice, seeds, or plumbs, are best baked with wooden girths, as thereby the heat will penetrate into the middle, which will not be the case if baked in pots or tins. The heat of the oven must be proportioned to the size of the cake.

A good Common Cake.

Take six ounces of ground rice, and the same quantity of

flour, the yolks and whites of nine eggs, half a pound of lump sugar, pounded and sifted, and half an ounce of carraway seeds. Mix these well together, and bake it an hour in a quick oven.

A rich Seed Cake

Take a pound and a quarter of flour, well dried, a pound of butter, a pound of loaf sugar, beaten and sifted, eight eggs, two ounces of carraway seeds, one nutmeg grated, and its weight in cinnamon. First beat your butter to a cream, then put in your sugar; beat the whites of your eggs by themselves, and mix them with your butter and sugar, and then beat up the yolks, and mix with the whites. Beat in your flour, spices, and seed, a little before you send it away. Bake it two hours in a quick oven.

A Pound Cake, plain.

Beat a pound of butter in an earthen pan till it is like a thick cream, then beat in nine whole eggs till it is quite light. Put in a glass of brandy, a little lemon-peel shred fine; then work in a pound and a quarter of flour. Put it into your hoop or pan, and bake it for one hour.

Gingerbread Cakes.

Take three pounds of flour, a pound of sugar, the same quantity of butter rolled in very fine, two ounces of beaten ginger, and a large nutmeg grated. Then take a pound of treacle, a quarter of a pint of cream, and make them warm together. Work up the bread stiff, roll it out, and make it up in thin cakes. Cut them out with a tea-cup or small glass, or roll them round like nuts, and bake them in a slack oven on tin plates.

Bath Cakes or Buns.

Take half a pound of butter, and one pound of flour; rub the butter well into the flour; add five eggs, and a tea-cupful of yeast. Set the whole well mixed up before the fire to rise; when sufficiently risen, add a quarter of a pound of fine powdered sugar, an ounce of carraways, well mixed in; then roll them out in little cakes, and bake them on tins: they may either be eaten for breakfast or tea.

Shrewsbury Cakes.

Beat half a pound of butter to a fine cream, and put in the same weight of flour, one egg, six ounces of beaten and sifted loaf sugar, and half an ounce of carraway seeds. Mix them with care; roll them thin, and cut them round with a small glass, or little tins ; prick them, lay tnem on sheets of tin ; and bake them in a slow oven.

Queen Cakes.

Take a pound of sugar, and beat and sift it ; a pound of well-dried flour, a pound of butter, eight eggs, and half a pound of currants washed and picked ; grate a nutmeg, and the same quantity of mace and cinnamon. Work your butter to a cream, and put in your sugar ; beat the whites of your eggs near half an hour, and mix them with your sugar and butter. Then beat your yolks near half an hour, and put them to your butter. Beat the whole well together, and when it is ready for the oven, put in your flour, spices, and currants. Sift a little sugar over them, and bake them in tins.

Little Plumb Cakes.

Take half a pound of sugar finely powdered, two pounds of flour well dried, four yolks and two whites of eggs, half a pound of butter washed with rose-water, six spoonfuls of cream warmed, and a pound and a half of currants unwashed, but picked and rubbed very clean in a cloth. Mix all well together, then make them up into cakes, bake them in a hot oven, and let them stand half an hour till they are coloured on both sides. Then take down the oven lid, and let them stand to soak. You must rub the butter well into the flour, then the eggs and cream, and then the currants.

Lemon Cakes.

Take the whites of ten eggs, put to them three spoonfuls of rose or orange-flower water, and beat them an hour with a whisk. Then put in a pound of beaten and sifted sugar, and grate into it the rind of a lemon. When it is well mixed, put in the juice of half a lemon, and the yolks of ten eggs beaten smooth. Just before you put it into the oven, stir in three quarters of a pound of flour, butter your pan, put it into a moderate oven, and an hour will bake it.

Currant Cakes.

Dry well before a fire a pound and a half of fine flour, take a pound of butter, half a pound of fine loaf sugar well beaten and sifted, four yolks of eggs, four spoonfuls of rose-water, the same of sack, a little mace, and a nutmeg grated. Beat the eggs well, and put them to the rose-water and sack. Then put to it the sugar and butter. Work them all together, and then stew in the currants and flour, having taken care to have them ready warmed for mixing. You may make six or eight cakes of them ; but mind to bake them of a fine brown, and pretty crisp.

Whigs.

Put half a pint of warm milk to three quarters of a pound of fine flour, and mix in it two or three spoonfuls of light barm. Cover it up, and set it before the fire an hour, in order to make it rise. Work into the paste four ounces of sugar, and the same quantity of butter. Make it into cakes or whigs, with as little flour as possible, and a few seeds, and bake them in a quick oven.

Common Biscuits.

Beat eight eggs well up together, and mix with them a pound of sifted sugar, with the rind of a lemon grated. Whisk it about till it looks light, and then put in a pound of flour, with a little rose-water. Sugar them over, and bake them on tins, or on papers.

Macaroons.

Blanch and beat fine a pound of sweet almonds, and put to them a pound of sugar and a little rose-water to keep them from oiling. Then beat the whites of seven eggs to a froth, put them in, and work the whole together. Drop them on wafer-paper, grate sugar over them, and put them into the oven.

CREAMS AND JAMS.

Orange Cream.

Pare off the rind of a Seville orange very fine, and then squeeze out the juice of four oranges. Put them into a stew-pan, with a pint of water, and eight ounces of sugar ; mix with them the whites of five eggs well beaten, and set the whole over the fire. Stir it one way till it becomes thick and white, then strain it through a gauze, and keep stirring it till it is cold. Then beat the yolks of five eggs very fine, and put it into your pan with some cream and the other articles. Stir it over a slow fire till it is ready to boil, then pour it into a basin, and having stirred it till it is quite cold, put it into your glasses.

Burnt Cream.

Take a little clarified sugar, put it into your sugar pan, and let it boil till it colours in the pan ; then pour in your cream, stirring it all the time till the sugar is dissolved. The cream may be made in the following manner : to a pint of cream take five eggs, a quarter of a pound of fine sugar, and a spoon-ful of orange-flower water; set it over the fire, stirring it till it is thick ; but be sure it does not boil, or else it will curdle.

Whipt Cream.

Take the whites of eight eggs, a quart of thick cream, and half a pint of sack. Mix them together, and sweeten it to your taste with double-refined sugar. You may perfume it, if you please, with a little musk or ambergris tied in a rag, and steeped a little in the cream. Whip it up with a whisk, and some lemon-peel tied in the middle of the whisk. Take the froth with a spoon, and lay it in your glasses or basins. This put over fine tarts has a pretty appearance.

Raspberry Cream.

Rub a quart of raspberries, or raspberry-jam, through a hair sieve, to take out the seeds, and then mix it well with cream. Sweeten it with sugar to your taste; then put it into a stone jug, and raise a froth with a chocolate-mill. As your froth rises, take it off with a spoon, and lay it upon a hair sieve. When you have got as much froth as you want, put what cream remains into a deep china dish, or punch-bowl, and pour your frothed cream upon it as high as it will lie on.

Ice Cream.

To a pound of preserved fruit, which may be of what kind you choose, add a quart of good cream, the juice of two lemons squeezed into it, and some sugar to your palate. Let the whole be rubbed through a fine hair sieve; and, if raspberry, straw-berry, or any red fruit, you must add a little cochineal to heighten the colour: have your freezing-pot nice and clean, and put your cream into it, cover it, and put it into your tub with ice beat small, and some salt; turn the freezing-pot quick, and as the cream sticks to the sides scrape it down with your ice-spoon, and so on till it is frozen. The more the cream is worked to the sides with the spoon, the smoother and better flavoured it will be. After it is well frozen, take it out, and put it into ice shapes, with fresh salt and ice; when you serve it, carefully wash the shapes for fear any salt should adhere to them; dip them in water lukewarm, and send them up to table.

Fruit Ices may be made either with water or cream. It water, two pounds of fruit, a pint of spring water, a pint of clarified sugar, and the juice of two lemons.

Raspberry Jam.

Let your raspberries be thoroughly ripe, and quite dry. Mash them fine, and strew in them their own weight of loaf sugar, and half their weight of the juice of white currants. Boil them half an hour over a clear slow fire, skim them well, and put them into pots or glasses. Tie them down with brandy papers, and keep them dry. Strew on the sugar as soon as you can after the berries are gathered, and in order to preserve their fine flavour, do not let them stand long before you boil them.

Strawberry Jam.

Bruise very fine some scarlet strawberries gathered when quite ripe, and put to them a little juice of red currants. Beat and sift their weight in sugar, strew it over them, and put them into a preserving-pan. Set them over a clear slow fire, skim them, boil them twenty minutes, and then put them into glasses

Gooseberry Jam.

Cut and pick out the seeds of fine large green gooseberries, gathered when they are full grown, but not ripe. Put them into a pan of water, green them, and lay them in a sieve to drain. Then beat them in a marble mortar, with their weight in sugar. Take a quart of gooseberries, boil them to a mash in a quart of water, squeeze them, and to every pint of liquor put a pound of fine loaf sugar. Then boil and skim it, put in your green gooseberries, and having boiled them till they are very thick, clear, and of a pretty green, put them into glasses.

Black Currant Jam.

Gather your currants when they are thoroughly ripe and dry, and pick them clean from the stalks. Then bruise them well in a bowl, and to every two pounds of currants, put a pound and a half of loaf sugar finely beaten. Put them into a preserving-pan, boil them half an hour, skim and stir them all the time, and then put them into pots.

Icings for Cakes and various Articles in Confectionary.

Take a pound of double-refined sugar pounded and sifted fine, and mix it with the whites of twenty-four eggs, in an earthen pan. Whisk them well for two or three hours till it looks white and thick, and then, with a broad thin board, or bunch of feathers, spread it all over the top and sides of the cake. Set it at a proper distance before a clear fire, and keep turning it continually, that it may not lose its colour; but a cool oven is best, where an hour will harden it.

JELLIES AND SILLABUBS.
Calf's Feet Jelly.

Boil two calf's feet, well cleansed, in a gallon of water till it is reduced to a quart, and then pour it into a pan. When it is cold, skim off the fat, and take the jelly up clean. Leave what settling may remain at the bottom, and put the jelly into a saucepan, with a pint of mountain wine, half a pound of loaf sugar, and the juice of four lemons. Add to these the whites of six or eight eggs well beaten up; stir all well together, put it on the fire, and let it boil a few minutes. Pour it into a large flannel bag, and repeat it till it runs clear; then have ready a large china basin, and put into it some lemon-peel cut as thin as possible. Let the jelly run into the basin, and the lemon-peel will not only give it a pleasing colour, but a grateful flavour. Fill your glasses, and it will be fit for use.

Black Currant Jelly.

Let your currants be thoroughly ripe, and quite dry; strip them clear from the stalks, and put them into a large stew-pot. To every ten quarts of currants, put one quart of water. Tie paper close over them, and set them for two hours in a cool oven. Then squeeze them through a fine cloth, and to every quart of juice add a pound and a half of loaf sugar broken into small pieces. Stir it gently till the sugar is melted, and when it boils, take off the scum quite clean. Let it boil pretty quick over a clear fire till it jellies, which is known by dipping the skimmer into your jelly and holding it in the air; when it hangs to the spoon in a drop, it is done. You may also put some into a plate to try, and if there come a thick skin it is done. If your jelly is boiled too long it will lose its flavour, and shrink very much. Pour it into pots, cover them with brandy papers, and keep them in a dry place. Red and white jelly is made in the same manner.

Common Sillabub.

Put a pint of cider and a bottle of strong beer into a large bowl; grate in a small nutmeg, and sweeten it to your taste. Then milk from the cow as much milk as will make a strong froth. Let it stand an hour, and then strew over it a few currants, well washed, picked, and plumped, before the fire, and it will be fit for use.

Whipt Sillabub.

Rub a lump of loaf sugar on the outside of a lemon, and put it into a pint of thick cream, and sweeten it to your taste. Then squeeze in the juice of a lemon, and add a glass of Madeira wine, or French brandy. Mill it to a froth with a chocolate mill, take off the froth as it rises, and lay it in a hair sieve. Then fill one half of your glasses a little more than half full with white wine, and the other half of your glasses a little more than half full with red wine Then lay on your froth as high as you can, but take care that it is well drained on your sieve, otherwise it will mix with the wine, and your sillabub be spoiled.

Flummery.

Take an ounce of bitter and the same quantity of sweet almonds, put them in a basin, and pour over them some boiling water to make the skins come off. Then strip off the skins, and throw the kernels into cold water; take them out, and beat them in a marble mortar, with a little rose-water to keep them from oiling; and when they are beat, put them into a pint of calves feet stock; set it over the fire, and sweeten it to your taste with loaf sugar. As soon as it boils, strain it through a piece of muslin or gauze; and when it is a little cold, put into it a pint of thick cream, and keep stirring it often till it grows thick and cold. Wet your moulds in cold water, and pour in the flummery. Let them stand about six hours before you turn them out; and, if you make your flummery stiff, and wet your moulds, it will turn out without putting them into warm water, which will be a great advantage to the look of the figures, as warm water gives a dulness to the flummery.

POSSETS, WHITE POTS, GRUELS, &c.
Wine Posset.

Boil the crumb of a penny loaf in a quart of milk till it is soft, then take it off the fire, and grate in half a nutmeg. Put in sugar to your taste, then pour it into a china bowl, and put in by degrees a pint of Lisbon wine. Serve it up with toasted bread upon a plate.

Ale Posset.

Take a small piece of white bread, put it into a pint of milk, and set it over the fire. Then put some nutmeg and sugar into a pint of ale, warm it, and when your milk boils, pour it upon the ale. Let it stand a few minutes to clear, and it will be fit for use.

A White Pot.

Take two quarts of milk, and beat up eight eggs, and half the whites, with a little rose-water, a nutmeg, and a quarter of a pound of sugar. Cut a penny loaf into very thin slices, and pour the milk and eggs over them. Put a little piece of butter on the top, send it to the oven, bake it for half an hour, and it will be fit for use.

White Caudle.

Take two quarts of water, and mix it with four spoonfuls of

oatmeal, a blade or two of mace, and a piece of lemon-peel. Let it boil, and keep stirring it often. Let it boil a quarter of an hour, and be careful not to let it boil over; then strain it through a coarse sieve. When you use it, sweeten it to your taste, grate in a little nutmeg, and what wine you think proper; and if it is not for a sick person, squeeze in the juice of a lemon.

White Wine Whey.

Put in a large basin half a pint of skimmed milk and half a pint of wine. When it has stood a few minutes, pour in a pint of boiling water. Let it stand a little, and the curd will gather in a lump, and settle at the bottom. Then pour your whey into a china bowl, and put in a lump of sugar, a sprig of balm, or a slice of lemon.

Water Gruel.

Put a large spoonful of oatmeal into a pint of water, and stir it well together, and let it boil three or four times, stirring it often; but be careful it does not boil over. Then strain it through a sieve, salt it to your palate, and put in a good piece of butter. Stir it about with a spoon till the butter is all melted, and it will be fine and smooth.

Barley Gruel.

Put a quarter of a pound of pearl barley, and a stick of cinnamon, into two quarts of water, and let it boil till it is reduced to one quart. Then strain it through a sieve, add a pint of red wine, and sweeten it to your taste.

Barley Water.

To two quarts of water put a quarter of a pound of pearl-barley. When it boils, strain it very clean, boil half away, and then strain it off. Add two spoonfuls of white wine, and sweeten it to your palate.

Rice Milk.

Boil half a pound of rice in a quart of water, with a little cinnamon. Let it boil till the water is wasted, but take care it does not burn. Then add three pints of milk, with the yolk of an egg beat fine, and keep stirring it while you put them in When it boils, pour it out, and sweeten it to your taste.

Sago.

Put a large spoonful of sago into three quarters of a pint of water. Stir it, and boil it gently till it is as thick as you would have it. Then put in wine and sugar, with a little grated nutmeg to your palate.

To mull Wine.

Grate half a nutmeg into a pint of wine, and sweeten it to your taste with loaf-sugar. Set it over the fire, and when it boils, take it off to cool. Beat up the yolks of four eggs, put them into a little cold wine, and mix them carefully with the hot, a little at a time. Then pour it backwards and forwards till it looks fine and bright. Set it on the fire again till it is quite hot and pretty thick, pour it again backwards and forwards several times, and serve it in chocolate cups, with long slices of bread toasted of a nice light brown.

Gooseberry Fool.

Set two quarts of gooseberries on the fire in about a quart of water. When they begin to simmer, turn yellow, and begin to plump, throw them into a cullender to drain the water out; then with the back of a spoon carefully squeeze the pulp through a sieve into a dish ; make them pretty sweet, and let them stand till they are cold. In the mean time, take two quarts of milk, and the yolks of four eggs, beat up with a little grated nutmeg ; stir it softly over a slow fire. When it begins to simmer, take it off, and by degrees stir it into the goose-berries. Let it stand till it is cold, and serve it up. If you make it with cream, you need not put in any eggs.

Lemonade.

Take two Seville oranges and six lemons, pare them very thin, and steep the parings four hours in two quarts of water. Put the juice of six oranges and twelve lemons upon three quarters of a pound of fine sugar, and when the sugar is melted, put the water to it in which the parings have been steeped. Add a little orange-flower water, and more sugar, if necessary. Press it through a bag till it is fine, and then pour it into bottles for use.

BREAD, &c.

To make Bread.

Let flour be kept four or five weeks before it is begun to bake with. Put half a bushel of good flour into a trough, or kneading-tub; mix with it between four and five quarts of warm water, and a pint and a half of good yeast; put it into the flour, and stir it well with your hands till it becomes tough. Let it rise about an hour and twenty minutes, or less if it rises fast ; then, before it falls, add four quarts more of warm water, and half a pound of salt ; work it well, and cover it with a cloth. Put the fire then into the oven ; and by the time it is warm enough, the dough will be ready. Make the loaves about five pounds each; sweep out the oven very clean and quick, and put in the bread; shut it up close, and two hours and a half will bake it. In summer the water should be milk-warm, in winter a little more, and in frosty weather as hot as you can well bear your hand in, but not scalding, or the whole will be spoiled. If baked in tins, the crust will be very nice.

The oven should be round, not long, the roof from twenty to twenty-four inches high, the mouth small, and the door of iron, to shut close. This construction will save firing and time, and bake better than long and high-roofed ovens.

Rolls, muffins, or any sort of bread, may be made to taste new when two or three days old, by dipping them uncut in water, and baking afresh or toasting.

American Flour

Requires almost twice as much water to make it into bread as is used for English flour, and therefore it is more profitable; for a stone of the American, which weighs fourteen pounds, will make twenty-one pounds and a half of bread, but the best sort of English flour produces only eighteen pounds and a half.

The Rev. Mr. Hagget's economical Bread.

Only the coarse flake bran to be removed from the flour: of this take five pounds, and boil it in rather more than four gallons of water; so that when perfectly smooth, you may have three gallons and three quarts of bran-water clear. With this knead fifty-six pounds of the flour, adding salt and yeast in the same way and proportions as for other bread. When ready to bake, divide it into loaves, and bake them two hours and a half.

Thus made, flour will imbibe three quarts more of bran-water than of plain; so that it not only produces a more nutritious substantial food, but makes an increase of one-fifth of the usual quantity of bread, which is a saving of one days consumption out of six; and if this was adopted throughout the kingdom, it would make a saving of ten millions sterling a year, when wheat was at the price it stood in the scarcity, reckoning the consumption to be two hundred thousand bushels a day. The same quantity of flour which, kneaded with water, produces sixty-nine pounds eight ounces of bread will, in the above way, make eighty-three pounds eight ounces and gain fourteen pounds. At the ordinary price of flour, four millions would be saved. When ten days old, if put into the oven for twenty minutes, this bread will appear quite new again.

Rice and wheat Bread.

Simmer a pound of rice in two quarts of water till it becomes perfectly soft, when it is of a proper warmth, mix it extremely well with four pounds of flour, and yeast and salt as for other bread; of yeast about four large spoonfuls; knead it extremely well; then set it to rise before the fire. Some of the flour should be reserved to make up the loaves. The whole expense, including baking, will not exceed three shillings, for which eight pounds and a half of exceeding good bread will be produced. If the rice should require more water, it must be added, as some rice swells more than other.

French Bread.

With a quarter of a peck of fine flour mix the yolks of three and whites of two eggs, beaten and strained, a little salt, half a pint of good yeast that is not bitter, and as much milk, made a little warm, as will work into a thin light dough. Stir it about, but do not knead it. Have ready three quart wooden dishes, divide the dough among them, set to rise, then turn them out into the oven, which must be quick. Rasp when done.

Excellent Rolls.

Warm one ounce of butter in half a pint of milk, put to it a spoonful and a half of yeast of small beer, and a little salt. Put two pounds of flour into a pan, and mix in the above. Let it rise an hour; knead it well; make into seven rolls, and bake in a quick oven.

If made in cakes three inches thick, sliced and buttered, they resemble Sally Lumm's, as made at Bath.

The foregoing receipt, with the addition of a little saffron boiled in half a tea-cupful of milk, makes them remarkably good.

French Rolls.

Rub an ounce of butter into a pound of flour; mix one egg beaten, a little yeast that is not bitter, and as much milk as will make a dough of a middling stiffness. Beat it well, but do not knead; let it rise, and bake on tins.

Brentford Rolls.

Mix with two pounds of flour, a little salt, two ounces of sifted sugar, four ounces of butter, and two eggs beaten with two spoonfuls of yeast, and about a pint of milk. Knead the dough well, and set it to rise before the fire. Make twelve rolls, butter tin plates, and set them before the fire to rise, till they become of a proper size; then bake half an hour.

Potato Rolls.

Boil three pounds of potatoes, bruise and work them with two ounces of butter, and as much milk as will make them pass through a colander. Take half or three quarters of a pint of yeast, and half a pint of warm water, mix with the potatoes, then pour the whole upon five pounds of flour, and add some salt. Knead it well: if not of a proper consistence, put a little more milk and water warm; let it stand before the fire an hour to rise; work it well, and make into rolls. Bake about half an hour in an oven not quite so hot as for bread.

They eat well, toasted and buttered.

Muffins.

Mix two pounds of flour with two eggs, two ounces of butter melted in a pint of milk, and four or five spoonfuls of yeast; beat it thoroughly, and set it to rise two or three hours. Bake on a hot hearth, in flat cakes. When done on one side, turn them.

Note. Muffins, rolls, or bread, if stale, may be made to taste new, by dipping in cold water, and toasting, or heating in an oven, or Dutch oven, till the outside be crisp.

Yorkshire Cakes.

Take two pounds of flour, and mix with it four ounces of butter melted in a pint of good milk, three spoonfuls of yeast, and two eggs; beat all well together, and let it rise; then knead it, and make into cakes; let them rise on tins before you bake, which do in a slow oven.

Another sort is made as above, leaving out the butter. The first sort is shorter; the last lighter.

Hard Biscuits.

Warm two ounces of butter in as much skimmed milk as will make a pound of flour into a very stiff paste, beat it with a rolling pin, and work it very smooth. Roll it thin, and cut it into round biscuits; prick them full of holes with a fork. About six minutes will bake them.

Plain and crisp Biscuits.

Make a pound of flour, the yolk of an egg, and some milk, into a very stiff paste; beat it well, and knead till quite smooth; roll very thin, and cut into biscuits. Bake them in a slow oven till quite dry and crisp.

PICKLES, &c.

It is too common to use brass kettles, and put in alum or

halfpence to make the pickles look green; but this is not only unnecessary, but highly pernicious. The colour may be preserved, if the receipts be properly attended to, without injuring health by such improper means. One principal thing is to see that the jars be sound and good, and not porous to admit the air; for this reason stone or glass is to be preferred. The vinegar should be good, the jars close tied down with a bladder, and kept in a dry place. Pickles are often spoiled by too frequently opening the jars to serve the table, and leaving them exposed to the air. To prevent this it would be better not to return what is left into the jar, but to keep them separate, and ready for use.

Alegar.

Take some good sweet wort before it is hopped, put it into a jar, add a little yeast when it becomes milk-warm, and cover it over. In three or four days it will have done fermenting; set it in the sun, and it will be fit for use in three or four months, or much sooner, if it be fermented with sour yeast, and mixed with an equal quantity of sour ale.

Barberries.

Gather them before they are quite ripe, pick them clean, put them into jars with strong salt and water, and tie them down with a bladder. When a scum rises, put them into fresh salt and water: they require no vinegar, but their own sharpness will preserve them. Currants may be done in the same way.

Cauliflowers.

Pull the white part into small bunches, salt them in a dish, and let them stand three days to draw out the water. Then put them into jars, pour on boiling water salted, let them stand one night, and drain them on a sieve. Preserve them in glass jars, filled up with vinegar that has been boiled, and tie them down carefully.

Codlings.

Gather them when about the size of a large walnut, put them into a pan, and cover them with vine leaves. Set them over a slow fire till the skins will come off; then take them up carefully in a hair sieve, peel them with a penknife, and return them into the pan, with the water and vine leaves as before. Set them again over a slow fire till they be of a fine green, and then drain them on a sieve: when cold, put them into white-wine vinegar which has been boiled and cooled.

Pour on a little mutton fat, and tie them down close with a bladder.

Cucumber Ketchup.

Pare some large old cucumbers, cut them in slices, and mash them; add some salt, and let them stand till the next day. Drain off the liquor, boil it with lemon-peel, mace, cloves, horse-radish, shalots, white pepper, and ginger. Strain it; and when cold, put it into bottles, with the mace, cloves and pepper corns, but not the rest. A little of this ketchup will give an agreeable taste to almost any kind of gravy sauce.

French Beans.

Gather them dry, pick them clean, and shake some salt over them. When the salt begins to dissolve, stir them frequently, and the next day drain them in a colander. Then put them in jars and cover them with boiled vinegar. Let the jars stand three or four days some distance from the fire put the vinegar and pickles into a stew pan, set it on the fire with vine leaves over the top to keep in the steam of the vinegar; and when the leaves are turned yellow, put in fresh ones till the pickles be of a good green. Let them simmer, but not boil: add some sliced ginger, and pepper corns.—Gherkins and radish pods are done in the same manner.

Gooseberry Vinegar.

Having bruised some ripe gooseberries, add three quarts of water that has been boiled and cooled to one quart of fruit, and let it stand a day. Then strain it through a flannel bag, put a pound of coarse sugar to a gallon of liquor, stir it well together, and let it stand several months till it be fit for use. It will improve by keeping, and is good for pickling.

Herbs for Winter.

Take any sort of sweet herbs, and three times the quantity of parsley, and dry them in the air, without exposing them to the sun. When they are quite dry, rub them through a hair sieve, put them in canisters or bottles, and keep them in a dry place. They will be very useful for seasoning in the winter. Mint, sage, thyme, and such kind of herbs, may be tied in small bunches, and hung up and dried in the air: then put each sort separately into a bag, and hang it up in the kitchen. Parsley should be picked from the stalks as soon as gathered, and dried in the shade to preserve the colour. Cowslips and marigolds should be gathered dry, picked clean, dried in a cloth, and kept in paper bags.

Indian Pickle

Break the heads of some good cauliflowers into small pieces, and add some slices of the inside of the stalk. Put to them a white cabbage cut in pieces, with inside slices of carrot, turnips, and onions. Boil a strong brine of salt and water, simmer the pickles in it one minute, drain them, put them on tins to dry over an oven till they are shrivelled up; then put them into a jar, and prepare the following pickle. To two quarts of good vinegar, put an ounce of the flour of mustard, one of ginger, one of long pepper, two of black pepper, four of cloves, a few shalots, and a little horse-radish. Boil the vinegar, put in the slices, and pour it hot on the pickles. When cold, tie them down, and add more vinegar afterwards if necessary, and in a week or two they will be fit for use.

Mangoes.

Cut off the tops of some large green cucumbers, take out the seeds, and wipe them dry. Then fill them with mustard-seed, horse-radish, onion, sliced ginger, and whole pepper. Sew on the tops, put them in a jar, cover them with boiling vinegar, and do them as directed for French beans. Melons may be done in the same way.

Mushrooms.

Rub some small mushrooms with a piece of flannel dipped in salt and water, boil them a few minutes in salt and water till the liquor is drawn out. Lay them on a cloth to cool, put them into jars, fill up the jars with cold vinegar, that has been boiled with mace, salt, and ginger in it. Add a spoonful of sweet oil to each bottle, cork them close, and tie them down.

Mushroom Ketchup.

Break some large mushrooms, throw over them a good quantity of salt, and let them stand two nights. Strain and press out the liquor, and put it into a stewpan with black pepper bruised, sliced ginger, shalots, and horse-radish. Boil it an hour, strain it, and bottle it up quite close when it is cold. If well boiled, tied down properly, and set in a dry place, it will keep two or three years; otherwise it will soon spoil.

Mushroom Powder.

Peel and cut some thick buttons, spread them on tins, and dry them in a slow oven till they will turn to powder. Beat them in a mortar, sift them through a sieve, add a little cayenne and pounded mace, and keep it dry in bottles.

Onions.

To prevent their affecting the eyes while peeling, put them first into a pot of boiling water, let them stand a few minutes, and drain them. Then peel them, put them into milk and water, with a little salt; and when it boils, strain off the onions, wipe them dry, and put them into wide-mouthed bottles. Have ready some cold white-wine vinegar in which whole white pepper, ginger, mace, and horse-radish have been boiled, pour it over the onions, and cover them down close with bladders. Small button onions are the best for this purpose.

Red Cabbage.

Slice a red cabbage cross-ways, put it in an earthen dish, and throw over it a handful of salt. Cover it over till the next day, drain it in a colender, and put it in the jar. Boil some good vinegar, with cloves and allspice; pour it hot on the cabbage till the jar is full, and tie it down close when it is cold.

Sliced Cucumbers

Cut some cucumbers into thick slices, drain them in a colender, and add some sliced onions. Use some strong vinegar, and pickle them in the manner directed for French beans and gherkins.

Sturtions.

Gather them young and dry, and put them into a jar of old vinegar which has been taken from green pickles and onions and boiled afresh; or boil some fresh vinegar with salt and spice, and when cold, put in the sturtions.

Verjuice

Lay some ripe crabs together in a heap to sweat; then take out the stalks and decayed ones, and mash up the rest. Press the juice through a hair cloth into a clean vessel, and it will be fit to use in a month. It is proper for sauces where lemon is wanted.

Walnuts.

Gather them before the shells begin to form, pick off the stalks, and put them into a jar. Boil some good vinegar with a little salt and horse-radish, some bruised pepper, ginger, and cloves, and pour it hot upon the walnuts. When cold, tie them down with a bladder, and let them stand a year. When the walnuts are all used, the vinegar may be improved and made useful for fish sauce and hashes, by boiling it up with anchovies, cloves, and garlic; then strain it, and cork it up in bottles.

Walnut Ketchup.

Take some green walnuts, or the green peel of ripe ones, and pound them in a mortar with some salt. Squeeze out the juice, pour it off clear, and boil it. To every quart of juice add half a pound of anchovies, half a pint of vinegar, a handful of shalots, a little whole pepper, mace, and cloves. Boil them together till the anchovies are dissolved, strain it off, cork it down close when it is cold, and let it stand at least for six months.

HOME-MADE WINES.

Sugar and water are the principal basis of home-made wine; and when these require to be boiled, it is proper to beat up the whites of eggs to a froth, and mix them with the water, when cold, in the proportion of one egg to a gallon of water. When the sugar and water have been boiled, the liquor should be cooled quickly; and if not for wines that require fermenting it may be put into the cask when cold. If the wine is to be fermented, the yeast should be put into it when it is milk-warm; but must not be left more than two nights to ferment before it is put into the cask. Particular care should be taken to have the cask sweet and dry, and washed within-side with a little brandy, before the wine is put in, but it should not be bunged up close till it has done fermenting. When it has stood three or four months, it will be necessary to taste the wine, to know whether it be fit to draw off. If not sweet enough, add some sugar to it, or draw it off into another cask, and put in some sugar candy; but if too sweet, let it stand a little longer. When the wine is drawn off, the dregs may be drained through a flannel bag; and the wine, if not clear enough for the table, may be used for sauce.

Balm Wine.

Boil three pounds of sugar in a gallon of water; skim it clean, put in a handful of balm, and let it boil ten minutes. Strain it off, cool it, put in some yeast, and let it stand two days. Put in the rind and juice of a lemon, and let it stand in the barrel six months.

Capillaire.

Take fourteen pounds of good moist sugar, three of coarse sugar, and six eggs beaten in well with the shells; boil it in three quarts of water, and scum it well. Then add a quarter of a pint of orange-flower water, cleanse it, and put it into bottles. When cold, mix a spoonful or two of this syrup in a little warm or cold water.

Cherry Wine.

Mash some ripe cherries, and press them through a hair sieve. Allow three pounds of lump sugar to two quarts of juice; stir them together till the sugar be dissolved; fill a small barrel with the liquor, add a little brandy, close down the bung when it has done hissing, and let it stand six months. —Strawberry, raspberry, mulberry, or blackberry wine may be made in the same way.

Cherry Brandy.

Stone ten pounds of black cherries, bruise the stones in a mortar, and put them into a gallon of the best brandy. Let it stand a month close covered, pour it clear from the sediment, and bottle it. Morello cherries managed in this way will make a fine rich cordial.

Cowslip Wine.

Allow four pounds of lump sugar to a gallon of water, and boil and scum it till it is quite clear. Add a gallon of the flowers picked from the stalks, and the rind of a lemon, and let them boil three minutes. Put it into a tub to cool, and then into the cask; add the juice of the lemon, and a little brandy.

Currant Wine.

Mix four pounds of moist sugar with two quarts of currant juice, two quarts of water, and a little brandy and raspberry juice. Let it stand two days, put in the bung, but do not close it till it has done hissing, and then let it stand a twelvemonth. Taste it after two or three months, as the sweetness will go off much sooner some years than others, and draw it off in a good state.

Currant Shrub.

Dissolve a pound and a half of loaf sugar in five pints of currant juice, put in a gallon of rum or brandy, and clear it through a flannel bag.

Damson Wine.

Mash eight pounds of damsons, and pour on a gallon of boiling water; let it stand two days, and draw it off. Add three pounds of sugar to a gallon of liquor; fill up the barrel, stop it close, and let it stand twelve months.

Elder Wine.

Put the berries into a jar, and let them stand all night in a cool oven To a quart of juice add three quarts of water, three pounds and a half of sugar, a little ginger and cloves, and boil it three quarters of an hour. When cool, put in a toast, or some yeast, and let it work till the next day: then put it into the cask, and put in the bung lightly till it has done fermenting.—To make elder wine to drink cold, pick sixteen pounds of raisins, and chop them small. Boil six pounds of sugar in five gallons of water, and pour it hot upon the raisins; stir them well together every day, and let them stand a week. Strain the liquor, press out the raisins, and add a pint of the juice of ripe elder berries to a gallon of liquor. Let it stand two or three days to ferment with a toast of yeast upon it, and put it into the barrel, leaving it room to work. Then stop it close, let it stand to be thoroughly fine, and till the sweetness is gone off, and then bottle it off.

English Sherry.

Boil thirty pounds of sugar in ten gallons of water, and scum it clear. When cold, put a quart of new ale-wort to every gallon of liquor, and let it work in the tub a day or two. Then put it into the cask with a pound of sugar candy, six pounds of fine raisins, a pint of brandy, and two ounces of isinglass. When the fermentation is over, stop it close; let it stand eight months, rack it off, and add a little more brandy. Put it in the cask again, and let it stand four months before it is bottled.

Frontiniac.

Boil twelve pounds of white sugar, and six pounds of sun raisins cut small, in six gallons of water. When the liquor is almost cold, put in half a peck of elder flowers; and the next day, six spoonfuls of the syrup of lemons, and four of yeast. Let it stand two days, put it into a barrel that will just hold it, and bottle it after it has stood about two months.

Ginger Wine.

Bruise ten ounces of ginger, put it into a muslin bag, boil it in ten gallons of water, with twenty pounds of moist sugar, and scum it well. Add the peel of ten Seville oranges and ten lemons, cool the liquor in a tub, and put the juice of the lemons and oranges into the barrel when the liquor is poured in. Allow a quart of brandy to every ten gallons, and let it stand four months: a little yeast, and a few raisins may be added

Gooseberry Wine.

Press out the juice of some ripe gooseberries; and to one quart of juice add three quarts of water, and four pounds of sugar. Make it as directed for currant wine; and to have it rich and good, let there be an equal quantity of juice and water

Grape Wine.

Dissolve three pounds and a half of loaf sugar in three quarts of water; and when cold, put in a quart of the juice of white grapes. Let it work two or three days, and put it into the barrel; when the fermentation is over, put it close, and let it stand six months.

Imperial Water.

Put four ounces of sugar and the rind of three lemons into an earthen pan; boil an ounce of cream of tartar in three quarts of water, and pour it on the sugar and lemon. Let it stand all night, clear it through a bag, and bottle it.

Lemon Brandy.

Pare two dozen of lemons, and steep the peels in a gallon of brandy; squeeze the lemons on two pounds of fine sugar, and add six quarts of water. The next day put the ingredients together, pour on three pints of boiling milk, let it stand two days, and strain it off.

Marigold Wine.

Boil three pounds and a half of lump sugar in a gallon of water, put in a gallon of marigold flowers, gathered dry and picked from the stalks, and make it as directed for cowslip wine. If the flowers be gathered only a few at a time, measure them when they are picked, turn and dry them in the shade; and when there is a sufficient quantity, put them into the barrel, and pour the sugar and water upon them. Put a little brandy into the bottles when it is bottled off.

Mixed Wine.

Take an equal quantity of white, red, and black currants, cherries, and raspberries; mash them, and press the juice through a strainer. Boil three pounds of moist sugar in three quarts of water, and scum it clean. When cold, mix a quart of juice with it, and put it into a barrel that will just hold it. Put in the bung, and after it has stood a week, close it up and let it stand three or four months. When the wine is put into the barrel, add a little brandy to it.

Mead.

Put four or five pounds of honey into a gallon of boiling water, and let it boil an hour and a half; take off the scum, and clear it well. Put in the rinds of three or four lemons, and two ounces of hops sewed up in a bag; when cold, put it into the cask, stop it close, and let it stand eight or nine months.

Orange Wine.

Boil ten gallons of water, and the whites of six eggs, with twenty-eight pounds of lump sugar, and scum it clean. Pour it boiling hot on the peels of a hundred oranges, when near cold, put in six quarts of orange juice, and let it stand three days. Strain off the peels, put the liquor into a cask, and in a month or six weeks, put in two quarts of brandy.—To make orange wine with raisins, take thirty pounds of good Malagas, pick them clean, and chop them small. Pare ten Seville oranges ; boil eight gallons of soft water till it be reduced one third, let it cool a little, and pour it upon the raisins and orange peel. Stir it well, cover it up, and let it stand five days ; then strain it through a sieve, and press it dry. Put it into a cask, add the rinds of ten more oranges cut thin, and make a syrup of the twenty oranges with a pound of white sugar. Stir it well together, stop it close, let it stand two months to clear, and bottle it off.

Orange Brandy.

Steep the peels of twenty Seville oranges in three quarts of brandy, and let it stand a fortnight in a stone bottle. Boil two quarts of water with a pound and a half of loaf sugar nearly an hour, clarify it with the white of an egg, strain it, and boil it till reduced nearly one half ; and when cold, strain the brandy into the syrup.

Quince Wine.

Gather twenty large quinces dry and ripe, wipe them with a cloth, and grate them so as not to touch the core   Put the quince into a gallon of boiling water, and let it boil gently a quarter of an hour : strain it into a pan on two pounds of re-fined sugar, put in the peels of two lemons, and squeeze the juice through a sieve. Stir it about till it is cool, put in a toast of bread with a little yeast on it, and let it stand close covered till the next day. Take out the toast and lemon, keep it three months, and bottle it off.

Raisin Wine.

Boil sixteen gallons of water ; when cold, put to it a hundred weight of raisins in a tub, and let it remain a month to ferment. When the raisins begin to rise to the top, it must be well stirred once a day for a fortnight ; and when the fruit begins to burst, press the liquor from it, put it into the cask, and leave it loosely stopped for two or three months. Examine it often ; when the fermentation abates, it will hiss and sparkle at the bung, the sweetness will subside, and it will have more the taste of wine. Put in a bottle of brandy, stop it close, keep it six months in the cask, rack it off from the lees, and fine it down with isinglass. When the lees are taken out, put the wine into the cask again, and stop it close; let it stand a few months, and bottle it off when fine.

Raspberry Brandy.

Put four pints of raspberries, half a pint of loaf sugar, and a pint of water to two quarts of brandy. Let it remain close covered for a week, strain it off, and bottle it a week afterwards.

Shrub.

To a gallon of rum, put a quart of the juice of Seville oranges, and two pounds and a half of loaf sugar beaten fine, and barrel it. Steep the rinds of half a dozen oranges in a little rum, the next day strain it into the vessel, and make it up ten gallons with water that has been boiled. Stir the liquor twice a day for a fortnight, or the shrub will be spoiled.

Spruce Beer.

Pour sixteen gallons of warm water into a barrel, with twelve pounds of molasses, and half a pound of the essence of spruce. When cool, add a pint of yeast, stir it well for two or three days, and put into stone bottles. Wire down the corks, pack the bottles in saw-dust, and it will be ripe in about a fortnight

Treacle Beer.

Put two quarts of boiling water to a pound of treacle, stir them together, add six quarts of cold water, and a tea-cupful of yeast. Put it into a cask, cover it close down, and it will be fit to drink in two or three days. If made in large quantities, or intended to keep, put in a handful of malt and hops, and stop it up close, when the fermentation is over.

CHAPTER XXXI.

USEFUL RECEIPTS IN DOMESTIC ECONOMY.

PERFUMERY

VARIOUS articles, imposed on the public under the description of cosmetics and perfumes, consist of metallic ingredients which are highly injurious to health. The safest way, therefore, as well as the cheapest, is to prepare these articles at home, of such productions as the garden generally affords, and which will be found to answer the purpose of foreign aromatics. Jessamines, tuberoses, lavender, and other odoriferous plants, may be so prepared as to form an agreeable variety, and yield an abundant fragrance, without endangering the constitution by the use of any foreign mixture. As the simplest perfume is, however, at best an article of luxury, and may prove injurious, particularly to nervous habits, we can only recommend a sparing use of what might otherwise be considered as agreeable and elegant.

Aromatic Vinegar.

Mix with common vinegar a quantity of powdered chalk or whitening sufficient to destroy the acidity; and when the white sediment is formed, pour off the insipid liquor. The powder is then to be dried, and some oil of vitriol poured upon it as long as white acid fumes continue to ascend. This substance forms the essential ingredient, the fumes of which are particularly useful in purifying rooms and places where any contagion is suspected.

Essence of Flowers.

Select a quantity of the petals of any flowers which have an agreeable fragrance, lay them in an earthen vessel, and sprinkle a little fine salt upon them : then dip some cotton into the best Florence oil, and lay it thin upon the flowers, continue a layer of flowers and a layer of cotton till the vessel is full. It is then to be closed down with a bladder, and exposed to the heat of the sun; in about a fortnight a fragrant oil may be squeezed away from the whole mass, which will yield a rich perfume.

Essence of Lavender.

Take the blossoms from the stalks in warm weather, and spread them in the shade for twenty-four hours on a linen cloth, then bruise and put them into warm water, and leave them closely covered in a still for four or five hours near the fire. After this the blossoms may be distilled in the usual way.

Essence of Soap.

For washing or shaving, the essence of soap is very superior to what is commonly used for these purposes, and a very small quantity will make an excellent lather. Mix two ounces of salt of tartar with half a pound of soap finely sliced, put them into a quart of spirits of wine, in a bottle that will contain twice the quantity. Tie it down with a bladder, prick a pin through the bladder to allow the air to escape, set it to digest in a gentle heat, and shake up the contents. When the soap is dissolved, filter the liquors through some paper to free it from impurities, and scent it with burgamot or essence of lemon.

Hungary Water.

Put some rosemary flowers into a glass retort, and pour on them as much spirits of wine as the flowers will imbibe. Dilute the retort well, and let the flowers stand for six days; then distil it in a sand-heat.

Incense.

Compound in a marble mortar great quantities of lignum rhodium and anise, with a little powder of dried Seville orange peel and gum benzoin. Add some gum dragon dissolved in rose-water, and a little civet; beat the whole together, form the mixture into small cakes, place them on paper to dry. One of these cakes being burnt, will diffuse an agreeable odour throughout the largest apartment.

Lavender Water.

Put a pound of lavender blossoms into a quart of water, and set them in a still over a slow fire; distil it off very gently till the water is all exhausted; repeat the process a second time, and cork it down close in bottles.

Milk of Roses.

Mix an ounce of oil of almonds with a pint of rose water, and then add ten drops of the oil of tartar.

Pomatum.

Hog's lard melted, and washed in clean water, laid an inch thick in a dish, and strewed over with jessamine flowers, will imbibe the scent, and make a very fragrant pomatum. For soft pomatum, the lard is to be cut in small pieces, covered with spring water for several days, and the water frequently removed. When the lard is well cleaned and whitened, melt it over a clear fire, strain it well, and add to it a little essence of lemon.

Rose-Water.

When the roses are full blown, pick off the leaves carefully, and allow a peck of them to a quart of water. Put them in a cold still over a slow fire, and distil it very gradually: bottle the water, and cork it up in two or three days.

Smelling Bottle.

Reduce to powder an equal quantity of sal-ammoniac and quick lime separately, put two or three drops of the essence of burgamot into a small bottle, then add the other ingredients, and cork it close. A drop or two of ether will improve it.

Wash.

An infusion of horse-radish in milk, makes one of the safest and best washes for the skin; or the fresh juice of house-leek, mixed with an equal quantity of new milk or cream. Honey-water made rather thick, so as to form a kind of varnish on the skin, is a useful application in frosty weather, when the skin is liable to be chapped; and if it occasions any irritation or un-easiness, a little fine flour or pure hair-powder should be dusted on the hands or face. A more elegant wash may be made of four ounces of potash, four of rose-water, two ounces of brandy, and two of lemon-juice, mixed in two quarts of water. A spoonful or two of this mixture, put into the bason, will scent and soften the waters intended to be used.

Windsor Soap.

Cut the best white soap into thin slices, melt it over a slow fire, and scent it with oil of carraway or any other agreeable perfume. Shaving boxes may then be filled with the melted soap, or it may be poured into a small drawer or any other mould; and after it has stood a few days to dry, it may be cut into square pieces ready for use.

MODES OF DETECTING ADULTERATION IN VARIOUS ARTICLES.

Beer.

Wholesome beer ought to be of a bright colour, and per-fectly transparent, neither too high nor too pale. It should have a pleasant and mellow taste, sharp and agreeably bitter, without being hard or sour. It should leave no particular sen-sation on the tongue; and, if drank in any considerable quan-tity, it must neither produce speedy intoxication, with the usual effects of sleep, nausea, headache, languor, &c.; nor should it be retained too long, or be too quickly discharged. If beer purchased at the alehouse be suspected of having been adulterated with the infusion of vitriol, for the purpose of add-ing to its strength, it may be discovered by putting in a few nut-galls, which will immediately turn it black, if it have been so adulterated.

Bread.

Bakers' bread is too frequently mixed with a quantity of alum, in order to give it a superior whiteness, but which is highly mjurious to health. Make a solution of lime in aqua fortis, steep the suspected bread in water, and add a little of the solution to it. If the bread be bad, the acid which was combined with the alum will form a precipitate, or chalky concretion at the bottom of the vessel. When much alum is mixed with bread, it may easily be distinguished by the eye : two loaves so adulterated will stick together in the oven, and break from each other with a much smoother surface, where they had adhered, than those loaves do which contain no alum.

Flour.

Mealmen and millers have been accused of adding chalk, lime and whitening, to the flour ; and there is reason to suspect thar this practice is but too prevalent. Adulterated meal or flour are generally whiter and heavier than the good, and may be ascertained by the following experiment. Mix a little good vinegar or the juice of a lemon with some flour : if the flour be genuine, the liquor will be at rest ; but if there be a mixture of chalk or whitening, it will produce a fermentation. Or pour boiling water on some slices of bread, and drop on it some spirits of vitriol. Put them in the flour ; and if there be any of the above ingredients in it, a violent hissing will ensue. Vitriol alone, dropped on a small quantity of bread or flour, will discover whether they be adulterated or not.

Good flour may be known by the quantity and quality of glutinous matter it contains, and which will appear when it is kneaded into dough. Take four ounces of fine flour, mix it with water, and work it together till it forms a thick paste. The paste is then to be well washed and kneaded with the hands under the water, and the water to be renewed till it ceases to become white by the operation. If the flour was sound, the paste which remains will be glutinous and elastic ; if heated, it will be brittle ; and if in a state of fermentation, no glutinous matter will be produced.

Hair-Powder.

To know whether hair-powder be adulterated with lime, put a little of the powder of sal-ammoniac into it, and stir it up with some warm water. If the powder has been adulterated with lime, a strong smell of alkali will arise from the mixture.

Perfumery.

Oil of lavender and other essences are frequently adulterated with a mixture of the oil of turpentine, which may be discovered by dipping a piece of paper or rag into the oil to be tried, and holding it to the fire. The fine scented oil will quickly evaporate, and leave the smell of the turpentine distinguishable, if the essence has been adulterated with this ingredient.

Spirits.

Good pure spirits ought to be perfectly clear, pleasant, and strong, though not of a pungent odour, and somewhat of a vinous taste. To try the purity of spirits, or whether they have been diluted with water, see whether the liquor will burn away without leaving any mixture behind, by dipping in a piece of writing paper, and holding it to the candle. As pure spirit is much lighter than water, place a hollow ivory ball into it: the deeper the ball sinks, the lighter the liquor, and consequently the more spirituous.

Wine.

The moderate use of wine is highly conducive to health, especially in weak and languid habits, and in convalescents who are recovering from the attacks of malignant fevers. Hence, it forms an extensive article of commerce, and immense quantities are consumed in this country; but no article is more capable of being adulterated, or of producing more pernicious effects on the human constitution, and therefore it requires the strictest attention. In order to expose such adulterations, and prevent their fatal consequences, we shall communicate a few simple means by which the fraud may be discovered, both by the taste and by the eye.

If new white wine be of a sweetish flavour, and leave a certain astringency on the tongue; if it have an unusually high colour, which is disproportionate to its nominal age and real strength; or if it have a strong pungent taste, resembling that of brandy, or other ardent spirits, such liquor may be considered as adulterated

When old wine presents either a very pale or a very deep colour, or possesses a very tart and astringent taste, and deposits a thick crust on the sides or bottom of glass vessels, it has then probably been coloured with some foreign substance; and which may be easily detected by passing the liquor through filtering paper, when the colouring ingredients will remain on the surface. The fraud may also be discovered by filling a small phial with the suspected wine, and closing its mouth with the fingers: the bottle is then to be inverted, and immersed into a basin of pure water. The fingers being withdrawn, the tinging or adulterating matter will pass into the water, so that the former may be observed sinking to the bottom by its greater weight.

Wines becoming tart or sour, are frequently mixed with the juice of carrots and turnips; and if this do not recover the sweetness to a sufficient degree, alum or the sugar of lead is sometimes added; but which cannot fail to be productive of the worst effects, and will certainly operate as slow poison. To detect the alum, let the suspected liquor be mixed with a little lime-water: at the end of ten or twelve hours, the composition must be filtered; and if crystals be formed, it contains no alum. But if it be adulterated, the sediment will split into small segments, which will adhere to the filtering paper on which it is spread.

In order to detect the litharge or sugar of lead, a few drops of the solution of yellow orpiment and quick lime should be poured into a glass of wine: if the colour of the liquor change, and become successively dark red, brown, or black, it is an evident proof of its being adulterated with lead. As orpiment is poisonous, it would be better, however, to use a few drops of vitriolic acid for this purpose, which should be introduced into a small quantity of the suspected liquor. This will cause the lead to sink to the bottom of the glass, in the form of a white powder. A solution of hepatic gas in distilled water, if added to wine sophisticated with lead, will produce a black sediment, and thus shew the smallest quantity of that poisonous metal; but in pure wine, no precipitation will take place.

The following preparation has been proved to be a sufficient test for adulterated wine or cider. Let one dram of the dry liver of sulphur, and two drams of the cream of tartar, be shaken in two ounces of distilled water, till the whole become saturated with hepatic gas: the mixture is then to be filtered through blotting paper, and kept in a phial closely corked. In order to try the purity of wine, about twenty drops of this test are to be poured into a small glass: if the wine only become turbid with white clouds, and a similar sediment be deposited, it is then not impregnated with any metallic ingredients. But if it turn black or muddy, its colour approach to a deep red, and its taste be at first sweet, and then astringent; the liquor certainly contains the sugar, or other pernicious preparation of lead. The presence of iron is indicated by the wine acquiring a dark blue coat, after the test is put in, similar to that of pale ink; and if there be any particles of copper or verdigris, a blackish grey sediment will be formed.

A small portion of sulphur is always mixed with white wines, in order to preserve them; but if too large a quantity be employed, the wine thus impregnated becomes injurious. Sulphur, however, may be easily detected; for if a piece of an egg-shell, or of silver, be immersed in the wine, it instantly acquires a black hue. Quick lime is also frequently mixed with wine, for imparting a beautiful red colour: its presence may be ascertained by suffering a little wine to stand in a glass for two or three days; when the lime, held in solution, will appear on the surface in the form of a thin pellicle or crust.

The least hurtful, but most common adulteration of wine, is that of mixing it with water, which may be detected by throwing into it a small piece of quick lime. If it slack or dissolve the lime, the wine must have been dilated; but if the contrary, which will seldom be the case, the liquor may be considered as genuine.

DIRECTIONS FOR CLEANING DIFFERENT ARTICLES.

As cleanliness in every department is a most essential requisite to an accomplished housekeeper, and as various domestic articles are difficult to manage, or may occasion much trouble to keep in proper order, a little assistance in the business will not appear unnecessary, especially to the less experienced, whose labour may in some instances be saved, or directed with better success.

Alabaster.

The proper way of cleaning elegant chimney-pieces, or other articles made of alabaster, is to reduce some pumice-stones to a very fine powder, and mix it up with verjuice: let it stand two hours, then dip into it a sponge, and rub the alabaster with it; wash it with fresh water and a linen cloth, and dry it with clean linen rags.

Bottles.

The common practice of cleaning glass bottles with shot is highly improper; for if through inattention any of it should remain, when the bottles are again filled with wine or cider, the metal will be dissolved, and the liquor impregnated with its pernicious qualities. A few ounces of pot-ash dissolved in water will answer the purpose much better, and clean a great number of bottles. If any impurity adhere to the sides, a few pieces of blotting paper put into the bottle, and shaken with the water, will remove it in an expeditious manner. Another way is to roll up some pieces of blotting paper, soak them in soap and water, put them into bottles or decanters with a little warm water, and shake them well for a few minutes: after this they will only require to be rinsed and dried.

Brass

Brass vessels, especially such as are used for culinary pur

poses, are constantly in danger of contracting verdigris. To prevent this, instead of wiping them dry in the usual manner, let them be frequently immersed in water, and they will be preserved safe and clean.

Carpets.

To clean a Turkey carpet, beat out all the dust with a stick; and if it be stained, take out the spots with sorrel or lemon juice. Wash it in cold water, and hang it out in the open air a night or two to dry; then rub it all over with the crumb of a hot loaf, and its colour will be revived.

Coppers.

In domestic economy, the necessity of keeping copper vessels always clean, is generally acknowledged; but it may not perhaps be so generally known, that fat and oily substances, and vegetable acids, do not attack copper while hot; and therefore, that if no liquor were suffered to remain and grow cold in copper vessels, they might be used for every culinary purpose with perfect safety. The object is to clean and dry the vessels well before they turn cold.

Feathers.

Feather beds may be cleared of dust and dirt by beating them well with a stick in the open air; but when the feathers have not been sufficiently cleared of the animal oil which they contain, they will require a different treatment. Dissolve a pound of quick lime in every gallon of water, and pour off the infusion at the time it is wanted. Put the feathers to be cleaned into another tub, and add a sufficient quantity of the lime water to cover the feathers, which require to be well soaked and stirred for three or four days: after this, the foul liquor should be separated from the feathers, by laying them in a sieve. They are then to be washed in clean water, shaken and dried on nets, and exposed as much as possible to the open air. The feathers being thus prepared, will want nothing more than beating for immediate use.

Floor-cloths.

After sweeping and cleaning the floor-cloths with a broom and wet flannel, wet them over with milk, and rub them with a dry cloth till they are beautifully white. This will be found a better mode of treatment than rubbing them with a waxed flannel, which renders them slippery, and liable to be clogged with dust and dirt.

Glasses

To restore the lustre of glasses, which have been tarnished by age or accident, strew on them some fullers' earth, carefully powdered and cleaned from sand and dirt, and rub them gently with a linen cloth or a little putty.

Mahogany.

Mahogany furniture may be cleaned and improved, by taking three-pennyworth of alkanet root, one pint of cold-drawn linseed oil, and two-pennyworth of rose pink ; or a part only of the alkanet and rose pink may be added, if the pinky shade occasioned by them should be disagreeable. These ingredients are put together into a pan, to stand all night : the mixture is then rubbed on tables and chairs, and suffered to remain one hour. After this, it is to be rubbed off with a linen cloth, and it will leave a beautiful gloss on the furniture.

Marble.

Chimney-pieces, or marble slabs, may be cleaned with muriatic acid, either diluted or in a pure state. If too strong, it will deprive the marble of its polish, but may be restored by the use of a piece of felt and a little putty powdered, rubbing it on with clean water. Another method is, making a paste of a bullock's gall, a gill of soap lees, half a gill of turpentine, and a little pipe-clay. The paste is then applied to the marble, and suffered to remain a day or two : it is afterwards rubbed off, and applied a second or third time, to render the marble perfectly clean and give it the finest polish

Paper.

To remove spots of grease from paper, mix together a dust of sulphur and burnt roach alum ; wet the spot a little, rub it gently with the finger dipped in the powder, and it will presently disappear. Pipe-clay, scraped and laid on both sides of the paper where the stain is, passing over it a heated ironing-box with a piece of paper under it, will soon discharge the grease.

Paper-hangings

Blow off all the dust from the paper to be cleaned, with a pair of bellows, beginning at the top of the room. Take some pieces of bread two days old, and rub it gently on the paper till the upper part of the room is cleaned all round : continue the operation downwards till the whole is finished. Care must be taken not to rub the paper too hard, and the pieces of bread must be renewed as soon as they begin to be soiled

Pewter and Tin.

Dish-covers and pewter requisites should be wiped dry immediately after being used, and kept free from steam or damp, which would prevent much of the trouble in cleaning them. Where the polish is gone off, let the articles be first rubbed on the outside with a little sweet oil laid on a piece of soft linen cloth: then clear it off with pure whitening on linen cloths which will restore the polish.

Polished Stoves.

Steel or polished stoves may be well cleaned in a few minutes, by using a piece of fine-corned emery-stone, and afterwards polishing with flour of emery or rotten-stone. If stoves or fire-irons have acquired any rust, pound some glass to fine powder; and, having nailed some strong woollen cloth upon a board, lay upon it a thick coat of gum-water, and sift the powdered glass upon it, and let it dry. This may be repeated as often as is necessary to form a sharp surface, and with this the rust may be easily rubbed off; but care must be taken to have the glass finely powdered, and the gum well dried, or the polish on the irons will be injured. Fire-arms, or similar articles, may be kept clean for several months, if rubbed with a mixture consisting of one ounce of camphor dissolved in two pounds of hog's lard, boiled and skimmed, and coloured with a little black lead. The mixture should be left on twenty-four hours to dry, and then rubbed off with a linen cloth.

Plate.

Whitening, properly purified from sand, applied wet, and rubbed till dry, is one of the safest and cheapest of all plate powders, many of which are highly injurious to the silver. Brass locks, and some articles of silver difficult to clean, may be boiled a little in three pints of water, with an ounce of hartshorn powder, and afterwards dried by the fire. Some soft linen rags should at the same time be boiled in the liquid; and, when dry, they will assist in cleaning the articles, which may afterwards be polished with a piece of soft leather.

Steel.

The method of cleaning and polishing steel, is to oil the rusty parts, and let it remain in that state two or three days: then wipe it dry with clean rags, and polish with emery or pumice-stone, or hard wood. After the oil is cleared off, a little fresh lime finely powdered will often be found sufficient; but where a higher polish is required, it will be necessary to use a paste composed of finely levigated blood stone and spirits of wine. See *Polished Stoves.*

Wainscots.

Dirtied painted wainscots may be cleaned with a sponge wetted in potatoe water, and dipped in a little fine sand. Grate a few raw potatoes into water, run it through a sieve, and let it stand to settle : the clear liquor will then be fit for use. If applied in a pure state, without the sand, it will be serviceable in cleaning oil paintings, and similar articles of furniture.

CLEANING AND IMPROVING WEARING APPAREL.

Among other articles of domestic economy, it would be improper not to notice those relating to wearing apparel, which form so essential a part of the expenditure, and require so much the care and attention of a superintendent of the family. Clothes are liable to injury from various accidents, as well as capable of being rendered more useful and comfortable ; and, in many instances, they are utterly spoiled for want of proper management. A few hints on this subject, therefore, will not be unacceptable to those who consult exterior appearance, or the convenience of a sound economy.

Boots.

Persons who travel much, or are often exposed to the weather, must be sensible of the importance of being provided with boots that will resist the wet.   The following is a composition for preserving leather, the good effects of which are sufficiently ascertained. One pint of drying oil, two ounces of yellow wax, two ounces of spirits of turpentine, and half an ounce of Burgundy pitch, should be carefully melted together over a slow fire ; with this mixture, new shoes and boots are rubbed in the sun, or at some distance from the fire, with a sponge or brush : the operation is to be repeated as often as they become dry, until they be fully saturated. In this manner, the leather becomes impervious to wet, the shoes or boots last much longer than those of common leather, acquire such softness and pliability that they never shrivel or grow hard, and in that state are the most effectual preservative against wet and cold.   It is necessary to observe, however, that boots or shoes thus prepared ought not to be worn till they are become perfectly dry and flexible ; otherwise, the leather will be too soft, and the boots unserviceable

Boot Tops.

Many of the compositions sold for the purpose of cleaning and restoring the colours of boot tops, are not found to answer the end, and are often injurious to the leather. A safe and easy preparation is made of a quart of boiled milk, which, when cold, is to be mixed with an ounce of the oil of vitriol, and an ounce of the spirits of salts, shaken well together ; an ounce of red lavender is then added, and the liquid is applied to the leather with a sponge. Or, mix a dram of oxy muriate of potash with two ounces of distilled water, and when the salt is dissolved, add two ounces of muriatic acid ; then shake together in another phial, three ounces of rectified spirits of wine, with half an ounce of the essential oil of lemon, and unite the contents of the two phials, keeping the liquid closely corked for use : it is to be applied with a clean sponge, and dried gently, after which the tops may be polished with a pro per brush so as to appear like new leather. This genuine composition will readily take out grease or any kind of spots from leather or parchment, and may be fully relied on as producing this desirable effect.

Coats.

To render great coats water-proof, it is only necessary to melt an ounce of white wax in a quart of spirits of turpentine ; and, when thoroughly mixed and cold, dip the coat in, and hang it up to dry. By this cheap and simple process, any kind of cloth may be rendered impenetrable to the hardest rains, without sustaining any injury.

Gloves.

Leather gloves may be repaired, cleaned, and dyed to a fine yellow, by steeping a little saffron in boiling water for about twelve hours ; and, having slightly sewed up the tops of the gloves, to prevent the dye from staining the insides, wet them over with a sponge or soft brush dipped in the liquid. A tea cupful will be sufficient for a single pair.

Leather.

To discharge grease from articles made of leather, apply the white of an egg, let it dry in the sun, and then rub it off. A paste made of dry mustard, potatoe meal, and two spoonsful of the spirits of turpentine, applied to the spot and rubbed off when dry, will be found to answer the purpose. If not, cleanse it with a little vinegar. Tanned leather is best cleaned with nitrous acid and salts of lemon, diluted with water, and afterwards mixed with skimmed milk. The surface of the leather should first be cleaned with a brush and soft water, adding a little free sand, and then repeatedly scoured with a brush dipped in the nitrous mixture. It is afterwards to be cleaned with a sponge and water, and left to dry.

Linen.

Linen in every form is liable to all the accidents of mildew, iron-moulds, ink-spots, and various other stains, which prove highly injurious, if not speedily removed. In case of mildew, rub the part well with soap, then scrape and rub on some fine chalk, and lay the linen out to bleach; wet it a little now and then, and repeat the operation if necessary. Ink spots and iron moulds may be removed, by rubbing them with the salt of sorrel, or weak muriatic acid, and laying the part over a tea-pot or kettle of boiling water at the same time, to be affected by the steam. Or some crystals of tartar powdered, and half the quantity of allum, applied in the same manner, will be found to extract the spots. The spirits of salts, diluted with water, will remove iron moulds from linen; and sal-ammoniac with lime, will take out the stains of wine. Fruit stains may generally be removed by wetting the part with water, and exposing it to the fumes of brimstone. When ink has been suddenly spilled on linens, wet the place immediately with the juice of sorrel, or lemon, or vinegar, and rub it with hard white soap. Or to the juice add a little salts, steam the linen over boiling water, and wash it afterwards in ley. If ink be spilled on a green table-cloth or carpet, the readiest way will be to take it up immediately with a spoon, and by pouring on fresh water, while the spoon is constantly applied, the stains will soon be removed.

Shoes.

The best way of cleaning shoes in the winter time is to scrape off the dirt with the back of a knife, or with a wooden knife made for that purpose, while the shoes are wet, and wipe off the remainder with a wet sponge or piece of flannel: set them to dry at a distance from the fire, and they will afterwards take a fine polish. This will save much of the trouble in cleaning when the dirt is suffered to dry on, and applying a little sweet oil occasionally, the leather will be prevented from growing hard.

Silks.

Silks and cotton may be cleaned in the following manner, without any injury to their colour or texture: grate two or three raw potatoes into a pint of clean water, and pass the liquid through a sieve, when it has stood to settle, pour off the clear part and it will be fit for use. Dip a clean sponge in the liquor, apply it to the silk till the dirt is well separated, and wash it several times in clear water. The coarse pulp of the potatoes, which does not pass the sieve, is of great use in cleaning worsted curtains, carpets, or other coarse goods.

To take the stains of grease from silk or woollen, mix together three ounces of spirits of wine, three of French chalk powdered, and five ounces of pipe-clay, rub it on the stain either wet or dry, and afterwards take it off with a brush. An equal quantity of spirits of wine and turpentine, mixed with pipe-clay, will also effectually remove spots or stains from cotton and silk. Sometimes a little of the spirits of turpentine alone will answer the purpose.

Silk Stockings.

To clean silk stockings properly, it is necessary first to wash them in lukewarm liquor of white soap, then to rinse them in clean water, and wash them again as before. They are to be washed a third time in a stronger soap liquor, made hot and tinged with blueing, and rinsed in clean water. Before they are quite dry, they are to be stoved with brimstone, and afterwards polished with glass upon a wooden leg. Gauzes are whitened in the same manner, only a little gum is put in the soap liquor before they are stoved.

Velvets.

When the pile of velvet requires to be raised, it is only necessary to warm a smoothing iron, cover it with a wet cloth, and hold it under the velvet; the vapour arising from the wet cloth will raise the pile of the velvet, with the assistance of a whisk gently passed over it. For spots and stains in velvet, bruise some of the plant called soap-wort, strain out the juice, and add to it a small quantity of black soap. Wash the stain with this liquor, and repeat it several times after it has been allowed to dry. To take wax out of velvet, rub it frequently with hot toasted bread.

Woollen.

If woollen cloth be spotted with oil or grease, the readiest way is to rub on some fullers' earth or pipe-clay a little moistened, and brush it out when dry. When the spot is occasioned by wax or tallow, it is necessary to heat the part carefully with an iron, while the cloth is drying; and in some instances, bran or raw starch may be used to advantage. Grease spots may be removed by using soap and water with a toothbrush, and cleansing the part with a wet sponge.

To take out all spots in cloths, stuff, and hats, whether from pitch, paint, or grease, the following mixture is perhaps the most effectual. Cut a lemon into two quarts of spring water, add a small spoonful of fine potash, and shake them well to gether : after standing all day in the sun, strain off the liquor. Rub some of it on the spot, and wash it with clean water ; if the cloth be of a deep colour, dilute a spoonful of the liquor with a little water, to prevent the colour being injured. This preparation will answer for silk, cotton, or linen, as well as for woollen cloths.

CEMENTS.

The destruction that is made of crockery, and other articles of brittle ware, is a frequent subject of complaint in most families : and though we cannot prevent such mischances, yet the damage may in some instances be repaired by the use of proper cement. We shall therefore notice a few common articles of this description, in which some expense and incon veniences may be avoided.

Boilers.

Coppers and boilers are apt to become leaky, when they have been joined or mended, or from bruises, which sometimes render them unfit for use. In this case a cement of pounded quick lime, mixed with ox's blood, applied fresh to the injured part, will be of great advantage and very durable. A valuable cement may also be made of equal parts of vinegar and milk mixed together so as to produce a curd : the whey is then put to the whites of four or five eggs after they have been well beaten, and the whole reduced to a thick paste by the addition of some quick lime finely sifted. This composition applied to cracks or fissures of any kind, and properly dried, will resist the effects of fire and water.

China.

A common cement for broken china may be made from a mixture of equal parts of glue, white of an egg, and white lead. The juice of garlic, bruised in a stone mortar, is a remarkably fine cement for broken glass or china ; and, if carefully applied, will leave no mark behind it. Isinglass glue mixed with a little fine chalk will answer the purpose, if the articles be required not to endure heat or moisture

Earthenware.

An ounce of dry lean cheese grated fine, and an equal quantity of quick lime mixed well together in three ounces of skimmed milk, will form a good cement for any articles of broken earthenware, when the rendering of the joint visible is reckoned of no consequence. A cement of the same nature may be made of quicklime tempered with the curd of milk, but the curd should either be made of whey or butter-milk. This cement, like the former, requires to be applied immediately after it is made, and will effectually join any kind of earthenware or china.

Glass.

Broken glass may be mended with the same cement as china, or if it be only cracked, it will be sufficient to moisten the part with the white of an egg, strewing it over with a little powdered lime, and instantly applying a piece of fine linen. Another cement for glass is prepared from two parts of litharge, one of quicklime, and one of flint glass, each separately and finely powdered; and the whole worked up into a paste with drying oil. This compound is very durable, and acquires a greater degree of hardness when immersed in water.

Iron pots.

To cure cracks or fissures in iron pots or pans, mix some finely-sifted lime with white of eggs well beaten, till reduced to a paste, then add some iron file dust, and apply the composition to the injured part · it will soon become hard and fit for use.

Marble

Alabaster, marble, or other stones, may be strongly cemented together in the following manner : melt two pounds of bees'-wax, and one pound of rosin, take about the same quantity of marble or other stones to be joined, reduce it to a powder, and stir it well together with the melted mixture, then knead the mass in water, till the powder is thoroughly incorporated with the wax and rosin. The parts to be joined must be heated and made quite dry, and the cement made hot when applied. Melted sulphur, laid on fragments of stone previously heated, will make a firm and durable cement. Little deficiencies in stones or corners that have been stripped or broken off, may be supplied with some of the stone powdered and mixed with melted sulphur ; but care must be taken to have both parts properly heated.

INDEX

312 INDEX